SOMETHING ABOUT THE AUTHOR

r

SOMETHING ABOUT THE AUTHOR

Facts and Pictures about Contemporary Authors
and Illustrators of Books for Young People

Anne Commire

VOLUME 9

GALE RESEARCH
BOOK TOWER
DETROIT, MICHIGAN
48226

Also Published by Gale

CONTEMPORARY AUTHORS:
A Bio-Bibliographical Guide to
Current Authors and Their Works

(Now Covers About 46,000 Authors)

Special acknowledgment is due to the members of the
Contemporary Authors staff who assisted in the prep-
aration of this volume, and to Gale's art director,
Chester Gawronski.

Associate Editor: Agnes Garrett
Assistant Editors: Linda Shedd, Rosemary DeAngelis Bridges

GRATEFUL ACKNOWLEDGEMENT

is made to the following publishers, authors, and artists, for their kind permission to reproduce copyrighted material. ■ **ABINGDON PRESS.** Illustration by Lorna Balian from *Humbug Witch* by Lorna Balian. Copyright © 1965 by Abingdon Press. Reprinted by permission of Abingdon Press. ■ **ADDISON-WESLEY PUBLISHING CO., INC.** Illustration by Normand Chartier from *Devin and Goliath* by Mary Blount Christian. Copyright © 1974 by Normand Chartier (a Young Scott Book). /Illustration by Gertrude Barrer-Russell from *Thor and the Giants* by Anita Feagles. Illustration copyright © 1968 by Gertrude Barrer-Russell. Both reprinted by permission of Young Scott Books and Addison-Wesley Publishing Co., Inc. ■ **ATHENEUM PUBLISHERS.** Illustration by Aline Amon from *Reading, Writing, Chattering Chimps* by Aline Amon. Copyright © 1975 by Aline Amon Goodrich. Reprinted by permission of Curtis Brown Ltd. /Drawings by Glo Coalson from *The Long Hungry Night* by E. C. Foster and Slim Williams. Copyright © 1973 by E. C. Foster and Slim Williams. /Illustration by Felix Hoffmann from *Hans in Luck* by Felix Hoffmann (a Margaret K. McElderry Book). U.S. translation copyright © 1975 by Atheneum Publishers. /Illustration by Miriam Morton from *Pleasures and Palaces* by Miriam Morton. Copyright © 1972 by Miriam Morton. /Illustration by Marvin Glass from *Ghosts Who Went to School* by Judith Spearing. Copyright © 1966 by Judith Spearing. /Illustration by Judith Gwyn Brown from *Chad and the Elephant Engine* by Marjorie Filley Stover. Illustration copyright © 1975 by Judith Gwyn Brown. All reprinted by permission of Atheneum Publishers. ■ **THE BOBBS-MERRILL CO.** Illustration by Robert Quackenbush from *The Bellfounder's Sons* by Lini R. Grol. Illustration copyright © 1971 by Robert Quackenbush. /Illustration by David Stone from *The Mystery of Ghost Burro Canyon.* Copyright © 1962 by The Bobbs-Merrill Co. /Illustration by Katherine Sampson from *John Philip Sousa: Marching Boy* by Ann Weil. Copyright © 1959 by The Bobbs-Merrill Co., Inc. All reprinted by The Bobbs-Merrill Co., Inc. ■ **CHATHAM PRESS, INC.** Illustration by Mary Lee Herbster from *Look What I Found!* Copyright © 1971 by Marshal T. Case. Reprinted by permission of Chatham Press, Inc. ■ **CHILDREN'S PRESS.** Decorations by Robert Corey from *Tomasito and the Golden Llamas* by Jane Castellanos. Copyright © 1968 by Jane Castellanos. Reprinted by permission of Golden Gate Junior Books. ■ **THOMAS Y. CROWELL CO.** Illustration by Allan Eitzen from *Ti Jacques* by Ruth Eitzen. Illustration copyright © 1972 by Allan Eitzen. /Drawings by Romare Bearden from *Poems from Africa* selected by Samuel Allen. Illustration copyright © 1973 by Romare Bearden. /Illustration by Glo Coalson from *At the Mouth of the Luckiest River* by Arnold A. Griese. Illustration copyright © 1973 by Glo Coalson. /Illustration by Richard Cuffari from *The Black Hawk War* by Miriam Gurko. Illustration copyright © 1970 by Richard Cuffari. /Illustration by Marilynne K. Roach from *Two Roman Mice* by Horace retold by Marilynne K. Roach. Copyright © 1975 by Marilynne K. Roach. All reprinted by permission of Thomas Y. Crowell Co. ■ **DESCLEE deBROUWER.** Illustration by Henri Maik from *The Foolish Bird* by Henri Maik. Copyright © 1966 by Desclée deBrouwer. Reprinted by permission of Desclée deBrouwer. ■ **DIAL PRESS.** Pictures by Lorence Bjorklund from *Cranes in My Corral* by Dayton O. Hyde. Illustration copyright © 1971 by Lorence Bjorklund. Reprinted by permission of the Dial Press. ■ **DODD, MEAD & CO., INC.** Illustration by Mircea Vasiliu from *Folk and Fairy Tales from Around the World* compiled by Ethna Sheehan. Copyright © 1970 by Ethna Sheehan. Reprinted by permission of Dodd, Mead & Co., Inc. ■ **DOUBLEDAY & CO., INC.** Illustration by Lee J. Ames from *The American Revolution* by Bruce Lancaster. Copyright © 1957 by Bruce Lancaster. /Illustration by Bernice Myers from *A Lost Horse* by Bernice Myers. Copyright © 1975 by Bernice Myers.

/Illustration by Judith Gwyn Brown from *Ben and Annie* by Joan Tate. Illustration copyright © 1974 by Judith Gwyn Brown. /Illustration by Gioia Fiammenghi from *Mrs. Arris Goes to Paris* by Paul Gallico. Copyright © 1958 by Paul Gallico. © 1957 by The Hearst Corp. All reprinted by permission of Doubleday & Co., Inc. ■ **E. P. DUTTON & CO., INC.** Illustration by Roz Abisch and Boche Kaplan from *Sweet Betsy from Pike* by Roz Abisch and Boche Kaplan. Copyright © 1970 by Roz Abisch and Boche Kaplan. /Illustration by Glen Rounds from *I'm Going on a Bear Hunt* by Sandra Stoner Sivulich. Illustration copyright © 1973 by Glen Rounds. /Illustration by David K. Stone from *Lost Bear* by Glen A. Hodges. Illustration copyright © 1975 by David K. Stone. /Illustration by Robert Clayton from *Ask Me No Questions* by Margaret Storey. Copyright © 1974 by Margaret Storey. All reprinted by permission of E. P. Dutton & Co., Inc. ■ **PAUL S. ERIKSSON INC.** Illustration by Brumsic Brandon, Jr. from *Luther Raps* by Brumsic Brandon, Jr. Copyright © 1971 by Brumsic Brandon, Jr. Reprinted by permission of Paul S. Eriksson. ■ **FABER AND FABER LTD.** Illustration by Tom Barling from *Bananas in Pyjamas: A Book of Nonsense* by Carey Blyton. Illustration © 1972 by Tom Barling. /Illustration by Charlotte Hough from *A Bad Child's Book of Moral Verse* by Charlotte Hough. © 1970 by Charlotte Hough. Both reprinted by permission of Faber and Faber Ltd. ■ **GARRARD PUBLISHING CO.** Illustration by Raymond Burns from *Colonel Meacham's Giant Cheese* by Rosemary Nesbitt. Copyright © 1972 by Rosemary Nesbitt. /Illustration by Cary from *Merrymaking in Great Britain* by Margaret Chittenden. Copyright © 1974 by Margaret Chittenden. /Illustration by Mimi Korach from *Hound Dog Zip to the Rescue* by William O. Steele. Copyright © 1970 by William O. Steele. /Illustration by Bert Dodson from *Fiesta Time in Mexico* by Rebecca B. and Judith Marcus. Copyright © 1974 by Rebecca B. Marcus and Judith Marcus. All reprinted by permission of Garrard Publishing Co. ■ **HARCOURT BRACE JOVANOVICH, INC.** Illustration by David Gwynne Lemon from *All American Ghost* by Chester Aaron. Illustration copyright © 1973 by Harcourt Brace Jovanovich, Inc. /Illustration by Fritz Eichenberg from *Ape in a Cape* by Fritz Eichenberg. Copyright © 1952 by Fritz Eichenberg. /Illustration by Beth and Joe Krush from *Gone-Away Lake* by Elizabeth Enright. © 1957 by Elizabeth Enright. /Illustration by Barbara Flynn from *Diego* by S. E. Moore. Illustration copyright © 1972 by Barbara Flynn. /Illustration by Robert Parker from *Ponies for Hire* by Margaret MacPherson. Copyright © 1967 by Margaret MacPherson. All reprinted by permission of Harcourt Brace Jovanovich, Inc. ■ **HARPER & ROW, PUBLISHERS.** Illustration by Syd Hoff from *Who Will Be My Friends?* by Syd Hoff. Copyright © 1960 by Syd Hoff. /Illustration by Kiyo Komoda from *The Incredible Detectives* by Don and Joan Caufield. Picture copyright © 1966 by Kiyo Kimoda. /Illustration by Edward Frascino from *The Little Mermaid* by Hans Christian Andersen. Translated by Eva Le Gallienne. Pictures copyright © 1971 by Edward Frascino. /Illustration by Anita Lobel from *Christmas Crafts* by Carolyn Meyer. Illustration copyright © 1974 by Anita Lobel. /Illustration by Louise Fitzhugh from *Bang Bang You're Dead* by Sandra Scoppetone and Louise Fitzhugh. Illustration copyright © 1969 by Louise Fitzhugh. /Illustration by Marc Simont from *The Happy Day* by Ruth Krauss. Illustration copyright 1949 by Marc Simont. All reprinted by permission of Harper & Row, Publishers. ■ **HARVEY HOUSE, INC.** Illustration by Harvey Kidder from *Wild Wings* by Walter B. Hendrickson. Illustration copyright © 1969 by Harvey Kidder. /Illustration by Kathleen Elgin from *African Treehouse* by James Tasker. Illustration copyright © 1973 by Kathleen Elgin. Both reprinted by permission of Harvey House, Inc. ■ **HAWTHORN BOOKS, INC.** Illustration by David Hodges from *The Bannekers of Bannaky Springs* by Deloris Harrison. Copyright © 1970 by Deloris Harrison. /Illustration by Paul Frame from *Mahatma Gandhi: Father of Nonviolence* by Catherine Owens Peare. Copyright © 1969 by Catherine Owens Peare. Both reprinted by permission of Hawthorn Books, Inc. All rights reserved. ■ **HOLT, RINEHART AND WINSTON, INC.** Illustration by Diane de Groat from *Luke Was There* by Eleanor Clymer. Illustration copyright © 1973 by Holt, Rinehart and Winston, Inc. Reprinted by permission of Holt, Rinehart and Winston, Inc. ■ **HOUGHTON MIFFLIN CO.** Illustration by Gertrude Allen from *Everyday Animals* by Gertrude Allen. Copyright © 1961 by Gertrude E. Allen. Reprinted by permission of Houghton Mifflin Co. ■ **HUMAN SCIENCES PRESS.** Illustration by Gloria Kamen from *Lisa and Her Soundless World* by Edna S. Wine. Copyright © 1974 by Human Sciences Press, a division of Behavioral Publications, Inc. Reprinted by permission of Human Sciences Press. ■ **LANTERN PRESS, INC.** Illustration by Charles H. Geer from *Young Visitor to Mars* by Richard M. Elam, Jr. Copyright © 1953 by Lantern Press, Inc. Reprinted by permission of Lantern Press, Inc. ■ **LERNER PUBLICATIONS CO.** Pictures by Joseph Folger from *Mr. Bumba's Tuesday Club* by Pearl Augusta Harwood. Copyright © 1966 by Lerner Publications Co. Reprinted by permission of Lerner Publications Co. ■ **THE LION PRESS, INC.** Illustration by Janet and Alex D'Amato from *Handicrafts for Holidays* by Janet and Alex D'Amato. Copyright © 1967 by KDI-Lion Press, Inc. Re-

PHOTOGRAPH CREDITS

SOMETHING ABOUT THE AUTHOR

The last Albie saw of her, the last he was ever to see of her, was her long, lean body loping directly into the morning's rusty sun. ■ (From *All American Ghost* by Chester Aaron. Illustrated by David Gwynne Lemon.)

CHESTER AARON

AARON, Chester 1923-

PERSONAL: Born May 9, 1923, in Butler, Pa.; son of Albert (a grocer and farmer) and Celia (Charleson) Aaron; married Margaurite Kelly (now a self-employed jeweler), March 17, 1954; stepchildren: Louis Daniel Segal. *Education:* University of California, Los Angeles, student; University of California, Berkeley, B.A., 1966; San Francisco State University, M.A., 1975. *Home:* 2927 Deakin St., Berkeley, Calif. 94705. *Agent:* Ellen Levine, Curtis Brown Ltd., 60 East 56th St., New York, N.Y. 10022. *Office:* English Department, Saint Mary's College, Moraga, Calif. 94575.

CAREER: X-ray technician in Berkeley, Calif., 1957-75; Saint Mary's College, Moraga, Calif., assistant professor of English and American literature, 1975—. *Military service:* U.S. Army, 1943-46. *Awards, honors:* Huntington Hartford Foundation grant, 1951, 1952; Chapelsrook Foundation grant, 1970.

WRITINGS: About Us, McGraw, 1967; *Better Than Laughter,* Harcourt, 1972; *An American Ghost* (Child Study Association book list), Harcourt, 1973. Contributor of short story to *Coastlines;* author of play produced at University of California, Berkeley, 1955; stories in *North American Review.*

WORK IN PROGRESS: A children's book; two novels.

FOR MORE INFORMATION SEE: New York Times Book Review, May 7, 1972; *Horn Book,* June, 1973.

ABELL, Kathleen 1938-

PERSONAL: Born September 8, 1938, in Timmins, Ontario, Canada; daughter of Harry Robert (a teacher) and Jean (a teacher; maiden name, Millican) Jenkins; married Norman Abell (an orthopedic surgeon), July 22, 1961; children: Leslie, Robert, Caroline, Kirsten. *Education:* McGill University, B.A. (honors), 1961. *Religion:* None. *Home:* 6 Farmingdale Rd., Willowdale, Ontario M2K IZ2, Canada.

WRITINGS: King Orville and the Bullfrogs (illustrated by Errol Le Cain), Little, Brown, 1974.

SIDELIGHTS: "I grew up in a small town in northern Canada. The nearest large city was 350 miles to the south. Although the first television antenna didn't appear in those parts until after my departure, I acquired a satisfactory background in culture and general education through exposure to comic books and movies. My first idols were Roy Rogers, Gene Autrey, the Lone Ranger, Batman, the

KATHLEEN ABELL

Something about the Author

Green Hornet, Tarzan, Superman, Amazon, Judy of the Jungle, Tom Sawyer, Huck Finn, Nancy Drew, the Hardy Boys, Robin Hood and John James Audubon.

"I read good literature and 'trash' in nearly equal amounts (large), and with nearly equal pleasure. I was an accomplished comic-book smuggler (into a house where comics were banned), an indifferent builder of tree forts and rafts, a good apple snitcher, an appalling violinist and the town's leading authority on birds. Although my teachers from the earliest grades had observed that I had a talent for writing, my ambition until adolescence was to become an ornithologist. During the diary-keeping years the urge to write became acute, and has (more-or-less) remained so.

"After graduating from university I married a doctor and moved with him to England. While he took his training in Orthopaedic Surgery, I became an appalling housekeeper,

"Very well," Queen Pamela agreed, "I shall announce the winner and present the prize." ■ (From *King Orville and the Bullfrogs* by Kathleen Abell. Illustrated by Errol Le Cain.)

an indifferent cook, a compulsive writer of long letters to absent friends, and the mother of four children. I discovered an ambition to write for children five minutes after entering the children's book section of a library with my first-born daughter.

"At present I live in a leafy suburb of Toronto on the edge of a beautiful ravine. I enjoy gardening, but I enjoy just sitting around watching the grass grow better. I continue to read good literature and bad with nearly equal pleasure. Some day I hope to rewrite the story of *The Grasshopper and the Ants* or *The Tortoise and the Hare* in favor of those who stop along the way to smell the flowers. In the meantime I am smelling them. CARPE DIEM!"

ABISCH, Roslyn Kroop 1927- (Roz Abisch, Mr. Sniff; joint pseudonym with Boche Kaplan: A. K. Roche)

PERSONAL: Born April 2, 1927, in Brooklyn, N.Y.; daughter of Benjamin and Frieda (Steinberg) Kroop; married Howard R. Abisch (an archietect), December 25, 1946; children: Janet, Ellen, Susan. *Education:* Brooklyn College, B.A., 1948. *Home and office:* 1095 Verbena Ave., North Merrick, N.Y. 11566.

CAREER: Advertising copywriter, 1944-48; teacher in New York (N.Y.) public schools, 1948-49; Kalle Studio, New York, N.Y., advertising copywriter, 1949-50; United Cerebral Palsy of Queens, N.Y., teacher-therapist assistant, 1954-56; Union Free School District 29, North Merrick, N.Y., administrator and curriculum coordinator for enrichment workshop program, 1959-61; lecturer on juvenile literature. Child Study Association, member of speakers' bureau, 1964—.

WRITINGS—With Boche Kaplan as illustrator: *Open Your Eyes,* Parents' Magazine Press, 1964; *Anywhere in the World,* McKay, 1966; *Monkeys Have Tails,* McKay, 1966; *Art is for You,* McKay, 1967; (under pseudonym A. K. Roche) *I Can Be,* Prentice-Hall, 1967; (under pseudonym A. K. Roche) *The Pumpkin Heads,* Prentice-Hall, 1968; (under A. K. Roche) *The Onion Maidens,* Prentice-Hall, 1968; *Do You Know What Time It Is?,* Prentice-Hall, 1969; *'Twas in the Moon of Wintertime,* Prentice-Hall, 1969; (under A. K. Roche) *The Clever Turtle,* Prentice-Hall, 1969; *Mai-Ling and the Mirror,* Prentice-Hall, 1969.

(Under pseudonym A. K. Roche) *Even the Promise of Freedom,* Prentice-Hall, 1970; (under A. K. Roche) *The City* (haiku), Prentice-Hall, 1970; *The Shoe for Your Left Foot Won't Fit on the Right,* McCall, 1970; *Sweet Betsy from Pike,* McCall, 1970; (under pseudonym Mr. Sniff) *Wishes, Whiffs, and Birthday Gifts,* Watts, 1971; (under Mr. Sniff) *Circus Tents and Circus Scents,* Watts, 1971; (under Mr. Sniff) *Scented Rhymes for Story Times,* Watts, 1971; (under Mr. Sniff) *Scents and Sun and Picnic Fun,* Watts, 1971; *If I Could, I Would,* Watts, 1971; *Silly Street,* Watts, 1971; *Smile If You Meet a Crocodile,* Watts, 1971; *Blast Off,* Watts, 1971; *Out in the Woods,* Watts, 1971; *Under the Ocean, Under the Sea,* Watts, 1971; *Let's Find Out about Butterflies,* Watts, 1972; *Around the House that Jack Built,* Parents' Magazine Press, 1972; *Easy-to-Make Holiday Fun Things,* Xerox Education Publications, 1973; *What's the Good Word?* (film strip), Urban Media Materi-

Did you ever hear tell of Sweet Betsy from Pike,
who crossed the wide prairie with her husband Ike? ■
(From *Sweet Betsy from Pike* by Roz Abisch and Boche Kaplan.
Illustrated by the authors.)

als, 1973; *Do Mixed Bag of Magic Tricks*, Walker & Company, 1974; *Textiles*, Watts, 1974; *The Make-It, Play-It Game Book*, Walker & Company, 1974; *Word Builders I and II* (film strips), Urban Media Materials, 1974.

SIDELIGHTS: "Ms. Kaplan and I have known each other since junior high school. At that time we planned to work together 'when we grew up.' Boche worked as a textile designer and wanted to do something less mechanical. She asked me to write a book. I did—*Open Your Eyes*, our first, and we've been working as a team since then."

Preliminary manuscripts and art work from *The Clever Turtle, 'Twas in the Moon of Wintertime*, and *Sweet Betsy from Pike*, have been included as part of the Kerlan Collection, Walter Library, University of Minnesota; preliminary and finished art from *Sweet Betsy from Pike* and *Around the House that Jack Built* are on display at the Portland Museum of Art in Oregon.

FOR MORE INFORMATION SEE: *Christian Science Monitor*, November 6, 1969.

AINSWORTH, Norma (Norma Paul Ruedi)

PERSONAL: Born in Clinton, Mo.; daughter of Paul J. and Minnie Lee (Morris) Ruedi; married Freedom H. Ainsworth (now president of Ainsworth Development Corp.), July 31, 1954. *Education:* Lindenwood College, A.B.; Southern Methodist University, M.A.; postgraduate study at University of Missouri and New York University. *Religion:* Episcopalian. *Home:* 27 West Tenth St., New York, N.Y. 10011.

CAREER: Columnist and feature writer for newspapers in Missouri and texas, 1932-35; teacher in high school and college, Bolivar, Mo., 1935-43; Colorado State University, Fort Collins, an assistant editor, 1943-44; U.S. Department of the Interior, radio assistant, later chief of editorial section, Bureau of Reclamation, 1944-49, director of publicity, Bureau of Land Management, 1949-54; publicity director

for various civic groups, Salisbury, Md., 1954-58; Mac-Fadden Publications, New York, N.Y., managing editor of *True Experiences,* 1960-61; Scholastic Magazines, Inc., New York, N.Y., fiction editor of *Practical English* and *Co-ed,* 1961-62; fiction editor of books and magazines, secondary school level, 1962-67, editor of manuscript department, 1967-75. Consultant, Institute of Children's Literature, 1973—. *Member:* Authors Guild, Mystery Writers of America (chairman, juvenile awards, 1963-64, 1974-75; secretary, 1973-74; board member, 1973-75), Alpha Sigma Tau.

WRITINGS: (Under name Norma Paul Ruedi) *If Dreams Came True and Other Poems,* Avondale Press 1927; (editor) *Hit Parade of Mystery Stories,* Scholastic Magazines, 1963; (editor) *14 Favorite Christmas Stories,* Scholastic Magazines, 1964; (editor) *The Last Bullet and Other Stories of the West,* Scholastic Magazines, 1965; (editor) *A Matter of Choice and Other Stories for Today,* Scholastic Magazines, 1965; *Mystery of the Crying Child,* Action Books, 1975; *The Ghost of Peaceful End,* Sprint Books, 1976. Contributor to *Writers' Yearbook,* 1964. Articles, short stories, and poetry have appeared in magazines and newspapers, including *Alaska Sportsman, Farm Journal, Saturday Review, Ozarkian, Popular Mechanics, Writer.*

WORK IN PROGRESS: *A Gothic novel.*

(From *Mystery of the Crying Child* by Norma Ainsworth. Photograph by Bob Van Lindt.)

tions were used in *Mystery of the Crying Child*. My husband, Freedom, was asked to take the part of Mr. Barnes in the story. He's the handsome, smiling man in the hat.

"When authors tell me they don't have time to write, I can't sympathize. There is always a little time—it may be lunch hour or in the early morning. Once I tried getting up at four and writing before breakfast, but I gave that up. Now I write nights and weekends, between working with my correspondence students in the Institute of Children's Literature."

ALLEN, Gertrude E(lizabeth)   1888-

PERSONAL: Born July 18, 1888, in Detroit, Mich. *Education:* School of Museum of Fine Arts, Boston, Diploma, 1911; Yale University, Mus. B., 1929. *Home:* 59 Sims Rd., Wollaston, Mass. 02170.

CAREER: Professional singer, and teacher of singing privately and in schools, 1951-28; concentrated on art and writing after 1931 when throat operation ended her singing

NORMA AINSWORTH

SIDELIGHTS: "*Mystery of the Crying Child* started with one small idea. I imagined how it would feel to discover something very odd happening in the apartment house where we live in New York City. It seemed more fun to have a teenager do the sleuthing.

"I wrote one chapter and outline and submitted these, without my own name, at Scholastic. And the book was accepted! But then I was asked to turn my boy hero into a girl, because Action Books needed girl stories. That was difficult, but as I have told authors at writers' conferences in Texas, Washington, New York, Indiana, Michigan and Missouri, an author should be willing to follow the editor's request.

"Now that I have written two juvenile mysteries, I am trying to decide whether I should tackle a Gothic for the young or a Gothic for adults. The setting will be Beckford which we are restoring near Princess Anne, Maryland. I keep thinking about Henry Jackson, merchant, who, it is said, built Beckford in 1776. We have the log book of his ship, the brig 'Peggy.' An historical novel would appeal to eleven-to-twelve year olds but not to teenagers.

"*Mystery of the Crying Child* and *The Ghost of Peaceful End* are both fast paced. Photographs instead of illustra-

GERTRUDE E. ALLEN

Rabbits like to play games. On moonlight nights they come together and play leapfrog. ■ (From *Everyday Animals* by Gertrude Allen. Illustrated by the author.)

career; began giving chalk talks on nature subjects around New England and Middle States in 1933, continuing to present programs for schools, libraries, and clubs until 1970. Illustrator for magazines and books; painter of nature tiles. *Member:* American Nature Society, Massachusetts Audubon Society, Audubon Society of New Hampshire, Massachusetts Horticultural Society, Society of Arts and Crafts (Boston; life member and master craftsman).

WRITINGS—Self-illustrated "Everyday Nature Books for Children" series, published by Houghton: *Everyday Birds*, 1943; *Everyday Animals*, 1961; *Everyday Insects*, 1963; *Everyday Wildflowers*, 1965; *Everyday Trees*, 1968; *Everyday Turtles, Toads and Their Kin*, 1970.

Other: *Tammy Chipmunk and His Friends*, Houghton, 1950. Author of a 75-year history of the Church of Our Saviour in Milton, Mass., privately printed.

WORK IN PROGRESS: Research on fish.

FOR MORE INFORMATION SEE: Christian Science Monitor, April 27, 1965.

ALLEN, Samuel (Washington) 1917-
(Paul Vesey)

PERSONAL: Born December 9, 1917, in Columbus, Ohio; son of Alexander Joseph (a clergyman) and Jewett (Washington) Allen; divorced; children: Marie-Christine. *Education:* Fisk University, A.B., 1938; Harvard University, J.D., 1941; further study at New School for Social Research, 1947-48, and Sorbonne, University of Paris, 1949-50. *Politics:* Democrat. *Religion:* African Methodist Episcopal Church. *Residence:* Winthrop, Mass. *Office:* Department of English, Boston University, Boston, Mass. 02215.

CAREER: County of New York, New York, N.Y., deputy assistant district attorney, Office of District Attorney, 1946-47; U.S. Armed Forces in Europe, civilian attorney, 1951-55; private practice of law, New York, N.Y., 1956-58; Texas Southern University, Houston, associate professor of law, 1958-60; U.S. Information Agency, Washington, D.C., assistant general counsel, 1961-64; Community Relations Service (U.S. Department of Commerce and U.S. Department of Justice), Washington, D.C., chief counsel, 1965-68; Tuskegee Institute, Tuskegee Institute, Ala., Avalon Professor of Humanities, 1968-70; Boston University, Boston, Mass., professor of English, teaching African and Afro-American literature courses, 1971—. Visiting professor at Wesleyan University, 1969-70, and Duke University, 1972-73, 1973-74. Vice-president and member of board of directors, Southern Education Foundation. *Military service:* U.S. Army, Adjutant Generals Corps, 1942-46; became first lieutenant.

MEMBER: African Studies Association, African Heritage Studies Association, National Council of Teachers of English, College English Association, College Language Association, Association of American University Professors, New York Bar Association.

WRITINGS: (Under pseudonym Paul Vesey) *Elfenbein Zahne* (title means "Ivory Tusks"; bilingual collection of poems with epilogue and translations by Jahnheinz Jahn), Wolfgang Rothe (Heidelberg), 1956; (translator) Jean Paul Sartre, *Black Orpheus* (original French title "Orphee Noir"; translation first published in *Presence Africaine,*

So let us roll over on our back
And again roll to the beat
of drumming all over the land
(From *Poems from Africa* selected by Samuel Allen. Drawings by Romare Bearden.)

1951), Presence Africaine (London), 1960; (author of introduction) *Pan-Africanism Reconsidered,* University of California Press, 1962; *Ivory Tusks and Other Poems,* Poets Press, 1968; (author of introduction) Naseer Aruri and Edmund Ghareeb, editors, *Enemy of the Sun: Poetry of the Palestinian Resistance,* Drum & Spear Press, 1970; (editor and author of introduction) *Poems From Africa,* Crowell, 1973; *Paul Vesey's Ledger* (collection of poems), Paul Breman (London), in press.

Contributor: Jacob Drachler, editor, *African Heritage,* Crowell, 1959; Arthur P. Davis and Saunders Redding, editors, *Cavalcade,* Houghton, 1970; Nathan Wright, Jr., editor, *What Black Educators Are Saying,* Hawthorn, 1970; Raymond F. Betts, editor, *The Ideology of Blackness,* Heath, 1971; Ruth Miller, editor, *Background to Black American Literature,* Glencoe Press, 1971. Poems have been reprinted in more than sixty anthologies and recorded for Library of Congress. Contributor of essays, poems, and translations to *Benin Review* (Nigeria), *Black World, Journal of Afro-American Studies,* and other periodicals.

WORK IN PROGRESS: A collection of essays dealing with African and Afro-American literature.

FOR MORE INFORMATION SEE: Black Orpheus, October, 1958; M. G. Cooke, editor, *Modern Black Novelists,* Prentice-Hall, 1971; Ezekiel Mphahlele, editor, *Voices in the Whirlwind and Other Essays,* Hill & Wang, 1972; *Publisher's Weekly,* April 23, 1973; *Horn Book,* June 6, 1973.

SAMUEL ALLEN

He went up, straight up, for over a mile. But the Enormous Room in the clouds was no longer there. Nothing was there. Only the timeless emptiness of space. ■ (From *High Spy* by Robert Edmond Alter. Illustrated by Albert Orbaan.)

ALTER, Robert Edmond 1925-1965
(Robert Raymond, Robert Retla)

PERSONAL: Born December 10, 1925, in San Francisco, Calif.; son of Retla and Irene (Kerr) Alter; married Maxine Louise Outwater, 1947; children: Sande. *Education:* Studied at University of Southern California, 1944, Pasadena City College, 1946, Pasadena Playhouse, 1948. *Home:* 2811 Alexander Dr., Laguna Beach, Calif. *Agent:* Larry Sternig, 2407 North 44th St., Milwaukee, Wis.

CAREER: In his youth was a migratory worker in Santa Paula, Calif., 1942, a stock boy for Vroman's Books, Pasadena, Calif., 1943-44, and a farm hand in Hamilton, N.D., 1945. U.S. Post Office, Altadena, Calif., carrier, 1949-62. *Military service:* U.S. Army, one year; National Guard, two years, becoming sergeant.

WRITINGS: Swamp Sister, Gold Medal, 1961, *Dark Keep,* 1962, *Listen, the Drum,* 1963, *Time of the Tomahawk,* 1963, *Shovel Nose and the Gator Grabbers,* 1963, *Treasure of Tenakertom,* 1964, *Rabble on a Hill,* 1964, *The Day of the Arkansas,* 1965, *Heroes in Blue and Gray,* Whitman, 1965, *Two Sieges of the Alamo,* 1965, *Who Goes Next,* 1966, *Carny Hill,* Gold Medal, *High Spy,* 1967,

Henry M. Stanley, the Man from Africa, 1967, *Red Water,* 1968, *First Comes Courage,* 1969, (all published by Putnam unless otherwise noted).

HOBBIES AND OTHER INTERESTS: Skin diving, history, and book collecting.

(Died May 26, 1965)

AMON, Aline 1928-

PERSONAL: Surname is pronounced to rhyme with "salmon"; born October 15, 1928, in Paris, France; daughter of American citizens, Will Rice (an architect) and Aline (Halstead) Amon; married Laurance Villers Goodrich (an attorney), October 31, 1953; children: Nielsen Halstead, Lauren Aline. *Education:* Wellesley College, B.A., 1950; Art Student's League of New York, further study, 1952, 1953. *Politics:* Democratic. *Religion:* None. *Home:* 295 Henry St., Brooklyn, N.Y. 11201. *Agent:* Curtis Brown Ltd., 60 West 56th St., New York, N.Y. 10022.

CAREER: Appleton-Century-Crofts, Inc., New York, N.Y., secretary in college text department, 1950-51; U.S. Air Force, Paris, France, executive secretary in military liaison office, 1951-52. Director of playground safety pro-

ALINE AMON

Running away is "funny" to a chimp. ■ (From *Reading, Writing, Chattering Chimps* by Aline Amon. Illustrated by the author.)

wildlife garden, but is less than a half-hour away by subway from the wealth of material in New York's research libraries.

"My first book was prompted by my son's interest in the Indian sign language. It had been discussed briefly in one of his classes, but he was unable to find any additional material on the subject in our local library. After the two years needed to research, write and illustrate *Talking Hands*, I temporarily retired to become reacquainted with my family and to supervise rather extensive renovations to our antique house.

"My new book is again the result of my children's interests. The one thing that most fascinated them among the many articles in natural history magazines that we sometimes discussed at dinner was the thought of 'talking' chimpanzees. I was very fortunate in having the help and cooperation of the scientists involved in the experiments in human-animal communication. They sent not only their scientific papers and photographs for the book, but also were remarkably patient in answering all my queries and in compiling mini-dictionaries of the signs, symbols and computer designs used with the apes—and also used in my illustrations."

gram, Brooklyn Heights, 1963-64. *Awards, honors:* New York Public Library listed *Talking Hands* as one of the ten best Christmas gift books, 1968.

WRITINGS—Self-illustrated: *Talking Hands: How to Use Indian Sign Language,* Doubleday, 1968; *Reading, Writing, Chattering Chimps* (Junior Literary Guild selection), Atheneum, 1975.

WORK IN PROGRESS: Natural science research, particularly in field of animal behavior.

SIDELIGHTS: "I was born in Paris of American parents, suddenly interrupting—and ending—their trip. I returned to the United States when six weeks old.

"The early death of my parents led to a wandering childhood. Until college, I never attended any school for longer than two years. However, I did have the opportunity to live, for periods ranging from a month to several years, in Pennsylvania, Kentucky, California, Arizona, Maine, New Hampshire and Massachusetts—although I always considered New York City my home base. During this time I had ample opportunities to develop my interests in the natural sciences and Indians—digging for relics, panning for gold, hiking, birdwatching and collecting nests, stones, shells, etc.

"After graduation [from college], I sensibly spent two months in secretarial school and then obtained a position at Appleton-Century-Crofts. After one year I left for Europe, having earned just enough for a one-way boat ticket and $100. Fortunately, I obtained a position in a military liaison office in the Paris Embassy just before the money was exhausted. After six months my finances had improved to the point where I could again resign and spend the next two or three months traveling in Europe and Egypt. . . . Since 1953, except for three years in the Mojave Desert, California, while my husband was in the Judge Advocate General's Office of the Air Force, I have lived in Brooklyn Heights. Our pre-Civil War house gives me space for a

ANDERSON, Eloise Adell 1927-

PERSONAL: Born May 13, 1927, in Warren, Minn.; daughter of Adam John and Marie (Hage) Rutkowski; married Samuel Anderson, December, 1953 (divorced, 1973); children: Suzanne, John. *Education:* Moorhead State College, B.S., 1948; University of Wyoming, M.Ed., 1968. *Politics:* Independent. *Religion:* Christian. *Home:* 24 Club Lane, Littleton, Colo. 80123. *Office:* Centennial School, 3306 West Berry Ave., Littleton, Colo. 80120.

ELOISE ADELL ANDERSON

Frank and I watch him steer the bus. When the driver turns the wheel, I turn and pull with my hands too. ■ (From *Carlos Goes to School* by Eloise A. Anderson. Illustrated by Harold Berson.)

10

CAREER: Elementary school teacher in Littleton Public Schools, Littleton, Colo., 1972—. *Awards, honors:* Scholarship to Colorado Women's College, 1971, for creative writing for children.

WRITINGS: Carlos Goes to School, Warne, 1973. Contributor of stories and poems to *Wee Wisdom, Quest,* and *Child Life.*

HOBBIES AND OTHER INTERESTS: Collecting old children's books, golf, swimming.

ARMER, Alberta (Roller)   1904-

PERSONAL: Born February 11, 1904, in Huntingburg, Ind.; daughter of Henry Bernard (a Methodist minister) and Mary (Katterhenry) Roller; married Austin Adams Armer (an agricultural engineer), December 25, 1928; children: Rollin, Beret (Mrs. Dwight Worsham), Elinor. *Education:* University of California at Berkeley, B.A. (with highest honors in English), 1926. *Politics:* Democrat. *Religion:* Unitarian Universalist. *Home and Office:* 725 Oak Ave., Davis, Calif. 95616.

CAREER: Charity Organization Society, New York, N.Y., secretary in research department, 1926-27; W. G. Swanson Publicity, San Francisco, Calif., writer, 1927-28; Federal Writers Project, Detroit, Mich., writer, 1933-34; University of California, Davis, editor, public information office, 1948-52, instructor, English department, 1958-59. *Member:* American Association for the United Nations, Authors Guild, United World Federalists, Guide Dogs for the Blind, Children's Home Society, Phi Beta Kappa. *Awards, honors: Steve and the Guide Dogs* chosen an American Ambassador book by the English-Speaking Union, 1965; *Screwball* listed in Fader & Shaevitz' "Hooked on Books"—one of five hundred paperbacks chosen by teen-agers.

WRITINGS: Cherry House, Beacon, 1958; *Hark the Herald Angel,* Arlington, 1959; *The Two Worlds of Molly O',* A. S. Barnes, 1962; *Screwball,* World Publishing, 1963; *Hi, the Story of a Giraffe,* Simmons Publishing, 1964; *Steve and the Guide Dogs,* World Publishing, 1965; *Troublemaker,* World Publishing, 1966; *The Ghost of Stevenson House,* World Publishing, 1967; *Runaway Girl,* World Publishing, 1970.

SIDELIGHTS: "When I was eight years old I began to write poems, but I can truly say they have improved over the years. I do not try to sell them. They are written out of a need to express a feeling, and when it is on paper I simply put it away—rather hoping some day it will be found and liked 'when I am gone.' If I am on a long automobile ride, since my husband prefers his driving to mine, I make *haiku* in my mind. They are only seventeen syllables—perfect ones, that is—and later they go into a notebook and help me remember countryside I have loved.

"I wrote a 'book' of 150 pages when I was twelve—in pencil in a lined writing tablet. I lay on my stomach in a cold locked bedroom after school and wrote and wrote, going into my other world that I alone could make and then enter. I sent this handwritten story to the A. L. Burt Publishing Company in Indianapolis and asked them please to print one copy for my family for Christmas. Someone very kind wrote back a whole single-spaced typed letter explaining why they could not print a single copy and closing, 'With best wishes for your success.' Believe it or not, my family made fun of me—all except my father, a minister who had written several religious books. He read the letter carefully and his blue eyes were soft as he looked up at me from his desk and said, 'My little girl is an author.'

"I feel that the most important service any adult can perform for a child is encouragement. This is usually possible if the adult is successful himself. If we are happily occupied in our lives we don't try to 'put down' other people. I have always disliked sarcasm and needless criticism. One may as well expect the best and compliment the second-best. I have loved talking to bright school children about writing. Once a whole class was seized with the desire to 'make books'. One boy, who has become a good artist, wrote a wonderful story about a falcon, made his own illustrations and initial-letters for chapter heads, learned book binding, even wrote title and publisher along the spine, and made a facsimile of a copyright page! I felt as though I had turned on a light.

"I no longer take speaking engagements since I turned seventy. But for three years now I have written a weekly familiar-essay column for the *Woodland Democrat,* a daily

ALBERTA ARMER

When it was finished, the hut was about four and a half by six feet, which is pretty crowded for six boys but pretty big for a city oak tree. ■ (From *Screwball* by Alberta Armer. Illustrated by W. T. Mars.)

with a wide circulation both professional and agricultural. I have made wonderful friendships sitting right here at my typewriter. I do not like to reread my old published things but want to get onto something new. I put myself to sleep imagining troubles my hero or heroine may encounter, and almost have a nightmare solving problems purely imaginary. An author, according to my family, is a queer fish who has to experience everything twice—once in life and once on paper. But not my husband, bless him! He will put up with any amount of note-taking when we travel, even help remember facts. Getting things down on paper saves many hours later looking up dates, names of flowers and birds, family histories, and so on.

I cannot resist a blank sheet, a good ballpoint pen, or a newly-sharpened pencil smelling faintly of cedar. I love music by the hour and am sorry I did not continue learning to play the pipe organ. (I once substituted for our church organist for two weeks while he was on vacation, and have never been the same since.) But I still like to play the recorder and piano and sing, especially old songs in groups, carols and the Messiah at Christmas time. I love friendly gatherings, fireplaces, many children, dogs, wild places. I have deeply enjoyed traveling in many countries, four visits to Ireland, several to Mexico; best of all Chile, when our grandchildren lived there.

"Colors become more important as I age, and I wish I had learned to paint. Once I caught a marlin and its wonderful iridescence brightened to intense rose and blue just before it faded in death. I have never gone marlin fishing since; but I have loved fishing in many places. My husband boasts that I always catch the big ones. I see I have not even mentioned cooking, but then don't most women really love to cook? Sewing is something else. I hate it.

"Live to the full in your own best way, I tell my descendants. And my greatest desire, by which I try to live, is to make good come out of something that was bad."

BAKELESS, John (Edwin) 1894-

PERSONAL: Born December 30, 1894, in Carlisle Barracks, Pa.; son of Oscar Hugh and Sara May (Harvey) Bakeless; married Katherine Little (a writer), June 16, 1920. *Education:* State Normal School, Bloomsburg, Pa., diploma in pedagogy, 1913; Williams College, B.A., 1918; Harvard University, M.A., 1920, Ph.D., 1936. *Home and office:* 179 Great Hill Rd., Great Hill, Seymour, Conn. 06483. *Agent:* Curtis Brown Ltd., 60 East 56th St., New York, N.Y. 10022.

CAREER: Started writing and editing career on city staff of *Morning Press,* Bloomsburg, Pa., 1911-14; *Living Age,* Boston, Mass., literary editor, 1921-23, managing editor, 1923-25, editor, 1928-29; *Independent,* literary adviser, 1925-26; *Forum,* New York, N.Y., managing editor, 1926-28; *Literary Digest,* literary editor, 1937-38. New York University, New York, N.Y., lecturer in journalism, 1927-29, 1947-54, instructor, 1929-30, assistant professor, 1930-40, associate professor, 1940-47, lecturer, 1947-54, member of graduate faculty, 1948-54. Sometime teacher of journalism at Finch College, Sarah Lawrence College. Visiting summer instructor at Harvard University, 1938, 1939, University of Colorado, 1962. Trumbull Lecturer at Yale University, 1948; Adams Lecturer at University of Michigan, 1960, Gray Lecturer at Yale, 1964. Seymour (Conn.) Board of Education, member, 1955-62. *Military service:* U.S. Army, 1918-53; became colonel; served with Infantry and General Staff Corps, 1940-46; received Bronze Star; awarded Order of Military Virtue by Bulgarian Army (acceptance of award not permitted by U.S. Army).

MEMBER: Company of Military Historians (fellow), Lepidopterists Society, Connecticut Entomological Society, Reserve Officers Association, Phi Beta Kappa; Harvard Club and University Club (both New York); Army and Navy Club (Washington, D.C.). *Awards, honors:* David A. Wells Prize, Williams College, for *Economic Causes of Modern War,* 1920; Guggenheim fellowships, 1936-37, 1946-47; American Revolution Round Table award for best book on Revolutionary War, 1960; award of New Haven (Conn.) Civil War Round Table.

WRITINGS: Economic Causes of Modern War, Moffat Yard, 1921; The *Origin of the Next War,* Viking, 1926; *Magazine Making,* Viking, 1931; *Christopher Marlowe, the Man in His Time,* Morrow, 1936; *Daniel Boone, Master of the Wilderness,* Morrow, 1939; *The Tragicall History of Christopher Marlowe,* two volumes, Harvard University Press, 1942; *Lewis and Clark, Partners in Discovery,* Morrow, 1947; *Fighting Frontiersman* (juvenile), Morrow, 1948.

Eyes of Discovery, Lippincott, 1950; *Background to Glory,* Lippincott, 1957; (with wife, Katherine Little Bakeless) *They Saw America First* (juvenile), Lippincott, 1957; *Turncoats, Traitors and Heroes,* Lippincott, 1959; *Adventures of Lewis and Clark,* Houghton, 1962; (with Katherine Little Bakeless) *Spies of the Revolution,* Lippincott, 1962; (contributor and adviser) *America's History Lands,* National Geographic Society, 1962; (with Katherine Little Bakeless) *Signers of the Declaration,* Houghton, 1969.

Spies of the Confederacy, Lippincott, 1970; (with Katherine Little Bakeless) *Confederate Spy Stories,* Lippincott, 1973.

Editor: *Report of Conferences and Round Tables,* Williamstown Institute of Politics, Yale University Press, 1932; *Journals of Lewis & Clark,* New American Library, 1964. Member of editorial board, *American Scholar,* 1937-41.

Contributor to *Dictionary of American Biography, Dictionary of American History, Collier's Encyclopedia, Britannica Junior Encyclopedia.* Contributor to magazines including *Atlantic Monthly, Forum, Saturday Review;* book reviews in New York newspapers.

WORK IN PROGRESS: Several books.

JOHN BAKELESS

SIDELIGHTS: "Being the child of two teachers I was born in the Carlisle Indian Industrial School. My father was civilian head of the strictly academic department, while the school itself also taught agriculture, carpentry, printing, blacksmithing, pipe-fitting and all sorts of trades to Indian boys and girls brought in from the Far Western Reservations (to get them away from tribal influences and accustom them to the white man's life, with a view to fitting them in).

"I naturally developed an interest in Indians, though I have no Indian blood myself. I was, therefore, amused when the editor of my book on *Daniel Boone* at William Morrow, complained that I seemed to understand my Indian characters better than my white characters! However, it was a book that has been almost steadily in print from 1939 (with a few years out) and is still selling. It has appeared in American hardcover and paperback editions and in German hard-cover and paperback editions, too. I think I did owe something to my memories of the Indian boys with whom I played, for I had practically no white boys for companions till I was about eight, when my father went to another school for white students.

"I have always loved teaching, hold a teachers' certificate, and the B.A., M.A. and Ph.D. degrees, but I hesitate to make a full-time career of teaching and have always held part-time professorships (except for a year or two) because the tyranny of deans and the jealousy one finds among teachers makes full-time academic life unpleasant and uncertain. On the other hand, a part-time teacher can always consign a dean or president to the infernal regions. I have done so once or twice and their faces, when you try it, are worth going miles to see.

"I have always been rather successful in teaching journalism. My women students in one small women's college had editorial or reportorial positions on something like twenty-five magazines and newspapers in five years! Of course, that made trouble on the faculty!"

Bakeless is competent in French, German, Russian, Latin, Greek, Gothic, Anglo-Saxon, Old French, Middle English.

HOBBIES AND OTHER INTERESTS: Gardening, nature (especially birds and insects), walking, camping, canoeing.

BAKELESS, Katherine Little   1895-

PERSONAL: Born December 5, 1895, in Bloomsburg, Pa.; daughter of Robert Robbins (an attorney and judge) and Deborah (Tustin) Little; married John Bakeless (an author), June 16, 1920. *Education:* Bloomsburg State Normal School (now Bloomsburg State College), graduate, college preparatory course, 1915, music certificate, 1916; additional music study at Peabody Conservatory, 1917-20, with Heinrich Gebhard in Boston, Mass., 1922-26, with Berta Jahn-Beer, Salzburg, Austria, Tobias Matthay, London, England, Arnold Dolmetsch, Haslemere, England. *Home:* 179 Great Hill Rd., Seymour, Conn. 06483.

CAREER: Music instructor at Belmont Hill School, Belmont, Mass., 1923-26, Child's Garden Music School, Summit, N.J., 1928-32, Windward School, Larchmont,

N.Y., 1932-36, City and Country Day School, New York, N.Y., 1933-36; also taught privately in New York, N.Y., 1926-38, Cambridge, Mass., Garden City, N.Y., and at own studio in New York, N.Y. *Member:* Society of Mayflower Descendants, Alliance Francaise (Waterbury, Conn.).

WRITINGS: Story Lives of Great Composers, 1940, revised edition, 1953, *Story Lives of American Composers,* 1941, revised edition, 1954, *Birth of a Nation's Song,* 1942, *Glory Hallelujah,* 1944, *In the Big Time,* 1953, (with husband, John Bakeless) *They Saw America First,* 1957, (with John Bakeless) *Spies of the Revolution,* 1962, (with John Bakeless) *Signers of the Declaration,* Houghton, 1969, (with John Bakeless) *Confederate Spy Stories,* 1973 (all published by Lippincott, unless otherwise noted).

Plays: *A Nation's Song is Born,* 1943, *Good Words for a Stirring Song,* 1945, *Most Memorable Voyage,* 1955, *My Patriot Mother,* 1959 (all published by Plays). A play anthologized in *Four Star Plays for Boys,* Plays, 1957.

SIDELIGHTS: "Being the youngest in the family, with two much-older brothers (the nearest eight years older than I) I had much time to myself, and spent much of it reading.

KATHERINE BAKELESS

I was given some excellent books for children, and kept them all these years, some that my grandmother gave me. I was encouraged to keep a diary and began my first one at the age of ten. I still have that! I wrote down my observations, activities, comments on things and people. It was supposed to be good for me to write something every day, and indeed it was. I would advise all children to be alone in a room a little every day, and write something.

"At six I was started on lessons on the piano. My mother could play piano well. She and her sisters had all been given piano and drawing lessons and were taught to sew. That would have been in the 1860's and '70's, when there was no T.V. and other distractions. As a child, a girl friend and I would spend time after school simply sitting quietly, each reading a book. Sometimes we told each other stories that we made up as we went along. Sometimes we read aloud to each other, laughing over the delightful stories in the fine *St. Nicholas Magazine* for children.

"I was fortunate in having an excellent teacher of piano, who had herself studied at the Boston Conservatory. As I grew up I was always playing in her spring concerts given by her pupils. She prepared me to play for my entrance audition at the Peabody Conservatory, Baltimore, where I studied for three years. After that, I studied wherever I lived; Heinrich Gebhard in Boston; Tobias Matthay in London; Berta Jahn-Beer in Austria. Except for Matthay, my teachers had been pupils of the great Leschetizsky. At the same time, I also taught.

"This does not mean that I was always indoors. Growing up, I was very active: roller-skating, bicycling, swimming. I loved camping, and after my marriage, my husband and I spent some wonderful summers canoeing in the great north woods of Ontario.

"While living in New York City—my husband was always writing when he was not at an office (he was editor of several magazines) or teaching journalism at NYU—he asked me one day if I would like to try writing a book for young people on life stories of composers. I shall never forget the thrill of delight when he told me that Helen Dean Fish, the excellent editor of children's books for Lippincott, would like to see me. She wanted a book on 'Story Lives' of the composers who were next in importance to the greatest ones that Harriet Brower had written in her *Story Lives of Master Composers.* I had read that book years before when I was in school. Miss Brower was now dead, and with the recording of music and the coming of radio, Miss Fish felt that young people should have information about other composers. This was the beginning of my writing books.

"Needless to say, I could not have done these things without my husband's help and advice. He knew style, correct writing, the publishing world.

"We have traveled much in Europe and the British Isles, and I have driven in many countries and in all but two States in the USA."

An Arabian translation of *In the Big Time* was published in Lebanon under auspices of the U.S. Information Agency; *Story Lives of American Composers* has been published in Hindi, Bengali, Gujarati, and Marathi. Bakeless speaks French, some German.

BALDWIN, James (Arthur) 1924-

PERSONAL: Born August 2, 1924, in New York, N.Y.; son of David (a clergyman) and Berdis (Jones) Baldwin. *Education:* Graduate of De Witt Clinton High School, New York, N.Y., 1942. *Agent:* Robert Lantz Literary Agency, 111 West 57th St., New York, N.Y. 10019.

CAREER: Along with writing, Baldwin has held a variety of jobs, most of them in New York but some in Paris, France, where he lived for ten years. Minister for over three years (while still in school) until he began to read again, "and I began, fatally, with Dostoevski." Congress of Racial Equality, member of advisory board. *Member:* National Committee for a Sane Nuclear Policy, Actors' Studio, Authors League, Dramatists Guild, International P.E.N. *Awards, honors:* Eugene F. Saxton fellowship, 1945, Rosenwald fellowship, 1948, Guggenheim fellowship, 1954; National Institute of Arts and Letters grant in literature, 1956; *Partisan Review* fellowship, 1956; Ford Foundation grant-in-aid, 1959; National Conference of Christians and Jews award, 1961.

WRITINGS: Go Tell It on the Mountain (novel), Knopf, 1953, Dial, 1963; *Notes of a Native Son* (essays), Beacon, 1955, Dial, 1963; *Giovanni's Room* (novel), Dial, 1956; *Nobody Knows My Name* (essays), Dial, 1961; *Another*

JAMES BALDWIN

Country (novel), Dial, 1962; *The Fire Next Time* (essays), Dial, 1963; (with Richard Avedon) *Nothing Personal* (photo essay), Atheneum, 1964; *Blues for Mister Charlie* (drama first produced in New York, 1964), Dial, 1964; *Going to Meet the Man* (short stories), Dial, 1965; *Tell Me How Long the Train's Been Gone* (novel), Dial, 1968; *The Amen Corner* (play, first produced Washington, D.C., 1955, New York, 1965), Dial, 1968; (with Margaret Mead) *A Rap on Race,* Lippincott, 1971; *No Name in the Street* (essays), Dial, 1972; *One Day When I Was Lost: A Scenario Based on "The Autobiography of Malcolm X"* (play first produced in New York, 1972), Dial, 1973; (with Nikki Giovanni) *Dialogue,* Lippincott, 1973; *If Beale Street Could Talk* (novel, ALA Best Young Adult Book list), Dial, May, 1974. Contributor to *Harper's, The Nation, Esquire, Mademoiselle, New Yorker, Liberator* (until 1967 when he severed his association to protest the publication of anti-Semitic articles), and other magazines in U.S. and abroad.

Screenplay: "The Inheritance", 1973.

SIDELIGHTS: James Baldwin was born on August 2, 1924, in New York City, the first of nine children, and grew up in Harlem where his father was a minister. He was graduated from De Witt Clinton High School in 1942 and held a number of minor jobs—handyman, porter, elevator operator, office boy, factory worker, dishwasher, file clerk. At twenty-four, he left the United States for a stay in Europe of almost ten years, broken only to return here for business reasons. Staying mainly in Paris but traveling in many parts of Europe, he wrote and published his first three books. In 1957, he came back to the United States, and, for the last several years has divided his time between a home in southern France and one in New York City. Recognized as one of America's finest writers, James Baldwin has also gained international prominence as a leader and spokesman for the civil rights movement.

FOR MORE INFORMATION SEE: Commonweal, May 22, 1953, December 8, 1961, October 26, 1962, December 7, 1962; *Commentary,* November, 1953, January, 1957; *New York Times Book Review,* February 26, 1956, July 2, 1961, June 24, 1962; *Saturday Review,* December 1, 1956, July 1, 1961, February 2, 1963, May 2, 1964; *Time,* June 30, 1961, June 29, 1962, November 6, 1964; *Atlantic,* July, 1961, July, 1962, March, 1963; *New Republic,* August 7, 1961, August 27, 1962, November 27, 1965; *New Yorker,* November 25, 1961, August 4, 1962; Alfred Kazin, *Contemporaries,* Little, 1962; *New York Herald Tribune Book Review,* June 17, 1962; *San Francisco Chronicle,* June 28, 1962; *New Statesman,* July 13, 1962, July 19, 1963; *Nation,* July 14, 1962, November 17, 1962, March 2, 1963; *Christian Science Monitor,* July 19, 1962; *Newsweek,* February 4, 1963; *Harper's,* March, 1963; *America,* March 16, 1963; *Times Literary Supplement,* July 26, 1963, December 10, 1964; Robert F. Sayre in *Contemporary American Novelists,* edited by Harry T. Moore, Southern Illinois University Press, 1964; *New York Review of Books,* May 28, 1964, December 17, 1964, December 9, 1965; *Book Week,* May 31, 1964, September 26, 1965; *Encounter,* July, 1965; Fern Marja Eckman, *The Furious Passage of James Baldwin,* Evans, 1966; *Contemporary Literary Criticism,* volumes 1, 2, and 3, edited by Carolyn Riley, Gale Research, 1973; *World Authors: 1950-1970,* edited by John Wakeman, H. W. Wilson, 1975.

BALIAN, Lorna 1929-

LORNA BALIAN

PERSONAL: Surname rhymes with "stallion"; born December 14, 1929, in Milwaukee, Wis.; daughter of Henry W. (with the telephone company) and Molly (Pope) Kohl; married John J. Balian (an artist), March 4, 1950; children: Heather, Japheth, Ivy, Aram, Lecia, Poppy. *Education:* Attended Layton School of Art, 1948-49. *Home and office address:* Route 2, Box 84, Hartford, Wis. 53207.

CAREER: American Lace Co., Milwaukee, Wis., artist, 1949-51; free-lance artist, 1948—. Teacher of crafts in adult vocational school. *Member:* Authors Guild of Authors League of America.

WRITINGS—Juvenile; all self-illustrated: *Humbug Witch* (Junior Literary Guild selection), Abingdon, 1965; *I Love You, Mary Jane* (Junior Literary Guild selection), Abingdon, 1967; *The Aminal,* Abingdon, 1972; *Sometimes It's Turkey-Sometimes It's Feathers,* Abingdon, 1973; *Where in the World Is Henry?,* Bradbury, 1973; *Humbug Rabbit,* (Junior Literary Guild selection), Abingdon, 1974.

WORK IN PROGRESS: Writing and illustrating *The Sweet Touch.*

When she wanted to cook up a batch of Magic Potion, she would dump all the very best things in her very best kettle. ■ (From *Humbug Witch* by Lorna Balian. Illustrated by the author.)

SIDELIGHTS: "My books are for very young children. They are primarily entertaining with illustration as important as the story. My six children inspired me and although I am forty-five years old now, I have good recall of my own childhood and clearly remember my feelings as a young child. I usually do my illustrations with pen and ink, or pencil, line drawings and watercolor. I write and illustrate books because it's the most fun thing I can imagine doing, and happily, children seem to have fun reading them."

HOBBIES AND OTHER INTERESTS: Gardening, cooking, sewing, painting.

FOR MORE INFORMATION SEE: Junior Literary Guild Catalog, September, 1974.

BARNABY, Ralph S(tanton) 1893-

PERSONAL: Born January 21, 1893, in Meadville, Pa.; son of Charles Weaver (an engineer) and Jennie (Christy) Barnaby; first wife, Charline Johnson; married Margaret Evans, March 19, 1936. *Education:* Columbia University, M.E., 1915. *Home:* 2107 Chancellor St., Philadelphia, Pa. 19103. *Office:* Franklin Institute, Philadelphia, Pa. 19103.

CAREER: Elco Co., Bayonne, N.J., engineer, 1915-16; Standard Aero Corp., Plainfield, N.J., assistant chief engineer 1917; U.S. Navy, regular officer, 1917-47, serving as naval constructor and naval aviator and retiring with rank of captain; Franklin Institute, Philadelphia, Pa., engineering executive, 1947-63, consultant, 1963—. Sculptor and painter; bronze busts are in collections of U.S. Naval Academy, Mariners Museum, and David Taylor Model

RALPH S. BARNABY

Basin; has done plaques for Wright Brothers Memorial at Kitty Hawk and naval air fields. *Awards, honors*—Military: Legion of Merit, Air Medal; Civilian: Columbia University Medal of Merit, Paul Tissandier diploma of Federation Aeronautique Internationale, Warren E. Eaton Soaring Trophy.

WRITINGS—Self-illustrated: *Gliders and Gliding: Design Principles, Structural Features and Operation of Gliders and Soaring Planes,* Ronald, 1930; *How to Make and Fly Paper Airplanes* (juvenile), Four Winds, 1968. Contributor of articles and papers to technical journals.

HOBBIES AND OTHER INTERESTS: Music.

BARTON, Byron 1930-

PERSONAL: Born September 8, 1930, in Pawtucket, R.I.; son of Toros and Elizabeth (Krekorian) Vartanian; married Harriett Wyatt, December, 1967 (divorced, April, 1973). *Education:* Attended Los Angeles City College, and Chouinard Art Institute. *Home:* 2 Washington Sq. Village, New York, N.Y. 10012. *Agent:* Marilyn Marlow, Curtis Brown, Ltd., 60 East 56th St., New York, N.Y. 10022.

CAREER: CBS-TV, New York, N.Y., designer, 1960-66. *Military service:* U.S. Army, 1950-52. *Awards, honors: The Paper Airplane Book,* 1971, and *Where's Al?,* 1973, were Children's Book Showcase Titles.

WRITINGS—All self-illustrated juveniles: *Elephant,* Seabury, 1971; *Where's Al,* Seabury, 1972; *Applebet Story,* Viking, 1973; *Buzz Buzz Buzz* (Junior Literary Guild selection), Macmillan, 1973; *Harry is a Scaredy-Cat,* Macmillan, 1974; *Jack and Fred,* Macmillan, 1974; *Hester,* Morrow, 1975.

Illustrator: Constance C. Greene, *Girl Called Al,* Viking, 1969; Alan Venable, *The Checker Players,* Lippincott, 1973; Seymour Simon, *The Paper Airplane Book,* Viking, 1973.

SIDELIGHTS: "I was born in Pawtucket, Rhode Island. My father sold coal and wood in the winter and ice in the summer. To a small boy, our home with its woodpiles, barns, and attics, made an ideal playground. When I was in the fourth grade, my parents moved with five children to California, and I grew up in Los Angeles.

"I went to Clifford Street Grammar School and because of a difference in teaching methods between this school and the Pawtucket school, my interest in drawing and art began. In class, when subjects I had already learned came up, I was allowed to go to the back of the room to play with paints. I remember making large paintings of Indians in their canoes, alongside their tepees, and hunting animals. My pictures were hanging all over the back walls of the class and the cloakroom. I became known as 'the artist'. At Christmas I was usually given paints, pencils, pads, and books on how to draw. Because some of the books were rather old, I began to develop a pen-and-ink style similar to artists popular during the time of Charles Dana Gibson."

FOR MORE INFORMATION SEE: Saturday Review/World, December 4, 1973; *Horn Book,* June, 1974.

(From *Applebet Story* by Byron Barton. Illustrated by the author.)

BEERS, Dorothy Sands 1917-

PERSONAL: Born June 17, 1917, in Rye, N.Y.; daughter of Benjamin Jerome (a physician) and Josephine (Willson) Sands; married Yardley Beers (a physicist), May 12, 1945; children: G. Jerome, Deborah Yardley. *Education:* Bennington College, A.B., 1938. *Home:* 740 Willowbrook Rd., Boulder, Colo. 80302.

CAREER: Massachusetts Institute of Technology, Radiation Laboratory, Cambridge, technician, 1943, staff member, 1944-46; free-lance writer. *Member:* American Pen Women, Colorado Authors League.

WRITINGS: ABC Alphabet Cookbook (juvenile), Schmitt, Hall & McCreary, 1973. Contributor of verse, fiction, and articles to children's magazines and newspapers; contributor of articles to *Denver Post* and *Christian Science Monitor.*

HOBBIES AND OTHER INTERESTS: Violin, hiking.

BEERS, V(ictor) Gilbert 1928-

PERSONAL: Born May 6, 1928, in Sidell, Ill.; son of Ernest S. (a farmer) and Jean (Bloomer) Beers; married Arlisle Felten, August 26, 1950; children: Kathleen, Douglas, Ronald, Janice, Cynthia. *Education:* Wheaton College, Wheaton, Ill., A.B., 1950; Northern Baptist Seminary, Chicago, M.R.E., 1953, M.Div., 1954, Th.M., 1955, Th.D., 1960; Northwestern University, Ph.D., 1963. *Politics:* Republican. *Home and office:* Route 1, Box 321, Elgin, Ill. 60120.

CAREER: Northern Baptist Seminary, Chicago, Ill., professor of religion, 1954-57; David C. Cook Publishing Co., Elgin, Ill., editor of senior high publications, 1957-59, executive editor, 1959-61, editorial director, 1961-67; Creative Designs, Elgin, Ill., president, 1967—. Presently member of board of directors, Summit Finance Corp., Fort Wayne, Ind., Scripture Press, Deerfoot Lodge (boys camp), Speculator, N.Y., and Wheaton College, Wheaton, Ill.; member of board of directors, Wheaton Youth Symphony, Wheaton, Ill., 1962-64, president, 1963-64; trustee of David C. Cook Foundation, 1965-67. *Member:* Children's Reading Round Table (Chicago), Wheaton College Alumni Association (president, 1972-73). *Awards, honors:* Distinguished Service Award of Midland Authors, 1973, for *Cats and Bats and Things Like That* and *The ABQ Book.*

WRITINGS—Adult: *Family Bible Library,* ten volumes, Southwestern Co., 1971; *Patterns for Prayer from the Gospels,* Ravell, 1972; *Joy Is . . .,* Revell, 1974; *The Discovery Bible Handbook,* Victor Books, 1974.

Juvenile: *A Child's Treasury of Bible Stories,* four volumes, Parent and Child Institute, 1970; *Cats and Bats and Things Like That,* Moody, 1972; *The ABQ Book,* Moody, 1972; *The House in the Hole in the Side of the Tree,* Moody, 1973; "Learning to Read from the Bible" series, four books titled *God Is My Helper, God Is My Friend, Jesus Is My Teacher,* and *Jesus Is My Guide,* Zondervan, 1973; *Coco's Candy Shop,* Moody, 1973; *Around the World with My Red Balloon,* Moody, 1973; *The Magic Merry-Go-Round,* Moody, 1973; *A Gaggle of Green Geese,* Moody, 1974; *Honeyphants and Elebees,* Moody, 1974; *Through Golden Windows,* Moody, 1975.

SIDELIGHTS: "As a father of five inquisitive children, I have spent many hours interacting with them where fun and learning touch. It has been my concern that we make learning fun and we make fun a means of learning. Add to this the dimension of Bible and Christian education, and we have the reason for my writing.

"Too often, the Bible and Christian education are presented in somber tones. This is inconsistent with the 'Good News' of One who came to bring life, and joy, and hope, and a new way. Thus *Honeyphants and Elebees* and *A Gaggle of Green Geese* help happy children learn about those happy truths."

BEYER, Audrey White 1916-

PERSONAL: Born November 12, 1916, in Portland, Me.; daughter of William Joseph and Hermon (Brand) White; married Walter Archer Beyer (teacher of mathematics), July 20, 1940 (died October, 1974); children: Henry G. II, Edmund Brand. *Education:* Westbrook Junior College, diploma, 1937; University of Maine, A.B., 1939; graduate study at Northeastern University and University of Maine (Portland). *Politics:* Independent (registered Republican). *Religion:* Episcopalian. *Home:* Belfield Rd., Cape Elizabeth, Me. 04107.

CAREER: Teacher of English at Westbrook Junior College, Portland, Me., 1939-43, Milton Academy Girls' School, Milton, Mass., 1956, Waynflete Summer School, 1957-59, Northeastern University, Boston, Mass., 1968-73, Milton Academy Boys' School, 1973-74, Westbrook College, 1974-75. *Member:* Maine Historical Society, *Awards, honors:* Jack and Jill Award, 1958; Westbrook Junior College Award for Alumnae Achievement, 1960.

WRITINGS: Capture at Sea (juvenile), Knopf, 1959; *The Sapphire Pendant,* Knopf, 1961, *Katharine Leslie,* Knopf, 1963; *Dark Venture,* Knopf, 1968.

WORK IN PROGRESS: A story for young adults based on nineteenth-century New England history.

SIDELIGHTS: "From a very early age I was encouraged in my writing by a sympathetic and understanding mother who listened attentively to anything I produced—short story, play, poem—and pronounced it 'lovely.' My teachers, too, were helpful as well as encouraging. They gave me many years of good, thorough training in composition. In high school I was co-editor of the newspaper and editor of the year book. In college, where I majored in English and minored in history, I continued to write and to edit. Here I was elected class poet.

"All my life I have been torn between teaching and writing. To me, teaching offers the stimulation of young minds, the challenge of getting across pertinent material, and the lively, often humorous, give and take of classroom discussion. Writing, on the other hand, offers a chance for research into history, always fascinating, and an opportunity to bring that history alive through the action of fictional characters whom I create. Here my aim is to present a story both accurate in historical detail and absorbing to the reader. All of my books are rooted in history: the War of 1812; Napoleon's preparations for an invasion of England; the burning in 1775 of Falmouth, Maine; and the 'triangle trade' with its horror and tragedy for both white and black men.

V. GILBERT BEERS

There came a cry, lost upon the wind, and Duval slumped to the ground. ■ (From *The Sapphire Pendant* by Audrey White Beyer. Illustrated by Robin Jacques.)

"Perhaps the two greatest joys writing offers me are, first, the actual creative process—getting words and ideas down on paper—and, second, the numerous letters from young readers who themselves write to say they enjoy my books."

Capture at Sea ran as a serial in *Jack and Jill.*

HOBBIES AND OTHER INTERESTS: Reading, walking, gardening.

BLAKE, Quentin 1932-

PERSONAL: Born December 16, 1932, in England. *Education:* Downing College, Cambridge, M.A., 1956. *Home:* Flat 8, 30 Bramham Gardens, London S.W.5, England. *Agent:* Curtis Brown Ltd., 60 East 56th St., New York, N.Y. 10022; and A. P. Watt & Son, 26-28 Bedford Row, London W.C.1, England.

CAREER: Primarily an illustrator, drawing for *Punch* and

1964; Rosemary Weir, *Further Adventures of Albert the Dragon,* Abelard, 1964; Richard Schickel, *Gentle Knight,* Abelard, 1964; Edward Korel, *Listen and I'll Tell You,* Lippincott, 1964; Ennis Rees, *Pun Fun,* Abelard, 1965; Thomas L. Hirsch, *Puzzles for Pleasure and Leisure,* Abelard, 1966; Ennis Rees, *Tiny Tall Tales,* Abelard, 1967; Nils-Olof Franzen, *Agaton Sax and the Diamond Thieves,* Delacorte, 1967; Robert Tibber, *Aristide,* Dial, 1967; Helen J. Fletcher, *Put on Your Thinking Cap,* Abelard-Schuman, 1968; John Yeoman, *The Bear's Winter House,* World, 1969; Nathan Zimelman, *The First Elephant Comes to Ireland,* Follett, 1969; John Yeoman, *Alphabet Soup,* Faber, 1969, Follett, 1970; S. Forst, *Agaton Sax and the Scotland Yard Mystery,* Delacorte, 1969; Ennis Rees, *Gillygaloos and the Gollywhoppers: Tall Tales About Mythical Monsters,* Abelard, 1969.

John Yeoman, *The Bear's Water Picnic,* Blackie, 1970, Macmillan, 1971; Thomas Corddry, *Kibby's Big Feat,* Follett, 1970; S. Forst, *Agaton Sax and the Incredible Max Brothers,* Delacorte, 1970; John Yeoman, *Sixes and Sevens,* Blackie, 1971, Macmillan, 1972; Helen J. Fletcher, *Puzzles and Quizzles,* Abelard, 1971; Sid Fleischman, *McBroom's Wonderful One-Acre Farm,* Chatto & Windus, 1972; John Yeoman, *Mouse Trouble,* Hamish Hamilton, 1972, Macmillan, 1973; Joan Aiken, *Tales of Arabel's*

QUENTIN BLAKE

One morning in early summer, many years ago, Sir Thomas Magpie was getting out of bed. He was unhappy because he'd just found that, in the night, the mice had been eating his boots again. ■ (From *Snuff* by Quentin Blake. Illustrated by the author.)

other British magazines and illustrating children's and educational books. Tutor in School of Graphic Design, Royal College of Art, London. *Awards, honors:* Whitbread Literary Award, 1974, for *How Tom Beat Captain Najork and His Hired Sportsmen;* Hans Christian Andersen honor book for illustration, 1975, for *How Tom Beat Captain Najork and His Hired Sportsmen.*

WRITINGS—All self-illustrated: *Patrick,* J. Cape, 1968, Walck, 1969; *Jack and Nancy,* J. Cape, 1969; *Snuff,* Lippincott, 1973; *Lester at the Seaside,* Collins Picture Lions, 1975; *Lester and the Unusual Pet,* Collins Picture Lions, 1975; (with John Yeoman) *Puffin Book of Improbable Records,* Puffin, 1975.

Illustrator: Weir, *Albert the Dragon,* Abelard, 1961; Ezo, *My Son-in-Law the Hippopotamus,* Abelard, 1962; Ennis Rees, *Riddles, Riddles Everywhere,* Abelard, 1964; Rosemary Weir, *Albert the Dragon and the Centaur,* Abelard,

Raven, J. Cape, 1974, published in America as *Arabel's Raven,* Doubleday, 1974; John Yeoman, *Beatrice and Vanessa,* Hamish Hamilton, 1974, Macmillan, 1975; Dr. Seuss, *Great Day for Up,* Random House, 1974; Russell Hoban, *How Tom Beat Captain Najork and His Hired Sportsmen,* Atheneum, 1974; Michael Rosen, *Mind Your Own Business,* S. J. Phillips, 1974; Bronnie Cunningham, *Puffin Joke Book,* Penguin, 1974; Russell Hoban, *A New Thing for Captain Najork,* J. Cape, 1975; John Yeoman, *Boy Who Sprouted Antlers,* Transatlantic.

SIDELIGHTS: Patrick was made into a film strip by Weston Woods.

FOR MORE INFORMATION SEE: Illustrators of Children's Books: 1957-1966, Horn Book, 1968; *Horn Book,* February, 1974; *New York Times Book Review,* November 3, 1974; *Signal,* January, 1975; *Graphis* (children's book edition), September, 1975.

BLYTON, Carey 1932-

PERSONAL: Born March 14, 1932, in Beckenham, Kent, England; son of Hanly Harrison (a company director) and Florence Maud (Pullen) Blyton; married Patricia Eileen Joan Dennis, April 4, 1953 (divorced April 16, 1957); married Mary Josephine Mills, October 28, 1961; children: (second marriage) Matthew James, Daniel Carey. *Education:* Attended University College, London, 1950-51; Trinity College of Music, London, A.Mus. T.C.L. and L.T.C.L., 1955, F.T.C.L. and B.Mus., 1957; attended Royal Danish Academy of Music, 1957-58. *Politics:* None. *Religion:* Church of England. *Home:* "Hawthornden," 55 Goldsel Rd., Swanley, BR8 8HA, England. *Agent:* John Farquharson Ltd., 15 Red Lion Square, London WC1R 4QW, England.

CAREER: Mills Music Ltd., London, England, music editor, 1958-63; Trinity College of Music, London, England, professor of music, 1963-73; Faber Music Ltd., London, England, music editor, 1963—; Guildhall School of Music and Drama, London, England, professor of composition for films, television, and radio, 1972—; composer, author, lec-

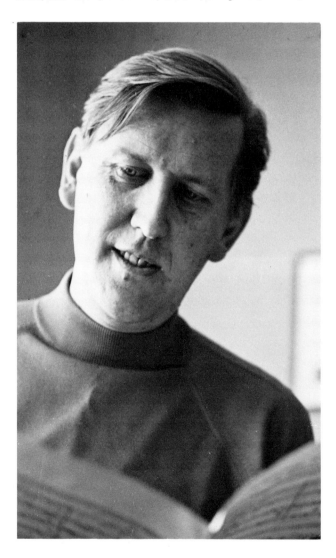

CAREY BLYTON

turer. Music tutor, Workers' Educational Association, 1964—; music adviser, Spottiswoode and Ballantyne, publishers, 1965-67; member of executive committee, Dartford Rural District Arts Council, 1966-72; member of lecture panel, British Film Institute, 1974—; member of Music Advisory Panel, South East Arts Association, 1974—. *Member:* Composers' Guild of Great Britain (member of executive committee, 1966-70), Society of Film & Television Arts, Mechanical-Copyright Protection Society, Performing Right Society. *Awards, honors:* Sir Granville Bantock Prize for Musical Composition, 1954. Sir Winston Churchill Endowment Fund scholarship to Royal Danish Academy of Music, 1957.

WRITINGS: (Arranger of music) *The Faber Book of Nursery Songs,* Faber, 1968, published as *Every Child's Book of Nursery Songs,* Crown, 1969; *Bananas in Pyjamas: A Book of Nonsense Songs and Nonsense Poems for Children,* Faber, 1972, Transatlantic, 1973. Also author of musical compositions. Contributor to *Musical Times, Composer, Music in Education, Musical Opinion, Making Music, BMG, Argosy,* and others.

WORK IN PROGRESS: Dr. Shinfiddler's Musical Zoo, a book of musical jokes, quodlibets, atrocious puns, and other musical nonsense.

SIDELIGHTS: "Although I am a professional composer, writing music for documentary films, television plays, television commercials, etc., I am intensely interested in writing words (though I haven't had much published in this way yet). My aunt, the children's writer, Enid Blyton, reckoned that 'the gift of the gab' was a Blyton trait, best put to some use like writing! Having changed horses in midstream (I was training to be a zoologist), I still remain deeply fascinated by natural history subjects (some of my best music scores are for natural history films), and I hope to try my hand eventually at television scripts involving pioneer naturalists and medical men, etc. I am also very involved with humour in all forms, and I hope to write more nonsense poetry in the future (which will be a lot easier than writing more in the past).

"I had been perpetrating nonsense poems—often 'set' to music spontaneously whilst dressing in the morning—ever since my eldest son, Matthew, was old enough to appreciate such things: say, since he was about two or three. I realised that I had almost two dozen of these extraordinary things, and it occurred to me—for no particular reason, other than I thought he might find them funny—to send some of them to Tom Barling. He loved them, and then it occurred to me that me might like to illustrate one or two. This he did. As soon as I saw them, I thought that maybe we would collaborate on a book—in other words, find a market for them a bit bigger than my bedroom and his studio. The rest is very simple. I showed the poems to Mr. Peter Crawley of Faber & Faber. (I naturally showed them first to Faber's, because of my connections with the firm) and he seemed to find them funny. Ever since then, no-one has had much rest. . . ."

FOR MORE INFORMATION SEE: Musical Times, July, 1964; *Kent Life,* June, 1969; *Music and Musicians,* December, 1971; *Strumenti e Musica,* May, 1973; *Woodwind World,* June, 1973; *Music in Education,* March/April, 1974; *Film,* April, 1975.

He's nitting nests for cobras
And Wellington boots for fleas.
(From *Bananas in Pyjamas: A Book of Nonsense* by Carey Blyton. Illustrated by Tom Barling.)

BOLES, Paul Darcy 1919-

PERSONAL: Born March 5, 1919, in Auburn, Ind.; son of Ernest Glendon and Gwendolyn (Marsden) Boles; married Dorothy Flory, December 25, 1941; children: Shawn Michael, Patric Laurence, Terence Ross. *Education:* Privately educated. *Politics:* Independent. *Home:* 4009 Wieuca Rd., N.E., Atlanta, Ga. *Mailing Address:* Lenox Square Station, Box 18582, Atlanta, Ga. 30326. *Agent:* A. L. Hart, Fox Chase Agency, 419 East 57th St., New York, N.Y. 10022.

CAREER: Writer. *Awards, honors:* Friends of American Writers $1,000 award for *Parton's Island*, 1959; Indiana University Writers' Conference, most distinguished work of fiction for young adults award, 1969, for *A Million Guitars;* Georgia Writers' Association literary achievement award for fiction, 1969, presented for entire body of work.

WRITINGS: The Streak, 1953; *The Beggars in the Sun,* 1954; *Glenport Illinois,* 1956; *Deadline,* 1957; (contributor) *The Living Novel,* edited by Granville Hicks, 1957, *Parton's Island,* 1958 (all published by Macmillan); *A Million Guitars* (short stories), Little, Brown, 1968; *I Thought You Were a Unicorn* (juvenile), Little, Brown, 1971; *The Limner,* Crowell, 1975. Short stories anthologized in *Best Post Short Stories,* 1958, 1961, *Seventeen's Stories,* 1958, *The Big Ones,* 1969, *Reading for You,* 1970, *The Rebel,* 1971, other collections. Short stories also have appeared in *Ladies' Home Journal, Cosmopolitan, McCall's, Good Housekeeping, Boy's Life, Argosy, Fantasy and Science Fiction, Seventeen, Saturday Evening Post, Playboy, Cavalier,* and in magazines in France, Germany, England, and Sweden; essays in *Writer, Writer's Digest;* reviews in *Saturday Review.*

SIDELIGHTS: "I suppose I started writing when I was about seven; I know when I was eight or nine I read chapters of a serial aloud to my English class, which was run by a most tolerant and magnificent lady. I was allowed ten minutes or so at the end of each class, each school day, and I learned to keep the class on edge and panting for more. It

PAUL DARCY BOLES

once in a while such writing reaches paper. I read anything and everything, always have; now and then I *re*-read Tolstoy, Proust, Mark Twain, Dostoyevsky, Balzac, Charles Dickens, just because what they all said, and say, is important today and we would have a better world if more people listened to it and loved it. Reading, and writing, can bring you closer to finding out who you are, it can sink you down into the earth like a blade of grass and lift you a lot higher than the sun, and that's more important to all people—learning who you are, the many things you are—than any politics have, so far, been.

"I live most of the time in Atlanta, which used to be a handsome city, and still is in places, where the real-estate beetles haven't chewed it away. I hate violence in any form, because it is only stupidity. And I know truly that pollution and greed are some of the worst kinds of violence, and that good writing—funny or tragic or in between—always deals with this kind of contest between good and evil, no matter what the writing may seem to be on the surface. And I know that one poet—John Keats or Dylan Thomas, a real poet, not a violent experimenter—is worth more to this earth than all its money, or a million steel and plastic buildings, or all the psychologists and psychiatrists, people have to pay to fix them up after they've chased the money and worked in the buildings."

was a strange sensation, learning to write to their reactions (and they made a tough audience). After class I would dash home, fair weather or foul, and immediately write the next chapter, partly because *I* wanted to know how it came out, just as much as my listeners did.

"I think writing, like the other arts, has to be done, to be done successfully, by somebody who cares more for it than for any other work on earth. I don't write for money, though money is always nice, and most welcome, and I'm not rich. I write because if I didn't I would die inside. Maybe I wouldn't look dead, but I'd feel that way. I don't need a cork-lined room for writing, I can do it, when I'm going good, in a telephone booth with a line of people waiting to get in, though this isn't smart practice.

"In old-time Ireland, before all the troubles, there were storytellers who went from home to home, castle to castle, and made their living by telling stories; they were called *schanacies*. If I'm anything, I'm a *schanacy*. As you write, through the years, you get better—you learn a little more of what to put in, what to leave out; you can feel more and more strongly what Robert Graves—the world's best living poet—called, *The reader over your shoulder*. You can hear your voice, your words, reaching the reader's ear. You can see his eyes read your words. I don't have any bright explanation for this; it just happens.

"For fun, I do a lot of things: archery, games of one kind and another, some traveling; but when I'm not with a typewriter or just some paper and a pen or pencil, I'm still writing in my head. I've written whole novels there, and

BRUMSIC BRANDON JR.

24   **Something about the Author**

(From *Luther Raps* by Brumsic Brandon, Jr.)

BRANDON, Brumsic, Jr. 1927-

PERSONAL: Born April 10, 1927, in Washington, D.C.; son of Brumsic and Pearl (Brooks) Brandon; married Rita Broughton (a teacher), September 30, 1950; children: Linda, Brumsic III, Barbara. *Education:* New York University, student, 1945-46. *Politics:* Independent. *Home:* 210 Rushmore St., Westbury, N.Y. 11590.

CAREER: RAC Service Co., Inc., Alexandria, Va., assistant art director, 1955-57; Bray Studios, Inc. (motion picture producers), New York, N.Y., designer and animator, 1957-69; WPIX-TV, New York, N.Y., television performer, 1969-73; Los Angeles Times Syndicate, Los Angeles, Calif., artist and writer for comic strip, "Luther," 1971—. Member of forum, White House Conference on Children, 1970; member of advisory board, Afro American Bicentennial Corp. *Military service:* U.S. Army, 1950-52; became sergeant. *Member:* American Federation of Television and Radio Artists.

WRITINGS: Luther's Got Class, Eriksson, 1975; *Luther from Inner City,* Eriksson, 1969; *Luther Tells It as It Is,* Eriksson, 1970; *Right On, Luther,* Eriksson, 1971; *Luther Raps,* Eriksson, 1971; *Outta Sight, Luther,* Eriksson, 1972; "Vegetable Soup," NBC, November, 1975. Publications include comic books for New York State Consumer Protection Board.

Illustrator: Matt Robinson, *The Six Button Dragon,* Random House, 1971.

WORK IN PROGRESS: Luther comic books and short stories; television adaptations of Luther.

SIDELIGHTS: "My objective, in my comic strip, is to bring to light not only the long ignored 'black perspective,' but the many various philosophical postures found therein."

BRIMBERG, Stanlee 1947-

PERSONAL: Born July 7, 1947, in New York. *Education:* Brooklyn College of the City University of New York, A.B., 1968. *Home:* 324 East 52nd St., New York, N.Y. 10022.

CAREER: Public School 23, Brooklyn, N.Y., teacher, 1968—.

WRITINGS: Black Stars (nonfiction children's book), Dodd, 1974.

WORK IN PROGRESS: Muffin's Trouble, novel for young readers.

SIDELIGHTS: "It's most important for me to *feel* deeply about what I write. This goes for non-fiction as well as fiction. No subject can be involving without feeling. I write, therefore, after I have come in contact with the feeling. The subject matter comes second.

"*Black Stars* came about because I saw a bunch of historical figures floating around in *facts,* in books that told me when they lived and died and went to school. I knew they had personalities, and that if I read enough about each, I'd get a sense of them. I only began writing after I felt I knew them personally."

STANLEE BRIMBERG

BROWN, Rosalie (Gertrude) Moore   1910-
(Rosalie Moore)

PERSONAL: Born October 8, 1910, in Oakland, Calif.; daughter of Marvin Alonzo (a railroad man) and Teresa (Wooldridge; a teacher and writer) Moore; married William Louis Brown (a writer), June 30, 1942 (died, September, 1964); children: Deborah Ann Turrietta, Celia Jeanne Barrett, Camas Eve. *Education:* University of California, Berkeley, A.B. (magna cum laude), 1932, M.A., 1934. *Home:* 11 Crescent Lane, Fairfax, Calif. 94930. *Agent:* McIntosh & Otis, Inc., 18 East 41st St., New York, N.Y. 10017.

CAREER: Oakland Tribune Radio Station KLX, Oakland, Calif., copywriter and announcer, 1935-37; Mexico City College, lecturer in creative criticism of contemporary literature, 1950; College of Marin, Kentfield, Marin County, Calif., instructor, 1965-76 (chairman, communications department, 1974-76); piano teacher and writer. Founder, with Lawrence Hart and Jeanne McGahey, of Activist Group of poets, under aegis of Lawrence Hart. Group work featured in poetry magazines. *Member:* American Federation of Teachers, Poetry Society of America, Phi Beta Kappa. *Awards, honors:* Charles H. Sergel Drama Prize, University of Chicago, for poetic drama, 1938; award for best poems, New York World's Fair, 1939; Albert Bender Award in literature, 1943; first award, Poetry Society of America, 1944; Yale Series of Younger Poets Award, 1948; Guggenheim fellowships in creative writing (poetry), 1950-51, 1951-52; Vachel Lindsay Award, *Poetry* magazine, 1957.

WRITINGS—Juvenile books with husband under names Bill and Rosalie Brown: *Forest Fireman,* Coward, 1954; *Whistle Punk,* Coward, 1956; *Boy Who Got Mailed,* Coward, 1957; *Big Rig,* Coward, 1959; *Department Store Ghost,* Coward, 1961; *Tickley and the Fox,* Lantern, 1962; *The Hippopotamus that Wanted to be a Baby,* Lantern, 1963. Several juvenile books and stories contributed to school readers.

Poetry under name Rosalie Moore: (Introduction by W. H. Auden) *The Grasshopper's Man and Other Poems,* Yale University Press, 1949. Poetry anthologized in: *Ideas of Order on Experimental Poetry* and *Accent on Barlow,* both Activist Group books; *New World Writing, 100 Best Modern Poems; Stars to Steer By* and *The Golden Treasury of Poetry,* both edited by Louis Untermeyer for Houghton, *Rising Tides,* Simon & Schuster, 1972. Also contributor to *New Yorker, Saturday Review, Accent, Poetry, Furioso, Southern Review, Poetry Now,* and *Chicago Tribune.*

WORK IN PROGRESS: A new volume of poetry, *Year of the Children* to by published by Brotherson & Woolmer, N.Y.

SIDELIGHTS: "At the time Bill and I started writing the children's books we had two little girls (later three) who were in school and many of the children felt a need for beginning books with strong stories. At that time they were mostly reading books like, *Run Spot Run.* At any rate we became interested in telling a funny or exciting story in simple, clear, sensory language. Bill was best at good stories, and because I was a poet, I did the most with trying to tell a story as if you could see, hear, and feel everything that was happening.

"This was also the case with my most reprinted poem, called 'Catalogue.' I was doing a lot of writing at the time, called Sensory Reporting, with the Hart (Activist) group. But no matter what I would start to write about, my cat, Jay Bird, would sit either on my paper or right up on my typewriter. I'd put him down, but he'd climb up again and look at me. Finally I decided to write about the cat, and I wrote the beginning line, 'Cats sleep fat and walk thin.'

"Since my husband's death I have been teaching and writing poetry, not for children but mainly a long narrative poem about children during the Middle Ages. It is not FOR children, but it is about children, and perhaps when the children grow up they will want to read it too. I am a teacher at College of Marin in Kentfield, California, where I have a poetry workshop and also teach courses in reading, basic writing, and the mass media. I no longer keep any cats, but my daughter, Camas, has five."

BRYSON, Bernarda   1905-
(Bernarda Bryson Shahn)

PERSONAL: Born March 7, 1905, in Athens, Ohio; daughter of Charles Harvey (an editor and publisher) and Lucy (a Latin professor; maiden name, Weethee) Bryson; married Victor Luster Parks, 1927 (divorced, 1930); married Ben Shahn (the artist), 1935 (died, 1969); children: (second marriage) Jonathan, Susanna Shahn Watts (deceased), Abby Shahn Slamm; stepchildren: Judith Shahn Dugan, Ezra. *Education:* Attended Ohio University, 1922-25, Ohio State University, 1926, Western Reserve University (now Case Western Reserve University), 1927, Cleveland School of Art, Columbus School of Art, and New School for Social Research. *Politics:* Generally Democrat. *Religion:* Protestant. *Residence:* Roosevelt, N.J.

CAREER: Illustrator for *Fortune, Harper's, Scientific American,* and other magazines. Columbus Gallery of Fine Arts School, Columbus, Ohio, instructor in etching and lithography, 1931. *Member:* Authors League, Society of Illustrators. *Awards, honors: The Twenty Miracles of Saint Nicolas* and *Gilgamesh* were chosen among the fifty books of the year by American Institute of Graphic Arts, 1962 and 1967 respectively.

WRITINGS: (Self-illustrated) *The Twenty Miracles of Saint Nicolas,* Little, Brown, 1960; (self-illustrated) *The Zoo of Zeus,* Grossman, 1964; (self-illustrated) *Gilgamesh* (*Horn Book* honor list), Holt, 1967; *Ben Shahn,* Abrams, 1973.

Illustrator: Charlton Ogburn, *The White Falcon,* Houghton, 1955; Rutherford Platt, *The River of Life,* Simon & Schuster, 1956; *Lives in Science,* Simon & Schuster, 1957; Jane Austen, *Pride and Prejudice,* Macmillan, 1962; Natalia M. Belting, *The Sun Is a Golden Earring,* Holt, 1962; Emily Bronte, *Wuthering Heights,* Macmillan, 1963; Pauline Clarke, *The Return of the Twelves,* Coward, 1963; Belting, *Calender Moon,* Holt, 1964; Norma Keating, *Mr. Chu,* Macmillan, 1965; Frank R. Stockton, *Storyteller's Pack,* Scribner, 1968; Carl Withers, *The Grindstone of God,* Holt, 1970. Also illustrator of *Bright Hunter of the Skies* and *The Son of the Sun.*

Contributor to *Penrose Annual, Graphis,* and *Image.* Editor of *Southside Advocate,* 1929-31; art columnist for *Ohio State Journal.*

WORK IN PROGRESS: Printmaking and writing.

FOR MORE INFORMATION SEE: Illustrators of Children's Books: 1946-1956, Horn Book, 1958; Diana Klemin, *The Art of Art for Children's Books,* Clarkson Potter, 1966; *Illustrators of Children's Books: 1957-1966,* Horn Book, 1968; Diana Klemin, *The Illustrated Book,* Clarkson Potter, 1970; *Third Book of Junior Authors,* edited by de Montreville and Hill, H. W. Wilson, 1972.

BURGER, Carl 1888-1967

PERSONAL: Born June 18, 1888, in Maryville, Tenn.; son of Joseph (a banker) and Elizabeth (Knox) Burger; married Margaret Rothery, September 18, 1920; children: Knox. *Education:* Attended Maryville College, Maryville, Tenn., and Stanford University; Cornell University, B.Arch., 1912; also studied for three years at School of Museum of Fine Arts, Boston. *Religion:* "No formal church." *Home and office:* 192 Bedford Rd., Pleasantville, N.Y. *Agent:* Marie Rodell, 141 East 55th St., New York, N.Y. 10022.

CAREER: Onetime art director of the advertising firms of N. W. Ayer & Sons in Philadelphia, Pa., and Batten, Barton, Durstine and Osborn in New York, N.Y.; illustrator of books and magazines, and writer. Work as an artist includes large murals for the Bronx Zoo and New York Aquarium, and landscapes in watercolor. *Military service:* U.S. Army, Infantry, 1917-20; became captain. *Member:* American Museum of Natural History, New York Zoological Society, Cornell Club of New York.

WRITINGS—All self-illustrated: *All About Fish,* Random, 1960; *All About Dogs,* Random, 1962; *All About Elephants,* Random, 1965; *All About Cats,* Random, 1966; *Beaver Skins and Mountain Men,* Dutton, 1968.

Illustrator: Will Barker, *Familiar Animals of North America,* Harper, 1957; Will Barker, *Winter-Sleeping Wildlife,* Harper, 1958; Fred Gipson, *Recollection Creek,* Harper, 1959; Will Barker, *Familiar Insects of America,* Harper, 1960; Sheila Burnford, *The Incredible Journey,* Little, Brown, 1960; Eugene Ackerman, *Tonk and Tonka,* Dutton, 1962; Fred Gipson, *Savage Sam,* Harper, 1962; Howard T. Walden, *Familiar Fresh Water Fishes,* Harper, 1964; Sterling North, *Little Rascal,* Dutton, 1965; Sterling North, *Hurry Spring!,* Dutton, 1966; Fred Gipson, *Old Yeller,* large type edition, Harper, and other books. Contributor to magazines, mostly articles on natural history subjects.

HOBBIES AND OTHER INTERESTS: Fly fishing for trout and salmon.

(Died, 1967)

The word for cat in Spanish is *gato,* in German *katze,* in French *chat,* in Arabic *kittah.* ▪ (From *All About Cats* by Carl Burger.)

RAY BURNS

BURNS, Raymond (Howard) 1924-
(Ray Burns)

PERSONAL: Born April 21, 1924, in New York, N.Y.; son of Mortimer (a jeweler) and Harriet (Baum) Burns; married Doris Williamson (a singer), May 3, 1953; children: John, David, Jane. *Education:* Graduate of high school in Stamford, Conn. *Home and studio:* 27 Warncke Rd., Wilton, Conn. 06897.

CAREER: Assistant to Alex Raymond (creator of Flash Gordon and Rip Kirby), Stamford, Conn., 1947-56; freelance illustrator and cartoonist, 1954—. *Military service:* U.S. Navy, 1942-46, 1950-52; received theater ribbons with three combat stars for service in Mediterranean and in Far East. *Member:* Westport Artists.

ILLUSTRATOR: Bradford Smith, *Stephen Decatur: Gallant Boy,* Bobbs, 1955; Marie Hammontree, *A. P. Giannini: Boy of San Francisco,* Bobbs, 1956; Ella Knox Evans, *The Adventure Book of Money,* Capitol Publishers, 1956; Marian T. Place, *Lotta Crabtree: Girl of the Gold Rush,* Bobbs, 1958; Olive Burt, *The Ringling Brothers: Circus Boys,* Bobbs, 1958; Joseph Bellafiore, *Literature for Today,* Noble, 1958; Dorothea Snow, *The Secret of the Stone Frog,* Bobbs, 1959.

Rosamund Morris, compiler, *Great Suspense Stories,* Hart Publishing, 1962; Miriam Gilbert, *Henry Ford's Dream,*

Science Research Associates, 1963; Marion Holland, *Billy's Raccoon,* Science Research Associates, 1963; Joan Heidemann, *The Russells of Hollytree Circle,* Macmillan, 1965; Jean Feidler, *Great American Heroes,* Hart Publishing, 1966; Dorothy Grider, *Peppermint,* Whitman Publishing, 1966; *Bear Cub Scout Book,* Boy Scouts of America, 1967; Basil Heatter, *The Sea Dreamers,* Farrar, Straus, 1968; Helen Stone Peterson, *Colony Leader: Roger Williams,* Garrard, 1968; Elizabeth Rider Montgomery, *When a Ton of Gold Reached Seattle,* Garrard, 1968; Wyatt Blassingame, *Jake Gaither: Winning Coach,* Garrard, 1969.

The Bicycle Story, Western Publishing, 1970; Susan Hall, *Benjie Beats the Mark,* Western Publishing, 1970; Samuel and Beryl Epstein, *Enrico Fermi: Father of Atomic Power,* Garrard, 1970; Stewart Graff, *A World Explorer: Hernando Cortes,* Garrard, 1970; James McCague, *When Chicago Was Young,* Garrard, 1971; Samuel and Beryl Epstein, *Michael Faraday: Apprentice to Science,* Garrard, 1971; Leland Jacobs, *Funny Folk in Limerick Land,* Garrard, 1971; May Justus, *Jumping Johnny Outwits Skedaddle,* Garrard, 1971; Wyatt Blassingame, *John Henry and Paul Bunyan Play Baseball,* Garrard, 1971; Rosemary Nesbitt, *Colonel Meacham's Giant Cheese,* Garrard, 1972; Franklin Meyer, *Me and Caleb,* Science Research Associates, 1972; Miriam Anne Bourne, *Second Car in Town,* Coward, 1972; John Dawkins, *The Story of a Paperbag,* Heath, 1973; Alvin Granowsky, *The Car That Hopped,* Heath, 1973; *Fun on a Log,* Jacaranda, 1974; *Ten Red Hens,* Jacaranda, 1974; Irwin Shapiro, *Paul Bunyan Tricks a Dragon,* Garrard, 1975; Barbara Klimowicz, *Ha, Ha, Ha, Henrietta,* Ábingdon, 1975; Yukiko Irwin, *Shiatzu,* Lippincott, 1976.

Also illustrator of "Power Boys Adventures" by Mel Lyle, published by Whitman Publishing: *Mystery of the Haunted Skyscraper,* 1964; *Mystery of the Flying Skeleton,* 1964; *Mystery of the Burning Ocean,* 1965; *Mystery of the Million Dollar Penny,* 1965; *Mystery of the Double Kidnapping,* 1966; *Mystery of the Vanishing Lady,* 1967.

Illustrator for textbooks, 1955—, with work in publications of Allyn & Bacon, American Book Co., D. C. Heath, Ginn & Co., Houghton Mifflin, Co., Prentice-Hall, Silver Burdett, Random House, Holt, Rinehart & Winston, Inc., Harcourt Brace, Jovanovich, and a number of other publishers. Also advertising illustration and assorted projects such as filmstrips and storyboards for agencies and industrial corporations.

SIDELIGHTS: "As assistant to the late Alex Raymond, one of our greatest cartoonists and illustrators, I learned the values of characterization and storytelling in pictures as well as the mechanics of perspective and composition. Bringing people in illustrations to life, to give them animation makes for compelling pictures. I am still mindful of these essentials as I now pursue a full time free-lance career employing various styles ranging from the dramatically realistic through stylized to offbeat cartoon.

"My use of color and technique has evolved through trial and error. I enjoy experimenting with various tools and surfaces and applying them in different ways. For one book project I was asked to use a different style and technique for nearly every one of some thirty-six illustrations to make it appear as though several artists had contributed their work.

"Happily, textbook and juvenile book publishers are anxious to have their books look as fresh and contemporary as possible. Advertising and magazine illustration had long been the models for a sophisticated new look but the work now being produced in books rival those fields in every way. So whether I am doing a TV storyboard, an insurance company brochure, a math text or a juvenile adventure story, the same creative and hopefully innovative approach applies for all.

"My wife and I share a common love of classical music. However I'm merely an avid listener while Doris is an active professional singer, having given numerous concerts, appeared in opera and musicals as a principal performer, and has been soloist for several area churches. In addition to dutifully serving our three cats I enjoy the care and feeding of my British MG-TD roadster that I've owned for twenty-three years and still drive daily."

FOR MORE INFORMATION SEE: Wilton Bulletin (Wilton, Conn.), November 4, 1970.

To top it all off, he was never without a furry white beaver hat that made him look eight feet tall. ■ (From *Colonel Meacham's Giant Cheese* by Rosemary Nesbitt. Illustrated by Raymond Burns.)

MARY CABLE

CABLE, Mary 1920-

PERSONAL: Born January 24, 1920, in Cleveland, Ohio; daughter of Robert Winthrop (an engineer) and Elizabeth (a painter; maiden name, Southwick) Pratt; married Arthur Goodrich Cable (a bookstore owner), May 25, 1949; children: Cassandra Southwick. *Education:* Mary C. Wheeler School, Providence, R.I., graduate, 1937; Barnard College, A.B., 1941; also studied at Cas'Alta School, Florence, Italy, 1939. *Home: 206 McKenzie St., Santa Fe, N.M. 87501.*

CAREER: Member of editorial staff of *New Yorker*, New York, N.Y., 1944-49, of *Harper's Bazaar*, New York, 1949-51, and of American Heritage Publishing Co., Inc., New York, 1963-65.

WRITINGS: Dream Castles, Viking, 1966; (with the editors of *American Heritage*) *American Manners and Morals*, American Heritage Press, 1969; *The Avenue of the Presidents*, Houghton, 1969; *Black Odyssey* (children's book), Viking, 1971; *El Escorial*, Newsweek Books, 1971; *The Little Darlings*, Scribner, 1975. Contributor of short stories and articles to *New Yorker, Horizon, Harper's Bazaar, Atlantic, Vogue*, and other periodicals.

SIDELIGHTS: While her husband was with the U.S. Information Service, Cable lived and traveled widely in Turkey, Germany, Rhodesia, and Thailand.

BENJAMIN CAPPS

CAPPS, Benjamin (Franklin) 1922-

PERSONAL: Born June 11, 1922, in Dundee, Tex.; son of Benjamin Franklin (a cowboy) and Ruth Kathleen (Rice) Capps; married Marie Thompson, December 12, 1942; children: Benjamin F., Jr., Kathleen Marie, Mark Victor. *Education:* Texas Technological College, student, 1938-39; University of Texas, B.A., 1948, M.A., 1949. *Home:* 2330 Southeast Eighth St., Grand Prairie, Tex. 75050. *Agent:* Malcolm Reiss, Paul R. Reynolds, Inc., 12 East 41st St., New York, N.Y. 10017.

CAREER: Northeastern State College, Tahlequah, Okla., instructor in English and journalism, 1949-51; tool and die maker for various companies, 1951-61; free-lance writer, 1961—. *Military service:* U.S. Army Air Forces, 1942-45; became first lieutenant; participated in Pacific campaigns. *Member:* Phi Beta Kappa. *Awards, honors: The Trail to Ogallala* selected by National Association of Independent Schools as one of ten best books of 1964 for pre-college readers; the same book received the Spur Award of Western Writers of America, as best western novel of 1964, and Golden Saddleman Award, as the best western writing of 1964, and was also chosen for the White House library by American Booksellers Association; *Sam Chance* received the Spur Award of the Western Writers of America, as best western novel of 1965; Western Writers of America Spur Award, 1969, for *The White Man's Road;* Wrangler Award of the Western Heritage Center, 1969, for *The White Man's Road,* 1974, for *The Warren Wagontrain Raid.*

WRITINGS: Hanging at Comanche Wells (novel), Ballantine, 1962; *The Trail to Ogallala* (novel), Duell, Sloan & Pearce, 1964; *Sam Chance* (novel), Duell, Sloan & Pearce,

1965; *A Woman of the People,* Duell, Sloan & Pearce, 1966; *The Brothers of Uterica* (novel), Meredith, 1967; *The White Man's Road* (novel), Harper, 1969; *The True Memoirs of Charley Blankenship* (novel), Lippincott, 1972; *The Indians* (non-fiction), Time-Life Books, 1973; *The Warren Wagontrain Raid* (non-fiction), Dial Press, 1974; *The Great Chiefs* (non-fiction), Time-Life Books, 1975.

SIDELIGHTS: "I grew up in a rather remote area in west Texas, rode horseback two years to a one-teacher school, later rode a school bus into town to finish high school. Early I learned the pleasures of reading and would devour every book I could get by hands on, including the Bible, Shakespeare, the works of Teddy Roosevelt, Zane Grey, Horatio Alger, Jr.—anything.

"My writing is not particularly intended for young people, however it is my ambition to write clearly and as simply and straightforwardly as the subject matter will permit. Therefore, it is with satisfaction that I have learned that many of my books have been acquired by high school libraries. I hope that I never bore my young readers."

CARINI, Edward 1923-

PERSONAL: Born May 27, 1923, in Glastonbury, Conn.; son of John A. (a realtor) and Rose (Quadiroli) Carini. *Education:* Art Institute of Chicago, B.F.A., 1950. *Home:* 85 Ridgeview Dr., Pleasantville, N.Y. 10570. *Office:* 15 Eward St., Ossining, N.Y. 10562.

CAREER: Self-employed producer of films for children, inventor of toys, and lyric writer, with office in Ossining, N.Y. Had one-man show in New York.

WRITINGS: What Is Big, Holt, 1964; (self-illustrated) *Take Another Look,* Prentice-Hall, 1970. Creator and producer of about forty children's films, including "Tadpole" Films, distributed by Denoyer-Geppert, and of "Kindle" Filmstrips, distributed by Scholastic Magazines. Writer of lyrics for more than one hundred songs.

CARTWRIGHT, Sally 1923-

PERSONAL: Born November 25, 1923, in New York, N.Y.; daughter of Henry (an engineer) and Anita (an artist; maiden name, Parkhurst) Willcox; married Roger Cartwright (a professor of education), December 25, 1943; children: Steven, Paul. *Education:* Cornell University, B.A., 1944; Harvard University, graduate study, 1970-71; Bank Street College of Education, M.S., 1971. *Politics:* Independent. *Religion:* Agnostic—no denomination. *Residence:* Cambridge, Mass. *Agent:* Evelyn Singer, P.O. Box 163, Briarcliff, N.Y. 10510.

CAREER: Junior high school teacher in Oak Ridge, Tenn., 1945-46; American Friends Service Committee, Bengal, India, founder and teacher of a school, 1946-49; elementary and junior high school teacher in public and private schools in New York, N.Y., at various times, 1949-70; KLH Child Development Center, Cambridge, Mass., head day care teacher, 1970-71; Watertown Cooperative Nursery School,

SALLY CARTWRIGHT

Inc., Watertown, Mass., teacher and educational director, 1971-75. *Awards, honors:* National Science Teachers Association and Children's Book Council outstanding trade book award, 1973, for *Water Is Wet.*

WRITINGS—Children's books: *The Tide,* Coward, 1970; *Why Can't You See the Wind,* Grosset, 1971; *Animal Homes,* Coward, 1973; *Water Is Wet,* Coward, 1973; *Sunlight,* Coward, 1974; *Sand,* Coward, 1974; *Who Rides the Red Engine,* Grosset, 1974. Contributor to *Young Children.* Editor of *City and Country News,* during 1950's.

WORK IN PROGRESS: More children's books; a book on the Watertown Cooperative Nursery School, *A Ground for Learning,* material for children, for Coward.

SIDELIGHTS: Sally Cartwright has sailed her own boat in the Atlantic and Pacific Oceans, Gulf of Mexico, Red Sea, and River Ganges. She also does cross-country skiing and walking, and she enjoys music and English country dancing.

CARY, Louis F(avreau) 1915-
(Cary)

PERSONAL: Born March 13, 1915, in Brockton, Mass.; son of Edgar Loring and Martha Aurelia (Favreau) Cary; married Mary Bradley, November 2, 1947; children: Elizabeth (Mrs. David Reese), Denison, Adele (Mrs. Thomas Aylmer). *Education:* Studied at Massachusetts College of Art, 1932-36. *Home and studio:* West Barnstable, Mass. 02668.

CAREER: Book and advertising illustrator, New York, N.Y., 1936—. Designer of sets, and actor with local drama group.

ILLUSTRATOR: Louise Dickinson Rich, *The First Book of New World Explorers,* Watts, 1960; Sheldon N. Ripley, *Ethan Allen,* Houghton, 1961; Mary Virginia Fox, *Treasure of the Revolution,* Abingdon, 1961; Natalia M. Belting, *The Long-Tailed Bear,* Bobbs, 1961; Solveig Paulson Russell, *Wonderful Stuff, The Story of Clay,* Rand, 1963; Gerald S. Craig, Bernice C. Bryan, *Science for You,* Ginn, 1965; Patrice Cutright, John Jarolimek, Mae Knight Clark, *Living in America Today and Yesterday,* Macmillan, 1966; Charles Leonard, Beatrice Pekham Krone, Irving Wolfe, Margaret Fullerton, *Discovering Music Together,* Follett, 1966; Eleanor Thomas, *Your Neighborhood and the World,* Ginn, 1966; Sam and Beryl Epstein, *Young Paul Revere's Boston,* Garrard, 1966; Harry W. Sartain, Hannah M. Lindahl, Katherine Koch, *English is our Language,* Heath, 1966; Cecil Malden, *The Borrowed Crown,* Viking, 1968; Lucille Wallower, *William Penn,* Follett, 1968; Irene R. Tamony, *Indian Tales,* Charles E. Merrill, 1968; Frank Sodwick, *Conversation in Spanish,* American Book, 1969; Polly Anne Graff, *Louisa May Alcott,* Garrard, 1969; Sally Glendinning, *Thomas Gainsborough: Artist of England,* Garrard, 1969; Cecil Maiden, *A Song for Young King Wenceslas,* Addison-Wesley, 1969.

Ralph F. Robinett, *On Sunfish Island,* Heath, 1970; Leo Tolstoy, *Anna Karenina,* Kawade-Shoto (Tokyo), 1970; Margery Greenleaf, *Letters to Eliza,* Follett, 1970; Esther Douty, *Mr. Jefferson's Washington,* Garrard, 1970; Adele Louis DeLeeuw, *Marie Curie: Woman of Genius,* Garrard, 1970; LaVere Anderson, *Sitting Bull: Great Sioux Chief,* Garrard, 1970; Virginia Frances Voight, *Stagecoach Days and Stagecoach Kings,* Garrard, 1970; Joy Dueland, *The Pine Tree that Went to Sea,* Ginn, 1971; Elizabeth Jane Coatsworth, *Daniel Webster's Horses,* Garrard, 1971; LaVere Anderson, *Abe Lincoln and the River Robbers,* Garrard, 1971; Virginia Frances Voight, *Massasoit: Friend of the Pilgrims,* Garrard, 1971; Pearle H. Schultz, *Isaac Newton: Scientific Genius,* Garrard, 1972; Jane Werner Watson, *The Mysterious Gold and Purple Box,* Garrard, 1972; Olive M. Price, *Rosa Bonheur: Painter of Animals,* Garrard, 1972; LaVere Anderson, *Black Hawk: Indian Patriot,* Garrard, 1972; Sharon Wagner, *Gypsy from Nowhere,* Western, 1972; Theodore L. Harris, Mildred Creekmore, Margaret H. Greenman, *Pug,* Economy Co., 1972; Harris, Creekmore, Greenman, *Green Feet,* Economy Co., 1972; Patricia Edwards Clyne, *The Corduroy Road,* Dodd, 1973; LaVere Anderson, *Martha Washington: First Lady of the Land,* Garrard, 1973; David R. Collins, *Linda Richards: First American Trained Nurse,* Garrard, 1973; Jane Werner Watson, *Dance to a Happy Song,* Garrard, 1973; Margaret Goff Clark, *Their Eyes on the Stars: Four Black Writers,* Garrard, 1973; Margaret Goff Clark, *John Muir: Friend of Nature,* Garrard, 1974; Selma Lola Chambers, *The Golden Book of Words,* Golden Press, 1974; Margaret Chittenden, *Merrymaking in Great Britain,* Garrard, 1974; Kathleen Arnott, *Dragons, Ogres and Scary Things: Two African Tales,* Garrard, 1974; *A Horse Called Lucky,* Western, 1974; Sharon Wagner, *Gypsy and Nimblefoot,* Western, 1975. For Western Publishing Co.: Sticker Books on dinosaurs, indians, fish, birds, American animals, African animals, planes, trains, cars, toys, American presi-

At once hundreds of eggs tumble down the slope together. Red, yellow, blue, green, purple— down they go, spinning and bouncing against each other in an avalanche of color. ■ (From *Merrymaking in Great Britain* by Margaret Chittenden. Illustrated by Cary.)

dents, heroes of the American revolution, dogs, horses. Also, many anthologies for various publishers, employing several artists.

SIDELIGHTS: "To me, the subject matter dictates the illustration style. I work in many styles. My favorite assignments are period, 15th through 19th centuries, although I have done everything from dinosaurs to moon landing."

CASE, Marshal T(aylor) 1941-

PERSONAL: Born February 21, 1941, in Buffalo, N.Y.; son of Melville (an engineer) and Helen (Taylor) Case; married Nancy Whiting, June 15, 1964; children: Laura Jean, Jennifer Lynn. *Education:* Cornell University, B.S., 1964. *Politics:* Republican. *Religion:* Episcopalian. *Home:* 2325 Burr St., Fairfield, Conn. 06430.

CAREER: Cape Cod Museum of Natural History, Brewster, Mass., director, 1964-69; Cape Cod Community College, West Barnstable, Mass., associate professor, 1967-69; Connecticut Audubon Society, Fairfield, executive director, 1969—; University of Bridgeport, Bridgeport, Conn., adjunct assistant professor of biology, 1972—. Research associate, Tufts University, 1968—. *Member:* Association of Interpretive Naturalists, American Nature Study Society (member of board of directors, 1972—), American Ornithol-

The friendly gerbil is a favorite with many small children. ■ (From *Look What I Found!* by Marshal T. Case. Illustrated by Mary Lee Herbster.)

ogists' Union, American Society of Mammalogists, American Society of Ichthyologists and Herpetologists, Connecticut Association for Environmental Education (president, 1971—), Eastern Bird Banding Association, Connecticut Botanical Society. *Awards, honors:* Award of Merit of Federated Garden Clubs of Connecticut, 1973, for "exceptional work with youth and conservation" and for *Look What I Found.*

WRITINGS: Look What I Found (Child Study Association book list), Chatham Press, 1971. Editor, *Connecticut Audubon Bulletin,* 1970—, and *Nutmeg Naturalist* (annual magazine), 1974—; associate editor, *Journal of Nature Study* (quarterly publication of American Nature Study Society), 1974—.

WORK IN PROGRESS: Feeder Birds of Connecticut, completion expected in 1976; a research paper on the birds of Exuma Cays, Bahamas.

SIDELIGHTS: "Subjects that will result in a benefit to conservation in general, nature appreciation and habitat preservation specifically, motivate me to write. Time is the factor that prevents me from doing more writing about what I think is necessary and of interest."

CASEY, Brigid 1950-

PERSONAL: Born January 11, 1950, in New York, N.Y.; daughter of Michael T. (an educator) and Rosemary (an editor; maiden name, Christmann) Casey; *Education:* St. Francis College, Brooklyn, N.Y., B.A., 1972; New York University, M.A. candidate. *Office:* 625 East 14th St., New York, N.Y. 10009.

MARSHALL T. CASE

WRITINGS: (With Sigmund A. Lavine) *Wonders of the World of Horses,* Dodd, 1972.

WORK IN PROGRESS: Further research on horses; a study of the elderly and their forms of recreation.

CASTELLANOS, Jane Mollie (Robinson) 1913-

PERSONAL: Born August 6, 1913, in Lansing, Mich.; daughter of Charles Summers (a biochemist) and Florence (Sherwood) Robinson; married Jose C. Castellanos, November 14, 1942; children: Esther, Elizabeth, Alice Marie. *Education:* Studied at University of Strasbourg, 1930, University of Munich, 1930-31; University of Michigan, B.A., 1934; Stanford University, M.A., 1935, Ph.D., 1938; postdoctoral study at Mills College, 1941, and University of California. *Home:* 2950 Brookdale Ct., Concord, Calif. 94518.

CAREER: San Francisco College for Women, San Francisco, Calif., instructor in languages, 1938-40; Mills College, Oakland, Calif., instructor in child development, 1942-50; Contra Costa Junior College District, Martinez, Calff., instructor in family life education and psychology, and counselor, 1950—, chiefly at Diablo Valley College, Concord, Calif. *Member:* Phi Beta Kappa.

WRITINGS: (With Louisa Wagoner) *The Observation of Young Children,* revised edition, privately printed, 1951; *A Shell for Sam,* Golden Gate Junior Books, 1963; *Something New for Taco,* Golden Gate Junior Books, 1965; *Tomasito and the Golden Llamas,* Golden Gate Junior Books, 1968.

The bells of Cuzco were pouring into the evening a silver melody that told him not all beauty had died with the Lord Inca.
■ (From *Tomasito and the Golden Llamas* by Jane Castellanos. Decorations by Robert Corey.)

ELIZABETH F. CHITTENDEN

CHITTENDEN, Elizabeth F. 1903-

PERSONAL: Born November 4, 1903, in Brandon, Vt.; daughter of Merritt Darrow (a teacher) and Gertrude (a teacher; maiden name, Cahee) Chittenden. *Education:* Smith College, A.B., 1924; University of Buffalo, M.A., 1936. *Politics:* Independent ("slanted liberal"). *Religion:* Episcopalian. *Home:* 310 Argonne Dr., Kenmore, N.Y. 14217.

CAREER: Teacher of English in Oswego, N.Y., 1924-25; teacher of English in Kenmore, N.Y., 1925-64, chairman of department of English, 1956-64; retired from teaching, 1964, and began free-lance writing. Director of religious education at Trinity Church, Buffalo, N.Y., 1966-69; volunteer tutor at Episcopal center. *Member:* National League of American Pen Women (recording secretary, Western New York branch, 1974—).

WRITINGS: (Translation editor) Katalin Ertavy-Barath, *Teaspoonful of Freedom,* American-Hungarian Literary Guild, 1968; *Profiles in Black and White: Stories of Men and Women Who Fought Against Slavery* (juvenile), Scribner, 1973. Contributor to *American West, Yankee, Negro History, Vermonter, Church Herald,* and other periodicals.

WORK IN PROGRESS: This Woman Question, a biography of Abigail Scott Duniway, the first woman's rights worker in the Northwest, for junior-high readers and up; *We Were a Procession,* a collective biography of little-known women who were early leaders in women's rights.

SIDELIGHTS: "Geographic loyalties: Always a Vermonter, who lives in New York State and summers in Maine. Yet, whenever I hear 'America the Beautiful,' I see in my mind's eye Mount Mansfield, Camel's Hump, Lake Champlain, my symbols of Vermont.

"I like the out-of-doors! I have a few friends who share the enthusiasm. In winter, we hike through the snow, always taking with us our golden retriever, Vickie, to add to the pleasure. We snowshoe and picnic in winter woods. . . .Summer brings daily swims in Casco Bay and long walks down sun-dappled roads and through bobolink meadows.

"Books at all seasons wherever I am! Thank heaven for the joy of losing 'me' in somebody else's life through a good tale, fiction or biography."

CHRISTIAN, Mary Blount 1933-

PERSONAL: Born February 20, 1933, in Houston, Tex.; daughter of George D. and Anna (Dill) Blount; married George L. Christian, Jr. (an assistant managing editor), September 22, 1956; children: Scott, Karen, Devin. *Education:* University of Houston, B.S., 1954. *Home:* 1108 Danbury Rd., Houston, Tex. 77055.

CAREER: Houston Post, Houston, Tex., reporter and columnist, 1953-57; free-lance writer in Houston, Tex., 1959—. Has taught writing for children at university workshops, adult education programs and seminars. Taught creative writing at Houston Community College, 1975—. *Member:* Society of Children's Book Writers (board of advisors, 1975-76, charter member), Associated Authors of Children's Literature (board of directors, 1975—; charter member), Authors Guild, Houston Writers Workshop.

WRITINGS—For children: *Scarabee: The Witch's Cat,* Steck, 1973; *The First Sign of Winter,* Parents' Magazine Press, 1973; *Nothing Much Happened Today,* Addison-Wesley, 1973; *Sebastian: Super Sleuth,* J. Philip O'Hara, 1974; *Devin and Goliath,* Addison-Wesley, 1974; *No Dogs Allowed, Jonathan!,* Addison-Wesley 1975 (also a sound film strip by Taylor Associates Corp.); *The Goosehill Gang and the Disappearing Dues,* Concordia, 1976; *When Time Began,* Concordia, 1976; *Jonah, Go to Nineveh!,* Concordia, 1976. Juvenile book critic, *Houston Post.*

WORK IN PROGRESS—For children: Readers for the "Concordia Easy Read Bible Series" and more "Goosehill Gang" adventures plus some short fiction and a novel. Also "Children's Bookshelf," a television program featuring news, interviews and reviews of children's books for Channel 8, public television in Houston.

SIDELIGHTS: "Everything I write comes both from a deep inner feeling and an experience (my own or someone else's), but they are so evolved by the time they are written that the original stimuli is invisible. I feel a deep responsibility for the reader. While I start out to entertain I never send anything out without being very sure that it contains nothing that will mislead or misinform a child about the world as I know it. I try to tell myself in one sentence just what theme, what universal message, each story conveys.

MARY BLOUNT CHRISTIAN

The turtle no longer held his long neck straight and high. He looked somehow smaller to Devin.
■ (From *Devin and Goliath* by Mary Blount Christian. Illustrated by Normand Chartier.)

After all, we can't follow the book around and add footnotes to the reader. It leads its own life apart from us and nothing we could say later can erase a misconception we may have caused. Children look much deeper into stories than adults—perhaps not consciously, but they decode everything into validity to life.

"I guess I was preparing for writing for children all of my life. An only child, I told stories to myself and my imaginary playmates, rewrote fairytales into plays to present to the neighborhood children and wrote stories (mostly scary ones) on every scrap of paper. It was Carol Ryrie Brink's *Caddy Woodlawn* that really made me know what I wanted to do. I read it in sixth grade—several times. From then on I rollerskated to the library (about a five mile round trip, I think) and started with the A's and worked my way around the shelves. My favorite writing is humor and poetic excursions into nature. Although my years of studying the piano never made me very good at that, it did develop an inner rhythm that helps me to 'hear' my work.

"If there are children who want to write they should not wait. They should get themselves little notebooks and write in them everyday—about their feelings, their needs, people they've observed, places that intrigued them. Why does that dark house at the corner make them feel creepy? What makes their best friend sometimes act so hostile? What would it take to change a person? Questions like that are the beginning of stories."

FOR MORE INFORMATION SEE: Houston Chronicle, December 24, 1972.

CLARKSON, Ewan 1929-

PERSONAL: Given name is pronounced *You*-an; born January 23, 1929, in England; son of Frank (a pharmacist) and Jenny (Johnston) Clarkson; married Jenny Maton, September 12, 1951; children: Bruce Andrew, Shelia Jane. *Education:* Attended schools in England until sixteen. *Home:* Moss Rose Cottage, Preston Kingsteignton, Newton Abbot, Devonshire, England.

CAREER: Has worked as a scientist, veterinarian, zookeeper, mink farmer, rabbit farmer, beach photographer, and truck driver; currently broadcasting short talks on local sound radio. Free-lance writer. *Military service:* British Army, national service, two years.

WRITINGS: Break for Freedom, George Newnes, 1967, published in America as *Syla The Mink,* Dutton, 1968; *Halic: The Story of a Grey Seal,* Dutton, 1970; *The Running of the Deer* (novel), Dutton, 1972; *In the Shadow of the Falcon* (novel), Dutton, 1973; *Wolf Country: A Wilderness Pilgrimage* (nonfiction), Dutton, 1975. Former author of "Clarkson's Commentary" for *Fishing* (monthly magazine published by Angling Times Co., now defunct).

SIDELIGHTS: "I was born in Cumberland, England in 1929 and grew up exploring the countryside of Cheshire. Now I live in Devon with my wife, Jenny, and two children, Bruce and Shelia, in the whitewashed, thatched cottage which belonged to my father. Here I make my own wine, brew my own beer, grow my own vegetables and marvel at the nature around me.

"Ever since I can remember, I have been interested in animals and nature. As a child I kept frogs and newts and stuffed or dissected every animal I could get my hands on. I have been fascinated with the balance of nature since the age of thirteen when I wrote a paper on the subject for school. Then I painted an idyllic picture of life in the animal kingdom, with man the destroyer as villain of the piece. I am still very interested in the ways in which nature balances and preserves her kingdom but have become increasingly concerned with the devastation man has wrought through his wanton destruction of the wilderness and thoughtless disposal of harmful chemicals.

"For twenty-five years I labored under the illusion that I was a scientist. I worked as a laboratory assistant after I left school to study for my Bachelor of Science. Then I was a veterinarian for the People's Dispensary for Sick Animals. When I realized that I became too emotionally involved with my charges and brooded for a week if I failed to save the life of an animal entrusted to my care, I rebelled against the objective, unemotional approach of the scientist and went to Devon where I could write."

EWAN CLARKSON

Clarkson's animal story, technically a youth book, was hailed as a potential classic when it appeared in England and "an outstanding story for readers of all ages." The author's motivation: "Believe man to be a part of nature and believe that it is only possible for man to survive as a species if he is prepared to co-exist in harmony with other species of life. If he destroys his environment he will destroy himself."

FOR MORE INFORMATION SEE: New York Times Book Review, August 4, 1968; *Best Sellers,* August 15, 1968; *Library Journal,* February 1, 1970; *Washington Post,* March 27, 1970.

CLYMER, Eleanor 1906-
(Janet Bell, Elizabeth Kinsey)

PERSONAL: Born January 7, 1906, in New York, N.Y.; daughter of Eugene (an engineer) and Rose (Fourman) Lowenton; married Kinsey Clymer (a former newspaperman and social worker, now retired), 1933; children: Adam. *Education:* Barnard College, student, 1923-25; University of Wisconsin, B.A., 1928; also studied at Bank Street College of Education and New York University. *Home:* 11 Nightingale Rd., Katonah, N.Y. 10536.

CAREER: In early 1930's worked for publishing house, in doctor's office, for social work agency, taught young children briefly; writer of children's books, 1943—. *Member:* Authors Guild (former chairman of children's book committee), Wilderness Society, Native American Rights Fund. *Awards, honors:* Woodward School Zyra Lourie book award, 1968, for *My Brother Stevie;* Juvenile Literature Award of Border Regional Library Association, Texas, 1971, for *The Spider, the Cave and the Pottery Bowl;* Children's Book Award of Child Study Association of America, 1975, for *Luke Was There.*

WRITINGS: A Yard for John (Junior Literary Guild selection), Dodd, 1943; *Here Comes Pete* (Junior Literary Guild selection), Dodd, 1944; *The Grocery Mouse* (Junior Literary Guild selection), Dodd, 1945; *Little Bear Island,* Dodd, 1945; *The Country Kittens,* Dodd, 1947; *The Trolley Car Family,* McKay, 1947; *The Latch-Key Club,* McKay, 1949.

Treasure at First Base, Dodd, 1950; *Tommy's Wonderful Airplane,* Dodd, 1951; *Thirty-Three Bunn Street,* Dodd, 1952; *Make Way for Water,* Messner, 1953; (with Lillian Gilbreth) *Management in the Home* (adult book), Dodd, 1954; *Chester,* Dodd, 1955; *Not Too Small After All,* Watts, 1955; *Sociable Toby,* Watts, 1956; (with Lillian Erlich) *Modern American Career Women,* Dodd, 1959.

Mr. Piper's Bus, Dodd, 1961; *The Case of the Missing Link,* Basic Books, 1962, revised edition, 1968; *Benjamin in the Woods,* Grosset, 1962; *Now That You Are Seven* (part of six-book series), Association Press, in cooperation with Child Study Association of America, 1963; *Search for a Living Fossil: The Story of the Coelacanth,* Holt, 1963 (published in England as *Search for a Fossil,* Lutterworth, 1965); *Harry, the Wild West Horse,* Atheneum, 1963; (with Ralph C. Preston) *Communities at Work* (textbook), Heath, 1964; *The Tiny Little House,* Atheneum, 1964; *Chipmunk in the Forest,* Atheneum, 1965; *The Adventure* of Walter, Atheneum, 1965; Wheels: A Book to Begin On, Holt, 1965; My Brother Stevie, Holt, 1967; The Big Pile of Dirt, Holt, 1968; Horatio, Atheneum, 1968; The Second Greatest Invention: Search for the First Farmers, Holt, 1969; Belinda's New Spring Hat (Junior Literary Guild selection), Watts, 1969.

We Lived in the Almont, Dutton, 1970; The House on the Mountain, Dutton, 1971; The Spider, the Cave and the Pottery Bowl, Atheneum, 1971; Me and the Eggman, Dutton, 1972; How I Went Shopping and What I Got, Holt, 1972; Santiago's Silver Mine, Atheneum, 1973; Luke Was There, Holt, 1973; Leave Horatio Alone, Atheneum, 1974; Take Tarts as Tarts Is Passing, Dutton, 1974; Engine Number Seven, Holt, 1975.

Under pseudonym Janet Bell: Monday-Tuesday-Wednesday Book, McBride, 1946; Sunday in the Park, McBride, 1946.

Under pseudonym Elizabeth Kinsey: Teddy, McBride, 1946; Patch, McBride, 1946; Sea View Secret, Watts, 1952; Donny and Company, Watts, 1953; This Cat Came to Stay!, Watts, 1955.

WORK IN PROGRESS: Books on Navajo Indians, the Indians of the Northeast, Ireland, Nova Scotia, and autobiographical fiction.

ELEANOR CLYMER

SIDELIGHTS: "I was born in New York City and spent most of my life there, living at different times in each of the five boroughs. My taste for stories came from my mother. When I was about six I started to make up my own poems and stories.

"Living in New York in those days meant freedom to wander all over the city, and I got to know many neighborhoods, including Harlem and the lower east side, the river fronts and the parks, as well as the Palisades across the Hudson.

"In high school I wrote for the school magazine and edited it. I was also introduced to the biological sciences, and at the Museum of Natural History I learned about paleontology and archaeology. These interests stayed with me through college.

"Later, at New York University, I studied story writing, but it wasn't till I was married and had a child that I discovered my real interest: children's books. I had worked with children at camps and settlement houses, telling stories and writing about children. Then I went to Bank Street College and studied with Lucy Sprague Mitchell, who was revolutionizing children's literature. She urged her students not to keep repeating time-worn fairy stories but to listen to the children themselves, watch their play, and find out what made sense to them, in other words to be guided by their interests and capacities. Since then I have written realistic fiction for the most part.

"My first books were for the very young, based on the everyday life of the children I knew. As they grew older I tried to write what would please them, stories about baseball, airplanes, photography, pets. Then I went back to an earlier interest and wrote several books about the history of science.

"About ten years ago I began to feel I had things I really wanted to say, but I hadn't settled on a way to say them. That was when I wrote My Brother Stevie. In that book I tried to write what a real child, living in the inner city, might have said in her own words if she had been telling the unvarnished truth about her life.

"I feel that children's emotions and their problems in dealing with the adult world are very important, and need interpretation, not necessarily in terms of everything turning out happily. At the same time I think that a book for children should not paint a picture that is too threatening or hopeless.

"That was the first of several books about the city. In the last few years I have been able to travel and to write about children in the Southwest, in Mexico and other places. Such books have to be carefully researched and I spend much time studying the history, archaeology and current life of the places I am writing about. I feel it is permissible for me, though I am not Indian or Mexican or black, to write about people who are, since human feelings are pretty much the same everywhere.

"Since moving from New York to the country village where I live now, I have become much involved with the village library. It is the center of cultural and community activity, and I find it very satisfying to help in various ways."

You know how it is when you're a kid, and you think somebody is going to be there to take care of you, and then they aren't? ■ (From *Luke Was There* by Eleanor Clymer. Illustrated by Diane de Groat.)

FOR MORE INFORMATION SEE: *Young Wings*, July, 1945, October, 1947; *New York Times Book Review*, May 9, 1965, August 4, 1968; *Saturday Review*, February 18, 1967, May 10, 1969, January 23, 1971; *Chicago Tribune Book World*, September 15, 1968; *Children's Book World*, November 3, 1968; *Library Journal*, July, 1969; *Horn Book*, August, 1971, April, 1974, June, 1974, October, 1974; *Bulletin of the Center for Children's Books*, October, 1973, July-August, 1974, March, 1975.

COLE, William (Rossa) 1919-

PERSONAL: Born November 20, 1919, in Staten Island, N.Y.; son of William Harrison (a businessman) and Margaret (O'Donovan-Rossa) Cole; married Peggy Bennett (a writer), May, 1947 (divorced); married Galen Williams (a cultural administrator), July 10, 1967; children: (first marriage) Cambria Bennett, Jeremy Rossa (both daughters); (second marriage) Williams, Rossa (sons). *Education:* High school graduate. *Politics:* Socialist. *Religion:* None. *Home and office:* 201 West 54th St., New York, N.Y. 10019.

CAREER: Alfred A. Knopf, Inc., New York, N.Y., publicity director, 1946-58; Simon and Schuster, Inc., New York, N.Y., publicity director, editor, 1958-61. Co-publisher, with Viking Press, William Cole Books. *Military service:* U.S. Army, Infantry, 1940-45; served in European theater; became sergeant; received Purple Heart. *Member:* International P.E.N. (vice-president, American Center, 1955-56; executive board member, 1956—), Authors Guild.

WILLIAM COLE

It has such long and lofty legs,
I'm glad it sits to lay its eggs.
　　　　　　　　—Ogden Nash

(From *OH, HOW SILLY!* poems selected by William Cole. Illustrated by Tomi Ungerer.)

WRITINGS: A Cat-Hater's Handbook; or, the Ailurophobe's Delight, Dial, 1963; *Frances Face-Maker: A Going-to-Bed Book,* World Publishing, 1963; *What's Good for a Six-Year-Old?,* Holt, 1965; *Uncoupled Couplets: A Game of Rhymes,* Taplinger, 1966; *What's Good for a Four-Year-Old?,* Holt, 1967; *What's Good for a Five-Year-Old?,* Holt, 1968; *That Pest, Jonathan,* Harper, 1970; *Aunt Bella's Umbrella,* Doubleday, 1970.

Anthologies edited: (With Marvin Rosenberg) *The Best Cartoons from Punch,* Simon & Schuster, 1952; *The Best Humor from Punch,* World Publishing, 1953; (with Florett Robinson) *Women Are Wonderful: A History in Cartoons of a Hundred Years with America's Most Controversial Figure,* Houghton, 1954; (with Douglas McKee) *French Cartoons,* Dell, 1954; (with McKee) *More French Cartoons,* Dell, 1955; *Humorous Poetry for Children,* World Publishing, 1955; *Story Poems, Old and New,* World Publishing, 1957; *I Went to the Animal Fair: A Book of Animal Poems* (ALA Notable Book), World Publishing, 1958; *The Fireside Book of Humorous Poetry,* Simon & Schuster, 1959.

Poems of Magic and Spells, World Publishing, 1960; (with Julia Colmore) *The Poetry-Drawing Book,* Simon & Schuster, 1960; *Poems for Seasons and Celebrations,* World Publishing, 1961; *Folk Songs of England, Ireland, Scotland and Wales,* Doubleday, 1961; (with Colmore) *New York in Photographs,* Simon & Schuster, 1961; (with McKee) *Touche: French Cartoons,* Dell, 1961; (with Colmore) *The Second Poetry-Drawing Book,* Simon & Schuster, 1962;

(with McKee) *You Damn Men Are All Alike: French Cartoons*, Gold Medal, 1962; *Erotic Poetry*, Random House, 1963; *The Most of A. J. Liebling*, Simon & Schuster, 1963; *The Birds and the Beasts Were There: Animal Poems* (ALA Notable Books), World Publishing, 1963; *Beastly Boys and Ghastly Girls*, World Publishing, 1964; *A Big Bowl of Punch*, Simon & Schuster, 1964; *A Book of Love Poems*, Viking, 1965; (with Mike Thaler) *The Classic Cartoons*, World Publishing, 1966; *Oh, What Nonsense!*, Viking, 1966; *The Sea, Ships, and Sailors: Poems, Songs and Shanties*, Viking, 1967; *D. H. Lawrence: Poems Selected for Young People*, Viking, 1967; *Poems of W. S. Gilbert*, Crowell, 1967; *Eight Lines and Under: An Anthology of Short, Short Poems*, Macmillan, 1967; *A Case of the Giggles*, two volumes, World Publishing, 1967; *Man's Funniest Friend: The Dog in Stories, Reminiscences, Poems and Cartoons*, World Publishing, 1967; *Poems of Thomas Hood*, Crowell, 1968; *A Book of Nature Poems*, Viking, 1969; *Rough Men, Tough Men: Poems of Action and Adventure*, Viking, 1969; *The Punch Line: Twenty-five Portfolios of Contemporary English Comic Artists*, Simon & Schuster, 1969; *Pith and Vinegar: An Anthology of Short Humorous Poetry*, Simon & Schuster, 1969.

Oh, How Silly!, Viking, 1970; *The Poet's Tales: A New Book of Story Poems*, World Publishing, 1971; *Poems from Ireland*, Crowell, 1971; *Poetry Brief*, Macmillan, 1971; *Oh, That's Ridiculous!*, Viking, 1972; *Pick Me Up: A Book of Short, Short Poems*, Macmillan, 1972; *. . . And Be Merry!: A Feast of Light Verse and a Soupcon of Prose About the Joy of Eating*, Grossman, 1972; *Poems One Line and Longer*, Grossman, 1972; *Poems from Ireland*, Crowell, 1972; *Half Serious: A Book of Short Short Poems*, Methuen, London, 1973; *A Book of Animal Poems*, Viking, 1973; (contributor) *Cricket's Choice*, Open Court, 1974; *Knock Knocks: The Most Ever*, Watts, 1976; *Making Fun! A Book of Verse*, Watts, 1976. Frequent contributor to the *New York Times Book Review;* writes the "Trade Winds" column in *The Saturday Review*, 1973—.

WORK IN PROGRESS: A second book of folksongs of the British Isles; poems from Ireland; a book of light verse; two children's books; contemplating an immense anthology of British and American humor from all periods.

SIDELIGHTS: Cole is a writer of books on his own, but, primarily, he belongs to that distinctive breed of bibliogoners known as *anthologists,* having gotten started some forty collections or so ago when he was an editor in search of an anthologist and suddenly realized that not only could he do the book he had in mind but that he'd *like* doing it.

"The first requisite for an anthologist," said Cole in a lively and informative article in *Junior Libraries* (May, 1960), "should be a crusading enthusiasm for his subject. He should be a practitioner of literary buttonholing—continually exclaiming, through the medium of his compilations, 'Hey! Take a look at *this* one!' An anthology done without enthusiasm is like a TV dinner: frozen, tasteless, and quickly forgotten."

The anthologist also needs, says Cole, some of the instincts of the pack rat, and since boyhood he has been accumulating files of anything which appealed to him, although in the beginning he had no particular reason for doing so except that "I felt somebody should do it the honor.

When, as Cole puts it, he "feels an anthology coming on," he mouses through his accumulated hoards, lives in libraries, and scouts used book shops carefully. In a month or so of intensive searching he generally uncovers everything he needs for a book—and much more. Then he begins the winnowing, the arranging, the re-arranging, the seeking of permissions and the negotiating of reprint fees.

Finally, the finished book arrives—"the biggest thrill of the year." There is excitement in examining the new volume and satisfaction in seeing that the desired mood is created by the selections. But there is a peculiar pleasure, Cole finds, in being able to say concerning little gems rescued from newspapers and magazines that, "Now, they've got a home."

HOBBIES AND OTHER INTERESTS: "Reading poetry, listening to folk songs, admiring pretty girls, eating exotically when possible, playing tennis and ping pong, making puns, and going to good movies."

FOR MORE INFORMATION SEE: Commonweal, May 26, 1967; *New York Times Book Review,* November 5, 1967, November 9, 1969, June 25, 1972; *Christian Science Monitor,* November 30, 1967; *Best Sellers,* December 1, 1967, December 15, 1969, January 1, 1970; *New Yorker,* March 30, 1968 *Poetry,* May, 1968; Lee Bennett Hopkins, *Books Are By People,* Citation, 1969; *Writers Digest,* March, 1969; *Saturday Review,* May 10, 1969; *Library Journal,* September, 1970; *Book World,* January 11, 1970; *Horn Book,* August, 1969, January 11, 1970, April 1971, June 1972, June 1973, April 1974; *Publishers' Weekly,* July 17, 1972; *American Libraries,* June 1974.

And even Kings
Have underthings.
—Arthur Guiterman

COOKSON, Catherine (McMullen) 1906-
(Catherine Marchant; Catherine McMullen)

PERSONAL: Born June 20, 1906, in Tyne Dock, Durham, England; married Thomas H. Cookson (now a schoolmaster), June 1, 1940. *Home:* Loreto, Saint Helens Park Rd., Hastings, Sussex, England. *Agent:* Anthony Sheil Associates, 52 Floral St., Covent Garden, London WC2 9DA, England.

CAREER: Author, Lecturer for women's groups and other organizations. *Member:* P.E.N. (England), Authors' Guild (America).

WRITINGS: Kate Hannigan, 1950, *The Fifteen Streets,* 1952, *Colour Blind,* 1953, Macmillan, 1955, *Maggie Rowan,* 1954, *Rooney,* 1957, *The Menagerie,* 1958, *Slinky Jane,* 1959, *Fenwick Houses,* 1960, *The Garment,* 1962, *The Blind Miller,* 1963, *Hannah Massey,* 1964, *The Long Corridor,* 1965, *Matty Doolin,* 1965, *Matty Doolin* (juvenile), 1965, *The Unbaited Trap,* 1966, *Katie Mulholland,* 1967, *The Round Tower,* 1968, *Joe and the Gladiator* (juvenile), 1968, *The Nice Bloke,* 1969, *Our Kate* (autobiography), 1969, *The Glass Virgin,* 1970, *The Invitation,* 1970, *The Nipper* (juvenile), Bobbs, 1970, *The Dwelling Place,* 1971, *Feathers in the Fire,* 1971, *Pure as the Lily,* 1972, *Blue Baccy* (juvenile), Bobbs, 1972, *The Mallen Streak,* 1973, *The Mallen Girl,* 1974, *Our John Willie* (juvenile), 1974, *The Mallen Lot,* 1975, *The Invisible Cord,* 1975 (all published by Macdonald & Co., except U.S. editions indicated).

"Mary Ann" series: *A Grand Man,* 1954, *The Lord and Mary Ann,* 1956, *The Devil and Mary Ann,* 1958, *Love and Mary Ann,* 1961, *Life and Mary Ann,* 1962, *Marriage and Mary Ann,* 1964, *Mary Ann's Angels,* 1965, *Mary Ann and Bill,* 1966 (all published by Macdonald & Co.).

Under pseudonym Catherine Marchant: *Heritage of Folly,* 1962, *The Fen Tiger,* 1963, *House of Men,* 1964, *Evil at Roger's Cross,* 1964 (all published by Macdonald & Co.).

SIDELIGHTS: "I think I write my books to please myself, the kind I personally would like to read. You see, my life is writing, I like writing; I do a fourteen-hour day, seven days a week, and am often at my desk at 6:30 a.m. seeing to mail. Illness, with which I am well acquainted, doesn't stop me, I write in bed; in fact, *Pure as the Lily* was completely written while in bed. This is the point, I think a writer must have the urge and should write every day, however little. I never take holidays much.

"When I write for children I do not talk down to them, but write the same as I would for adults; the only thing that is different is the story line. My only real recreation is the daily dip in the pool. This has proved to be so beneficial to me that I look upon it as a small miracle."

Rooney and *A Grand Man* were made into films, the latter as 'Jacqueline." All of the "Mary Ann" books have been published in Germany, where they have a large following, and in Holland and Italy.

CATHERINE COOKSON

HOBBIES AND OTHER INTERESTS: Gardening, particularly cultivating a two-acre woodland plot; painting, swimming.

FOR MORE INFORMATION SEE: Children's Literature in Education/8, APS Publications, Inc., July, 1972.

COX, John Roberts 1915-
(Jack Cox, David Roberts, John Havenhand)

PERSONAL: Born January 15, 1915, in Worsley, Lancashire, England; son of Frank Clarkson (a local educational official) and Elizabeth (Roberts) Cox; married Kitty Margaret Forward, August 26, 1943; children: David John, Martin Andrew, Lindsay Robert. *Education:* University of Geneva, traveling scholar, 1936; Manchester University, B.A., 1941. *Religion:* Anglican. *Home:* Wychwood 113, Wolsey Rd., Moor Park, Northwood, Middlesex, England. *Agent:* Rupert Crew, Ltd., King's Mews, Gray's Inn Rd., London WC1, and Alec Harrison & Associates, 118 Fleet St., London, EC4, England.

CAREER: *Manchester Guardian,* Manchester, England, news and feature reporter, 1937-40; Lutterworth Press, London, England, editor of *Boy's Own Paper,* 1946-67, managing editor, Lutterworth Periodicals, Ltd., 1953-63; Purnell Group/B.P.C., London, editor of *Family Pets,* 1964-67, general editor of book department, 1966-68, editor of *Boy's Own Annual,* 1959—; International Publishing Corp., Hamlyn Group, managing editor of Practical Books Division, 1968-71; consultant editor and author, 1971—. Geographer. *Military service:* British Army, 1940-46, served in Royal Engineers; became captain. *Member:* National Union of Journalists, British Society of Authors, Association of Radio Writers, London Press Club, Sports Writers Club, Wasps Rugby Football Club (vice-president, 1951), Manchester University Convocation (treasurer, 1948-58; chairman, 1958-68; vice-president, 1969—), Surrey University Rugby Club (vice-president, 1966).

WRITINGS—Nonfiction: *Richard Hakluyt* (Elizabethan play for schools), 1937; *Camping for All,* Ward Lock, 1951; *Ideas for Rover Scouts,* Jenkins, 1953, 5th edition, 1959; *Ideas for Scout Troops,* Jenkins, 1954, 8th edition, 1963; *The Outdoor Series,* Lutterworth, 1954, 6th edition, 1970; *Camp and Trek,* foreword by Lord Hunt, Lutterworth, 1956, 3rd new and revised edition, 1970; *Portrait of B-P.: The Life Story of Lord Baden-Powell,* Lutterworth, 1957; *The Hike Book,* Lutterworth, 1960, 3rd revised edition, 1968; *Don Davies: "An Old International"* (biography), Hutchinson, 1962; *Camping in Comfort,* Lutterworth, 1963; *The Rugby Union Football Book,* Purnell, *Volume 1,* 1968, *Volume 2,* 1970; *Modern Camping,* Hutchinson, 1968; *The International Rugby Book,* Hamlyn Group, 1970; *Lightweight Camping,* Lutterworth, 1971; *Fun and Games Outdoors,* Pan Books, 1970. Also author of numerous radio and television plays, scripts, and documentaries for the BBC and Rediffusion and Granada I.T.A. programs; author of a BBC documentary on Lord Baden-Powell for the 1957 Centenary of his birth.

Fiction for young people: *Dangerous Waters* (originally written and broadcast as a BBC radio serial), Lutterworth, 1955; *Calamity Camp,* Lutterworth, 1957; *Majorca Moon,* Lutterworth, 1960; (under pseudonym David Roberts) *The Mushroom God,* Parrish, 1961.

Editor: *World Rover Moot Handbook,* Munro Press, 1939; *The Boy's Book of Popular Hobbies,* Burke, 1954, revised edition, 1968; *The Boy's Own Book of Hobbies,* Lutterworth, 1957, revised edition published as *The Boy's Book of Hobbies,* 1966, new edition, 1968; (and contributor) Frank Showell Styles, *Getting to Know Mountains,* George Newnes, 1958; *The Boy's Own Companion, Volumes 1-5,* Lutterworth, 1959-64; *Serve by Conserving: A Study of Conservation,* UNESCO [Paris], amended edition by Arco Publications, 1959; *The Boy's Own Book of Outdoor Hobbies,* Lutterworth, 1960, revised edition, 1968; *They Went to Bush: Forestry in Ghana,* Collins and MacGibbon & Kee, 1961; *Fred Buller's Book of Rigs and Tackles,* Purnell, 1967; (and reviser) Stuart Petre Brodie Mais, *An English Course for Everybody,* 5th edition, Frewin Publishers, 1969. Editor, with Enid Blyton, of the "Children's Library of Knowledge" series, published by Odhams Books, 1957-62.

Editor of books by Gilbert Davey, all published by Kaye & Ward: *Fun with Radio,* 1957, *Fun with Short Wave Radio,*

1960, *Fun with Electronics,* 1962, *Fun with Transistors,* 1964, *Fun with Hi-Fi,* in press; revised edition of all titles, 1970-71.

Author of weekly columns for children in the *Daily Graphic* (Kemsley), 1946-59, the *Sunday Graphic,* 1959-61, and the *Birmingham Weekly Post,* 1957-58. Contributor of sport and recreation articles, book reviews, and interviews to the (London) *Sunday Times,* 1951-68, *Daily Telegraph,* 1956—, *The Guardian,* 1960—, *Smith's Trade News,* and various periodicals.

WORK IN PROGRESS: A detailed history of *Boy's Own Paper,* founded in 1879, with all original source material and illustrations for important authors.

HOBBIES AND OTHER INTERESTS: Music of all kinds; playing the piano; conservation, ornithology, outdoor interests.

FOR MORE INFORMATION SEE: Brian Doyle, *The Who's Who of Children's Literature,* Schocken, 1968.

CRAIG, Margaret Maze   1911-1964

PERSONAL: Born January 16, 1911, in Ridgway, Pa.; daughter of Henry Riley and La Belle (Sutton) Maze; married Roy H. Craig, 1937; children: Judith, Jane. *Education:* Indiana State College, B.S., 1934. *Politics:* Republican. *Religion:* Presbyterian. *Home:* 121 Wyllis St., Oil City, Pa. 16301.

CAREER: West Penn Power Co., Pittsburgh, Pa., home economist, 1934-37; author, 1950-64. Oil City Area Schools, Oil City, Pa., teacher, 1956-57, 1959-64. *Member:* National League of American Pen Women (treasurer, 1952-56), Belles Lettres Club, Young Women's Christian Association, Parent-Teacher Association, Hospital Auxiliary. *Awards, honors:* Named to top ten by *Seventeen* in 1962 Salute to Homemaking Teachers of the Year.

WRITINGS: *Trish,* 1951, *Julie,* 1952, *Marsha,* 1955, *Three Who Met,* 1958, *Now That I'm Sixteen,* 1959, *It Could Happen to Anyone,* 1961 (all published by Crowell). Stories and articles have appeared in magazines.

SIDELIGHTS: Books have been published in Sweden, Germany, and Japan.

HOBBIES AND OTHER INTERESTS: Camping, fishing, bridge, baseball, square dancing, work with young adults.

FOR MORE INFORMATION SEE: *Seventeen-at-School,* May, 1962; *More Junior Authors,* edited by Muriel Fuller, H. W. Wilson, 1963.

(Died December 5, 1964)

CRARY, Margaret (Coleman)   1906-

PERSONAL: Born September 27, 1906, in Carthage, S.D.; daughter of James V. (a lumberman) and Ellen (Brown) Coleman; married Ralph W. Crary (a lawyer), August 19, 1926; children: Bruce Albert, David Ralph, Nancy Jean

Crary Veglahn (author of juvenile books). *Education:* Morningside College, B.A., 1926. *Politics:* Republican. *Religion:* Methodist. *Home:* 3213 Viking Dr., Sioux City, Iowa 51104. *Agent:* MacIntosh & Otis, 18 East 41st St., New York, N.Y.

CAREER: Free-lance writer. *Member:* National League of American Pen Women, Sioux Writers (past president). *Awards, honors:* Doctor of letters, Morningside College, 1965.

WRITINGS: The Calico Ball (Junior Literary Guild selection), Prentice-Hall, 1961; (with Carroll Voss) *Corn for the Palace,* Prentice-Hall, 1963; *The Secret of Blandford Hall,* Funk, 1963; *Pocketful of Raisins* (Junior Literary Guild selection), McKay, 1964; *Jared and the Yankee Genius,* McKay, 1965; *Secret of the Unknown Fifteen,* Funk, 1966; *Rookie Fireman,* Washburn, 1967; *Mexican Whirlwind,* Ives Washburn, 1969; *Susette La Flesche: Voice of the Omaha Indians,* Hawthorn, 1973.

Plays: *Beware the Bear,* Harper, 1953; *Song of the Cuckoo,* Harper; two Doctor Christian Award radio plays, "The Black Patch," and "The Old Gray Mare."

MARGARET CRARY

The two of them ran to the edge of the cut. Phil aimed the camera and pressed the shutter release. ■ (From *Secret of the Unknown Fifteen* by Margaret Crary. Illustrated by Vic Donahue.)

SIDELIGHTS: "I lived all the years of my growing up in a large victorian house in the middle-sized, midwestern city of Sioux City, Iowa. All the events of my childhood were colored by curiosity and imagination so I suppose the seeds for becoming a writer were always there. The material for most of my books was gleaned from the people and the happenings around me. Because the history of our community is closely involved with the American Indian, in one way or another, Indian characters appear in my stories."

HOBBIES AND OTHER INTERESTS: Golf, hunting, fishing, boating, and travel, particularly in rural and wilderness areas.

CRICHTON, (J.) Michael 1942-
(Jeffery Hudson, John Lange)

PERSONAL: Born October 23, 1942, in Chicago, Ill.; son of John Henderson (a corporation president) and Zula (Miller) Crichton; married Joan Radam, January 1, 1965 (divorced, 1970). *Education:* Harvard University, A.B. (summa cum laude), 1964, M.D., 1969. *Agent:* Lynn Nesbit, ICM, 40 West 57th St., New York, N.Y. 10019.

CAREER: Crichton writes: "Was a student for 80% of my life and never held a real job." But after a stint as post-doctoral fellow at Salk Institute for Biological Studies, La Jolla, Calif., 1969-70, "I subsequently have lived in Los Angeles where I have devoted full time to writing books, and writing and directing films." *Member:* Mystery Writers of America, Writers Guild of America West, Aesculaepian Society, Phi Beta Kappa. *Awards, honors:* Mystery Writers of America award, 1968, for *A Case of Need.*

WRITINGS: *The Andromeda Strain* (Book-of-the-Month Club and Literary Guild selection), Knopf, 1969; *Five Patients* (Doubleday Book Club selection), Knopf, 1970; *The Terminal Man* (ALA Notable Book; Book-of-the-Month Club selection), Knopf, 1972; *Westworld* (screenplay), Bantam, 1973; *The Great Train Robbery* (Book-of-the-Month Club selection), Knopf, 1975; *Eaters of the Dead,* Knopf, 1976.

Under pseudonym Jeffery Hudson: *A Case of Need,* World Publishing, 1968.

Under pseudonym John Lange: *Odds On,* New American Library, 1966; *Scratch One,* New American Library, 1967; *Easy Go,* New American Library, 1968; *Zero Cool,* New American Library, 1969; *The Venom Business,* World Publishing, 1969; *Drug of Choice,* New American Library, 1970; *Grave Descend,* New American Library, 1970; *Binary,* Knopf, 1972.

Screenplay: "Westworld" (also directed), M-G-M, 1973.

SIDELIGHTS: Introductory psychology textbooks would undoubtedly call six-foot-nine-inch Crichton an "achiever." He sold a travel article to the *New York Times* when he was fourteen; in the fourteen years that followed, he earned a bachelor's degree with highest honors and a medical degree, both from Harvard, and published ten novels. What's more, most of his fiction has been well-reviewed. But it was the publication of *The Andromeda Strain,* that, in 1969, catalyzed Crichton's bid for literary recognition.

The Andromeda Strain, a "science-nonfiction" novel, is concerned with the attempts of four scientists, mobilized on a minute's notice and sent to a top-secret laboratory installation five stories beneath the Nevada desert, to save the world from an alien bacterial strain, code named Andromeda, which was dropped on Earth by a Project Scoop

Hall, climbing up the core wall, was aware only of the distance and his fatigue. He felt strangely and totally exhausted, as if he had been climbing for hours. Then he realized that the gas was beginning to affect him. ■ (From the movie *"The Andromeda Strain,"* © Universal Pictures, 1971.)

MICHAEL CRICHTON

satellite. If the scientists fail, and if the germ invades the uncontrolled atmosphere, the laboratory will "self-destruct" and the scientists will thereby be sacrificed. As John Allen writes, "under the scientific-fictional gloss there's an old-fashioned Whodunit in the form of a Whatdunit."

The following have been made into films: *The Andromeda Strain,* Universal, 1971; *Dealing,* Warner Bros., 1972; *A Case of Need* (under the title, *The Carey Treatment*), M-G-M, 1973; *The Terminal Man,* Warner Bros., 1973; *The Great Train Robbery,* Paramount, 1976.

FOR MORE INFORMATION SEE: Library Journal, June 1, 1968; *New York Times Book Review,* August 18, 1968; *New Yorker,* October 5, 1968; *New York Times,* February 9, 1969, May 30, 1969; *Life,* May 30, 1969; *Time,* June 6, 1969; *Book World,* June 8, 1969; *Variety,* June 25, 1969; *Christian Science Monitor,* June 26, 1969; *Newsweek,* June 26, 1969; *Saturday Review,* June 28, 1969, August 30, 1969; *Writer's Digest,* July, 1969; *National Observer,* July 14, 1969; *Harper's,* August, 1969; *Commonweal,* August 8, 1969; *Times Literary Supplement,* October 16, 1969; *Vogue,* September 15, 1970; *Life,* March 3, 1972; *Harper's Bazaar,* April, 1972, October, 1973; *Time,* May 8, 1972; *Vogue,* September, 1973; *Horn Book,* October 1975.

CUTLER, (May) Ebbitt 1923-

PERSONAL: Born September 4, 1923, in Montreal, Quebec, Canada; daughter of William Henry (a policeman) and Francis (Farrelley) Ebbitt; married Philip Cutler (an attorney), January 17, 1952; children: Keir, Michael, Adam, Roger. *Education:* McGill University, B.A. (first class honors), 1945, M.A., 1952; Columbia University, M.S., 1946. *Politics:* "Liberal; mildly socialist, mostly fem-

inist." *Religion:* Atheist. *Home:* 3200 The Blvd., Westmount, Montreal, Quebec, Canada. *Agent:* Paul R. Reynolds, Inc., 599 Fifth Ave., New York, N.Y. 10017. *Office:* Tundra Books of Montreal, 1374 Sherbrooke St. W., Montreal, Quebec H3G 1J6, Canada.

CAREER: Canadian Press, Montreal, Quebec, and New York, N.Y., writer-editor, 1945-46; journalist on *Montreal Herald,* Montreal, 1947-48, *Standard,* Montreal, 1947-53; Tundra Books of Montreal, Montreal, founder, president, and editor-in-chief, 1967—; Tundra Books of Northern New York, Plattsburgh, N.Y., president, 1971—. *Awards, honors:* Canadian Centennial literary competitions first prize, 1967, for *The Last Noble Savage.*

WRITINGS: The Last Noble Savage, Tundra Books, 1967, reissued as *I Once Knew An Indian Woman,* Houghton, 1973. Contributor to *Canadian Art.*

WORK IN PROGRESS: Research on why Canada's literary output is so slim.

SIDELIGHTS: "I decided to start my own publishing company in 1967 under the name of Tundra Books. First publications were a series of brochures on the arts, at EXPO 67, followed by the publication of my own book *The Last Noble Savage.* The book sold 200 copies during its first year of existence in Canada, even though it had won

EBBITT CUTLER

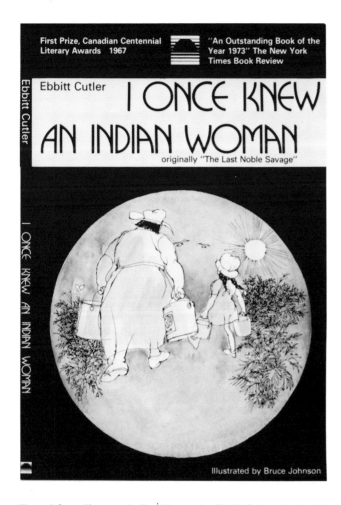

First Prize, Canadian Centennial Literary Awards 1967

"An Outstanding Book of the Year 1973" The New York Times Book Review

Ebbitt Cutler

I ONCE KNEW AN INDIAN WOMAN

originally "The Last Noble Savage"

Illustrated by Bruce Johnson

(From *I Once Knew an Indian Woman* by Ebbitt Cutler. Illustrated by Bruce Johnson.)

the Centennial Library Award and every public, university, and high-school librarian in Canada had been circularized on it—an indication of Canadian library interest in new Canadian books at that time. (Since then, the first printing has sold out, the book sold U.S. rights, and Houghton Mifflin brought out a new edition in 1973 which was chosen by *The New York Times* as 'One of the outstanding books of the year 1973.')

"In spring of 1968 I opened a bookstore in Old Montreal, selling only Canadian books in English and French. Although financially unsuccessful—people used it as a library rather than a bookstore—it was an education on the state of Canadian publishing, and how, with the exception of a few publishers, generally awful it was.

"Although I am an anti-nationalist, and remain so, a year before the sale of Gage and Ryerson, I was writing all the small publishers in Canada protesting the attitude of the Canadian Book Publishers Council regarding small Canadian publishers. This was not because these publishers were not Canadian but because most of them weren't publishers at all. They were merely importers and jobbers. There's nothing wrong with that, but for them to exclude small publishers who really were publishing (which they were doing by charging $1600.00 annual fees and assessments) seemed unjust. It was largely due to my efforts and

those of Maynard Gertler of Harvest House in Montreal, that the first meeting of Canadian publishers was called by the Canada Council in Montreal in December, 1969—out of which the Independent Publishers Association eventually grew—an association with which I have become increasingly unhappy in the last few years.

"In the years of its existence, Tundra Books has published a small amount of books, but these have won an impressive series of literary and design awards. Tundra does not believe that Canada needs more books, but it needs more *good books*. It has avoided bandwagons, and all of its books are highly original in concept. It has made them often difficult of immediate acceptance, particularly in Canada, which I consider almost pathetically backward today as it was in my youth thirty years ago. I still believe it is necessary for a creative Canadian to gain acceptance outside Canada—although he may no longer have to live outside Canada, since the new electronic world has made it less important not only where one lives, but even where one publishes.

"It is because I felt that the Canadian book world was increasingly claustrophobic that I set up a small American company in 1971, Tundra Books of Northern New York (in Plattsburgh, N.Y.—65 miles from Montreal). This meant that Tundra Books could be published simultaneously on both sides of the border at once, in those cases where none of the larger U.S. publishers were interested."

FOR MORE INFORMATION SEE: New York Times Book Review, June 3, 1973.

D'AMATO, Janet   1925-

PERSONAL: Born June 5, 1925, in Rochester, N.Y.; daughter of Earle H. and Florence (an artist; maiden name, Cowles) Potter; married Alex D'Amato (a book designer), February 28, 1949; children: Sandra (Mrs. Harry Tompkins, Jr.), Donna. *Education:* Pratt Institute, diploma, 1946. *Residence:* Bronxville, N.Y.

CAREER: Display designer; Art Studio, Mt. Vernon, N.Y., illustrator for filmstrips, 1946-47; free-lance artist, 1952—.

WRITINGS—With husband, Alex D'Amato: *Wendy and the Wind,* Grosset, 1957; *U.S.A. Fun and Play,* Doubleday, 1960; *My First Book of Jokes,* Grosset, 1962; *Animal Fun Time,* Doubleday, 1964; *Fun Till Christmas,* Whitman Publishing, 1965; *Cardboard Carpentry,* Lion Press, 1966; *Handicrafts for Holidays,* Lion Press, 1967; *Indian Crafts,* Lion Press, 1968; *African Crafts for You to Make,* Messner, 1968; *African Animals Through African Eyes,* Messner, 1971; *What's in the Sky,* Nutmeg Press, 1971; *Houses,* Nutmeg Press, 1971; *Animals,* Nutmeg Press, 1971; *American Indian Craft Inspirations,* M. Evans, 1972; *Gifts to Make for Love or Money,* Golden Press, 1973; *Colonial Crafts for You to Make,* Messner, 1975; *Quillwork—The Craft of Paper Filligree,* M. Evans, 1975.

Illustrator: Sophie Ruskay, *Discovery at Aspen,* A. S. Barnes, 1960; Shari Lewis and Jacquelyn Reinach, *Headstart Book of Looking and Listening,* McGraw, 1960; Constantine Georgiou, *Wait and See,* Harvey House, 1962;

The train engine can be made from cookie, cereal, candy or gift boxes—whatever you can find. ■ (From *Handicrafts for Holidays* by Janet and Alex D'Amato. Illustrated by the authors.)

Azriel Eisenberg, editor, *Tzedakah*, Behrman, 1963; Hyman Ruchlis, *Your Changing Earth*, Harvey House, 1963; Mary Elting, *Water Come, Water Go*, Harvey House, 1964; Elting, *Aircraft at Work*, Harvey House, 1964; Norah Smaridge, *The Light Within*, Hawthorne, 1965; Arnold Sundgaard, *How Lovely is Christmas*, Western Publishing, 1966; Joan W. Jenkins, *A Girls' World*, Hawthorne, 1967; Samm S. Baker, *Miracle Gardening Encyclopedia*, Grosset, 1967; Arthur Liebers, *50 Favorite Hobbies*, Hawthorne, 1968; Margaret Bevans, *Weather and Weather Forecasting*, Nutmeg Press, 1975. Also creator, with husband, of kits and book and record cover designs.

Contributor to *Creative Crafts* and *Humpty Dumpty*.

SIDELIGHTS: "When my husband started freelancing on children's books I began doing a few illustrations. By the time the girls were school age, free-lance illustration had become full time. The first book I wrote (an illustrated), *Wendy and the Wind* was about a three year old when my daughter was about that age. In the years that followed, I did many books specializing in children, and animals; books to go with records, record jackets, workbooks, activity books, etc.

"Meanwhile my husband and I were always involved in crafts, spending much of our free time all year making all our Christmas gifts and children's toys. Some of our activity books had pages on how-to make things, and gradually we were doing books about projects of things for children to make. In 1966 we did our first hard-cover book on crafts and have been doing them ever since.

"Our machine age has produced a huge gap between the creation of a product and its user. As I believe children should be aware of basic crafts and how household essentials were originally made in the home, most of our books give some history of the origins of crafts, methods and designs used by early people.

"I am constantly discovering new crafts or new applications of old crafts and usually start experimenting on something long before it finds its way into a book. I hope the people who work from my books find as much satisfaction and excitement in creating, as I do."

"In 1962 we bought a larger house in Bronxville, with a studio room over the garage, a garage workshop and every room finds some sort of craft activity in it. For instance: sewing, jewelry supplies in the guest room; papier mache in the laundry room; collage in the game room and at the moment, the dining room is full of quillwork materials. In the studio we have our drawing boards, spend most of our time there, doing the drawings, illustrations and mechanicals, etc., needed for all sorts of jobs. Besides books, I've been designing and making models for craftwork kits, creating games and toys and still do a few illustrations; write articles for craft magazines.

"I'd like to do more experiments, creating with fabric and thread manipulation for wall hangings and soft sculptures (which I exhibit occasionally) but I haven't been able to devote enough time to really explore this art.

"One daughter is now married, the other just finishing college. In the twenty years we have free lanced, we have done many enjoyable projects and books; had considerable frustration (mostly with budget cuts on producing books) and lots of deadlines to meet. Despite the fact we've never had time for a vacation, there is nothing I'd rather be doing than this type of creative work. And I hope some young people will also find this kind of enjoyment of life through our books."

FOR MORE INFORMATION SEE: Horn Book, February, 1970.

DARLING, Mary Kathleen 1943-
(Kathy Darling)

PERSONAL: Born September 8, 1943, in Hudson, N.Y.; daughter of Andrew J. (a major in the U.S. Army) and Helen C. (McCourt) Sipos; married Joseph Darling; children: Tara Ann. *Education:* Attended Russell Sage College. *Home:* 46 Cooper Lane, Larchmont, N.Y. 10538. *Office:* Garrard Publishing Co., 2 Overhill Rd., Scarsdale, N.Y. 10583.

CAREER: Garrard Publishing Co., Scarsdale, N.Y., children's book editor and promotion director, 1968—.

WRITINGS—For children; under name Kathy Darling: *The Jelly Bean Contest,* Garrard, 1972; (with Leland B. Jacobs) *April Fool!,* Garrard, 1973; *Little Bat's Secret,* Garrard, 1974. Contributor to magazines about dogs.

HOBBIES AND OTHER INTERESTS: Raising Irish wolfhounds.

DAVIDSON, Mary R.   1885-1973

PERSONAL: Born December 20, 1885, in Auburndale, Mass.; daughter of Frank F. (a jeweler) and Rachel (Allen) Davidson. *Education:* Smith College, A.B., 1908; Boston University, special courses, 1923-25. *Politics:* Progressive Republican. *Religion:* Congregationalist. *Home:* Ponce de Leon Hotel, St. Augustine, Fla. (winter); South China, Me. (summer).

CAREER: Newton High School, Newton, Mass., English teacher, 1910-13; St. Johnsbury Academy, St. Johnsbury, Vt., head of English department; Garland Junior College, Boston, Mass., head of English department, 1926-51; retired. *Awards, honors:* Second prize for one-act plays for children, National Womens' Clubs.

WRITINGS: Christmas to Christmas, Baker's Plays, 1924; *Buffalo Bill, Wild West Showman,* Garrard, 1962; *The Life of Dolly Madison* (juvenile), Garrard, 1966. Writer of radio scripts, and of plays for children.

HOBBIES AND OTHER INTERESTS: Music, birds, gardening.

(Died, 1973)

DAVIS, Mary L(ee)   1935-

PERSONAL: Born March 21, 1935, in Worthington, Minn.; daughter of Homer L. (a businessman) and Minnie E. (Pearson) Davis; children: Laura Eileen. *Education:* University of Minnesota, A.A., 1954. *Politics:* Democrat. *Religion:* "No affiliation." *Home:* 316 Oak Grove St., Minneapolis, Minn. 55403.

CAREER: Staff writer for *St. Paul Dispatch,* 1958-60; political press aide in Washington, D.C., 1960; public relations representative in Minnesota, 1961-71; teacher of English in a Montana junior high school, 1966; free-lance writer. *Awards, honors:* Page One award from Newspaper Guild, 1959, for feature story.

WRITINGS—Juveniles; all published by Lerner: *Polly and the President,* 1967; *Careers in Baseball,* 1973; *Careers in the Bank,* 1973; *Careers in the Telephone Company,* 1973; *Careers in the Medical Center,* 1973; *Careers in Printing,* 1973. Contributing editor and feature writer for *Metropolitan Magazines,* St. Paul.

WORK IN PROGRESS: An adult novel set in contemporary Britian; a ten-book series in "women in American life," for Denison.

MARY LEE DAVIS

SIDELIGHTS: "I began writing children's books because I thought the market would be easier to crack than adult fiction. It happens that I was right. From juvenile fiction I switched to biography. History was my minor field in college, journalism was my major. I consider myself a news writer. Perhaps that is why I like doing biography better than fiction. At least I can deal with facts and with real people."

DE CAMP, L(yon) Sprague   1907-
(Lyman R. Lyon, J. Wellington Wells)

PERSONAL: Born November 27, 1907, in New York, N.Y.; son of Lyon and E. Beatrice (Sprague) de Camp; married Catherine A. Crook, 1939; children: Lyman Sprague, Gerard Beekman. *Education:* California Institute of Technology, B.S., 1930; Massachusetts Institute of Technology, student, 1932; Stevens Institute of Technology, M.S., 1933. *Politics:* Democrat. *Home:* 278 Hothorpe Lane, Villanova, Pa. 19085. *Agent:* Berthold Fles, 507 Fifth Ave., New York, N.Y. 10017.

CAREER: Inventors Foundation, Inc., Hoboken, N.J., editor and instructor, 1933-36; International Correspondence Schools, Scranton, Pa., principal, 1936-37; Fowler-Becker Publishing Co., New York, N.Y., editor, 1937-38;

American Society of Mechanical Engineers, New York, N.Y., editor, 1938; now a self-employed writer. Member, board of elections, Nether Providence Township, Pa., 1955-60. *Military service:* U.S. Navy, three and a half years during World War II; became lieutenant commander. *Member:* History of Science Society, Society for the History of Technology (advisory board), Association Phonétique Internationale, Authors Club of New York, Bread Loaf Writers Conference (fellow), Philadelphia Science Fiction Society, Hydra Club, Trap Door Spiders Club, Hyborian Legion. *Awards, honors:* International Fantasy Award for *Lands Beyond,* 1953; Cleveland Science Fiction Association award for *Tales from Gavagan's Bar,* 1953; fiction award, Athenaeum of Philadelphia, for *An Elephant for Aristotle,* 1958.

WRITINGS—Nonfiction: (With Alf K. Berle) *Inventions and Their Management,* International Textbook Co., 1937; *The Evolution of Naval Weapons,* U.S. Government textbook, 1947; (with Willy Ley) *Lands Beyond,* Rinehart, 1952; *Science-Fiction Handbook,* Hermitage, 1953; *Lost Continents: The Atlantis Theme in History, Science and Literature,* Gnome, 1954; (with Alf K. Berle) *Inventions, Patents and Their Management,* Van Nostrand, 1959.

The Heroic Age of American Invention, Doubleday, 1961; *The Ancient Engineers,* Doubleday, 1963; *Elephant,* Pyramid, 1964; (with Catherine C. de Camp) *Ancient Ruins and Archaeology,* Doubleday, 1964; (with Catherine C. de Camp) *Spirits, Stars, and Spells,* Canaveral, 1966; *Fantastic Swordsmen,* Pyramid, 1966; (with Catherine C. de Camp) *The Day of the Dragon,* Doubleday, 1968; *The Conan Reader,* Mirage Press, 1968; *The Great Monkey Trial,* Doubleday, 1968; (with George H. Scithers) *The Conan Swordbook,* Mirage Press, 1969; (with George H. Scithers) *The Conan Grimoire,* Mirage Press, 1972; *Great Cities of the Ancient World,* Doubleday, 1972; *Lovecraft: A Biography,* Doubleday, 1975; *The Miscast Barbarian: A Biography of Robert R. Howard (1906-1936),* Gerry de la Ree, 1975.

Juveniles: *Engines,* Golden Press, 1959; *Man and Power,* Golden Press, 1962; (with Catherine C. de Camp) *The Story of Science in America,* Scribner, 1967; *Darwin and His Great Discovery,* Macmillan, 1972.

Historical fiction: *An Elephant for Aristotle,* Doubleday, 1958; *The Bronze God of Rhodes,* Doubleday, 1960; *The Dragon of the Ishtar Gate,* Doubleday, 1961; *The Arrows of Hercules,* Doubleday, 1965; *The Golden Wind,* Doubleday, 1969.

Science fiction: *Lest Darkness Fall,* Holt, 1941; (with Fletcher Pratt) *The Incomplete Enchanter,* Holt, 1941; (with Fletcher Pratt) *The Land of Unreason,* Holt, 1942; (with Fletcher Pratt) *The Carnelian Cube,* Gnome, 1948; *Divide and Rule,* Fantasy Press, 1948; *The Wheels of If,* Shasta, 1948; (with Fletcher Pratt) *The Castle of Iron,* Gnome, 1950; (with P. Schuyler Miller) *Genus Homo,* Fantasy Press, 1950; *The Undesired Princess,* Fantasy, 1951; *Rogue Queen,* Doubleday, 1951; *The Continent Makers,* Twayne, 1953; (with Fletcher Pratt) *Tales from Gavagan's Bar,* Twayne, 1953; *The Tritonian Ring,* Twayne, 1953; *Cosmic Manhunt,* Ace, 1954; (with Robert E. Howard) *Tales of Conan,* Gnome, 1955; (with Björn Nyberg) *The Return of Conan,* Gnome, 1957; *Solomon's Stone,* Avalon, 1957; *The Tower of Zanid,* Avalon, 1958;

L. SPRAGUE DE CAMP

The Glory That Was, Avalon, 1960; (with Fletcher Pratt) *Wall of Serpents,* Avalon, 1960; *The Search for Zei,* Avalon, 1962; *A Gun for Dinosaur,* Doubleday, 1963; *The Hand of Zei,* Avalon, 1963; (editor) *Swords and Sorcery* (anthology), Pyramid, 1963; (editor) *The Spell of Seven* (anthology), Pyramid, 1965; (editor) *The Fantastic Swordsmen,* Pyramid, 1966; (editor) *Warlocks and Warriors,* Putnam, 1970; *The Goblin Tower,* Pyramid, 1968; *The Clocks of Iraz,* Pyramid, 1971; *The Fallible Fiend,* Pyramid, 1973; (with Catherine C. de Camp) *3000 Years of Fantasy and Science Fiction,* Lothrop, 1972; (with Catherine C. de Camp) *Tales Beyond Time,* Lothrop, 1973. Contributor to anthologies and symposia, author of about one-hundred-forty articles and one-hundred-five short stories. Other writings include technical and public relations articles, book reviews, fillers, verses, phonetic transcriptions, letters and stories in fan magazines. Between 1948 and 1956, he wrote seventy-six radio scripts for "Voice of America," most of which were on current developments in science. Has also done ghost writing and editing.

Verse: *Demons and Dinosaurs,* Arkham House, 1970; *Phantoms and Fancies,* Mirage Press, 1972.

Miscellany: *Scribblings,* Nesfa Press, 1972.

WORK IN PROGRESS: The Ragged Edge of Science; Swordsmen and Sorcerers: The Creators of Heroic Fantasy; Shadows Out of Time.

SIDELIGHTS: Has traveled widely in the Americas, Europe, Africa, Asia, the Pacific. Speaks several languages. During World War II, served as civilian engineer and as officer doing test and development engineering on aircraft. At one time was a uranium prospector. His books have been translated into at least seven foreign languages and he has translated stories from the French and the Italian. He lectures and makes radio appearances occasionally. Special interests are travel, gardening, language study, and collecting the works of R. E. Howard, Lord Dunsany and C. A. Smith.

FOR MORE INFORMATION SEE: Everybody's Weekly, January 11, 1948; *Chester Times,* Pennsylvania, June 15, 1955; *Delaware County Times,* May 21, 1958, January 4, 1960; *Fantasy and Science Fiction,* January, 1963; *Amazing Stories,* February, 1964; Sam Moskowitz, *Seekers of Tomorrow,* World, 1966.

DEMAS, Vida   1927-

PERSONAL: Born March 30, 1927, in Pittsburgh, Pa.; daughter of Benjamin Morris (a businessman) and Cecelia (Shapiro) Kramer; married Nicholas James Demas (a professor of law), March 25, 1953; children: Rebecca. *Education:* University of Pittsburgh, B.A., 1948; Radcliffe College, further study, 1952. *Politics:* Democrat. *Religion:* None. *Home:* 1460 Graham Ave., Monessen, Pa. 15062. *Agent:* Elizabeth Otis, McIntosh & Otis, Inc., 18 East 41st St., New York, N.Y. 10017.

CAREER: Carnegie Museum, Pittsburgh, Pa., promotion assistant, 1949; University of Pittsburgh, Pittsburgh, Pa.,

VIDA DEMAS

public relations writer, 1950-52, 1955-57, promotion assistant for University Press, 1952-55; Chatham College, Pittsburgh, Pa., assistant director of public relations, 1962-63. *Awards, honors: School Library Journal* listed *First Person, Singular,* as one of best books of 1974.

WRITINGS: First Person, Singular (ALA Notable Book), Putnam, 1974. Contributor of news and feature articles to newspapers and magazines.

WORK IN PROGRESS: A novel, not yet titled.

SIDELIGHTS: "I write because I must; it makes me happy."

DEVEREUX, Frederick L(eonard), Jr. 1914-

PERSONAL: Born April 20, 1914, in New York, N.Y.; son of Frederick Leonard (an executive) and Frances (Clark) Devereux; married Ruth Wentworth Foster, June 26, 1936; children: Foster, Frances Clark, Frederick Leonard III. *Education:* University of Chicago, A.B., 1937; U.S. Army Command and General Staff College, Diploma, 1943. *Politics:* Republican. *Religion:* Episcopalian. *Home:* 24 The Green, Woodstock, Vt. 05091.

CAREER: R. H. Macy & Co., New York, N.Y., buyer, 1936-38; Young and Rubicam, Inc., New York, N.Y., merchandizing executive, 1939-40, 1946-52; Oneita Knitting Mills, Utica, N.Y., general sales manager, 1953-59; Allied Stores, Corp., New York, N.Y., marketing manager, 1960-64; Merit Stores, Inc., Middletown, N.Y., president, 1964-66. Lecturer at Graduate School of Business Administration, New York University, 1959-60; instructor for U.S. Power Squadrons classes, 1969-72. Judge at National Horse Show and other horse shows and hunter trials. *Military service:* U.S. Army, Cavalry, 1941-45; instructor in horsemanship at U.S. Military Academy, 1942-43; later assistant chief of staff, Intelligence, 86th Infantry Division; became lieutenant colonel. *Member:* Institute of Navigation, American Horse Shows Association, U.S. Power Squadrons, American Yacht Club.

WRITINGS: Practical Navigation for the Yachtsman, Norton, 1972; *Famous Horses—Past and Present* (juvenile), World Publishing, 1972; *Ride Your Pony Right* (juvenile), Dodd, 1974. Former editor, *Vermont Horse.*

WORK IN PROGRESS: Horses, A First Book and *The Backyard Pony* for Watts; *Horse Problems and Problem Horses* for Devin-Adair; *The Oxford Companion to the American Revolution* for Oxford University Press.

DICK, Trella Lamson   1889-1974

PERSONAL: Born May 29, 1889, in Orleans, Neb.; daughter of Junius Truesdale and Harriet Elvira (Derrick) Lamson; married Robert Payne Dick, November 30, 1912; children: Trella Margaret (Mrs. Erwin Laurance), Elizabeth Leslie (Mrs. Richard Clark), Kathleen Roberta (Mrs. Roger Stewart), Robert Frederick. *Education:* Attended University of Nebraska. *Politics:* Republican. *Religion:* Episcopal. *Home:* 1417 University, Walla Walla, Wash. 99362. *Agent:* Ruth Cantor, 120 West 42nd St., New York, N.Y. 10036.

CAREER: Teacher in elementary and high schools in Orleans, Neb., Fairfield, Idaho, and Maxwell, Neb., for ten years; free-lance writer. *Member:* Daughters of the American Revolution, Delta Kappa Gamma. *Awards, honors:* Follett award 1953, and award certificate of Boys' Clubs of America, both for *Tornado Jones.*

WRITINGS: Tornado Jones, Follett, 1953; *Tornado Jones on Sentinel Mountain,* Follett, 1955; *Tornado's Big Year,* Follett, 1956; *Flag in Hiding,* Abelard, 1959; *Valiant Vanguard,* Abelard, 1960; *The Island on the Border* (Junior Literary Guild selection), Abelard, 1963; *Bridger's Boy,* Follett, 1965; *Burro at the Beach,* Follett, 1967.

Contributor to textbooks, *Let's Travel On,* Macmillan, 1940, and *Exploring Near and Far,* Follett, 1955. Contributor of short stories to *Child Life, Sentinel, Young Catholic Messenger, Capper's Farmer, Omaha Herald, Christian Herald, Junior World, Wee Wisdom,* and other publications, and of articles to *Better Homes and Gardens.* Several books serialized in young peoples' periodicals.

WORK IN PROGRESS: A mystery story set in the Blue Mountains.

SIDELIGHTS: "I think all juvenile books should include the three E's—ethics, education, and entertainment."

HOBBIES AND OTHER INTERESTS: Gardening.

(Died May 10, 1974)

DONNA, Natalie   1934-

PERSONAL: Born December 25, 1934; daughter of P(atrick) B. and Maryanne (Tritto) Donna. *Education:* New York University, B.A. *Home:* 320 East 73rd St., New York, N.Y. 10021.

NATALIE DONNA

You will be amused and amazed at the artful creatures you can conjure at a moment's notice, once you really start to look at peanuts. ■ (From *Peanut Craft* by Natalie Donna. Illustrated by the author.)

CAREER: Advertising agency copywriter, working in all media, in New York, N.Y., Boston, Mass., and Montreal, Canada. Package and product design consultant and copywriter; designer of three historically-based games for children; creator of history, science, math, literature, and geography quizzes for children; currently free-lance writer.

WRITINGS: Boy of the Masai, Dodd, 1964; *Bead Craft,* Lothrop, 1972; *Peanut Craft,* Lothrop, 1974.

WORK IN PROGRESS: A major work on jewelry, for Chilton Publishing, illustrated and photographed by the author; a cookbook, for Lothrop.

SIDELIGHTS: "I cannot remember a time when I did not write. As soon as I was technically able to manage a pencil I scribbled poetry and stories. Later I delved into scripts, film and communications. Encouraged to enter the field professionally, I did so as an advertising copywriter.

"Creativity is my career. My activities are diversified. I see my endeavors reach the public in varied media. It is all fun and I love it. To pursue a career that is a combination of best-loved hobbies, is to enjoy work a great deal; things mesh beautifully."

FOR MORE INFORMATION SEE: Horn Book, June, 1974.

DUVALL, Evelyn Millis   1906-

PERSONAL: Born July 28, 1906, in Oswego, N.Y.; daughter of Charles Lieb and Bertha (Palmer) Millis; married Sylvanus Milne Duvall, 1927; children: Jean (Mrs. Paul Walther), Joy (Mrs. Ray M. Johnson, Jr.). *Education:* Syracuse University, B.S. (summa cum laude), 1927; Vanderbilt University, M.S., 1929; Northwestern University, postgraduate study, 1935-40; University of Chicago, Ph.D., 1946. *Home and office:* 700 John Ringling Blvd., Plymouth Harbor #804-805, Sarasota, Fla. 33577.

CAREER: Association for Family Living, Chicago, Ill., initial director, 1934-45; National Council on Family Relations, Chicago, Ill., executive, 1945-51; National Congress of Parents and Teachers, Chicago, Ill., director of adolescent study course, 1954—. Southern Illinois University, Carbondale, Distinguished Visiting Professor of Family

Life, 1962. Co-leader with husband, S. M. Duvall, of Southeast Asia Conference on Family Life, Manila, 1954; conductor of Around the World Leaders' Conferences, 1954-55; leader of seminars through Scandinavia, 1958, and through British West Indies, 1963-1968; leader, World Congress on the Family, New Delhi, 1966; consultant to government of New Zealand in Family Life Education, 1967; keynoter, Family Life Section, White House Conference on Aging, 1971; Program Coordinator, Sarasota Institute of Lifetime Learning, 1972—; incorporator and advisor, Sarasota Council on Aging, 1973—.

MEMBER: American Association of Marriage and Family Counselors (fellow), American Institute of Family Relations (regional consultant), American Sociological Association (fellow), Child Study Association of America (advisory board), International Union of Family Organizations (general council), National Council on Family Relations (honorary life member; chairman of committee on international liaison, 1963—), Sex Information and Education Council of the United States (charter member, board of directors, 1964—), Society for Research in Child Development, Phi Kappa Phi, Pi Delta Nu, Pi Lambda Theta, Sigma Xi. *Awards, honors:* George Arents Medal from Syracuse University; Doctor of Humane Letters, Hood College, 1970.

WRITINGS: (With Reuben Hill) *When You Marry,* Heath (textbook), and Association Press, 1945, high school edition, 1961; *Leading Parents' Groups,* Abingdon, 1946; *Family Living* (high school text), Macmillan, 1950, 2nd edition, 1961; *Facts of Life and Love for Teen-Agers,* Association Press, 1950, 3rd edition, 1963; *In-Laws: Pro and Con,* Association Press, 1954, 2nd edition, 1961; *Family Development,* Lippincott, 1957, 2nd edition, 1962, 4th edition, 1971; (with Joy Duvall Johnson) *The Art of Dating,* Association Press, 1958; (with Reuben Hill) *Being Married,* Heath (textbook), and Association Press, 1961; (editor with S. M. Duvall) *Sex Ways—in Fact and Faith,* Association Press, 1961; (with S. M. Duvall) *Sense and Nonsense about Sex,* Association Press, 1962; *Love and the Facts of Life,* Association Press, 1963; (with David Mace and Paul Popenoe) *The Church Looks at Family Life,* Broadman, 1964; *Why Wait Till Marriage?,* Association Press, 1965; *Today's Teen-Agers,* general and Roman Catholic editions, Association Press, 1966; *Faith in Families,* Rand, 1970; *Coping with Kids,* Broadman, 1974; *Handbook for Parents,* Broadman, 1974; *Journal of Marriage and the Family,* Broadman, 1976; *Parents and Teenagers,* Broadman, 1976.

Contributor to *Journal of Marriage and the Family, Coordinator,* and other journals.

WORK IN PROGRESS: A revised text edition of *Family Development,* for Lippincott, 1977.

HOBBIES AND OTHER INTERESTS: Philately, photography, swimming and gardening.

EICHENBERG, Fritz   1901-

PERSONAL: Born October 24, 1901, in Cologne, Germany; came to United States in 1933, naturalized in 1941; son of Siegfried and Ida (Marcus) Eichenberg; married Mary Altmann, 1926 (died, 1937); married Margaret Ladenburg, 1941 (divorced, 1965); married Antonie Ida Schulze-

Forster (a graphic designer), January 7, 1975; children: (first marriage) Suzanne Eichenberg Jensen; (second marriage) Timothy. *Education:* School of Applied Arts, Cologne, student, 1916-20; State Academy of Graphic Arts, Leipzig, M.F.A., 1923. *Religion:* Society of Friends (Quakers). *Home and studio:* 142 Oakwood Dr., Peace Dale, R.I. 02879.

CAREER: Graphic artist and illustrator of classics and other books. Started as newspaper artist in Germany, 1923, and worked as artist and traveling correspondent for Ullstein Publications, Berlin, before settling in United States; New School for Social Research, New York, N.Y., member of art faculty, 1935-45; Pratt Institute, Brooklyn, N.Y., professor of art, 1947-72, chairman of department of graphic arts, 1956-63, founder-director of Graphic Arts Center, 1956-72; University of Rhode Island, Kingston, professor of art, 1966-71, chairman of department, 1966-69; Albertus Magnus College, New Haven, Conn., professor of art, 1971-72. Had one-man shows at New School for Social Research, 1939, 1949, Associated American Artists Gallery, 1967, Pratt Manhattan Center Gallery, 1972, and retrospective show at Klingspor Museum, Offenbach, Germany, 1974; work has been shown in Xylon International exhibitions in Switzerland, Yugoslavia, and other countries, in U.S. Information Agency traveling exhibits, and Society of American Graphic Artist shows; represented in collections of National Gallery of Art, Hermitage Museum (Moscow), Metropolitan Museum of Art, Philadelphia Museum of Art, and other museums. Member of Pennell Committee, Library of Congress, 1959-65.

MEMBER: National Academy of Design, Royal Society of Arts (London; corresponding fellow), Society of American Graphic Artists, Xylon International, Bund Deutscher Buchkuenstler. *Awards, honors:* Joseph Pennell Medal of Pennsylvania Academy of Fine Arts, 1944; first prize for print, National Academy of Design, 1946; Silver Medal of Limited Editions Club, 1954; runner-up for Caldecott

FRITZ EICHENBERG

X for Rex

(From *Ape in a Cape* by Fritz Eichenberg. Illustrated by the author.)

Something about the Author

Medal, 1957, for *Ape in a Cape;* grant from John D. Rockefeller III Fund, 1968; D.F.A., Southeastern Massachusetts University, 1972; S.F.B. Morse Medal of National Academy of Design, 1973; D.F.A., University of Rhode Island, 1974.

WRITINGS: (Self-illustrated) *Ape in a Cape: An Alphabet of Odd Animals* (juvenile), Harcourt, 1952; (self-illustrated) *Art and Faith* (booklet), Pendle Hill, 1952; (self-illustrated) *Dancing in the Moon: Counting Rhymes* (ALA Notable Book), Harcourt, 1955; (translator with William Hubben) Helmut A. P. Grieshaber, *H.A.P. Grieshaber,* Arts, 1965; (author of text) Naoko Matsubara, *Nantucket Woodcuts,* Barre Publishers, 1967; (contributor) *Education in the Graphic Arts,* Boston Public Library, 1969; (editor) *Artist's Proof: A Collector's Edition of the First Eight Issues of the Distinguished Journal of Print and Printmaking,* New York Graphic Society, 1971; (translator and illustrator) Desiderius Erasmus, *In Praise of Folly,* Aquarius, 1972; *The Print: Art, History and Techniques,* Abrams, 1975. Numerous articles contributed to *Artist's Proof, American Artist, Friends Journal, Publishers' Weekly, Horn Book,* and *Print Magazine.*

Illustrator: *Puss in Boots,* Holiday House, 1936; Joel Chandler Harris, *Uncle Remus Stories,* limited edition, Peter Pauper Press, 1937; Moritz A. Jagendorf, *Tyll Ulenspiegel's Merry Pranks,* Vanguard, 1938; Therese Lenotre, *Mystery of Dog Flip,* translated from the French by Simone Chamoud, Stokes, 1939; Robert Davis, *Padre: The Gentlemanly Pig,* Holiday House, 1939, enlarged edition, 1948; Rosalys Hall, *Animals to Africa,* Holiday House, 1939.

Stewart Schackne, *Rowena, the Skating Cow,* Scribner, 1940; Eula Griffin Duncan, *Big Road Walker,* Stokes, 1940; Babette Deutsch, *Heroes of the Kalevala: Finland's Saga,* Messner, 1940; Jonathan Swift, *Gulliver's Travels,* Heritage Press, 1940, junior text edition, 1947, new edition, 1961; Richard A. W. Hughes, *Don't Blame Me* (short stories), Harper, 1940; William Shakespeare, *Tragedy of Richard the Third,* Limited Editions Club, 1940; Henry Beston, *The Tree That Ran Away,* Macmillan, 1941; Marjorie Fischer, *All on a Summer's Day,* Random House, 1941; Irmengarde Eberle, *Phoebe-Bell,* Greystone Press, 1941; Ivan S. Turgenev, *Fathers and Sons,* translated from the Russian by Constance Garnett, Heritage Press, 1941; Mabel Leigh Hunt, *"Have You Seen Tom Thumb?,"* Stokes, 1942; Charlotte Brontë's *Jane Eyre* and Emily Brontë's, *Wuthering Heights* (companion volumes in one slipcase), Random House, 1943; Hendrik Ibsen, *Story of Peer Gynt,* retold by E. V. Sandys, Crowell, 1943; Irmengarde Eberle, *Wide Fields: The Story of Henry Fabre,* Crowell, 1943; Eleanor Hoffman, *Mischief in Fez,* Holiday House, 1943; Lev N. Tolstoi, *Anna Karenina,* translated from the Russian by Constance Garnett, two volumes, Doubleday, 1944, two volumes in one, 1946, deluxe edition, Garden City Publishing, 1948; Edgar Allen Poe, *Tales,* Random House, 1944; Mark Keats, *Sancho and His Stubborn Mule,* W. R. Scott, 1944; Rose Dobbs, *No Room: An Old Story Retold,* Coward, 1944; Fedor M. Dostoevski, *Crime and Punishment,* translated from the Russian by Constance Garnett, Heritage Press, 1944; Glanville W. Smith, *Adventures of Sir Ignatius Tippitolio,* Harper, 1945; Stephen Vincent Benet, *The Devil and Daniel Webster,* Kingsport Press, 1945; Anna Sewell, *Black Beauty,* Gros-

set, 1945; Terence H. White, *Mistress Masham's Repose,* Putnam, 1946, Maurice Dolbier, *The Magic Shop,* Random House, 1946; Felix Salten, compiler, *Favoriete Animal Stories,* Messner, 1948; Fedor M. Dostoevski, *The Grand Inquisitor,* Haddam House, 1948; Fedor M. Dosteovski, *The Brothers Karamazov,* translation from the Russian by Constance Garnett revised, with introduction by Avrahm Yarmolinsky, Limited Editions Club, 1949; Ruth Stiles Gannett, *Wonderful House-Boat-Train,* Random House, 1949.

Mark van Doren, *The Witch of Ramoth,* Maple Press, 1950; Rudyard Kipling, *Jungle Book,* Grosset, 1950; Wilkie Collins, *Short Stories,* Rodale Books, 1950; Nathaniel Hawthorne, *Tale of King Midas and the Golden Touch,* Limited Editions Club, 1952; (with Vassily Verestchagin) Lev N. Tolstoi, *War and Peace,* translated from the Russian by Louise and Aylmer Maude, two volumes in one, Heritage Press, 1951; Margaret Cousins, *Ben Franklin of Old Philadelphia,* Random House, 1952; Dorothy Day, *Long Loneliness* (autobiography), Harper, 1952; Johann Wolfgang von Goethe, *Story of Reynard the Fox,* translated by Thomas J. Arnold from original German poem, Heritage Press, 1954; Fedor M. Dostoevski, *The Idiot,* translation from the Russian by Constance Garnett revised, with introduction by Avrahm Yarmolinsky, Heritage Press, 1956; Elizabeth J. Coatsworth, *The Peaceable Kingdom and Other Poems,* Pantheon, 1958; Edna Johnson and others, compilers, *Anthology of Children's Literature,* 3rd edition (Eichenberg did not illustrate earlier editions), Houghton, 1959, 4th edition, 1970.

Fedor M. Dostoevski, *The Possessed,* translated from the Russian by Constance Garnett, Heritage Press, 1960; Lev N. Tolstoi, *Resurrection,* translation by Leo Wiener, Limited Editions Club, 1963; Jean Charlot, *Posada's Dance of Death,* Graphic Arts Center, Pratt Institute, 1965; Etienne Decroux, *Mime: The Art of Etienne Decoux,* Pratt Adlib Press, 1965; Dylan Thomas, *A Child's Christmas in Wales,* limited edition, New Directions, 1969.

Lev N. Tolstoi, *Childhood, Boyhood, Youth,* translation by Leo Wiener, Limited Editions Club, 1972; John M. Langstaff, *The Two Magicians,* Atheneum, 1973; Feodor M. Dostoevski, *A Raw Youth,* translation by Constance Garnett, Limited Editions Club, 1974; *The Wood and the Graves,* Clarkson Potter, 1976.

Founder and chief editor, *Artist's Proof: An Annual of Prints and Printmaking,* Pratt Institute, 1960-72. Contributor to *American Artist* and other journals.

WORK IN PROGRESS: Fables with a Twist; illustrating J. C. Grimmelshausen's *The Adventurous Simplicissimus.*

SIDELIGHTS: Eichenberg's favorite mediums are lithographs, wood engravings and woodcuts. Many of the classics he illustrated have been reissued several times and there have been British and Japanese editions of some of the children's books.

FOR MORE INFORMATION SEE: American Artist, December, 1944, October, 1975; *Graphis,* volume 8, number 43, 1952; *Library of Congress Quarterly,* April, 1965; *The Rhode Islander,* August 12, 1973; *Idea Magazine,* January, 1974.

Ti Jacques' whole family was up. Their breakfast of hot coffee warmed them against the chilly morning breeze. ■ (From *Ti Jacques* by Ruth Eitzen. Illustrated by Allan Eitzen.)

EITZEN, Allan 1928-

PERSONAL: Born May 25, 1928, in Mountain Lake, Minn.; son of George P. (a bank clerk) and Agatha (Warkentin) Eitzen; married Ruth Carper (a writer and artist), 1953; children: Hilda, Dirk, Anne, Laura, John. *Education:* Studied at Gustavus Adolphus College, 1946-48, Minneapolis Institute of Art, 1949, and Philadelphia College of Art, 1951-53. *Politics:* Liberal. *Religion:* Mennonite. *Home:* Route 1, Box 60, Barto, Pa. 19504. *Agent:* (Art) Frank Crump—Bookmakers Inc., 12 Burnham Hill, Westport, Conn. 06880.

CAREER: Staff artist for Herald Press, Scottdale, Pa., summers, 1950-53; art therapist at state hospital in Delaware, 1954; free-lance artist and illustrator, 1955—. *Awards, honors:* Print Council of America Illustration Award, 1953.

ILLUSTRATOR: (Story without words) *Birds in Wintertime,* Holt, 1963; Lois Kauffmann, *What's That Noise?,* Lothrop, 1966; Roland Bertol, *The Two Hats: A Story of Portugal,* Crowell, 1969; Barbara Corcoran, *A Row of Tigers,* Atheneum, 1969; Thomas C. O'Brien, *Odds and Evens,* Crowell, 1971; Beman Lord, *On the Banks of the Delaware: A View of Its History and Folkore,* Walck, 1971; Ruth Eitzen, *Ti Jacques: A Story of Haiti,* Crowell, 1972; Alvin and Virginia Silverstein, *The Long Voyage: The Life Story of a Green Turtle,* Warne, 1972; Alan M. Fletcher, *Fishes and Their Young,* Addison-Wesley, 1974; Dina Anastasio, *A Museum of Time,* Macmillan, 1975.

ALLAN EITZEN

WORK IN PROGRESS: Illustrating a book on the Boston Massacre, for Crowell; *City Talk* illustrations for Allyn & Bacon.

SIDELIGHTS: "I particularly enjoy assignments which involve sketching trips (*Two Hats*-to Portugal, *Ti Jacques*-to Haiti, etc.)." Eitzen has been remodeling a country home.

EITZEN, Ruth (Carper) 1924-

PERSONAL: Born July 20, 1924, in Lititz, Pa.; daughter of Reuben R. and Eva (Weber) Carper; married Allan Eitzen (an artist), June 12, 1954; children: Hilda, Dirk, Ann, Laura, John. *Education:* Goshen College, B.A., 1946; also studied at Eastern Mennonite School, Basel Gewerbeschule, and Pennsylvania Academy of Art; studied art privately. *Religion:* Mennonite. *Home address:* Route 1, Box 60, Barto, Pa. 19504.

CAREER: Mennonite Publishing House, Scottdale, Pa., writer and illustrator, 1945-49; Mennonite Central Committee, Akron, Pa., volunteer in editorial and educational capacity in Europe, 1950-54; free-lance artist and writer, 1954—.

WRITINGS: *Ti Jacques: A Story of Haiti,* Crowell, 1972. Contributor of poems, articles, and short stories to journals.

WORK IN PROGRESS: Writing poems; research in American history for children's books.

ELAM, Richard M(ace, Jr.) 1920-

PERSONAL: Born July 16, 1920, in Richiond, Va.; son of Richard Mace (an accountant) and Louise S. Elam. *Education:* Student at Richmond Professional Institute, 1946-47, Phoenix College, 1947-48, and Arizona State University, 1948-50. *Home:* 1333 Stevens Ridge Dr., Dallas, Tex. 75211. *Office:* Precision Silkscreen, Inc., 2926 Congressman Lane, Dallas, Tex. 75220.

CAREER: Started as bank teller at age seventeen; later show card writer and photographer; secretary-treasurer of Precision Silkscreen, Inc., Dallas, Tex., 1970—. *Military service:* U.S. Army Air Forces, 1942-46; became sergeant.

WRITINGS: *Teen-Age Science Fiction Stories,* Lantern Press, 1952; *Young Visitor to Mars,* Lantern Press, 1953; *Young Readers Science Fiction Stories,* Lantern Press, 1957; *Teen-Age Super Science Stories,* Lantern Press, 1957; *Cave of Living Treasure,* Lantern Press, 1958; *Young Stowaways in Space,* Lantern Press, 1960; *Young Visitor to the Moon,* Lantern Press, 1965. Writer of juvenile stories and articles and creator of puzzles.

SIDELIGHTS: "I started in juveniles originally just to get published, but through the years I have come to believe this field to be more satisfying to me than adult work. In fact, I find juvenile writing easier, with greater freedom of imagination. I haven't published since 1965 but hope to resume shortly, still in the imaginative vein."

Ted thought his father's voice sounded queer coming over his helmet receiver, but he guessed he would get used to it in time.
■ (From *Young Visitor to Mars* by Richard M. Elam Jr. Illustrated by Charles H. Geer.)

Elam's books have been reprinted in the United States, and *Young Visitor to Mars* translated into Dutch and Japanese.

HOBBIES AND OTHER INTERESTS: Music, gardening, psychic and other reading on unusual subjects.

ELLIS, Harry Bearse 1921-

PERSONAL: Born December 9, 1921, in Springfield, Mass.; son of Harry Dutton and Helen (Bearse) Ellis; married Ann Michelson, 1949; children: Andrew B. *Education:* Wesleyan University, B.A., 1947. *Home:* 13107 Parkridge Circle, Oxon Hill, Md. 20022.

CAREER: Christian Science Monitor, Boston, Mass., staff writer, 1947-51, Middle East correspondent, Beirut, Lebanon, 1952-54, assistant overseas news editor, 1955-58, Mediterranean correspondent, Beirut, 1959-60, chief of Paris Bureau, 1961-1964, central European correspondent, Bonn, West Germany, 1965-71, economics correspondent, Washington, D.C., 1972—. Radio and television commentary for NBC, CBS, Group W, BBC, National Public Radio, National Public Affairs Center for Television (NPACT), VOA, and USIA. Lecturer on foreign affairs. *Military service:* U.S. Army; attained rank of second lieutenant; awarded Bronze Star, Combat Invasion Arrowhead,

Combat Infantryman's Badge, five battle stars. *Member:* Phi Beta Kappa. *Awards, honors:* L.H.D. from Wesleyan University, 1959.

WRITINGS: Heritage of the Desert: The Arabs and the Middle East, Ronald, 1956; *Israel and the Middle East,* Ronald, 1957; *The Arabs* (for children), World Publishing, 1958; *Challenge in the Middle East,* Ronald, 1960; *The Common Market* (for young people), World Publishing, 1965; *Ideals and Ideologies: Communism, Socialism, and Capitalism* (for teenagers), World Publishing, 1968; *The Dilemma of Israel,* American Enterprise Institute, 1970; *Israel: One Land, Two Peoples* (for teenagers), Thomas Y. Crowell, 1972; (contributor) *The United States and the Middle East,* Prentice-Hall, 1974.

SIDELIGHTS: "The experience on which I base my books is firsthand—that is, extensive travels through the lands I write about, as a foreign correspondent of the *Christian Science Monitor.* My hope, particularly in books for young people, is to bring alive to readers the special qualities of each people and country, as well as their problems and relationship to the United States.

"To cite the Arab-Israeli dispute, for example, both sides should have a hearing, and this I attempt to give, aware that my books may be the first in-depth contact young readers have with the problem. Thus I strive for fairness, and a reflection of the wonderful vivacity of both Arabs and Jews.

HARRY B. ELLIS

Unfortunately, most of the music composed during this period was never written down or was lost at the downfall of the empire. ■ (From *The Arabs* by Harry B. Ellis. Illustrated by Leonard Everett Fisher.)

"In comparing Communist, Socialist, and capitalist systems of government, I try to show how common experience—the experience of coping with rapid industrialization, for example—blurs political distinctions and is shaping basic approaches to the needs of young people, the elderly, and others.

"Each nation, whether small like Luxembourg or Iceland or huge like the Soviet Union, has woven its own rich tapestry of culture. To give insights into these people and lands is a great challenge and joy."

ENGLE, Eloise Katherine 1923-

PERSONAL: Born April 12, 1923, in Seattle, Washington; daughter of Floyd and Lois (Best) Hopper; married Paul R. Engle, M.D., 1943, (divorced, 1968); married Lauri A. Paananen, 1973; children (first marriage): David, Paula and Margaret Engle. *Education:* George Washington University, Washington, D.C., 1944-47. *Home and office:* 6348 Cross Woods Drive, Falls Church, Va.

CAREER: Self-employed author of books for adults and young adults; contributor to national magazines in a variety of fields; film scriptwriter for U.S. Government, contract writing for United States Intelligence Agency; teaching writing at Northern Virginia Community College. *Member:* Society of Magazine Writers, Author's Guild, Virginia Press Women, Society of Woman Geographers. *Awards:* American Federation of Press Women, first prize for book *The Winter War,* 1973; Outstanding Science Books for Children by Children's Book Council and National Science Teachers Association, 1972, for *Parachutes: How They Work.*

WRITINGS: Dawn Mission, 1962, *Sea Challenge,* Hammond, 1962, *Princess of Paradise,* 1962, *Countdown for Cindy,* Hammond, 1962, *Escape,* 1963, *Sea of the Bear,* U.S. Naval Institute, 1963, *Pararescue,* 1964, *Sky Rangers,* 1965, *Earthquake!,* 1966, *Medic,* Day, 1969 (all published by John Day, except as indicated); *The House that Half-Jack Built,* Scholastic, 1971; *Parachutes—How They Work,* Putnams, 1972; *Do's and Don'ts of Delightful Dieting,* Westover, 1972; *National Governments Around the World,* Fleet Press, 1974; *The Winter War,* Scribner, 1973; *America's Maritime Heritage,* U.S. Naval Institute Press, 1975. Four paperback books about the American scene for Librairie Hachette in Paris, France, 1972-75. Contributor to *Above and Beyond* encyclopedia of space, and *Encyclopedia for Young People,* Funk & Wagnall.

WORK IN PROGRESS: The Finns in North America, the story of American and Canadian Finns.

SIDELIGHTS: "People often ask me 'What do you write about?' and my answer is, 'Just about anything that interests me at the moment.' I have an insatiable curiosity about so many things that I never seemed to specialize. To me, this is what makes writing fun.

"Admittedly, when you open one door to a subject you find yourself opening other doors along the way, mentally filing side subjects for future use; it's a subconscious, almost automatic process that comes after many years of writing and researching. I often suspect that I would be quite content just to research on and on, but then I realize that would be like dressing up for a party and staying home instead. And so I force myself to call a halt finally when I begin to read things I already know and talk to people who are supposed to be experts and realize that 'Hey, I'm ahead of you on that.' The moment of truth is at hand, the traveling, the interviews, the reading and note-taking and picture collecting and browsing through archives and reports must be orchestrated into something readable, exciting, useful, factual and worthy of people's confidence in me.

"Writing to me is such a responsibility that it often scares me, particularly since I know so many of my books are in libraries where they are read by thousands of young people. Although I have written five books that are labeled as fiction and were well received, I think I am much better at non-fiction. I say this regretfully because I would love to write suspense novels but I'm afraid that's not for me.

"Now that my three children are grown I can feel free to travel with my husband and nowadays we are on the go quite a lot. Alaska, California, Florida, Europe and my husband's native country of Finland are some of the trips we have made this year. Although he is a business man he has caught the writing 'bug' and has sold a number of his

ELOISE KATHERINE ENGLE

stories and photos to popular magazines. My 24-year-old son who recently graduated from the University of Michigan at Ann Arbor and is a Phi Beta Kappa has had three papaerback books published, along with a number of newspaper feature stories. Many of my students at Northern Virginia Community College have gotten into print for the first time after taking my course. So, all in all I seem to be responsible for quite a few words finding their way into print.''

ENRIGHT, Elizabeth   1909-1968

PERSONAL: Born September 17, 1909, in Oak Park, Ill.; daughter of Walter J. (a political cartoonist) and Maginel (a magazine illustrator; maiden name, Wright) Enright; married Robert Marty Gillham (an advertising man and television executive), April 24, 1930; children: Nicholas Wright, Robert II, Oliver. *Education:* Studied at Edgewood School, Greenwich, Conn., at Art Students League of New York, 1927-28, in Paris, 1928, and at Parsons School of Design. *Residence:* New York, N.Y.

CAREER: Began as magazine illustrator but started writing the stories to accompany her drawings and eventually stopped illustrating; author of books for children and of short stories for adults, appearing in *New Yorker* and other national magazines and published as collections. Lecturer in creative writing at Barnard College, 1960-62, and at writing seminars at Indiana University, University of Connecticut, and University of Utah.

ELIZABETH ENRIGHT

I hastily performed the little sleight-of-hand trick that my father had taught me. Very useful. Very adroit. Suddenly in my hand, instead of my plain pocketknife, I held a golden one. ■ (From *GONE-AWAY LAKE* by Elizabeth Enright. Illustrated by Beth and Joe Krush.)

MEMBER: Authors League of America, Pen and Brush Club. *Awards, honors:* John Newbery Medal of American Library Association, 1939, for *Thimble Summer; New York Herald Tribune* Children's Spring Book Festival Award, 1957, runner-up for Newberry Award, 1958, both for *Gone-Away Lake;* named by American Library Association as U.S. nominee for International Hans Christian Andersen Award, 1963, for outstanding literary quality of complete works; *Tatsinda* was an Honor Book in *New York Herald Tribune* Children's Spring Book Festival, 1963; LL.D., Nasson College, 1966.

WRITINGS—Juvenile fiction; books 1935-51 were self-illustrated: *Kintu: A Congo Adventure,* Farrar, 1935; *Thimble Summer,* Farrar, 1938; *The Sea Is All Around,* Farrar, 1940; *The Saturdays* (ALA Notable Book), Farrar, 1941; *The Four-Story Mistake,* Farrar, 1942; *Then There Were Five,* Farrar, 1944; *The Melendy Family,* three volumes in one (containing *The Saturdays, The Four-Story*

Mistake, and *Then There Were Five*), Rinehart, 1947; *Christmas Tree for Lydia,* Rinehart, 1951; *Spiderweb for Two: A Melendy Maze,* Rinehart, 1951; *Gone-Away Lake* (ALA Notable Book), Harcourt, 1957; *Return to Gone-Away,* Harcourt, 1961; *Tatsinda* (fairy tale), Harcourt, 1963; *Zeee* (fairy tale), Harcourt, 1965.

Adult story collections: *Borrowed Summer and Other Stories,* Rinehart, 1946 (published in England as *The Maple Tree and Other Stories,* Heinemann, 1947); *The Moment Before the Rain,* Harcourt, 1955; *The Riddle of the Fly and Other Stories,* Harcourt, 1959; *Doublefields: Memories and Stories* (autobiographical sketches, short stories, and one novella), Harcourt, 1966.

Illustrator: Marian King, *Kees,* Harper, 1930; Nellie M. Rowe, *The Crystal Locket,* Albert Whitman, circa, 1931; Marian King, *Kees and Kleintje,* Albert Whitman, 1934.

Bulk of her short stories were first published in *New Yorker,* but others appeared in *Ladies' Home Journal, Cosmopolitan, Mademoiselle, Redbook, Yale Review, Harper's, McCall's,* and *Saturday Evening Post.* Her stories were included in *Prize Stories: The O. Henry Awards,* 1946, 1949, 1951, 1955, 1958, 1960, and *Best American Short Stories,* 1950, 1952, 1954. Contributor of reviews of children's books to *New York Times.*

All but one or two of Elizabeth Enright's children's books still are in print, published now by Holt, Rinehart & Winston and Harcourt Brace Jovanovich, with some paperback editions by Dell. Most of them were published in England by Heinemann, as were the adult story collections.

FOR MORE INFORMATION SEE: Current Biography, 1947; Stanley Kunitz and Howard Haycroft, editors, *Junior Book of Authors,* 2nd edition revised, H. W. Wilson, 1951; *New York Times,* January 24, 1967, June 10, 1968; *Antiquarian Bookman,* June 24, 1968; *Horn Book,* December, 1969, February, 1970; Virginia Haviland, *Children and Literature: Views and Reviews,* Scott, Foresman, 1973.

(Died June 8, 1968)

FARALLA, Dana 1909-
(Dorothy W. Faralla; Dana Wilma, pseudonym)

PERSONAL: Born August 4, 1909, in Renville, Minn.; daughter of John Frederick (a merchant) and Estella (Gilger) Wein; married Dario Faralla (a film executive and producer), August 6, 1935 (died May 31, 1944). *Education:* Attended University of Minnesota, 1927-28; Williams School of Drama, Bachelor of Oral English, 1930. *Religion:* Protestant. *Agent:* Curtis Brown Ltd., 60 East 56th St., New York, N.Y. 10022.

CAREER: Has worked as a professional actress, private secretary, screen story analyst in Hollywood, Calif., and New York, N.Y., also employed in a rare book shop in New York City; *Poets Magazine,* New York, N.Y., associate editor, 1930-31; novelist and author of children's books. *Member:* Poetry Society of America.

WRITINGS—Novels: The Magnificent Barb, Messner, 1947; *Dream in the Stone,* Messner, 1948; *Black Renegade,*

DANA FARALLA, from the portrait
by Comte le Serrec de Kervily

Lippincott, 1954; *A Circle of Trees,* Lippincott, 1955; *The Madstone,* Lippincott, 1958; *Children of Lucifer,* Lippincott, 1964; *The Straw Umbrella,* Gollancz, 1968.

Children's books: *The Willow in the Attic,* Lippincott, 1960; *The Singing Cupboard,* Lippincott, 1962; *Swanhilda-of-the-Swans,* Lippincott, 1964; *The Wonderful Flying-Go-Round,* World Publishing, 1965; *The Wooden Swallow,* World Publishing, 1966.

Also author, under pseudonym Dana Wilma, of original screen story for film, "El Otro Soy Yo," 1939; author of original story and collaborator on screenplay, "Papa Soltero," 1939. Contributor of travel articles to *New York Times* and *New York Herald Tribune.*

SIDELIGHTS: "Here, briefly, is something of the strange alchemy that occurred in the writing of five books for children, a blending of personal experiences and imagination, of recollection and reflection—a certain nostalgia.

"In the opening chapter of *The Willow in the Attic,* an aging willow tree is being cut down. There was such a tree in my Minnesota childhood. I recalled it so vividly one day in Rome, Italy, that I began writing the story. My room at the Flora Hotel overlooked the Aurelian Wall and the Borghese Gardens of umbrella pines, ilex, and tall cypress, alien to my childhood. The story was perhaps born out of sudden nostalgia for other trees that I had known. Then too, I had spent the previous summer in Istanbul in the home of friends, where the four children had an insatiable appetite for stories—read or invented. They were of French-English parentage, and yet they 'transplanted' easily from their flat on the Bosphorus to the Minnesota prairie. They became the characters in the book.

"There are four seasons in the life of the willow branch that Catherine nurtures in the attic. The Autumn Tree decorated with paper butterflies came from a childhood memory of my father excitedly summoning the family to look upon a breathtaking spectacle; a tall maple tree in our front yard upon which thousands of migrating milkweed butterflies had alighted at sunset. The Winter Tree of paper snowflakes was a remembrance of a Christmas in Copenhagen when I was ill, and a Danish artist in the Hotel Vestersoehus where I was staying brought me a vase with a barren branch of shrubbery on which were suspended by fine thread exquisite lacy 'snowflakes' she had cut from tissue paper. The idea of the Easter Tree adorned with beribboned, painted hollow eggs came from my childhood. Our mother drew lovely flowers with a soft pencil on the eggs and taught my sisters and me to paint them with watercolors for our friends. However, we had never thought of tying them to a miniature tree. Oddly, some years after I had published the book, I was residing in Beirut; at Easter in the little panelled dining room at Myrtom House there was a china pitcher filled with green branches of shrubbery on which Madame Marie, the Lebanese housekeeper had tied hollow, painted eggs. The Summer Tree with its green leaves and Chinese paper lanterns was also a memory from childhood, of garden parties, church bazaars, and 'Ice-Cream Socials.' I submitted a design to my publishers; somehow they ignored it, and the artist's conception of a Chinese lantern was far afield from mine, but when I saw the illustration, it was too late—the book had already been printed.

"I wrote *The Singing Cupboard* one cold, dark winter in Copenhagen when the sun rarely appeared. The prototype of the cupboard was a tall cupboard of polished wood that stood in the living room of an endearing Danish family. Peter, the father, had made a small harp of piano wires and affixed it to the inner side of the cupboard door. Whenever this door swung open there was a humming, musical sound; little hammers had been set in motion on the strings. Ulla and Nils were children in this family, and became characters in the book. Hans Mus existed in my childhood as a small grey velvet mouse with black beady eyes that my Danish Aunt Kristine had made for me. He emerged in imagination that bleak winter in Denmark with remarkable talents as a story-teller and harpist—a *real* mouse.

"*Swanhilda-of-the-Swans* was written in Montreux, Switzerland during one of the coldest winters ever known in Europe. From my window overlooking Lac Léman I could see the swans buffeted on the grey waves, and nearly every day I walked along the shores of the lake to the Embarcadere where they were daily fed by the municipality. I remembered too, a little painted sleigh in the shape of a swan on a postcard a friend had sent me from Holland. But primarily the source was a newspaper item concerning a swan that had been trapped in a frozen pond. And then, of course, I love swans. Denmark became the setting for the story because it is, to me, the true country of swans.

"*The Wonderful Flying-Go-Round* was also written in Montreux, Switzerland. On a day in early autumn I saw a

children's carrousel being dismantled at the Place du Marche. It was, I thought, a rather ugly modern carrousel of garish paint and plastic, but as I walked along the quai I could hear in my mind the gay and happy tunes played on the Merry-go-rounds of my childhood. I began imagining a very special carrousel for children, one that had never before existed: a Flying-Go-Round. And thus began the story and the Florabellas' song, 'Take your feet off the ground, on a Flying-Go-Round.' The Land of Mira-Rami was a Dump Yard seen through the enchanted vision of childhood. The House-of-Twelve-Doors had its inception in a playhouse my father had once constructed out of oddments from derelict buildings—discarded doors, window frames, and even part of a wagon he had fitted for fishing-camping trips at the Minnesota River—a jumble-tumble house that had never really pleased us, but which in retrospect acquired a certain charm.

"*The Wooden Swallow* was written on the °island of Rhodes, Greece, which is the setting of the story. On a cruise to various Grecian islands in the Aegean Sea in the autumn of 1958 I resolved to return to Rhodes one day for a long sojourn. The following year in London I was casually reading a book about bird lore, and noticed a footnote regarding a pottery perfume vessel in the shape of a swallow found on the island of Rhodes. It was perhaps from the sixth century B.C. and supposedly patterned after a wooden swallow used in spring rites connected with the Temple of Athena on the acropolis in Lindos. The clay vessel was housed in the British Museum. I made a notation.

"Some years later I returned to Rhodes and throughout a rainy winter did much research in the library of the Museum of Antiquities in the medieval infirmary of the Knights of Saint John of Jerusalem and Rhodes. I could discover nothing at all regarding the wooden swallow. Then one day a young archaeologist doing research at the same table in the library told me that his father, a scholar, collected Rhodian folklore. He made a prose translation of the context of an ancient Greek song used in the spring ritual. From this rather incomplete material, I wrote the poem, *The Song of the Swallow,* on a Sunday afternoon in March in my hotel room during a heavy rain storm. Thus the poem was completed before I had even begun the book, which was still vague and unformed in my mind. The characters in the book are all imaginary, other than Yannis, the vendor of *pastelli,* who still stands at the Freedom Gate leading into the old City of the Knights; and Nikos, the crippled lad of Lindos, who in actuality was a little hump-backed tailor's apprentice I encountered in the Rhodian village of Maritsà. The cats too, are hardly imaginary.

"Travel has been a motivation for my writing. More than twenty-five years of residence abroad: Europe, the Middle East, East Africa, Bermuda, Jamaica, Virgin Islands, Haiti, Cyprus, Malta, Madeira, Baleric Islands, Teneriffe. I have lived for long periods in Italy, Denmark, England, Switzerland, Greece, Cyprus, Lebanon. Languages in which I am most proficient are Italian and French."

FEAGLES, Anita MacRae (Travis MacRae)

PERSONAL: Born September 27, in Chicago, Ill.; daughter of Cuyler Scott (editor) and Anita (Foley)

ANITA FEAGLES

MacRae; married Robert West Feagles (banker), September 14, 1951; children: Wendy, Cuyler, Priscilla, Patrick. *Education:* Knox College, A.B., 1947; City College of New York, M.S., 1950. *Politics:* Democrat. *Religion:* Society of Friends. *Home:* 41 Ashland Ave., Pleasantville, N.Y. *Agent:* James O. Brown, 405 East 54th St., New York, N.Y. 10022.

CAREER: New York State Prison for Women, Bedford Hills, N.Y., teacher, 1949. *Member:* Junior League (Mt. Kisco), Phi Beta, Pi Beta Phi.

WRITINGS: (With Gretchen Mockler) *Trial by Slander*, Rinehart, 1960; (with Gretchen Mockler) *Death in View*, Holt, Rinehart & Winston, 1961; *Casey, The Utterly Impossible Horse*, Scott, 1961; (with Gretchen Mockler) *Twenty Percent*, Holt, 1962; *The Genie and Joe Maloney*, Scott, 1962; *The Tooth Fairy*, Scott, 1962; *A Stranger in the Spanish Village*, Scott, 1964; *27 Cats Next Door*, Scott, 1965; *He Who Saw Everything,* Scott, 1966; *Autumn and the Bear*, Scott, 1967; *Queen Sara and the Messy Fairies*, Young Scott Books, 1968; *Sea Rock*, Bobbs, 1968; *Me, Cassie* (Child Study Association book list), Dial, 1968; *Thor and the Giants*, Young Scott Books, 1968; *Emergency Room*, Cowles, 1968; *The Addicts*, Cowles, 1969; *Ladies of the Afternoon* (adult), Curtis Brooks, 1972; *Cutting Out* (adult), Curtis Books, 1973.

SIDELIGHTS: "I live in London now. I am writing regu-

larly but have changed my main focus to first young adult and now adult books. I am trying to investigate larger themes. I don't think in terms of age, but in general, hope to write for relatively mature readers."

FIAMMENGHI, Gioia 1929-

PERSONAL: Given name is pronounced Joya, and surname Fya-men-gi (hard "g"); born September 29, 1929, in New York, N.Y.; daughter of Luigi (a banker) and Jeanne (Elmo) Fiammenghi; married Guido Caputo (an industrialist), October 24, 1959; children: Jean-Guy, Marco, Giorgio. *Education:* Parsons School of Design, graduate, 1950; also studied at Art Student's League of New York, on and off for fifteen years. *Religion:* Roman Catholic. *Home:* 3 Avenue d'Alsace, Nice, Alpes-Maritimes, France.

CAREER: Pettinella Advertising Agency, New York, N.Y., assistant art director, 1951-52; free-lance artist and book illustrator, 1951—. Fashion model for a time in earlier career; before going to Europe to live did advertising illustration, record covers, and book jackets for adult books. Work has been shown at several exhibitions in New York and at American Consulate in Nice; drawings and sketches included in Kerlan Collection at University of Minnesota and in collection of Alexis Dupont Library, Wilmington, Del.

AWARDS, HONORS: The Golden Doors was chosen by *New York Times* as one of the hundred outstanding children's books of 1957 and *First Book of England* received the same honor, 1958; *Rimbles* was selected by American Institute of Graphic Arts as one of the fifty best designed books of 1961; Child Study Association of America's Best Books of the Year, 1965, included *Lizard Comes Down from the North* and *Little Raccoon and the Outside World*.

ILLUSTRATOR: Loretta Marie Tyman, *Michael Mcgillicudy,* Abelard, 1951; Rachel Learnard, *Lucky Pete,* Abelard, 1954; Moritz A. Jagendorf, compiler, *The Priceless Cats, and Other Italian Folk Stories,* Vanguard, 1956; Edward Fenton, *The Golden Doors,* Doubleday, 1957; Lois Allen, *Mystery of the Blue Nets,* Coward, 1957; Elizabeth F. Abell, reteller, *The First Book of Fairy Tales,* Watts, 1958; Paul Gallico, *Mrs. 'Arris Goes to Paris,* Doubleday, 1958; Noel Streatfeild, *The First Book of England,* Watts, 1958; Margaret E. Martignomi, compiler, *Every Child's Storybook: A Horn of Plenty of Good Reading for Boys and Girls,* Watts, 1959; Lilian Moore, *Once Upon a Holiday* (stories and poems), Abingdon, 1959.

Guy H. Hansen, *Burrhead's Confessions,* Doubleday, 1960; Patricia Evans, *Rimbles: A Book of Children's Classic Games, Rhymes, Songs and Sayings,* Doubleday, 1961; Irene Kampen, *Life Without George* (autobiography), Doubleday, 1961; Lilian Moore, *Once Upon a Season,* Abingdon, 1962; Lilian Moore, *Little Raccoon and the Thing in the Pool,* McGraw, 1963; Barbee O. Carleton, *Chester Jones,* Holt, 1963; Susan Bartlett, *A Book to Begin On: Libraries,* Holt, 1964; LouAnn Gaeddert, *Noisy Nancy Norris,* Doubleday, 1964; Lilian Moore, *Papa Albert,* Atheneum, 1964; Paul Gallico, *Mrs. 'Arris Goes to Parliament,* Doubleday, 1965 (published in England as *Mrs. Harris, M.P.,* Heinemann, 1965); Lilian Moore, *Little Racoon and the Outside World,* McGraw, 1965; Anita Hewett, *Lizard Comes Down from the North,* McGraw,

Thor liked to travel, for there was nothing the gods enjoyed more than adventure. ■ (From *Thor and the Giants* by Anita Feagles. Illustrated by Gertrude Barrer-Russell.)

1965, adapted as *Dragon from the North,* McGraw, 1965; Scott Corbett, *The Cave above Delphi,* Holt, 1965; Paul Gallico, *The Day Jean-Pierre Went Round the World,* Doubleday, 1965; Mildred O. Knopf, *Around the World Cookbook for Young People,* Knopf, 1966; Frederic Rossomando and others, *Spending Money,* Watts, 1967; Frederic Rossomando and others, *Earning Money,* Watts, 1967; Aileen Lucia Fisher, *Skip Around the Year,* Crowell, 1967; Ray Broekel, *Hugo the Huge,* Doubleday, 1968; Phyllis R. Naylor, *Meet Murdock,* Follett, 1968; Philip M. Sherlock, *The Iguana's Tail: Crick Crack Stories from the Caribbean,* Crowell, 1969; Eleanor L. Clymer, *Belinda's New Spring Hat* (Junior Literary Guild selection), Watts, 1969; Alex Rider, *When We Go to Market: Cuando vamos al mercado* (text in English and Spanish), Funk, 1969; Paul Gallico, *The Day Jean-Pierre Joined the Circus,* Heinemann, 1969.

GIOIA FIAMMENGHI, with husband

And since the char's hands were spotless from the soap and water in which they were immersed most of the time, she let her touch the material, which the little drudge did as though it were the Grail. ■ (From *Mrs. 'Arris Goes to Paris* by Paul Gallico. Drawings by Gioia Fiammenghi.)

LouAnn Gaeddert, *Noisy Nancy and Nick,* Doubleday, 1970; Barbara Ireson, compiler, *Puffin Book of Poetry,* Puffin, 1970; Michael Bond, *Mr. Cram's Magic Bubbles,* Puffin, 1970; Robert Froman, *Bigger and Smaller,* Crowell, 1971; William C. McGraw, under pseudonym William Corbin, *The Day Willie Wasn't,* Coward, 1971; Robert K. Smith, *Chocolate Fever,* new edition, Coward, 1972; Lilian Moore, *Little Raccoon and No Trouble at All,* new edition, McGraw, 1972; Shulamith Oppenheim, *A Trio for Grandpapa,* Crowell, 1974; Carlo Collodi, *Pinocchio,* Puffin, 1974; Paul Gallico, *The Day the Guinea Pig Talked,* Pan Books, 1975; Paul Gallico, *The Day Jean-Pierre Was Pignapped,* Pan Books, 1975; Thom Roberts, *The Barn,* McGraw, 1975.

WORK IN PROGRESS: Illustrating another *Little Raccoon* and *Poems from the Woods;* activity cards for Crowell based on *Bigger and Smaller.*

SIDELIGHTS: "My father worked in Venezuela and Colombia for several years, and my husband has business in Colombia. I've lived in Colombia on and off for a total of about five years, for two or three months at a time. We go to Bogota every summer.

"The whole family speaks English, Italian, Spanish and French. Both my husband and I are of Italian extraction. When I am working on a drawing, I often ask the boys' opinion about it. I like to get a child's viewpoint. The two younger boys draw very well and we have gone sketching together. All three boys play the piano very well.

"I love to go antique hunting and like to collect antiques from different countries we go to. I also am very interested in folk art. Playing the piano and dancing are favorites with me and often give me inspiration and a lift when I'm blue or stuck on a drawing. I did and still do outdoor sketching and painting whenever I can. I especially like to draw people in South America. . . . I've also done some portrait painting. When I have a job I must finish, I get up at five in the morning to work. I love the stillness of the household when everyone is asleep.

"I started drawing very young and always knew I would do something in the arts. I used to sew outfits and costumes for a mannequin doll I had. I even snitched a tiny piece of my mother's fur coat for the doll. When I was about fifteen I started going to life classes at the Art Student's League. I continued going on and off until I came to live in Europe. After high school I got a scholarship to Parsons School of Design, graduated, and went to their European school. The charm and artistic monuments of Europe impressed me very much. My favorite cities were, and still are, Rome and Florence.

"The arts were considered very important in my family when I was a child. Many members of my mother's family were artists and the tradition continues in one form or another. On my father's side is a well-known painter in Italy. Our family name comes from the Italian word Fiamminghi which means 'Flemish' (plural form). About five hundred years ago my father's family went to Italy from Belgium to study painting.

"I love cats and always had one before I got married. Each one I had used to come and sit on my drawing table as I worked. My cat was a model for the jacket of *Thomasina* by Paul Gallico and for several other books I did about cats.

"When I start a book I might just read it [the manuscript] and think about it for a couple of days. I do all the research I can to really get into the atmosphere of the story. I do thumbnail sketches first in black and white, then in color. Then I go ahead and do the dummy exact size. By doing the thumbnails first I feel I get a better view of the design as a whole. When I need models I ask my husband or children to pose for me. I might also go out to sketch a place or object I think will be good for the story. I use acetate film for color separation washes and vidalon heavy tracing paper for color separation in pen and pencil work. I like pen and ink very much but now I'm experimenting with collage and crayon prints.

"I love to read and always have a book in my bag to read on the bus or in offices, etc. I enjoy cooking (special dishes) and like to try new ones on the men in the house."

Thomasina and *Love of Seven Dolls,* for which Gioia Fiammenghi also did the book jacket, both were made into motion pictures. Two of the books she illustrated, *Noisy Nancy Norris* and *Bigger and Smaller* were made into film strips.

FIGUEROA, Pablo 1938-

PERSONAL: Surname is pronounced Fee-geh-*ro*-ah; born

January 26, 1938, in Santurce, Puerto Rico; son of Sotero and Natividad (Davila) Figueroa. *Education:* City College (now City College of City University of New York), B.A., 1962. *Home and office:* 321 West 22nd St., New York, N.Y. 10011.

CAREER: New York Public Library, New York, N.Y., technical assistant, 1965-70; free-lance television producer for National Broadcasting Co., New York, N.Y., 1971—. Photographer and theatrical director.

WRITINGS: Enrique (children's book), Hill & Wang, 1971; "El King Cojo" (play), was produced off-off Broadway by INTAR, February, 1973. Television programs include "Bienvenido Means Welcome," and "We, Together," and "The Hispanic Policeman." Writer of filmstrip, "Los Puertorriquenos," and other materials on Puerto Rico.

WORK IN PROGRESS: Cofresi, a short novel for children.

SIDELIGHTS: "Believe in no ideology, a few people and all children. Interested in all aspects of the communication arts."

FLEMING, Alice Mulcahey 1928-

PERSONAL: Born December 21, 1928, in New Haven, Conn.; daughter of Albert Leo and Agnes (Foley) Mulcahey; married Thomas J. Fleming (writer), January 19, 1951; children: Alice, Thomas, David, Richard. *Education:* Trinity College (Washington, D.C.), A.B., 1950; Columbia University, M.A., 1951. *Politics:* Democrat. *Religion:* Roman Catholic. *Home:* 315 East 72nd St., New York, N.Y. 10021. *Agent:* Joan Raines, Raines and Raines, 244 Madison Ave., New York, N.Y. 10016.

WRITINGS—Young people's books: *The Key to New York,* Lippincott, 1960; *Wheels,* Lippincott, 1960; *A Son of Liberty,* St. Martins, 1961; *Doctors in Petticoats,* Lippincott, 1964; *Great Women Teachers,* Lippincott, 1965; *The Senator from Maine,* Crowell, 1969; *Alice Freeman Palmer: Pioneer College President,* Rutledge Books, 1970; *General's Lady,* Lippincott, 1971; *Reporters at War,* Cowles, 1970; *Highways Into History,* St. Martin's Press, 1971; *Pioneers in Print,* Reilly and Lee, 1971; *Ida Tarbell: First of the Muckrakers,* Crowell, 1971; *Psychiatry: What's it all About,* Cowles, 1972; (editor) *Hosannah the Home Run!,* Little, Brown, 1972; *The Moviemakers,* St. Martin's Press, 1973; *Alcohol: The Delightful Poison,* Delacorte, 1975; *Trials that Made Headlines,* St. Martin's Press, 1975; *Contraception, Abortion, Pregnancy,* Thomas Nelson, 1975.

Adult Books: *Nine Months: An Intelligent Woman's Guide to Pregnancy,* Stein and Day, 1972; *New on the Beat: Woman Power in the Police Force,* Coward, 1975.

SIDELIGHTS: "I spent most of my childhood with, as my mother used to put it, my nose in a book. I started with *Winnie the Pooh* and went on to *Oliver Twist, The House of the Seven Gables, Gone With the Wind,* and every Nancy Drew mystery in the series. (My tastes were, and still are, varied.)

"Although I won an essay contest sponsored by *Child Life* magazine when I was seven, I enjoyed writing only in small doses. In grammar school I was always delighted when there was a writing assignment (the rest of the class usually groaned). Later, I worked on my high school and college newspapers and, still in love with reading, became an English major in college.

"I did occasionally think of becoming a writer but the idea of putting enough words on paper to fill a book absolutely staggered me. Within a year after I graduated from college, however, I married a young man who wanted to be a writer, Thomas Fleming (he has since become a well-known novelist and historian). He encouraged me to write and he also made me realize that it isn't such a formidable job after all.

"Since then, I've put enough words on paper to fill nineteen books. Most of them are non-fiction because I am fascinated by facts and enjoy presenting them in what I hope is a lively way."

FOR MORE INFORMATION SEE: New York Times Book Review, February 25, 1973, May 4, 1975.

FLEMING, Ian (Lancaster) 1908-1964 (Atticus)

PERSONAL: Born May 28, 1908, in London, England; son of Valentine (a major and a Conservative member of the British Parliament) and Evelyn Beatrice (Ste. Crois Rose)

ALICE FLEMING

IAN FLEMING

Fleming; younger brother of Peter Fleming, also an author; married Anne Geraldine Charteris (formerly Lady Rothermere), March 24, 1952; children: Caspar. *Education:* Attended Eton, Royal Military Academy at Sandhurst, University of Munich, and University of Geneva. *Home:* 16 Victoria Sq., London S.W.1, England; also maintained a home in Jamaica, and a flat on Pegwell Bay, Sandwich, Kent, England.

CAREER: Moscow correspondent for Reuters Ltd., London, England, 1929-33; associated with Cull & Co. (merchant bankers), London, England, 1933-35; stockbroker with Rowe & Pitman, London, England, 1935-39; returned to Moscow, 1939, officially as a reporter for *The Times,*

London, unofficially as a representative of the Foreign Office; Kemsley (later Thomson) Newspapers, foreign manager, 1945-59; publisher of *The Book Collector,* 1949-64. *Military service:* Royal Naval Volunteer Reserve, 1939-45; lieutenant; did secret service work as a personal assistant to the director of Naval Intelligence. *Member:* Turf Club, Broodle's Club, Portland Club (all London).

WRITINGS—All fiction unless otherwise noted: *Casino Royale,* J. Cape, 1953, Macmillan (New York), 1954, published in paperback as *You Asked for It,* Popular Library, 1955; *Live and Let Die,* J. Cape, 1954, Macmillan (New York), 1955; *Moonraker,* Macmillan, 1955, published in paperback as *Too Hot to Handle,* Perma Books, 1957; *Diamonds are Forever,* Macmillan, 1956; *The Diamond Smugglers,* J. Cape, 1957, Macmillan (New York), 1958; *From Russia, With Love,* Macmillan, 1957; *Doctor No,* Macmillan, 1958; *Goldfinger,* Macmillan, 1959.

For Your Eyes Only: Five Secret Exploits of James Bond, Viking, 1960; *Gilt-Edged Bonds* (omnibus volume), introduction by Paul Gallico, Macmillan, 1961; *Thunderball,* Viking, 1961; *The Spy Who Loved Me,* Viking, 1962; *On Her Majesty's Secret Service,* New American Library, 1963; *Thrilling Cities* (thirteen essays), J. Cape, 1963, New American Library, 1964; *You Only Live Twice,* New American Library, 1964; *Chitty-Chitty-Bang-Bang* (juvenile), Random, 1964; *Bonded Fleming: A James Bond Omnibus,* Viking, 1965; *The Man with The Golden Gun,* New American Library, 1965; *More Gilt-Edged Bonds* (omnibus volume), Macmillan, 1965; *Ian Fleming Introduces Jamaica* (nonfiction), edited by Morris Cargill, Hawthorn, 1966; *Octopussy: The Last Great Adventures of James Bond 007,* New American Library, 1967, published with an additional story, Signet, 1967. Columnist, under pseudonym Atticus, for *The Sunday Times,* London, during the fifties. Contributor to *Horizon, Spectator,* and other magazines.

SIDELIGHTS: "If I understand children at all," wrote Rex Stout, "my guess is that four out of five of them would love [*Chitty-Chitty-Bang-Bang*]. The danger is that many of them might love it too much; they might want to trade in

(From *Chitty-Chitty-Bang-Bang* by Ian Fleming. Illustrated by John Burningham.)

(From the movie "*Chitty-Chitty-Bang-Bang*," © United Artists, 1969.)

the family car for one like ... the magical car. Furthermore, they might want to trade in their father for one like Caractacus Pott and their mother for one like Mrs. Pott. But for any parent willing to take a chance this book is a find."

Chitty-Chitty-Bang-Bang is being adapted into a musical and was filmed by United Artists in 1968. Various young readers' editions of the book have been published including: *Meet Chitty-Chitty-Bang-Bang: The Wonderful Magical Car*, and *Ian Fleming's Story of Chitty-Chitty-Bang-Bang*, both by Al Perkins, Random House, 1968, also *The Adventures of Chitty-Chitty-Bang-Bang* by Albert G. Miller, Random House, 1968.

The Book of Bond; or, Every Man His Own 007, by Lt. Col. William (Bill) Tanner, is a guide for gentlemen who would like to be as glamorous as Fleming's hero. Many of Fleming's books have been filmed, with Sean Connery generally in the lead, including: *From Russia With Love*, 1964, *Thunderball*, United Artists, 1965, *Dr. No, Goldfinger,* *You Only Live Twice*, United Artists, 1967, *Casino Royale*, Columbia, 1967, *On Her Majesty's Secret Service* (with George Lazenby as Bond), United Artists, 1969, *Diamonds Are Forever*, United Artists, 1971, *Live and Let Die*, United Artists, 1974; *The Spy Who Loved Me*, United Artists, 1976.

HOBBIES AND OTHER INTERESTS: Swimming, gambling, and golf.

FOR MORE INFORMATION SEE: New York Times Book Review, July 4, 1961, November 5, 1961, April 1, 1962, November 1, 1964, December 11, 1966; *Books for Children, 1960-1965*, American Library Association, 1966; *New York Times*, February 16, 1967; Ann M. Currah, *Best Books for Children*, Bowker, 1967; *Reporter*, July 13, 1967; *Commentary*, July, 1968; *South Atlantic Quarterly*, winter, 1968; *Contemporary Literary Criticism*, edited by Carolyn Riley, Gale Research, 1975; *World Authors: 1950-1970*, edited by John Wakeman, HW Wilson, 1975.

(Died August 12, 1964)

JOHN THOMAS FLEXNER, from the
portrait by Joseph Hirsch

FLEXNER, James Thomas 1908-

PERSONAL: Born January 13, 1908, in New York, N.Y.;
son of Simon (a medical scientist) and Helen (Thomas)
Flexner; married Beatrice Hudson (a singer), August 2,
1950; children: Helen Hudson. *Education:* Harvard University, B.S. (magna cum laude), 1929. *Address:* 530 East
86th St., New York, N.Y. 10028.

CAREER: New York Herald Tribune, New York, N.Y.,
reporter, 1929-31; New York City Department of Health,
Noise Abatement Commission, executive secretary, 1931-
32; professional writer, 1932—. Colonial Williamsburg,
consultant, 1956-57. *Member:* P.E.N. (president, American
Center, 1954-55), Century Association, Society of Amer-
ican Historians (fellow), Authors League. *Awards, honors:*
Library of Congress grant-in-aid for studies in the history of
American civilization, 1945; Life in America Prize for
American Painting: First Flowers of Our Wilderness, 1946;
Guggenheim fellowship, 1953; Parkman Prize for *That
Wilder Image,* 1963; National Book Award, Pulitzer Prize,
and Christopher Award, 1973, for *Washington.*

WRITINGS: Doctors on Horseback, Viking, 1937; *Ameri-
ca's Old Masters,* Viking, 1939; (with father, Simon
Flexner) *William Henry Welch and the Heroic Age of
American Medicine,* Viking, 1941; *Steamboats Come True:
American Inventors in Action,* Viking, 1944; *American
Painting: First Flowers of Our Wilderness,* Houghton,

1947; *John Singleton Copley,* Houghton, 1948; *A Pocket
History of American Painting,* Houghton, 1950; *The
Traitor and the Spy,* Harcourt, 1953, Little, Brown, 1975;
American Painting: The Light of Distant Skies, Harcourt,
1954; *Gilbert Stuart,* Knopf, 1955; *Mohawk Baronet: Sir
William Johnson of New York,* Harper, 1959.

*That Wilder Image: The Painting of America's Native
School from Thomas Cole to Winslow Homer,* Little,
Brown, 1962; *George Washington: The Forge of Experi-
ence, 1732-1775,* Little, Brown, 1962; *The World of
Winslow Homer, 1836-1910,* Time, Inc., 1966; *George
Washington in the American Revolution, 1775-1783,* Little,
Brown, 1968; *The Double Adventure of John Singleton
Copley,* Little, Brown, 1969; *George Washington and the
New Nation, 1783-1793,* Little, Brown, 1970; *Nineteenth-
Century American Painting,* Putnam, 1970; *George Wash-
ington: Anguish and Farewell, 1793-1799,* Little, Brown,
1972; *Washington: The Indispensible Man,* Little, Brown,
1974; *The Face of Liberty,* Clarkson Potter, 1975.

Writer of television drama, "Treason 1780," 1954.

WORK IN PROGRESS: A biography of Alexander Hamilton.

FOR MORE INFORMATION SEE: Horn Book, December, 1969.

Each one held a fishhook and plucked at his string as the
tune required it. One of them tapped on the wood and the
music stopped. When it started again, there was less buzzing
on the low notes. ■ (From *Diego* by S. E. Moore. Illustrated by
Barbara Flynn.)

FLYNN, Barbara 1928-

PERSONAL: Born October 12, 1928, in Culver City, Calif.; daughter of Harold Squire and Helen (Dunlap) Johnston; married Robert Flynn, 1967 (died, 1970); children: Kathleen. Education: University of Iowa, B.A., 1950. Politics: Democrat. Religion: Catholic. Home: 914 Wynnewood Rd., Pelham Manor, N.Y. 10803.

CAREER: Textile designer and art teacher in New York; illustrator of children's books.

ILLUSTRATOR: J. B. Priestley, Snoggle, Harcourt, 1972; S. E. More, Diego, Harcourt, 1972; Emily Buchwald, Gildaen, Harcourt, 1973; Gladys Yessayan Cretan, Sunday for Sona, Lothrop, 1973.

WORK IN PROGRESS: Fabric designs and illustrations relating to the American Revolution and the Bicentennial; wallpaper and fabric design in various techniques and subject matter; decorative display design; exhibits of pen and ink illustrations.

FOSTER, E(lizabeth) C(onnell) 1902-

PERSONAL: Maiden name is accented on second syllable; born January 11, 1902, in Chicago, Ill.; daughter of William Perry and Anna (Ahlberg) Connell; married Robert Eugene Foster, June 19, 1937. Education: Attended University of Chicago, Art Institute of Chicago, and Chicago Musical Hall offered lectures and sometimes films as well as music.

ELIZABETH C. FOSTER

College. Politics: "Current biased news reporting is strengthening my conservative Republican tendencies." Religion: "Certainly I am no materialist, far from it. But I have never been able to accept the teaching of any organized religion." Home: 713 Apalachicola Rd., Venice, Fla. 33595.

CAREER: Commonwealth Edison Co., Chicago, Ill., secretary, 1920-37; secretary to Ashton Stevens, columnist and drama critic for Hearst newspaper, 1922-47, did secretarial work for physician, 1928-37; writer. Volunteer worker for Institute of International Education, and North Shore Mental Health Association. Awards, honors: First place juvenile award from Friends of American Writers, 1974, for The Long Hungry Night.

WRITINGS: (With Slim Williams) The Friend of the Singing One (Eskimo story), Atheneum, 1967; (with Williams) The Long Hungry Night (Eskimo story; Junior Literary Guild selection), Atheneum, 1973.

WORK IN PROGRESS: A third Eskimo story with Slim Williams; research for a book about Shelley; revising an adventure story about the sea and the Oriental arts of self-defense, originally written with a sea-captain.

SIDELIGHTS: "Whatever I write about my life comes out a lovesong to Chicago. Although I was born there, on the South Side, we moved to Los Angeles before I was three, so my earliest memories are of poppy-covered foothills and towering Pacific breakers. I attended the Sixteenth Street School, but before my first year was over we returned to Chicago. My father's death a few months later suddenly and forever destroyed the warm sense of security that had sheltered me until that time.

"There had been music, and trips to the theater, and animals, always animals while William Perry Connell, my Scottish father, lived. After his death my grieving mother and I shared an apartment with her mother and her youngest brother. Grandmother Ahlberg, as compulsive a reader as I grew to be, had a great fund of stories, but would speak only Swedish. I quickly learned to understand her, and to speak her language easily. That pleased her. From my young progressive Uncle Fernie I learned about politics (socialism) and poker and poetry. My interest in the first two faded; but from those early poetry readings—Robert Service and Rudyard Kipling to the Greek anthology—probably grew my unending interest in the words and rhythms of language, especially English.

"There were rarely any children to play with. We lived a long way from Scott School, but the kindness of the adults around me filled every vacancy except the loss of my father. I was never athletic, but I loved the out of doors. I used to pretend the vacant lot next door was an Oriental garden. The graceful weeds that grew taller than my head had a look of bamboo, I thought. It was half a lifetime later, and the vacant lot had long been occupied by a six-flat before I realized my pretty Oriental garden was a thriving growth of marijuana!

"Jackson Park was near enough for frequent walks, and in the great expanse of night sky above, the constellations were pointed out to me, and I learned the myths associated with their names. There were rowboat rides on the lagoon in summer, and ice skating in the winter. The Field Museum, too, was in the park. Every child should be fortunate enough to grow up near a museum.

"For just plain fun there were still vaudeville shows (I think my family frowned on movies), even an occasional trip to Comiskey Park to see the White Sox with my uncle. In the summers, with the stepsons of my Aunt Jennie Sandberg, who lived on the North Side, I experienced the wonders of Riverview Park, and saw the Cubs at Wrigley Field.

"After graduating from high school I immediately started working at the Commonwealth Edison Company in the Loop. I would have wished to go to college as my closest friends did; but my mother had worked hard all those school years, and it was high time I made some contribution. But there was no stop to studying. There were plenty of schools offering instruction in every imaginable subject.

"The Loop was a wonderful place to work. That roughly mile-square area outlined by the grey steel elevated tracks of the Rapid Transit lines, and the blocks bordering it, held everything anybody might ever need or want, all within a lunch hour's walk. Crowded and noisy and exciting, there were, beside the downtown branches of half-a-dozen colleges, theatres, night clubs, restaurants, hotels, shops of every description, and stores from Woolworth's to Fields. And beside all this, the beautiful public library. Orchestra (I travelled the world with Burton Holmes.) And across Michigan Boulevard there was the most fascinating place of all, the Art Institute; Grant Park was just beyond, and the lake front, and to the north the busy bridges that spanned the river that runs backwards.

"Those were the years of jazz and Dixieland and the tea dance. Every restaurant offered a small orchestra and a smaller dance floor. We danced at lunch, and we danced before dinner. I guess it was also the years of gangsters and prohibition, but that side of Chicago's life touched me only lightly.

"Ashton Stevens, the Hearst drama critic and columnist, and his wife Kay (with whom I had gone to school) lived at the Congress Hotel at the edge of the Loop, and I 'moonlighted' taking Ashton's dictation of reviews and columns. This very dearly remembered association continued for many years, almost to the end of his life.

"During the mid-1930's Robert E. Foster and I met and married. Some years later, following the death of my dear mother, we sold the little house my father's brother had left to my mother and me, and moved to an apartment in an old converted townhouse on the near North Side. Those were the war years, and sometimes my husband (whose work kept him out of the military services) and our little dog were the only males in the building. Stubby was the best walked dog in the neighborhood.

"Several years ago my husband's nephew introduced me to Slim Williams. The Alaskan sourdough was a long-time friend of his and of his father. Out of that pleasant association came our first book, *The Friend of the Singing One*, and then *The Long Hungry Night*.

"Since 1967 we have been away from Chicago. At that time my husband's work necessitated a move to Nashville, in the beautiful Tennessee hills. And for the past year we have been living near the shores of the Gulf of Mexico, in Venice, Florida.

Ancient Grandmother knelt beside him, and with a spoon carved from a hollow curve of walrus ivory, touched his cold lips with a drop of the warm broth. ■ (From *The Long Hungry Night* by E. C. Foster and Slim Williams. Drawings by Glo Coalson.)

"Reading is really my only hobby. History, criticism, essays, travel, archaeology, poetry, drama, nature writing, mystery stories. Like Paul Darrow and his father Clarence, I always carry a book. Even to parties.

"I love a garden—we have usually chosen our homes for the trees on the property—but my green thumb is neither wise nor educated. If I could draw I would be always sketching faces. But I only disappoint myself. Lately I've done a little needlepoint designing and stitching."

HOBBIES AND OTHER INTERESTS: Reading, poetry, gardens, needlework, travel.

FOR MORE INFORMATION SEE: Sarasota Herald-Tribune/Journal, March 25, 1973; *Venice Gondolier,* April 8, 1974, May 13, 1974; *Sarasota Journal* March 20, 1974.

FRANKEL, Bernice

PERSONAL: Born in New York, N.Y.; married Ray Hunold (a photographer). *Home:* 900 Bay St., San Francisco, Calif. 94109.

CAREER: In earlier years was children's book editor and reviewer in New York, N.Y.; did the work of junior author for Macmillan Co. on Harris-Clark readers, writing original stories as well as selecting and adapting material as texts for lower grades; children's book editor for Abelard-

Schuman Ltd. and then for Parents' Magazine Press; weekly columnist, "Books for Children," for Saturday Review Newspaper Syndicate running in the 1950's. *Awards, honors: Half-as-Big and the Tiger,* illustrated by Leonard Weisgard, was one of fifteen picture books on *New York Times* list of the hundred best children's books of 1961.

WRITINGS—Picture books: *Half-as-Big and the Tiger,* Watts, 1961; *Timothy and Alexander the Great,* A. S. Barnes, 1962; *The Seven Monkeys,* A. S. Barnes, 1962; *Tag-Along,* Parents' Magazine Press, 1962; *Two Stories About Rickey,* Whitman Publishing, 1966; *Tom and the Zoo,* Whitman Publishing, 1967; *Grandpa's Policemen Friends,* Whitman Publishing, 1967. Contributor of articles on children's books to *Town and Country, American Home,* and other national magazines.

WORK IN PROGRESS: Travel articles illustrated with her husband's photographs.

SIDELIGHTS: "My husband and I have photographed close to a dozen different deserts, as well as seacoasts from Washington down through Oregon and California to Baja, Mexico. Also woodlands, rain forest in Olympia, most national parks and monuments, rock country such as the Grand Canyon—and most of all our beloved city by adoption, San Francisco. We moved here from New York in 1970 and love it more with each year." The Hunolds have a German shepherd named Homer and a mini-motorhome named Half-as-big.

FOR MORE INFORMATION SEE: Commonweal, May 20, 1961.

FRIEDLANDER, Joanne K(ohn)   1930-

PERSONAL: Born August 22, 1930, in Chicago, Ill.; daughter of Isidore E. (a physician) and Carolyn (Newman) Kohn; married Stanley Friedlander (a business executive), September 10, 1955; children: Mark, Susan. *Education:* University of Colorado, student, 1948-49; Northwestern University, B.A., 1954; Chicago Teachers College, Teacher's Certificate, 1965. *Politics:* Independent. *Religion:* Jewish. *Home:* 1300 Rosemary Lane, Northbrook, Ill. 60062. *Office:* Kahn Realty, 640 Vernon, Glencoe, Ill. 60022.

CAREER: Former newspaperwoman and teacher; realtor with Kahn Realty, Glencoe, Ill., 1970—. *Member:* League of Women Voters.

WRITINGS: (With Jean Neal) *Stock Market ABC,* Follett, 1969.

SIDELIGHTS: "When my own children received a gift of stock, they asked 'What is the stock market?' Since I could find no simple book to answer their questions and since one million other youngsters own stock, I decided to write my own book."

FULLER, Catherine L(euthold)   1916-

PERSONAL: Born December 31, 1916, in Bucyrus, Ohio; daughter of Godfrey (a lawyer) and Mila (Bomgardner) Leuthold; married Leonard F. Fuller, Jr. (an engineer),

CATHERINE L. FULLER

November 24, 1952. *Education:* Mount Holyoke College, B.A., 1938; Oberlin College, M.A., 1945. *Politics:* Independent. *Religion:* Christian. *Home:* 1135 Hillcrest Blvd., Millbrae, Calif. 94030.

CAREER: Worked as an art historian at Dudley Peter Allen Memorial Art Museum of Oberlin College, Oberlin, Ohio, and at National Gallery of Art, Washington, D.C.; employed in the fields of economics and history with several organizations and projects including Republic Steel Corp., Cleveland Council on World Affairs, and Stanford Study of Undergraduate Education. *Member:* The Print Club of Cleveland, Phi Beta Kappa.

WRITINGS: Beasts: An Alphabet of Fine Prints (introduction to fine prints for young people), Little, Brown, 1968.

SIDELIGHTS: "Because my mother was a librarian, excellent children's books were always a part of my life. As an art historian I combined in *Beasts* my special study of fine prints with my love for children's books. The serious purpose underlying my creation of *Beasts* was to lead young people to fine original prints and suggest a scholarly approach to their appreciation. In this area of the graphic arts there is a huge gap between scholarly publications and the books readily available to the general public. My present research is directed toward another book for young people to narrow this gap and increase their technical and aesthetic understanding of the graphic arts."

FOR MORE INFORMATION SEE: *New York Times Book Review,* November 3, 1968; *Chicago Tribune Children's Book World,* November 3, 1968.

GAY, Kathlyn 1930-

PERSONAL: Born March 4, 1930, in Zion, Ill.; daughter of Kenneth Charles and Beatrice (Anderson) McGarrahan; married Arthur L. Gay (now an elementary principal), August 28, 1948; children: Martin, Douglas, Karen. *Education:* Attended Northern Illinois University, two years. *Politics:* Registered Democrat. *Religion:* "No affiliation." *Home and office:* 1711 East Beardsley Ave., Elkhart, Ind. 46514. *Agent:* Hoffman & Sheedy, 145 West 86th St., New York, N.Y. 10024.

CAREER: Church World Service, Christian Rural Overseas Program (CROP), editor and public relations writer in Elkhart, Ind., and New York, N.Y., 1962-65; Juhl Advertising Agency, Elkhart, Ind., publicity and public relations writer, 1966; free-lance writer, 1957—, full-time, 1966—. Instructor of creative writing class for adults, Elkhart Area Career Center, 1970—. *Member:* Authors Guild. *Awards, honors:* Honorable mention in *Writer's Digest* short story contest, 1962; first prize in literary section, Northern Indiana Arts Festival, 1965, for one-act play.

WRITINGS: Girl Pilot, Messner, 1966; *Money Isn't Everything: The Story of Economics,* Delacorte, 1967; *Meet the Mayor of Your City,* Hawthorn, 1967; *Beth Speaks Out,* Messner, 1968; *Meet the Governor of Your State,* Hawthorn, 1968; *Careers in Social Service,* Messner, 1969; *Where the People Are: Cities and Their Future,* Delacorte, 1969; *The Germans Helped Build America,* Messner, 1971; *A Family is for Living,* Delacorte, 1972; *Proud Heritage on Parade,* Contemporary Drama Service, 1972; *Be a Smart Shopper,* Messner, 1974; *Body Talk,* Scribner, 1974; (with Ben E. Barnes) *The River Flows Backward,* Ashley Books, 1975. Contributor of feature articles to *American Home, Ebony, Women's World, Ave Maria, Marriage, Family Digest, Harvest Years, Popular Medicine, True Confessions, Better Camping, Women in Business, P.T.A. Magazine,* and other periodicals; contributor of short stories to *Child Life, Twelve/Fifteen, Catholic Miss, St. Anthony's Monthly,* and other magazines. Major writing responsibilities for teachers' manuals published by Science Research Associates, Lyons & Carnahan, and Ginn & Co.

WORK IN PROGRESS: Care & Share for Messner, a book on teenagers and volunteerism; a book for teens who have alcoholic parents; an adult work on interracial marriages; a teen novel about an interracial family; an adult novel about an interracial couple; a juvenile book on how to write and produce your own play.

SIDELIGHTS: "Writing, for me, has become a way of life, and I could not imagine trying to function as an individual without exercising this form of communication. I have always considered myself a rather shy person, but also one who can 'walk in another's shoes.' These traits, more than any others, have probably motivated me to write both fiction and non-fiction.

"Through the written word, I feel I have been able to share with young people and adults some of the observations and impressions I have had on what it means to be a person, a productive human being. So many different conditions and factors shape each one of us as individuals that I am often amazed we are able to understand one another at all. Happily, though, there are many experiences in life that are common to all of us and a writer can draw on these in stories and articles to help readers see, hear, feel with real or imaginary people.

"For as long as I can remember I have always been concerned about the way people get along with each other. I believe we are all of one humankind, but have differences that we can learn to respect. So, much of my writing has been about our pluralistic society—the variety of different cultures and backgrounds which shape people in this country.

"At first I began writing about my own background which was rather unique. I was born and raised in the town of Zion, Illinois, a religious community founded about 1900 by a faith healer and a man who called himself a prophet. The town was controlled by the church group, with all property, industries and businesses under church ownership. 'Outsiders' were seldom welcome in this community and it was here I learned the real dangers of 'exclusiveness' and isolation. Even at nine and ten years old I felt there was little opportunity for growth in a closed community. What is good and right and productive in life takes many forms, not just one. Each of us may come from a different place and still arrive at the same goal or end.

KATHLYN GAY

"With this view, I have felt part of many groups, not just the White Anglo-Saxon Protestant majority. As an example, my husband and I have joined with a black couple to form a business partnership which covers a variety of activities such as rental properties, advertising and promotion. I also feel very fortunate that through my oldest son—who was accepted by and himself has accepted Judaism—we have an extended family that is multi-cultural. Married to a young woman of Jewish heritage, my son's link has given both families the opportunity to share and communicate our differences as well as our similarities.

"Besides human relationships, other interests have determined some types of writing I do. Since my husband has been a teacher, counselor and principal in elementary schools, I have had many first-hand experiences with new educational programs. Much of this has been shared in textbooks and teaching materials I've helped prepare.

"Also, my husband and I have been active in amateur theater groups and I have been involved in some sort of drama ever since childhood when I staged my own plays in our basement or backyard. This has led to writing a few plays and a variety of articles on how dramatic skills can be used in teaching, the way our bodies and facial expressions are used to send silent messages, and how to use speech effectively.

"Of course being a part of the development of my three children, who are all grown now, has provided material for articles and stories, too. One childrens' story, for example, came about because my middle child was having problems with his size—he was unhappy about being the smallest in his class. The story, called, *He Wasn't Too Small,* dealt with the idea that physical size has little to do with what one can accomplish.

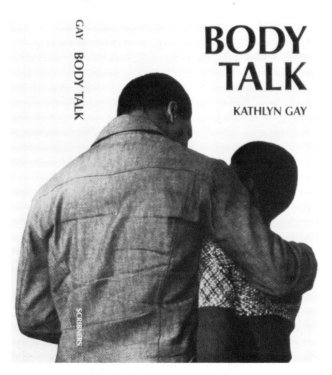

Even without seeing their faces, you could read the body language of these two. ■ (From *Body Talk* by Kathlyn Gay. Photographs by David Sassman.)

"In summary, I write daily about people and things that arouse my curiosity. I have always been eager to *know;* I hope I never lose that desire to learn. That is the stuff from which one keeps developing not only as a writer, but also as a productive human being."

GILL, Derek L(ewis) T(heodore) 1919-

PERSONAL: Born December 23, 1919, in Kampala, Uganda; son of William Bridson (a missionary) and Lilian (Moore) Gill; married Erica Elizabeth McPherson (an editor-in-residence), January 5, 1945; children: Diana Jane, A. Malcolm, Duncan R. *Education:* University of London, M.B. (first), 1938; Cambridge University, graduate study, 1939-40. *Religion:* Episcopalian. *Home and office:* 421 Via Almar, Palos Verdes Estates, Calif. 90274.

CAREER: Daily Representative, Queenstown, South Africa, editor, 1948-60; *Pretoria News,* Pretoria, South Africa, city editor, 1960-63; *World* (daily newspaper), Johannesburg, South Africa, editorial director, 1963-66; *Pace* (magazine), Los Angeles, Calif., senior editor, 1966-70; researcher for author, Irving Stone, 1970—. Lecturer and broadcaster to creative writing classes and other groups; painter; exhibiting in one-man shows in Europe, the United States, and South Africa. *Military service:* British Army, 1940-44; served in Africa, Europe, and Southeast Asia; became captain. *Member:* Screen Writers Guild (West), Round Table (chairman).

WRITINGS: (With Robin Graham) *Dove* (ALA Notable book), Harper, 1972; *The Boy Who Sailed Around the World* (children's book), Western Publishing, 1973; (with Tom Sullivan) *You Can See What I Hear,* Harper, 1974; *Adventure in the Dark* (children's book), Western Publishing, in press. Author of screenplay, "The Dove," based on own book. Contributor to journals and newspapers in the United States and abroad, including *Reader's Digest, Women's Own, London Times, New York Times, Modern Maturity,* and *Tokyo Times.*

WORK IN PROGRESS: Home Is the Sailor, a sequel to *Dove,* publication by Harper.

SIDELIGHTS: I believe passionately that writing—and indeed all art—is meant to illustrate the highest aims of society, of humanity. What distresses me is that so many great writers—far better writers than I am—use their pens to reflect and exaggerate the worst of human nature, and thus debase humanity. After thirty years of writing, I still sweat out every line, every paragraph. Yet it is this striving that I relish—striving to reach for the finest, freest, fullest, most creative work of which I'm capable.

"Some write for cash. I do not; although I hope that cash will flow from my endeavors. Some write for fame. I would be content to write in a Tibetan monastery. The richest reward from my writing is in those letters which come from strangers—from people who say, in essence, 'I read your book and feel the better for it.' Perhaps the surgeon feels the same way when he sees his patient regaining strength.

"I am an optimist. Point to the cynic and you have found my enemy, for I am convinced that mankind will climb out of the cold gray valleys of privation and prejudice and reach the sunlit uplands of promise.

Coffee House Club (New York). *Awards, honors:* Silver Medal of U.S. Treasury Department for war bond work during World War II; other awards and prizes for radio, television, and films, and from American Society of Composers, Authors and Publishers.

WRITINGS—Compiler: *A New Treasury of Folk Songs,* Bantam, 1961; *Tom Glazer's Treasury of Songs for Children* (arranged for piano, with guitar chords), Grosset, 1964; *On Top of Spaghetti* (collection of children's songs with notes on their origin and background; arranged for piano, with guitar chords), Grosset, 1966; *Songs of Peace, Freedom and Protest,* Fawcett World, 1972; *Eye Winker, Tom Tinker, Chin Chopper: Fifty Musical Fingerplays* (arranged for piano, with guitar chords), Doubleday, 1973.

Recordings sung, or sung and played, include: "Activity and Game Songs," two albums; "Music for 1's and 2's"; "Children's Songs from Latin America" (sung in English and Spanish); "The Musical Heritage of America," two albums; "The Twelve Days of Christmas"; "Do Not Go Gentle ..." (song-settings of lyrics of Dylan Thomas, Yeats, Shakespeare, and other poets). Also has written poetry and liner notes for albums.

WORK IN PROGRESS: A large collection of children's songs, tentatively titled *The Complete Book of Children's Songs,* publication by Open Court expected in 1976.

SIDELIGHTS: "My motivation among many is to provide

DEREK L. T. GILL

"I think that every writer shares the experience of feeling that life and color and warmth and vitality will not be known by him again. But, of course, they are. And it is in these moments of rediscovery that a writer experiences his greatest joy."

Gill's books have been published in German, French, Italian, Japanese, Spanish, Swedish, and Finnish. "The Dove" was produced as a movie by Gregory Peck, in 1973.

FOR MORE INFORMATION SEE: P. V. Review, May, 1973; *Star* (Johannesburg), June 15, 1973.

GLAZER, Tom 1914-

PERSONAL: Born September 3, 1914, in Philadelphia, Pa.; married Miriam Reed Eisenberg (a remedial reading teacher), June 25, 1944; children: John Prescott, Peter Reed. *Education:* Studied at City College (now City College of City University of New York), but left in final year, 1941. *Politics:* Independent. *Religion:* Unaffiliated. *Address:* Box 102, Scarborough, N.Y. 10510. *Agent:* Julian Bach, Jr., 3 East 84th St., New York, N.Y. 10017; and other agents.

CAREER: Folksinger, songwriter, and composer. *Member:* American Federation of Musicians, American Guild of Authors and Composers, American Society of Composers, Authors and Publishers, Screen Actors Guild.

TOM GLAZER

Something about the Author

instruction and/or entertainment to as many people as can find my efforts useful. The most vital thing I know of today is to prevent violence while changing the world for the better if possible. All else is secondary, certainly books. Next we must preserve the remaining beauty of the world. I have had a long drawn out love affair with the French language, but the more I study it, the more I realize how few people master their own tongue.''

FOR MORE INFORMATION SEE: Horn Book, April, 1974.

GOLD, Sharlya

PERSONAL: Given name is pronounced to rhyme with ''Carla''; born in Los Angeles, Calif.; daughter of Albert (an accountant) and Selma (a pianist and concert singer; maiden name, Mayer) Isenberg; married Leonard Gold (an elementary school principal), 1951; children: Alison, Sheridan, Hilary, Darien. *Education:* San Bernardino Valley College, A.A.; University of California, Berkeley, B.A. *Religion:* Jewish. *Residence:* Capitola, Calif.

CAREER: Former elementary school teacher; reading specialist; instructor of adult classes in writing for children and of children's classes in bookbinding. *Member:* National Writers Club, National League of American Pen Women. *Awards, honors:* First prize in juvenile short story contest conducted by Southern California branch of National League of American Pen Women.

SHARLYA GOLD

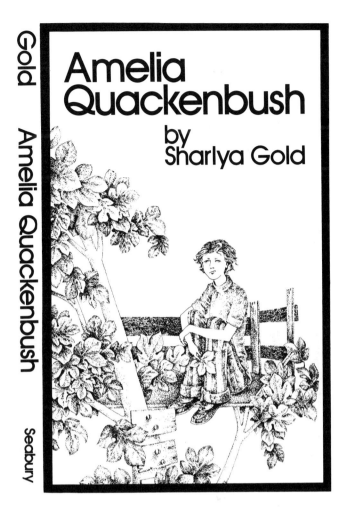

Amelia had seen the grown-ups world and wanted no part of it—until absolutely necessary. ■ (From *Amelia Quackenbush* by Sharlya Gold. Jacket by John C. Wallner.)

WRITINGS: The Potter's Four Sons, Doubleday, 1969; *Amelia Quackenbush,* Seabury, 1973. Contributor to *The Porcupine Storybook,* Concordia, 1974, and to juvenile magazines, including *Child Playmate, Friend, Working for Boys,* and *Together.*

WORK IN PROGRESS: Two books.

SIDELIGHTS: ''Most of my writing, both fiction and non-fiction, is based on what I see, hear, and experience. A part comes from my dreams, those of the night and the day. At times, buried ideas and thoughts, triggered by reading or television-watching, surface and find their way into stories and articles.

''Because I usually write for children, I think back into my own childhood experiences to recall the emotions and feelings of those years, the frustrations and yearnings that were so consuming. But that isn't always necessary. Even today, when I enroll in a class that I know nothing about, such as calligraphy or photography which I'm currently studying, I'm again gripped by a lack of confidence, a feeling of inferiority, a dread of failure—and the emotions of childhood come rushing back at me.''

ELAINE GOODMAN

GOODMAN, Elaine 1930-

PERSONAL: Born January 23, 1930, in New York, N.Y.; daughter of Abraham and Dorothy (Dean) Egan; married Walter Goodman (a writer), February 10, 1951; children: Hal, Bennet. Education: Syracuse University, B.A., 1951; University of Reading, Reading, England, M.A., 1953. Religion: Jewish. Home: 4 Crest Dr., White Plains, N.Y. 10607.

MEMBER: Phi Beta Kappa. Awards, honors: Christopher Award, 1971, for The Rights of the People.

WRITINGS: (With husband, Walter Goodman) The Rights of the People, Farrar, Straus, 1971; (with Walter Goodman) The Family, Yesterday, Today, and Tomorrow, Farrar, Straus, 1975.

GOODMAN, Walter 1927-

PERSONAL: Born August 22, 1927, in New York, N.Y.; married Elaine Egan (now an artist), February 10, 1951; children: Hal, Bennet. Education: Syracuse University, B.A. (magna cum laude), 1949; University of Reading, M.A., 1953.

CAREER: New Republic, Washington, D.C., staff writer, 1954-55; Playboy, Chicago, Ill., contributing editor, 1960-

61; Redbook, New York, N.Y., senior editor, 1957-74; New York Times, New York, N.Y., assistant editor of Arts & Leisure section of Sunday New York Times, 1974—.

WRITINGS: The Clowns of Commerce, Sagamore, 1957; All Honorable Men, Atlantic-Little, Brown, 1963; Smoking and the Public Interest (Part IV), Consumer's Union, 1963; The Committee, Farrar, Straus, 1968; Black Bondage, Farrar, Straus, 1970; A Percentage of the Take, Farrar, Straus, 1970; (with wife, Elaine Goodman) The Rights of the People, Farrar, Straus, 1971; (with Patsy Anthony Lepera) Memoirs of a Scam Man, Farrar, Straus, 1974; (with Elaine Goodman) The Family: Yesterday, Today, Tomorrow, Farrar, Straus, 1975. Writer of magazine articles and book reviews.

WALTER GOODMAN

The privileged domestics, some of whom even had servants of their own, tended to look down on the less fortunate field hands. ■ (From *Black Bondage: The Life of Slaves in the South* by Walter Goodman. Sketch appeared in a Baltimore newspaper in 1861.)

GORDON, Margaret (Anna) 1939-

PERSONAL: Born May 19, 1939, in London, England; daughter of Stanley Alan (a violinist) and Florence (Lunnon) Eastoe; married Giles Alexander Esme Gordon (a writer and literary agent), March 21, 1964; children: Callum Giles, Gareth Alexander, Harriet Miranda. *Education:* Studied in England at St. Martin's School of Art, 1955, and Camberwell School of Arts and Crafts, 1956-59.

The yellow vapor wrapped them in its hundred arms; the oak staff stood firm, stronger than them all. ■ (From *The Callow Pit Coffer* by Kevin Crossley-Holland. Illustrated by Margaret Gordon.)

Politics: Labour Party. *Religion:* Christian. *Home:* 9 St. Ann's Gardens, London NW5 4ER, England. *Agent:* Laura Cecil, 10 Exeter Mansions, 106 Shaftesbury Ave., London W1V 7OH, England.

CAREER: Teacher of art in Bexhill-on-Sea, England, 1961-63, and London, England, 1963-65; illustrator of books, 1965—. *Awards, honors: The Green Children* received Arts Council of Great Britain Award as best book for young children published during 1966-68.

ILLUSTRATOR: George MacBeth, *Noah's Journey* (long poem for children), Viking, 1966; Kevin Crossley-Holland, *The Green Children,* Macmillan (London), 1966, Seabury, 1968; Kevin Crossley-Holland, *The Callow Pit Coffer,* Macmillan (London), 1968, Seabury, 1969; George Mac-Beth, *Jonah and the Lord* (long poem for children), Macmillan (London), 1969, Holt, 1970; Mervyn Horder, arranger, *On Christmas Day: First Carols to Play and Sing,* Macmillan (New York), 1969; Helen Cresswell, *A House for Jones,* Benn, 1969.

Kevin Crossley-Holland, *The Pedlar of Swaffham,* Seabury, 1971; Peter John Stephens, *Lillapig,* Benn, 1972; Malcolm Carrick, *All Sorts of Everything,* Heinemann, 1973; Giles Gordon, *Walter and the Balloon,* Heinemann, 1974; Elaine Bastable, *Recipes and Rhymes,* Heinemann, 1975; author anonymous, *Paper of Pins,* Macmillan (London), 1975, Seabury, 1975.

Illustrator of "Albert" series by Alison Jezard: *Albert,* Gollancz, 1968, Prentice-Hall, 1970; *Albert in Scotland,* Gollancz, 1969; *Albert and Henry,* Gollancz, 1970; *Albert's Christmas,* Gollancz, 1970; *Albert Up the River,* Gollancz,

WORK IN PROGRESS: Illustrating a second book by her 1971; *Albert and Digger,* Gollancz, 1972; *Albert and Tum Tum,* Gollancz, 1973; *Albert Goes to Sea,* Gollancz, 1973; *Albert Police Bear,* Gollancz, 1975.

Also illustrator of several "Wombles" books by Elisabeth Beresford and of "numerous very early and very bad educational books."

husband, Giles Gordon; research on cats, peacocks, and children.

SIDELIGHTS: "Chief motivation to career so far is that it is possible (just) to illustrate books while looking after small children."

FOR MORE INFORMATION SEE: Illustrators of Children's Books: 1957-1966, Horn Book, 1968.

GORELICK, Molly C. 1920-

PERSONAL: Born September 19, 1920, in New York, N.Y.; daughter of Morris and Jean Chernow; married Leon Gorelick, April 12, 1941; children: Walter, Peter. *Education:* University of California, Los Angeles, B.A., 1948, M.A., 1955, Ed.D., 1962; University of Southern California, graduate study, 1950. *Home:* 600 North June St., Los Angeles, Calif. 90004.

CAREER: Licensed psychologist, and marriage, family, and child counselor. Los Angeles (Calif.) city schools, teacher, 1948-62, counselor, 1957-58; University of California, Los Angeles, instructor in psychology and education departments, 1957-64, research assistant, 1961-62, super-

MOLLY C. GORELICK

visor in school psychology clinic, 1962-63; University of Southern California, School of Education, Los Angeles, assistant professor, 1964-66; Exceptional Childrens Foundation, Los Angeles, Calif., chief of guidance services, 1963-70; California State University, Northridge, professor, 1970—. University of Hawaii, visiting associate professor, summer, 1967, 1969, 1971, 1973. *Member:* American Association on Mental Deficiency (regional executive board), Council for Exceptional Children, National Rehabilitation Association, American Psychological Association, and Western branch; Phi Beta Kappa, Pi Gamma Mu, Pi Lambda Theta.

WRITINGS—"Rescue Series," with Jean Boreman: *Fire on Sun Mountain,* 1967, *Flood at Dry Creek,* 1967, *Storm at Sand Point,* 1967, *Fog Over Sun City,* 1968, *Snow Storm at Green Valley,* 1968 (all published by Ritchie). Contributor to *Human Behavior, American Journal of Mental Deficiency,* and other educational and guidance journals.

GOVAN, Christine Noble 1898-
(Mary Allerton, J. N. Darby)

PERSONAL: Born 1898, in New York, N.Y.; daughter of Stephen Edward and Mary (Quintard) Noble; married Gilbert Eaton Govan, 1916; children: Emily Payne Govan West, Mary Q. Govan Steele, James F. *Education:* University of Chattanooga, student, one year. *Politics:* Democrat. *Home and office:* 400 Laurel Lane, Lookout Mountain, Tenn. *Agent:* Bill Berger and Associates.

CAREER: Writer, primarily of children's books. *Member:* Authors League.

*WRITINGS—*Juveniles: *Those Plummer Children,* Houghton, 1934; *Five at Ashefield,* Houghton, 1935; *Judy and Chris,* Houghton, 1936; *The House with the Echo,* Houghton, 1937; *Narcissus and de Chillun,* Houghton, 1938; *String and the No-Tail Cat,* Houghton, 1939; *Sweet 'Possum Valley,* Houghton, 1940; *Carolina Caravan,* Houghton, 1942; *Mr. Hermit Miser,* Aladdin, 1949; *The Pink Maple House,* Aladdin, 1950; *The Surprising Summer,* Aladdin, 1951; *The Super-duper Car,* Houghton, 1952; *Tilly's Strange Secret,* Aladdin, 1952; *Rachel Jackson, Tennessee Girl,* Bobbs, 1955, illustrated edition, 1962; *The Year the River Froze,* World Publishing, 1959; *Willow Landing,* World Publishing, 1961; *The Delectable Mountain,* World Publishing, 1962; *Number 5 Hackberry Street,* World Publishing, 1964; *Return to Hackberry Street,* World Publishing, 1967; *The Curious Clubhouse,* World Publishing, 1967; *Phinny's Fine Summer,* World Publishing, 1968; *The Trash-Pile Treasure,* World Publishing, 1970.

Juveniles, with daughter, Emmy Govan West: *Mystery at Shingle Rock,* 1955, *Mystery at the Mountain Face,* 1956, *Mystery at the Shuttered Hotel,* 1956, *Mystery at Moccasin Bend,* 1957, *Mystery at the Indian Hide-out,* 1957, *Mystery at the Vanishing Stamp,* 1958, *Mystery at the Deserted Mill,* 1958, *Mystery at the Haunted House,* 1959, *Mystery at Plum Nelly,* 1959, *Mystery at Fearsome Lake,* 1960, *Mystery at Rock City,* 1960, *Mystery at the Snowed-in Cabin,* 1961, *Mystery of the Dancing Skeleton,* 1962, *Mystery at Ghost Lodge,* 1963, *Mystery at the Weird Ruins,* 1964, *Mystery at the Echoing Cave,* 1965 (all published by Sterling); *Alexander and the Witch,* Viking, 1972; *Danger Downriver,* Viking, 1972.

CHRISTINE NOBLE GOVAN

Adult novels: *Murder on the Mountain,* Houghton, 1937; *Plantation Murder,* Houghton, 1938; (under pseudonym Mary Allerton) *Shadow and the Web,* Bobbs, 1939; *Murder in the House with the Blue Eyes,* Bobbs, 1939; *Jennifer's House,* Houghton, 1945.

Short stories in *O. Henry Memorial Award Prize Stories,* 1947, *Timeless Stories for Today and Tomorrow,* edited by Ray Bradbury, 1952; and in magazines. Book reviewer for *Chattanooga Times.*

WORK IN PROGRESS: The Green Blade, a novel for adults; *Each Heart Knows the Secret,* a juvenile.

SIDELIGHTS: "I was born in New York City one of a long line of New Yorkers. We came south after my father's death to Sewanee, Tennessee—The University of the South, because my great uncle, Bishop Quintard, had been one of the founders and because Sewanee was virtually a Paradise occupying only a few acres in the middle of the most primitive and gorgeous Appalachian wilds. *The Delectable Mountain* gives a fairly good partial picture of our move. The night trip from New York to Sewanee is almost entirely factual.

"Later we moved to Nashville and to Franklin, close by, and my 'Plummer' books tell the story of my life in Franklin, Tennessee probably the happiest time of my entire youth. The 'Hackberry Street' books have a good deal of material taken from my later life in Nashville.

"Our last move was to Chattanooga, where I finished elementary school, got through high school by the skin of my teeth and taught in rural schools for about two years before

I married during World War I. I was given a scholarship to the University of Chattanooga but had to give it up after a few months to help financially in my family. I had been so poorly prepared in high school—and too busy having fun there—that I was at a loss in college and spent most of my time hiding under a library table reading authors I had not met before—chiefly essayists and poets. Years later my husband, then university librarian, wrote a history of the school and said at all the faculty meetings someone asked, 'Where is this Miss Noble? Has anybody seen her?'

"By some twist of fate—probably a shortage of teachers—I got a certificate to teach the first grade in a rural school. There were twenty-five children in my room ranging from four years to fifteen. Three were congenital idiots. All walked miles to school—I walked five each way myself—and brought their lunches in buckets. We had no running water—nothing but the bare rooms and the teachers. I could write a whole book on my brief teaching experience there—I left to get married. I always loved Edna Ferber's *So Big* because I identified so closely with the heroine's school teaching days.

"My husband ran one of the most excellent book stores in the south and we entertained a constant stream of traveling book salesmen, editors, artists, authors and publishers. Our

One boy with a tangle of fair hair walked up with his stomach stuck out in what he must have thought was a manly posture.
■ (From *Danger Downriver* by Emmy West and Christine Govan. Illustrated by Charles Robinson.)

children grew up in an atmosphere of 'bookishness' and there are now seven members of our family who write—three generations.

"I used to write two books a year. Sometimes I would publish a book and sell one in the same week and have one 'in the typewriter' at the same time. But now I am plagued with arthritis and older so that I am much slower.

"At present I am just finishing up a children's book on a subject dear to my heart—The Kindness Clubs and kindness to 'dumb' creatures in general. It is to be called, *Each Heart Knows the Secret,* from a poem by John Boyle, 'Each heart knows the secret. Kindness is the word.' I am also half way through a Gothic novel about a man who is obsessed by his Viking ancestry and maintains a sort of 'indentured' estate made possible by blackmail.

"We live on Lookout Mt. which is a beautiful place—all azaleas, pines, hemlocks, laurel and dogwoods—in a little house almost a hundred years old. I used to travel a great deal giving book talks, etc., but I seldom do now. I have a very satisfactory life with my garden, housework, writing, children and grandchildren and good friends.

"Practically all my books are autobiographical. I lived for years in the scenes of *Jennifer's House,* my novel about middle Tennessee. It got a snide review from a southern paper because the jacket said I was born in New York. The review, in total, was, 'Some Yankee's idea of the south.' As I knew the people I was writing about personally and had, practically, all my life it made me furious.

"My husband has retired but still writes a newspaper column on local history and an occasional article. We have our own work rooms and lead I suppose, the quiet satisfactory life of all married writers."

Several of Govan's adult novels have been published in England, and one in Finland.

GRAFF, (S.) Stewart 1908-

PERSONAL: Born May 8, 1908, in Worthington, Pa.; son of John Francis and Martha Grier (Stewart) Graff; married Polly Anne Colver (a free-lance writer and author of children's books), March 3, 1945; children: Jeremy M. Harris (stepson); Kate G. (Mrs. Stephen L. Danielski). *Education:* Attended Taft School, Watertown, Conn., 1921-25; Williams College, student, 1925-28; Harvard University, A.B., 1930, LL.B., 1936. *Politics:* Independent. *Religion:* Lutheran. *Home:* 157 West Clinton Ave., Irvington, N.Y. 10533.

CAREER: Brown, Cross & Hamilton (law firm), New York, N.Y., associate attorney, 1936-48; Synthetic Organic Chemical Manufacturers Association, New York, N.Y., executive secretary, 1948-68; writer of children's books, 1968—. Member of board of directors of Donald R. Reed Speech Center; member of Irvington Narcotics Guidance Council and Irvington Jobs for Youth Committee. *Military service:* U.S. Army Air Forces, 1942-46; became captain. *Member:* New York County Lawyers Association, Harvard Club (New York, N.Y.), Chemists Club (New York, N.Y.).

STEWART GRAFF, with wife, Anne Colver

WRITINGS—For children: *John Paul Jones,* Garrard, 1961; *George Washington,* Garrard, 1964; *Theodore Roosevelt's Boys,* Garrard, 1967; *Hernando Cortes,* Garrard, 1970.

With wife, Polly Anne (Colver) Graff: *Squanto: Indian Adventurer,* Garrard, 1965; *Helen Keller: Toward the Light,* Garrard, 1965; (co-edited) *Wolpert's Roost,* Washington Irving Press, 1971; *The Wayfarer's Tree,* Dutton, 1973.

WORK IN PROGRESS: Research on the periods of the American Revolution and World War Two.

HOBBIES AND OTHER INTERESTS: Travel.

GREEN, Jane 1937-

PERSONAL: Born June 27, 1937, in New York, N.Y.; daughter of Samuel (an attorney) and Mollie (Schmerzler) Oliphant; married Daniel Green, September 20, 1959; children: Matthew, Simon. *Education:* Cornell University, student, 1955-57. *Residence:* Great Neck, N.Y. *Agent:* Marilyn Marlow, Curtis Brown Ltd., 60 East 56th St., New York, N.Y. 10021. *Office:* National Foundation for Sudden Infant Death, Inc., 1501 Broadway, New York, N.Y. 10036.

JANE GREEN

CAREER: National Foundation for Sudden Infant Death, New York, N.Y., 1974—.

WRITINGS: (With Virginia Pasley) *You Can Do Anything with Crepes,* Simon & Schuster, 1970; (with Judith Choate) *The Gift-Givers Cookbook,* Simon & Schuster, 1972; (with Choate) *Scrapcraft: 50 Easy-to-Make Handicraft Projects* (juvenile), Doubleday, 1973; (with Choate) *Patchwork* (juvenile), Doubleday, 1975.

WORK IN PROGRESS: A book on beachcraft; research on the canning and preserving of foods.

GRIEDER, Walter   1924-

PERSONAL: Born November 21, 1924, in Basel, Switzerland; married Bona Beretta; children: Lorenz-Alain. *Education:* Studied at a normal school in France and at art schools in Basel and Paris. *Politics:* "Open for freedom, efficiency, humanity, without any prejudice, for modern solutions—big thinking!" *Religion:* "My own." *Home:* Baeumleingasse 16, 4051 Basel, Switzerland.

CAREER: Painter, graphic artist, and writer, designer, and illustrator of books. *Member:* Swiss Graphic Designers. *Awards, honors:* Prizes for posters and for books.

WRITINGS: Die Geburtstagsreise, Herder Verlag, 1961; *Pierrot and His Friends in the Circus* (translation), Delacorte, 1967; *Das Grosse Fest,* translation published as *The Great Feast,* Parents' Magazine Press, 1968; *Die Verzauberte Trommel,* Sauerlaender, 1968, translation by Doris Orgel published as *The Enchanted Drum,* Parents' Magazine Press, 1969; *Nimm Mich Mit, Frau Vogeluase,* Otto Maier Verlag, 1972; *Die Gute Tat dev Dicken Kinder,* Auuelle Betz Verlag, 1972; *The Wonderchild,* Broschek Verlag, 1972; *Das Geschuk des Oparis,* Atlantis Verlag, 1972. Contributor of short stories and articles on art to periodicals.

WORK IN PROGRESS: Designing "very modern books" for Diogenes, Atlantis, Otto Maier, Broschek, and other publishers.

SIDELIGHTS: "My father was an important manager and art collector, so I arrived in France, in artists surroundings, Henry Miller style! I designed thousands of drawings (all destroyed) when very young. I was a student of philosophy, and Indian and Chinese traditional thoughts. Then I became interested in graphic design. I made a name through posters and illustrations for all ages! It was Henry Verlag, who asked first by accident for a children's book. Because the first book was a success, there came other demands. I took my material from my childhood (like Chaplin). I do not want to create fairy-tales, but show confrontations between the child and his actual problems. I do not want to specialize for scholarly people, but art-illustration in general."

WALTER GRIEDER

(From *The Enchanted Drum* by Maria Aebersold. Illustrated by Walter Grieder.)

Grieder has traveled in most countries of Europe, in Africa, and in India, where he designed a booklet, *Grieder meets the Maharajah,* for Air India.

HOBBIES AND OTHER INTERESTS: "Everything that is really important. Painting, work, work, work."

FOR MORE INFORMATION SEE: Graphis 155, Volume 27, 1971/72.

GRIESE, Arnold A(lfred) 1921-

PERSONAL: Surname rhymes with "rice"; born April 13, 1921, in Lakota, Iowa; son of Helmut Adam (a farmer) and Augusta (Meltz) Griese; married Jane Warren (owner of Jacyn School of Modeling, Fairbanks, Alaska), January 14, 1943; children: Warren, Cynthia (Mrs. Les Blakely). *Education:* Georgetown University, B.S., 1948; University of Miami, Coral Gables, Fla., M.Ed., 1957; University of Arizona, Ph.D., 1960. *Politics:* Independent. *Religion:* Episcopalian. *Home:* 3070 Riverview Dr., Fairbanks, Alaska 99701. *Office:* Department of Education, University of Alaska, Fairbanks, Alaska 99701.

CAREER: McGraw-Hill Publishing Co., New York, N.Y., sales representative in Colombia, South America,

1948-50; elementary school teacher in the Bureau of Indian Affairs at Tanana, Alaska, 1951-56; University of Alaska, Fairbanks, assistant professor, 1960-65, associate professor, 1965-71, professor of education, 1971—. *Military service:* U.S. Army Air Forces, 1942-46; became captain. *Member:* National Council of Teachers of English, Alaska Council of Teachers of English, Delta Phi Epsilon, Phi Delta Kappa.

WRITINGS: (Contributor) Miriam Hoffman, editor, *Authors and Illustrators of Children's Books,* Bowker, 1972; *At the Mouth of the Luckiest River* (juvenile), Crowell, 1973; *The Way of Our People* (juvenile), Crowell, 1975. Contributor to *Elementary English.*

WORK IN PROGRESS: A children's book on the Alaskan Aleuts on Attu Island.

SIDELIGHTS: "I was born and lived until I was seventeen on a farm in Iowa. That was long ago. Most of you who read my books would find it hard to understand what it was like to live without electricity, without running water, and without indoor toilets. But we really didn't miss these things because no one else had them either. There were other things, pleasant things, like riding in a horse-drawn sled on a cold clear Christmas Eve, tucked in snugly with my brothers and sisters under a heavy buffalo robe; seeing the stars shining overhead and hearing the happy voices of adults singing carols. And all the while thinking about Christmas morning, just like you still do today.

ARNOLD A. GRIESE

84   **Something about the Author**

Tatlek moved from the back of the sled and put his arms around him. The dog licked his face and Tatlek held him close.
■ (From *At the Mouth of the Luckiest River* by Arnold A. Griese. Illustrated by Glo Coalson.)

"The thing I missed most when I was young was books. I went to a one-room country school which had only four short shelves of books and they had to last for the seven years I spent there. It wasn't enough and I read anything else I could find. I read the Bible through, more than once, and I read my Dad's weekly Western story magazines even though I didn't understand most of what I read. Reading took me to far away places and helped me to understand people who were different from those who lived around me. Finally, when I was seventeen, I left the farm and traveled a great deal; to most of the states, to Mexico, Hawaii, Puerto Rico, South America. I enjoyed it all and learned first hand about people and places. But I never stopped reading books. I am interested in people and I find that authors have a special way of sharing their ideas about people. That is why I read a lot, and that is the reason I like to write for young people.

"I write about the Indians, Eskimos, and Aleuts of Alaska because Alaska is now our home. Also, although we have lived among these people for twenty years, I still find them interesting."

HOBBIES AND OTHER INTERESTS: Reading, flying (pilots his own plane), chess, swimming, travel.

GROL, Lini Richards 1913-

PERSONAL: Born October 7, 1913, in Nijmegen, Netherlands; daughter of Johannes and Catharine (Engel) Grol.

Education: Trained in Netherlands for R.N. and public health nursing; has since taken writing courses at McMaster University, Brock University, and Columbia University. *Politics:* Conservative. *Religion:* Christian. *Home and studio:* Fonthill Studio, 53 South Pelham St., Fonthill, Ontario LOS 1EO, Canada.

CAREER: Nurse in Netherlands before coming to Canada; presently part-time registered nurse on pediatrics ward in Welland County Hospital, Welland, Ontario; instructor and lecturer in scissorcraft. Scissor-cutting illustrations in black and white and in color have been shown in Netherlands and at art gallerys and libraries in Ontario. *Member:* Canadian Authors Association, Professional Association of Woman Writers, St. Catharines Arts Council, Hamilton Arts Council, Niagara Falls Arts Association (Ontario), Media Club.

WRITINGS: Repetitorium (a referendum for the mental nursing student), De Bussy, 1950; (self-illustrated) *Silent Thoughts and Silhouettes* (poems), privately printed by Trillium Books (Fonthill Studio), 1967; (self-illustrated) *Scissorcraft,* Sterling, 1970; *The Bellfounder's Sons* (juvenile), Bobbs, 1971; (self-illustrated) *Lelawala* (juvenile), privately printed by Trillium Books, 1972; (self-illustrated) *Tales from the Niagara,* privately printed by Trillium Books, 1973; (self-illustrated) *Three Fables* (juvenile), privately printed by Trillium Books, 1974; (self-illustrated) *Insiders or Outsiders* (poems), privately printed by Trillium Books, 1974. Stories, articles, poems, and illustrations have been published in magazines in Netherlands, England, Canada, and United States.

LINI R. GROL

As he grew up, Peter quiet and serious, liked to go on long hikes in the country with only his sketchbook for company. ■ (From *The Bellfounder's Sons* by Lini R. Grol. Illustrated by Robert Quackenbush.)

WORK IN PROGRESS: Two novels, *Out of the Dark* and *The Stepmother.*

SIDELIGHTS: "My viewpoints can be found in my writing, and depend very much on the audience, age or theme I try to convey. I am a Christian and rather conservative in my views. Consideration of the fellowmen is my main theme in life."

Three of Lini Grol's poems were read at the National Arts Centre in Ottawa on May 17, 1970, as part of the program marking the 25th anniversary of the liberation of the Netherlands. The celebration was organized by Canadians from Holland.

FOR MORE INFORMATION SEE: The St. Catharines Standard, May 25, 1972.

GROSS, Sarah Chokla 1906-

PERSONAL: Born October 13, 1906, in New York, N.Y.; daughter of Louis Moses (a civil engineer) and Bassetta (Shore) Chokla; married Benjamin Gross (a manufacturer of house dresses), August 9, 1937 (died August 29, 1974); children: Emily Jane (deceased). *Education:* Southern Methodist University, B.A., 1926, M.A., 1928; further graduate studies at Columbia University, 1934-35, and University of Texas, 1935-37. *Home:* 11 Newkirk Ave., East Rockaway, N.Y. 11518.

CAREER: Teaching fellow, 1926-28; instructor in English at Southern Methodist University, Dallas, Tex., 1928-34, University of Texas, Austin, instructor in English, 1935-37, and School of General Studies, Columbia University, New York, N.Y., 1956-57; Franklin Watts, Inc., New York, N.Y., an editor of children's books, 1959-70. Regular reviewer for *Dallas Morning* News, 1930-32 (associate editor of book page in the 1930's), *Sunday New York Times* Book Section, 1947-62, and *Library Journal,* 1963—; editor of *Broadside* (printed newsletter of Theatre Library Association), 1940-72. *Member:* Women's National Book Association, Theatre Library Association, Long Island Book Collectors.

WRITINGS: (Translator) Claude Cenac, *Four Paws into Adventure,* Watts, 1965; (translator) Rene Guillot, *Fonabio and the Lion,* Watts, 1966; (translator) Charles Perrault, editor, *Famous Fairy Tales,* Watts, 1967; (editor) *Every Child's Book of Verse,* Watts, 1968. Editor, *Long Island Book Collector's Journal,* 1972, 1975.

WORK IN PROGRESS: Editing a personal journal, *Green Girl.*

SIDELIGHTS: "Miniature books, children's books, books on theatre and costume, [and] fine presses are among my collecting interests—as are antiques, especially glass. I started the Book Fair at Marion Street School in Lynbrook, Long Island—the oldest continuously observed annual

SARAH CHOKLA GROSS

Under her breath—but loud enough for her anger to be known—she said ugly words. ■ (From *Famous Fairy Tales* by Charles Perrault. Illustrated by Charles Mozley. Translated by Sarah Chokla Gross.)

school book fair in the U.S. as far as I know (it began in 1949).''

Her interest in book fairs brought about a little manual she prepared for the Children's Book Council, *Planning a School Book Fair,* 1970.

GUNSTON, William Tudor 1927- (Bill Gunston)

PERSONAL: Born March 1, 1927, in London, England; son of William John (a professional soldier and linguist) and Stella Hazelwood (Cooper) Gunston; married Margaret Anne Jolliff, October 10, 1964; children: Jeannette Christina, Stephanie Elaine Tracy. *Education:* University of Durham, Inter-B.Sc., 1946; attended Northampton College of Advanced Technology (now The City University), London, 1948-51. *Politics:* Conservative. *Religion:* Church of England. *Home and office:* Foxbreak, Courts Mount Rd., Haslemere, Surrey GU27-2PP, England. *Agent:* Donald Copeman, 52 Bloomsbury St., London WC1B-3QT, England.

CAREER: Iliffe & Sons, London, England, member of editorial staff of *Flight International,* 1951-54, and technical editor, 1955-64, technology editor of *Science Journal,* 1964-70; free-lance writer, 1970—. *Military service:* Royal Air Force, flying instructor, 1945-48. *Member:* Association of British Science Writers, Circle of Aviation Writers (chairman, 1956, 1961).

WRITINGS—All under name Bill Gunston: *Your Book of Light* (juvenile), Faber, 1968; *Hydrofoils and Hovercraft,* Doubleday, 1968; *Flight Handbook,* Iliffe, 1968; (with John W. R. Taylor, Kenneth Munson, and John W. Wood) *The Lore of Flight,* Time-Life, 1970; *The Jet Age,* Arthur Barker, 1972; *Transport Problems and Prospects,* Dutton, 1972; *Transport Technology,* Crowell-Collier, 1972; (contributor) Edward de Bono, editor, *Technology Today,* Routledge & Kegan Paul, 1972; (with Frank Howard) *The Conquest of the Air,* Random House, 1973; *Bombers of the West,* Scribner, 1973; *Shaping Metals* (young adult), Macdonald & Co., 1974; *Attack Aircraft of the West,* Scribner, 1974; *Philatelist's Companion,* David & Charles, 1974.

Writer of materials for industry, business, government, and education and research institutions, including Nuffield Foundation, Ford Foundation, UNESCO, British Government, Rutherford High Energy Laboratory, oil companies, British Broadcasting Corp., Hughes Aircraft, and Rolls-Royce.

Contributor to encyclopedias and yearbooks, including *National Encyclopedia, Aviation Encyclopedia, Junior Encyclopedia, Brassey's Annual and Defence Yearbook, Aircraft Annual, Jane's All the World's Aircraft* (annual), *Young Scientist's Annual,* and *Look and Learn Annual.*

Contributor to about seventy magazines, juvenile periodicals, and newspapers all over the world, including *New Scientist, Aircraft* (Australia), *Speed and Power, Battle* and *Aeroplane Monthly.*

WORK IN PROGRESS: A large dictionary of advanced technology, especially about aerospace subjects; a book about NADGE, the European and NATO defense system;

eleven other adult nonfiction books; seven juvenile books.

SIDELIGHTS: "I left my old firm in 1970 ... and cast around looking for a job (and the best offers were all outside the United Kingdom), but first I had to clear a vast backlog of free-lance work. I am still trying to clear it, but the pile is now twice as large. I have a golden rule for authors: if you are daunted at the size of the task, or the amount of research needed, just sit down and write the book. When it is finished you will wonder why you were worried.''

GURKO, Leo 1914-

PERSONAL: Born January 4, 1914, in Warsaw, Poland; son of Adolph (merchant) and Renia (Kaye) Gurko; married Miriam Berwitz (writer), February 3, 1934; children: Stephen, Jane. *Education:* College of the City of Detroit, B.A., 1931; University of Wisconsin, M.A., 1932, Ph.D., 1934. *Home:* 258 Riverside Dr., New York, N.Y. 10025. *Office:* Hunter College, 695 Park Ave., New York, N.Y. 10021.

CAREER: G. P. Putnam's Sons, New York, N.Y., member, editorial staff, 1934-36; free-lance writer, 1936-38; Hunter College, New York, N.Y., 1938—, began as instructor in English, now professor of English, served as chairman of English department, 1954-60. Macmillan Co., New York, N.Y., publisher's reader, 1936-62. *Member:* Modern Language Association, National Council of Teachers of English, American Association of University

LEO GURKO

Professors. *Awards, honors:* Dodd, Mead faculty fellowship, 1946; fellowship, Ford Foundation fund for the advancement of education, 1953-54.

WRITINGS: The Angry Decade, Dodd, 1947; *Heroes, Highbrows, and the Popular Mind,* Bobbs, 1953; *Tom Paine, Freedom's Apostle,* Crowell, 1957; *Joseph Conrad: Giant in Exile,* Macmillan, 1962; *The Two Lives of Joseph Conrad,* Crowell, 1965; *Ernest Hemingway and the Pursuit of Heroism,* Crowell, 1968; *Thomas Wolfe: Beyond the Romantic Ego,* Crowell, 1975. Contributor to professional journals.

SIDELIGHTS: Competent in French and German.

FOR MORE INFORMATION SEE: Third Book of Junior Authors, edited by de Montreville and Hill, H. W. Wilson, 1972; *Horn Book,* October, 1975.

GURKO, Miriam

PERSONAL: Born in Union City, N.J.; daughter of Jacob and Rebecca (Littauer) Berwitz; married Leo Gurko (an English professor and writer), February 3, 1934; children: Stephen, Jane. *Education:* New York University, student, 1929-31; University of Wisconsin, B.A., 1934. *Home:* 258 Riverside Dr., New York, N.Y. 10025.

CAREER: Editorial work, publicity, and research, New York, N.Y., 1934-38. *Member:* Authors Guild of Authors League of America, Phi Beta Kappa.

In Washington, President Andrew Jackson was indignant. It seemed inconceivable to the old Indian fighter that a large and powerful white army could not seek out and destroy one small fraction of an Indian tribe. (From *The Black Hawk War* by Miriam Gurko. Illustrated by Richard Cuffari.)

WRITINGS: The Lives and Times of Peter Cooper, Crowell, 1959; *Restless Spirit: The Life of Edna St. Vincent Millay,* Crowell, 1962; *Clarence Darrow,* Crowell, 1965; *Indian America: The Black Hawk War,* Crowell, 1970; *The Ladies of Seneca Falls: The Birth of the Woman's Rights Movement,* Macmillan, 1974. Contributor to magazines.

SIDELIGHTS: "I have always been fascinated by history and by the lives of those individuals who have contributed to our history. I feel that we cannot fully understand our own times and even ourselves without some knowledge of where we came from and how we arrived at our present ways of living and thinking. My aim in writing for young people is to disclose their own backgrounds to them and to kindle their interest in further exploration along these lines. My last book, *The Ladies of Seneca Falls,* was written especially to portray the lives and accomplishments of the many remarkable women who have been so regrettably ignored in the pages of most historical works."

FOR MORE INFORMATION SEE: Third Book of Junior Authors, edited by de Montreville and Hill, 1972; *Horn Book,* October, 1974.

MIRIAM GURKO

HAHN, James (Sage) 1947-

PERSONAL: Born May 24, 1947, in Chicago, Ill.; son of James Peter (a designer and manufacturer) and Joan (Redfern) Hahn; married Mona Lynn Lowery (a writer), April 17, 1971. *Education:* Attended Wright City College, 1965-67; Northwestern University, B.A., 1970. *Politics:* Independent. *Religion:* Roman Catholic. *Home and office:* 1500 Chicago Ave., Apt. 622, Evanston, Ill. 60201.

CAREER: Free-lance writer and photographer for newspapers, magazines, and books. Lecturer. *Member:* Children's Reading Round Table.

WRITINGS—Children's books with wife, Lynn Lowery Hahn: *Recycling: Re-Using Our World's Solid Wastes,* Watts, 1973; *Plastics: A First Book,* Watts, 1974; *The Metric System,* Watts, 1975; *Environmental Careers,* Watts, 1976.

WORK IN PROGRESS: Rock n' Roll Boy Is Gone, a novel; two books of environmental science fiction for children, with wife, Lynn Lowery Hahn.

SIDELIGHTS: "Young people, returning newspapers, magazines, bottles, tin and aluminum cans to recycling centers, inspired me to begin researching and writing *Recycling: Re-using Our World's Solid Wastes.* Since many of these young people wanted to know more about recycling (and so did I), more about what happens to the paper, glass, and metal once it leaves the recycling center, and why it is important to recycle, I decided to begin researching the topic full time. After one year of researching and writing, and one year of finding the right publisher, *Recycling* was published.

"Plastics, plastics, and more plastics! Plastics are everywhere today! I was really curious about plastics and wanted to know all about their history, how they are made, how they are used in medicine, and how they will be used in the future. After one year of curious research and writing, the result was the book, *Plastics.*

"Because I am a curious person, I write for people of any age who are also curious, so we can share a learning experience together. Research for non-fiction books takes a lot of time. I read every newspaper and magazine article and book published on the topic I am curious about. Then, I write letters and talk to people who are involved in the topic, asking them questions that satisfy my curiosity.

"Then, I sit down with my notes and write, in long hand for about three hours every day, the first draft of the book. I type the second, third, and as many other drafts as it takes to make my writing understandable. And when the book is finally published, I just want to share my curious experiences with as many people as I can, and hope that their curiosities are satisfied through my writings."

HOBBIES AND OTHER INTERESTS: Avant garde poetry and fiction, "walking in the uncommon area of large cities."

FOR MORE INFORMATION SEE: *Evanston Review*, February 21, 1974.

HAHN, (Mona) Lynn 1949-

PERSONAL: Born July 3, 1949, in Cleveland, Ohio; daughter of James William (a boilermaker) and Mona Alice (Benjamin) Lowery; married James Hahn (a writer), April 17, 1971. *Education:* Northwestern University, B.S., 1971. *Politics:* Independent. *Religion:* United Church of Christ. *Home and office:* 1500 Chicago Ave., Apt. 622, Evanston, Ill. 60201.

CAREER: Writer for newspapers, magazines, and books. Lecturer and photographer. *Member:* Children's Reading Round Table, Kappa Tau Alpha.

WRITINGS—Children's books with husband, James Hahn: *Recycling: Re-Using Our World's Solid Wastes,* Watts, 1973; *Plastics: A First Book,* Watts, 1974; *The Metric System,* Watts, 1975; *Environmental Careers,* Watts, 1976. Contributor to Chicago newspapers.

WORK IN PROGRESS: The Scrapbook from the Blue Jean Queen, a novel; two books of environmental science fiction for children, with husband, James Hahn.

SIDELIGHTS: "I began writing stories and thinking about writing as a career, when I was in the second grade. My elementary school published a weekly newspaper, so I had the thrill of seeing my work in print. During the third, fourth, fifth, and sixth grades, I was lucky enough to receive a great deal of encouragement and guidance from my teacher, Mrs. Doris Griffith. She organized a creative writing seminar, for which students wrote poems and stories; advised our class on the publication of our school newspaper; and taught her students to thoroughly research, organize, and write about subjects that interested us. I am sure that early training made writing easier for me in high school and college and still helps me with my writing today.

"I began writing non-fiction books because I wanted to find out more about the world around me. Some of my books, such as *Recycling,* began as a result of personal experience. I developed ideas for other books after seeing a topic mentioned in newspapers or magazines or hearing about it on radio or television.

"The idea for *The Metric System* really developed as a combination of news exposure and personal experience. I knew that the U.S. Congress was considering making the metric system the official system of measurement in the United States. At the same time I began to notice that the canned goods, bottles, and soaps I bought were labeled with both metric and customary units of quantity. The patterns I used for sewing included metric measurement and I began to see advertisements for metric tools in newspapers and catalogs. I wondered why almost all of the rest of the world used the metric system while the United States used the customary system, so I began to do some research on the history of the metric system. Correspondence with the International Bureau of Weights and Measures in Sevres, France, provided a lot of fascinating information and photographs, and encouraged me to search further.

Environmental Careers was also a result of personal experience combined with media exposure. While talking with young people at many schools and libraries about *Recycling,* I discovered they have a great interest in all kinds of environmental topics. Those I talked with wanted to do things to help our environment, but many thought the only environmental careers available were as conservationists

LYNN HAHN

and park rangers. I had seen many help-wanted ads in newspapers for environmental engineers, sewage chemists, aquatic biologists, so I decided to find out more about these and other environmental career opportunities.

I think one of the writer's most important jobs is to be observant and aware of changes in the world. This means reading all kinds of newspapers, magazines, and books, listening to news reports, and observing people, nature, and other aspects of the world.

HOBBIES AND OTHER INTERESTS: Creative photography and photographic processing, designing and sewing clothing, baking, Russian studies (has studied in the Soviet Union).

FOR MORE INFORMATION SEE: Evanston Review, February 21, 1974.

HAMMERMAN, Gay M(orenus) 1926-

PERSONAL: Born May 14, 1926, in Richmond, Va.; daughter of Richard Thomas (an architect) and Constance (Gay) Morenus; married Herbert Hammerman (an economist), September 3, 1955; children: Joseph Richard, Daniel Aaron. *Education:* University of North Carolina at Greensboro, student, 1943-45; University of North Carolina at Chapel Hill, A.B., 1947; Radcliffe College, M.A., 1949. *Politics:* Democrat. *Residence:* Arlington, Va. *Office address:* Historical Evaluation & Research Organization, P.O. Box 157, Dunn Loring, Va. 22027.

CAREER: Mount Vernon Seminary and Junior College, Washington, D.C., teacher of history and government, 1949-51; Department of the Army, Office of the Chief of Military History, Washington, D.C., copy editor, then editor and indexer, 1951-55; U.S. Department of State, Washington, D.C., editor, 1955-57; Historical Evaluation & Research Organization (HERO), Dunn Loring, Va., writer and editor, 1963—. *Member:* Phi Beta Kappa.

WRITINGS: (Contributor) Trevor Nevitt Dupuy, editor, *Holidays: Days of Significance for All Americans* (young adult), Watts, 1965; (with Dupuy) *The Military History of World War I, Volume III: Stalemate in the Trenches: November 1914-March 1918* (young adult), Watts, 1967; (contributor) Dupuy, editor, *The Almanac of World Military Power,* T. N. Dupuy Associates, in association with Stackpole, 1970; (with Dupuy) *The Military History of Revolutionary War Land Battles* (juvenile), Watts, 1970.

WORK IN PROGRESS: A documentary history of arms control and disarmament; research on public opinion and public attitudes on national and international issues; research on the American Revolution.

HOBBIES AND OTHER INTERESTS: Modern dance, cats, gardening, conservation, cooking, comparative religion, mythology, the Bible.

HANCOCK, Sibyl 1940-

PERSONAL: Born November 10, 1940, in Pasadena, Tex.; daughter of Briten E. (a department manager for Shell Oil Co.) and Floreine (Fisher) Norwood; married Thomas L. Hancock (a school administrator), August 21, 1965; chil-

SIBYL HANCOCK

dren: Kevin Thomas. *Education:* Attended Sam Houston State University, 1959-61, and University of Houston, 1963-65. *Religion:* Methodist. *Home:* 210 Coronation, Houston, Tex. 77034.

CAREER: Free-lance writer. Stenographer for Ellington Air Force Base, 1962. *Member:* National Writers Club, Society of Children's Book Writers (charter member), Associated Authors of Children's Literature (charter member), Pasadena Writers Club (president, 1966, 1973), Houston Writers Workshop, Friends of the Pasadena Public Library (vice-president, 1973). *Awards, honors:* First prize for best children's book from Texas Pen Women, 1970, for *Let's Learn Hawaiian.*

WRITINGS—For children, except where noted: (With Doris Sadler) *Let's Learn Hawaiian,* Tuttle, 1969; *Mario's Mystery Machine,* Putnam, 1972; *Mosshaven* (adult gothic novel), Beagle, 1973; *The Grizzly Bear,* Steck, 1974; *The Blazing Hills,* Putnam, in press; *Theodore Roosevelt,* Putnam, in press; *Bill Pickett,* Harcourt, in press; *Noah's Ark,* Concordia, in press. Contributor to *Texas Star, Humpty Dumpty,* and *Kidstuff.* Juvenile book critic, *Houston Chronicle,* 1973—.

WORK IN PROGRESS: A see-and-read history book.

SIDELIGHTS: "I was born in Pasadena, Texas and have lived all my life in this area. Living in a Texas coastal town has influenced my writing in a number of ways. I am lucky to be able to draw upon a heritage of cowboys riding the range, of booming oil wells, and of the experiences in riding out hurricanes. In this part of Texas we also enjoy the traditions of the Deep South. These things often can be found in the stories I create.

"My childhood was a happy one. My mother read to me every day when I was small, and I have loved books for as long as I can remember. I spent many hours playing with my sister in a playhouse in our backyard. Our playhouse had electricity, glass windows and a door, because it had once been someone's workshop. There were shelves filled with not only books, but comic books which I also enjoyed.

"I had many pets, and a favorite of mine was a calico cat who produced many beautiful kittens. I used to write stories about my pets, my family and even about comic book characters.

"As I grew older I began to re-write scenes in books, making the characters act and talk the way I believed they should. I suppose the groundwork was being laid for my career as a writer, but I really didn't know it at the time.

"My father has always had an interest in science and in unusual science-based stories. My mother loves mysteries, as well as nature stories. So, with both my parents influencing me, I developed an interest in many fields. I liked reading science-fiction, historical fiction, mysteries, biographies, and books about animals. In time all my reading gave me a good background for my writing.

"I began to write during my last years in college. I was so full of stories and ideas that I just began writing them down. There was no big decision made to become an author. I just started writing because it seemed the natural thing for me to do. And before I knew it, my stories began to sell to publishers. My family has always helped by encouraging me in my writing. My husband has been very understanding and helps care for our little boy when I'm sometimes so involved in a story, it's hard to put my pencil aside."

HOBBIES AND OTHER INTERESTS: Collecting old children's books, reading, astronomy.

HANNA, Paul R(obert) 1902-

PERSONAL: Born June 21, 1902, in Sioux City, Iowa; son of George Archibald and Regula (Figi) Hanna; married Jean Shuman (a writer of textbooks), August 20, 1926, children: Emily-Jean (Mrs. Lester H. Clark), John Paul, Robert Shuman. *Education:* Hamline University, A.B. (magna cum laude), 1924; Columbia University, A.M., 1925, Ph.D., 1929. *Politics:* Republican. *Religion:* Methodist. *Home:* 12371 Cabrillo Hwy., Pescadero, Calif. 94060; and Mitchell Pl. #20, Stanford, Calif. 94305.

CAREER: Superintendent of schools, West Winfield, N.Y., 1925-27; Columbia University, New York, N.Y., research associate, Lincoln School, 1928-35, assistant professor of education, Teachers College, 1930-35; Stanford University, Stanford, Calif., associate professor, 1935-37, professor of education, 1937-54, director of Stanford Services (war contracts—research and training), 1942-44; Lee L. Jacks Professor of Child Education, 1954-68, director of Stanford International Development Education Center, 1963-68, emeritus Jacks Professor and emeritus director of International Development Education Center, 1968—. National director of U.S. Council for Conservation Education, 1936-39; U.S. Agency for International Development (originally U.S. Mutual Security Agency), director of Educational Division, Philippines, 1952-53, coordinator of University of the Philippines-Stanford University Contract, 1953-56, coordinator of Philippine Department of Education-Stanford University Contract, 1956-60; U.S. Department of State, chairman of educational and cultural exchanges team to Yugoslavia, 1966, specialist-consultant to four African governments on educational reform, 1967. American Council on Education, member of Commission on International Education, 1964-68; Atlantic Council and Atlantic Institute, member of committee on Atlantic stud-

What he planned to build was a secret! ■ (From *Mario's Mystery Machine* by Sibyl Hancock. Illustrated by Tomie de Paola.)

PAUL R. HANNA

ies, 1964-72. Educational consultant to U.S. National Resources Planning Board, 1939-42, War Department, 1942-44, War Relocation Authority, 1942-45, U.S. Secretary of War (on German education), 1947, U.S. Office of Education, 1963-72, to universities and colleges in United States and abroad, and U.S. school systems. Member of international board, Atlantic Colleges, 1966-69; member of board of directors, W. Clement and Jessie V. Stone Foundation, 1969-72, Videorecord Corp. of America, 1971-73, Infomedia, Inc., 1972-75, U.S. National Commission for UNESCO, 1972—; member of National Trust for Historic Preservation, 1968—, Environmental Defense Fund, 1969—; trustee of Castilleja School and United World Colleges.

MEMBER: National Education Association, American Educational Research Association (chairman of committee on international relations, 1964-66), National Society for the Study of Education, Childhood Education Association International, American Association for the Advancement of Science (fellow), American Overseas Educators Association, Society for International Development, Comparative Education Society (member of board of directors), American Academy of Political and Social Science, National Planning Association, Asia Society, John Dewey Society, Society for the History of Technology, Society for Architectural Historians, American Institute of Biological Sciences, National Council of Teachers of English, Foreign Policy Association (member of national council), World Affairs Council, American Forestry Association, Phi Delta

Kappa, Kappa Delta Pi, Phi Gamma Mu, Theta Chi, Cosmos Club (Washington, D.C.), Bohemian Club (San Francisco). *Awards, honors:* D.Ped., Hamline University, 1937; senior fellow, East-West Center, University of Hawaii, 1965.

WRITINGS—Adult books: (With others) *Youth Serves the Community,* Appleton, for Progressive Education Association, 1936; (editor) *Aviation Education Source Book,* Hastings House, 1946; (editor) *Education: An Instrument of National Goals,* McGraw, 1962; (with others) *Geography in the Teaching of Social Studies: Concepts and Skills,* Houghton, 1966; (with others) *Phoneme-Grapheme Correspondences as Cues to Spelling Improvement,* U.S. Office of Education, 1966; (with wife, Jean S. Hanna, and Richard E. Hodges) *Spelling: Structure and Strategies,* Houghton, 1971.

Textbooks, published by Scott, Foresman, except as noted: (With Mary Elizabeth Barry) *Wonder Flights of Long Ago,* Appleton, 1930; (with Jesse H. Newlon) *The Newlon-Hanna Speller,* Houghton, 1933, and other variously titled spellers, including *The Day-by-Day Speller,* seven books, 1942; (with Genevieve Anderson and William S. Gray) *Peter's Family,* 1935, 4th edition, 1949; (with Anderson and Gray) *David's Friends at School,* 1936, revised edition published as *Hello, David,* 1943; (with Anderson and Gray) *Susan's Neighbors at Work,* 1937, revised edition published as *Someday Soon: A Study of a Community and Its Workers,* 1947; (with Anderson and Gray) *Centerville,* 1938, revised edition published as *New Centerville,* 1948; (with Gray and Gladys Potter) *Without Machinery,* 1939; (with Potter and I. James Quillen) *Ten Communities,* 1940; (with Paul B. Sears) *This Useful World,* 1941; (with Edward A. Krug) *Marketing the Things We Use,* 1943, 2nd edition, 1953; (with Quillen and Sears) *Making the Goods We Need,* 1943, 2nd edition, 1953.

(With Clyde F. Kohn) *Cross-Country: Geography for Children,* 1950; (with Genevieve Anderson and William S. Gray) *Tom and Susan,* 1951; (with Edna Fay Campbell) *Our World and How We Use It,* 1953; (with Jean S. Hanna) *Building Spelling Power,* seven books, Houghton, 1956; (with Anderson and Gray) *At School,* 1956; (with Anderson and Gray) *At Home,* 1956; (with Anderson and Gray) *In the Neighborhood,* 1958; (with Anderson and Kohn) *In City, Town, and Country,* 1959; (with Kohn and Robert A. Lively) *In All Our States,* 1960; (with Kohn and Lively) *In the Americas,* 1962; (with Kohn, Lively, and Helen F. Wise) *Living and Learning Together,* 1962; (with Jean S. Hanna) *First Steps: A Speller for Beginners,* Houghton, 1963; (with Kohn and Lively) *Beyond the Americas,* 1964; (with others) *Power to Spell,* eight books, Houghton, 1967. Co-author of teacher's editions and guidebooks accompanying many of the textbooks above.

Member of editorial board, *Building America,* 1930-44, *World Book Encyclopedia,* 1936-66, *Review of Educational Research,* 1961-65, American Educational Press, 1964-70, *My Weekly Reader,* and Encyclopaedia Britannica Films; editorial adviser, "Elementary School Professional Textbook" series, Houghton, 1964-69.

WORK IN PROGRESS: A book on his Stanford University home which was designed by Frank Lloyd Wright; linguistic research for cues to voice typewriter; an autobiography.

SIDELIGHTS: "I grew up in Minnesota in a minister's family where we were encouraged to value the literature of the mind and the spirit. I knew when I entered high school that I wanted to be a teacher and a writer. My college years helped enormously to give me a structure of knowledge and writing skills.

"As a young teacher just out of college, I became aware of the inferior quality of school books and decided to do something about it. My first effort was a children's book on mythical flying, entitled *Wonder Flights of Long Ago.* School children helped collect over fifty of the great stories—'The Magic Carpet,' 'The Flying Trunk,' 'Daedalus and Icarus,' 'Pegasus,' etc. We selected the dozen stories most loved by the children and prepared them for printing. Lynd Ward, the famous artist, drew the sketches for the stories.

"With this book on the library shelves, my wife and I proceeded to lay out a forty-year plan of research and publishing in the language arts curriculum of the elementary schools, emphasizing linguistics and orthography (spelling). More then twenty-seven million copies of these textbooks have been used by school children of this nation. We have sought to help the pupil discover the sets of rules which will give him the power to spell a very large vocabulary without having to memorize each spelling word as a separate learning act. This approach to encoding (spelling) is generally followed today in textbooks throughout the English speaking world.

"Very early I became conscious of the need for a comprehensive, multi-discipline approach to textbooks in the elementary school social sciences. In the 1920's and 30's only geography and history were taught in the lower schools. So we assembled a team of scholars in economics, political science, sociology, anthropology, geography, and history and our team planned a series of school texts for grades one through eight that would introduce young people to the entire set of interdependent communities of men—from the family community, the neighborhood, the local, state, region, national communities, to the global communities. This endeavor resulted in more than ten million social science textbooks being used by U.S. schools.

"I have written for adults but it is more satisfying to read letters from school children who have read these texts and have expressed pleasure as well as offered comments for improvements in the series."

HARDY, David A(ndrews) 1936-

PERSONAL: Born April 10, 1936, in Birmingham, England; son of Arthur (a violinist) and Lilian (Andrews) Hardy; married Ruth Margaret Fearn (a music teacher), 1975; children: (prior marriage) Karen Dawn. *Education:* Attended private school in England until eleven, and grammar school, 1947-52. *Religion:* Church of England. *Home:* 99 Southam Rd., Hall Green, Birmingham B28 OAB, England. *Office:* Astro Art, 99 Southam Rd., Hall Green, Birmingham B28 OAB, England.

CAREER: Laboratory technician, 1952-54; commercial artist with Cadbury Bros. Ltd., Bournville, England, 1956-65; free-lance artist and writer, 1965—. *Military service:* Royal Air Force, 1954-56. *Member:* Royal Astronomical Society (fellow), British Interplanetary Society (associate fellow), British Astronomical Association, Lincoln Astronomical Society (president, 1969-72; vice-president, 1972—).

ILLUSTRATOR: M. T. Bizony, general editor, *The Space Encyclopedia: A Guide to Astronomy and Space Research,* 2nd revised edition, Dutton, 1960; Patrick Moore, *Astronomy,* Oldbourne Press, 1961, second edition, 1967, published as *Story of Astronomy,* Macdonald, 1972; Colin Ronan, *The Stars,* Bodley Head, 1965; Colin Ronan, *The Universe,* Oxford University Press, 1966; W. E. Swinton, *The Earth Tells Its Story,* Bodley Head, 1967; J. Petrie, *The Earth,* Oxford University Press, 1967; Patrick Moore, *Space,* Lutterworth Press, 1968; *The New Space Encyclopedia,* Artemis, 1969; Patrick Moore, *Astronomy for "O" Level,* Duckworth, 1970; Patrick Moore, *Mars: The Red World,* World's Work, 1971; co-author with Patrick A. Moore, *The Challenge of the Stars: A Forecast of the Future of the Universe,* Rand, 1972; Brenda Thompson, editor, *Volcanoes,* Sidgwick and Jackson, 1974; Brenda Thompson, editor, *Spaceship Earth,* Sidgwick and Jackson, 1975; *The Solar System,* World's Work, 1975; *Rockets and Satellites,* World's Work, 1976. Also illustrated various children's books, including Methuen's "Outlines," between 1957-1961. Writings include science and art articles, illustration and designing of book jackets, including science fiction in the United States, United Kingdom and Germany and many film strips for visual publications.

SIDELIGHTS: "My chief motivation, since the early 1950's, has been to present an *accurate* picture of space

DAVID A. HARDY

(From *Challenge of the Stars* by Patrick Moore and David A. Hardy. Illustrated by David A. Hardy.)

Something about the Author

and astronomy—in fact any science—especially to children, as so many bad books, cheaply illustrated, have been on sale."

FOR MORE INFORMATION SEE: Science in Action, February 6, 1969; *Canvas,* June, 1969; *Spaceflight,* January, 1970; *Pictures & Prints,* spring, 1970.

HARMELINK, Barbara (Mary)

PERSONAL: Born in Ningpo, China; daughter of Albert Allan (a clergyman) and Florence (Searle) Conibear; married Herman Harmelink III (a clergyman and author), August 11, 1959; children: Herman Alan, Lindsay Alexandra. *Education:* University of Birmingham, B.A. (honors in history), 1952, Certificate of Education, 1953. *Religion:* Reformed Church in America. *Residence:* Poughkeepsie, N.Y. 12603.

CAREER: Kingsley School for Girls, Horley, Surrey, England, head of history department, 1953-55; Selhurst Grammar School for Girls, Croydon, Surrey, England, teacher of history, 1955-59. Member of women's committee, Japanese International Christian University; member of Board of World Missions, Reformed Church in America; director, Reformed Church Weekday Nursery, 1972-1975.

WRITINGS: (Contributor) *Program Book for 1965,* Half Moon Press, 1965; *A White Christmas Worship Service,* Japan International Christian University, 1965; *Florence*

BARBARA HARMELINK

Nightingale: Founder of Modern Nursing (juvenile), Watts, 1969.

WORK IN PROGRESS: Research on Queen Victoria and other nineteenth-century material in English history, and on African history, especially the roots of the American Negro and folklore.

SIDELIGHTS: "My chief hobby, besides gardening, is music. I play the piano, spent two years at the Guildhall School of Music in London studying classical Spanish guitar, was a member of the Royal Choral Society in London under the direction of Sir Malcolm Sargent, and currently sing in my local church choir.

"I am an avid opera and ballet-goer wherever possible, mostly in New York, sometimes in Europe. My children take me to zoos and science museums, but I prefer art galleries, cathedrals, country estates, arboretums and botanical gardens. Latin America fascinates me so I have started to study Spanish, which I have practised in Spain, Peru and Venezuela. I have also visited Brazil, West Africa, and spent two months in South Africa on a leader-exchange programme with my husband. I also speak French, have a working knowledge of German, and have travelled extensively in Western Europe."

HARRISON, Deloris 1938-

PERSONAL: Born February 4, 1938, in Bedford, Va.; daughter of Ernest and Lucy (a hospital administrator; maiden name, Hall) Harrison; children: Germaine Auguste Netzband. *Education:* St. Joseph's College for Women, Brooklyn, N.Y., A.B., 1958; New York University, A.M., 1963. *Home address:* P.O. Box 698, Hanover, N.H. 03755. *Agent:* Phyllis Westberg, Harold Ober Associates, Inc., 40 East 49th St., New York, N.Y. 10017. *Office:* Orford High School, Orford, N.H. 03777.

CAREER: High school teacher of English in New York, N.Y., 1961-68; Dartmouth College, Dartmouth, N.H., assistant professor of English, 1970-72; Windham College, Putney, Vt., assistant professor of creative writing, 1972-74; Orford High School, Orford, N.H., teacher of English, 1974—. *Awards, honors:* Fulbright exchange teacher in the Netherlands, 1966-67; Bread Loaf Writers' Conference fellowship, 1969.

WRITINGS: (Editor) *We Shall Live in Peace: The Teachings of Martin Luther King* (juvenile), Hawthorn, 1968; *The Bannekers of Bannaky Springs* (juvenile), Hawthorn, 1970; *Journey All Alone* (young adult book), Dial, 1971.

WORK IN PROGRESS: The Notebook of Jason Ellis, a novel told in diary form about a college student who lost both his white mother and black father.

SIDELIGHTS: "Although I grew up in New York City's Harlem, I was born on a farm in Virginia in the same house that my mother and all her eight brothers and sisters were born in. As an only child myself, I have always been fascinated by my parents who both came from large families (my father was one of eight children) and by the lives of people who differed from me.

"My first two published books deal with the thinking and

lives of two black men who were influential to their times: Banneker to the Revolutionary period and Martin Luther King, Jr., to the period of civil rights struggles in the South. These books were exciting to research, to uncover and develop as it has always been exciting for me to learn about other people's lives.

"But when I think of what I have always loved about writing and what has kept me enthralled with it since the fourth grade, it has been the ability to recall and spin the tales of my own experiences and those of the people I have known and grown up with. That I guess is why writing *Journey All Alone* was so easy for me because Mildren's life was so close to the life I knew so well. Still for me writing is an art and not a reproduction. It is the art of carving out of actual experience a new and fresh view of life that will enlighten and enrich everyone."

. . . the idea that he would go to school and have new books to read pleased him. He only wished that his grandmother were alive to see him on the first day of school. ■ (From *The Bannekers of Bannaky Springs* by Deloris Harrison. Illustrated by David Hodges.)

HARWOOD, Pearl Augusta (Bragdon) 1903-

PERSONAL: Born December 21, 1903, in Grafton, Mass.; daughter of Clifford Sawyer (a school superintendent) and Helen (Woodside) Bragdon; married Lester E. Harwood (now a life underwriter), 1933. *Education:* Mount Holyoke College, A.B.; Boston University, M.Ed.; San Jose State College, library training. *Religion:* Protestant. *Home:* San Marcos, Calif.

CAREER: San Jose (Calif.) Unified School District, home teacher, 1948-54; Las Lomitas (Calif.) School District, elementary librarian at Atherton, 1955-57; public library work with children in Alameda and Ventura counties, and Los Gatos, Calif., 1955, and 1958-62; Vista (Calif.) School District, home teacher, 1963—. Sometime worker in psychological and nursery school fields.

DELORIS HARRISON

PEARL AUGUSTA HARWOOD

WRITINGS: Mr. Bumba's New Home, Lerner, 1964; *Mr. Bumba Plants a Garden*, Lerner, 1964; *Mr. Bumba and the Orange Grove*, Lerner, 1964; *Mr. Bumba's New Job*, Lerner, 1964; *Mr. Bumba Keeps House*, Lerner, 1964; *Mr. Bumba Has a Party*, Lerner, 1964; *Mr. Bumba Draws a Kitten*, Lerner, 1966; *Mr. Bumba's Four-Legged Company*, Lerner, 1966; *Mr. Bumba Rides a Bicycle*, Lerner, 1966; *Mr. Bumba's Tuesday Club*, Lerner, 1966; *The Widdles*, Lerner, 1966; *Mrs. Moon's Story Hour*, Lerner, 1967; *Mrs. Moon and Her Friends*, Lerner, 1967; *Mrs. Moon's Polliwogs*, Lerner, 1967; *Mrs. Moon's Picnic*, Lerner, 1967; *Mrs. Moon Goes Shopping*, Lerner, 1967; *Mrs. Moon's Harbor Trip*, Lerner, 1967; *Mrs. Moon and the Dark Stairs*, Lerner, 1967; *Mrs. Moon's Rescue*, Lerner, 1967; *Mrs. Moon Takes a Drive*, Lerner, 1967; *Mrs. Moon's Cement Hat*, Lerner, 1967.

A Long Vacation for Mr. and Mrs. Bumba, Lerner, 1971; *The Rummage Sale and Mr. and Mrs. Bumba*, Lerner, 1971; *A Special Guest for Mr. and Mrs. Bumba*, Lerner, 1971; *The Make-It Room of Mr. and Mrs. Bumba*, Lerner, 1971; *A Thief Visits Mr. and Mrs. Bumba*, Lerner, 1971; *A Happy Halloween for Mr. and Mrs. Bumba*, Lerner, 1971; *New Year's Day with Mr. and Mrs. Bumba*, Lerner, 1971; *The Carnival with Mr. and Mrs. Bumba*, Lerner, 1971; *Climbing a Mountain with Mr. and Mrs. Bumba*, Lerner, 1971; *The Very Big Problem of Mr. and Mrs. Bumba*, Lerner, 1971. Contributor of over eighty children's stories to periodicals.

SIDELIGHTS: "My husband and I live in southern California, but we came here from the other side of the country—Massachusetts. We do not have any children, but I have been a teacher, a children's librarian, and a camp counsellor—as well as a part-time author! I still work with children as a volunteer, helping pupils who need extra practice in learning to read. My husband gives talks in schools about the care of pets and about the many interesting habits of wild animals. So you see we both have quite a bit to do with children.

"The reason I like to write about *lots* of children is that I was an only child—well, almost. My one sister was so much older that she seemed like another grown-up. I longed to be one of a large family, since there were never many playmates living close to us. Often in the summers our family would make visits to relatives who lived on farms in Maine, where I was always happy. Two of these families had five children each, and the others had four, or at least three. We had wonderful times just being together and playing all sorts of games.

"So many times I have been asked where I got the idea for Mr. Bumba himself. I think it was partly from a book, *The Little Auto*, by Lois Lenski. In that book, Mr. Small was the hero. I noticed how interested children were in that little man. Boys and girls do like to read about the everyday doings of some grown-up, especially if that grown-up is fond of children and enters into their lives with enthusiasm and fun. If they can help him do what he wants to do (or if he can help them), then that makes the story all the more interesting.

"I didn't have any model for Mrs. Moon, but she turned out to be the kind of person who would get along very well with Mr. Bumba. She also had many adventures with the children who lived near her. So when these two people finally met each other, it was easy to see why they would want to get married.

"Many letters ask where I get the ideas for my stories. Well, it's hard to say, but one question I keep asking myself is 'What if ... ?' 'What if Mr. Bumba gets a bicycle and doesn't know how to ride it? What if Mrs. Moon tries to rescue two cats that are up in a tree, and the ladder breaks, leaving her stranded? What if a ball of yarn disappears from Mrs. Bumba's "Make-It" room, and no one knows who the thief is?'

"Some of the ideas for the Mr. and Mrs. Bumba books came from real life happenings that I have watched or lived through myself. For instance, I've seen school carnivals and I've been to rummage sales and folk dancing parties. I've planned new houses and watched them being built. I've climbed mountains with youngsters from a camp, and I used to live in a mobile park. I know how Nicky's social worker would go about finding the right foster home for her. And, of course, everyone at one time or another has visited neighbors on Halloween—only Mr. and Mrs. Bumba helped the boys and girls do it in a new way!

"When I think about the things I've seen and done, and when I ask myself 'What if ... ?', a story just seems to grow and grow. The boys and girls in the story always try to help solve the problem, and usually they succeed."

HASKINS, James 1941-
(Jim Haskins)

PERSONAL: Born September 19, 1941, in Alabama; son of Henry and Julia Haskins. *Education:* Georgetown University, B.A., 1960; Alabama State University, B.S., 1962; University of New Mexico, M.A., 1963; further graduate study at New School for Social Research and Queens College, Flushing, N.Y. *Home:* 668 Riverside Dr., New York, N.Y. 10031. *Agent:* Ronald Hobbs, 211 East 43rd St., New York, N.Y. 10017.

CAREER: Smith Barney & Co., New York, N.Y., stock trader, 1963-65; New York City Board of Education, New York, N.Y., teacher, 1966-68; New School for Social Research, New York, N.Y., instructor in urban education, 1970-72, instructor in psychology of black language, 1971-72; Staten Island Community College, Staten Island, N.Y., instructor in English, 1970-71, director, black writers workshop, 1971-72, assistant professor in urban education, the psychology of black language, 1970—; assistant professor in folklore, children's literature, ethics and morality of education, 1972—. Manhattanville College, Purchase, N.Y., visiting lecturer in urban education and psychology of black language, 1972—; Indiana University-Purdue University, Indianapolis, Ind., visiting summer lecturer in Afro-American folklore and recent black American writing, 1973—;

The Psychology of Black Language, Barnes & Noble, 1973; Snow Sculpture and Ice Carving, Macmillan, 1974.

Juveniles—under name Jim Haskins: Ralph Bunche: A Most Reluctant Hero, Hawthorn, 1974.

FOR MORE INFORMATION SEE: New York Post, February 7, 1970; Manhattan Tribune, March 7, 1970; Christian Science Monitor, March 12, 1970; New Leader, April 16, 1970.

HECHT, Henri Joseph 1922- (Henri Maik)

PERSONAL: Born March 27, 1922, in Paris, France; son of Joseph (a painter and engraver) and Ingrid (Morssing) Hecht; married Irma Chevalier (director of a school), January 22, 1946; children: Sylvain, Frederic, Ingrid. Education: Attended primary and secondary schools in France. Home: Atelier 34 Blvd. Clichy, Paris 18, France.

CAREER: Painter with his own studio in Paris, France, 1956—.

WRITINGS—Self-illustrated children's books under pseudonym Henri Maik: L'Oiseau charmant, Desclee de Brouwer, 1966, translation published in America as The Foolish Bird, Luce, 1968; Flegmatique le Lion, Desclee de Brouwer, 1967, translation published in England as Livingstone the Lion, Evans Brothers, 1969, and in America as

JAMES HASKINS

Manhattan Community Board No. 9; 1972-73; Manhattan Advisory Board, N.Y. Urban League, 1973—; board of directors, The Speedwell Services for Children, 1974—.

WRITINGS—Juveniles: Resistance: Profiles in Nonviolence, Doubleday, 1970; The War and the Protest: Viet Nam, Doubleday, 1971; Revolutionaries: Agents of Change, Lippincott, 1971; A Piece of the Power: Four Black Mayors, Dial, 1972; From Lew Alcindor to Kareem Abdul Jabbar, Lothrop, 1972; Religions, Lippincott, 1973; Jobs in Business and Office, Lothrop, 1974; Adam Clayton Powell: Portrait of a Marching Black, Dial, 1974; Street Gangs: Yesterday and Today, Hastings, 1974; Witchcraft, Mysticism and Magic in the Black World, Doubleday, 1974; Babe Ruth and Hank Aaron: The Home Run Kings, Lothrop, 1974; The Picture Life of Malcolm X, Watts, 1975; The Consumer Movement, Watts, 1975; Fighting Shirley Chisholm, Dial, 1975; The Creoles of Color of New Orleans, Crowell, 1975; The Rights of Youth: Past and Present, Hawthorn, in press; The Story of the Special Olympics, Doubleday, in press.

Adult books—Under name Jim Haskins: Diary of a Harlem Schoolteacher, Grove, 1969; Pinckney Benton Stewart Pinchback, Macmillan, 1973; (editor) Black Manifesto for Education, Morrow, 1973; (with Hugh F. Butts)

HENRI JOSEPH HECHT

(From *The Foolish Bird* by Henri Maik. Illustrated by the author.)

remarked on the absence of meaning in certain texts. After which, I was challenged to do better!

"A difficult task, obviously—all the more so, because I am not a writer, and because I like doing my books solely drawing on my talents as a painter, trying, all the same, to include in them a certain sense of the unexpected and adventure, and the childlike freshness that lies in the heart of all painters. I was equally committed to giving the story a certain moral ending—moral which is, in addition, the result of a sort of comprehension of the heart, rather than a legalistic thought.

"Children thus penetrate a world which, certainly, has its difficulties, and where, as in traditional tales, the hero must of course wage certain battles; but even if it is a question of exterior battles, they are only the symbol of the interior battle which every man must wage if he wants to achieve peace in his own life, which could only result from a new understanding.

"If the children's book is of great importance to me, it is no less true, that, painting remains my principal preoccupation. For the painter, it is not necessary to pass via the Word!"

Hecht traveled in the United States and Mexico, 1967.

FOR MORE INFORMATION SEE: Times Literary Supplement, October 16, 1969.

HEINLEIN, Robert A(nson) 1907- (Anson MacDonald, Lyle Monroe, John Riverside, Caleb Saunders)

PERSONAL: Born July 7, 1907, in Butler, Mo.; son of Rex Ivar and Bam (Lyle) Heinlein; married Virginia Gerstenfeld, 1948. *Education:* Graduate of U.S. Naval Academy, 1929; University of California at Los Angeles, graduate work, 1934. *Agent:* Lurton Blassingame, 60 East 42nd St., New York, N.Y. 10017.

CAREER: Commissioned lieutenant, U.S. Navy, 1929, retired, 1934, because of physical disability in line of duty; writer of science fiction since 1939. *Member:* American Institute of Astronautics and Aeronautics, Authors' League of America, Navy League, Air Force Association, Air Power Council, Association of the Army of the United States, United States Naval Academy Alumni Association, American Association for the Advancement of Science. *Awards, honors:* Hugo award for best science fiction novel, 1956, 1960, 1962, 1966; Boys' Clubs of America Book Award, 1959; Sequoyah Book Award, 1961; Science Fiction Writers of America first "Grand Master" *Nebula*, 1975.

WRITINGS: (With others) *Of Worlds Beyond,* Fantasy Press, 1947 (published in England as *The Science of Science Fiction Writing,* Dobson, 1965); *Rocket Ship Galileo,* Scribner, 1947; *Beyond This Horizon,* Fantasy Press, 1948; *Space Cadet,* Scribner, 1948; *Red Planet,* Scribner, 1949; *Sixth Column,* Gnome, 1949.

Farmer in the Sky, Scribner, 1950; *Man Who Sold the Moon,* Shasta, 1950; *Waldo [and] Magic, Inc.,* Doubleday, 1950; *Between Planets,* Scribner, 1951; *Green Hills of*

The Flying Lion, Putnam, 1970; *Hermes le Crocodile bleu,* Desclee de Brouwer, 1968; *Bismuth le Tigre,* Desclee de Brouwer, 1972.

SIDELIGHTS: "I began to write my first children's book following a discussion with the head of the children's book department of Desclee de Brouwer Publishers.

"I found particularly blameworthy the mediocrity of the illustrations—I especially disliked the plastic side. I also

ROBERT A. HEINLEIN

Earth, Shasta, 1951; *Puppet Masters,* Doubleday, 1951; *Rolling Stones,* Scribner, 1952; *Tomorrow, The Stars,* Doubleday, 1952; *Assignment in Eternity,* Fantasy Press, 1953; *Revolt in 2100,* Shasta, 1953; *Starman Jones,* Scribner, 1953; *Star Beast,* Scribner, 1954; *Tunnel in the Sky,* Scribner, 1955; *Double Star,* Doubleday, 1956; *Time for the Stars,* Scribner, 1956; *Citizen of the Galaxy,* Scribner, 1957; *Door Into Summer,* Doubleday, 1957; (with others) *Famous Science Fiction Stories,* Random, 1957; *Have Space Suit, Will Travel,* Scribner, 1958; *Methusalah's Children,* Gnome Press, 1958; *Starship Troopers,* Putnam, 1959; *Unpleasant Profession of Jonathan Hoag,* Gnome Press, 1959; *The Menace from Earth,* Gnome Press, 1959, Dobson, 1966.

Stranger in a Strange Land, Putnam, 1961; *Glory Road,* Putnam, 1963; *Podkayne of Mars: Her Life and Times,* Putnam, 1963; *Orphans of the Sky,* Gollancz, 1963, Putnam, 1964; *Farnsham's Freehold,* Putnam, 1964; (contributor) Lloyd A. Eshbach, editor, *Of Worlds Beyond: The Science of Science Fiction,* Advent, 1964; *The Moon Is a Harsh Mistress,* Putnam, 1966; *History of the Future,* Putnam, 1967; *The Past Through Tomorrow,* Putnam, 1967; *The Door into Summer,* Gollancz, 1967; *Time Enough For Love,* Putnam, 1973. Author of more than one hundred fifty science fiction stories and novelettes.

Omnibus volumes: *Three by Heinlein: The Puppet Masters, Waldo, [and] Magic, Inc.,* Doubleday, 1965 (published in England as *A Heinlein Triad,* Gollancz, 1966); *A Robert Heinlein Omnibus: Beyond This Horizon, The Man Who Sold the Moon, and The Green Hills of Earth,* Sidgwick & Jackson, 1966; *The Worlds of Robert A. Heinlein,* Ace, 1969.

Motion pictures: "Destination Moon," Eagle Lion, 1950; "Project Moonbase," Lippert Productions, 1953.

SIDELIGHTS: "I was born in 1907 in Butler, Missouri, a small country town where my grandfather was a horse-and-buggy doctor, who strongly influenced me. I have been influenced by my parents and six siblings and everything I have seen, touched, eaten, endured, heard and read. I served as an officer in the United States Navy after graduation from the Naval Academy at Annapolis, Maryland, was disabled in line of duty and retired, and later attended post-graduate school at the University of California in Los Angeles, concentrating my studies in the field of mathematics and physics. A relapse into illness forced me to drop out without a degree.

"I began writing 'more or less by accident' and when my first short story was accepted for publication in 1939, I decided to continue. When an editor assigned me the task of writing a juvenile novel, I entered the field with determination not to 'write down' to children. My greatest challenge is to write a new story each time, despite the restrictions of editors or readers who clamor for one 'just like the last.'

"Although my primary purpose in writing is to entertain, my work naturally reflects my personal evaluations. 'A man without learning is crippled; nothing in this life is free; the universe does not forgive stupidity; honesty, courage, loyalty and duty are not only their own reward, but the only reward a self-respecting person needs.'

"I'm married to Virginia Gerstenfeld Heinlein, a former lieutenant in the United States Navy. She appears in my stories and has strongly influenced my writing, often supplying theme, title and invaluable criticism. She and I have gone around the world three times, visited more than eighty countries and flown over the North Pole. The first-hand knowledge which I have acquired through my travels has influenced my writing and I will not use a setting that I have not seen myself, except when I put the scene on a planet other than earth. My supplementary interests include astronomy, semantics, fiscal theory, politics and civil liberties. My hobbies include figure-skating, sculpture, stone masonry and fencing. I am an expert rifleman and pistol shot, both right and left-handed, though I have rarely fired a shot except professionally. We prefer living in the country and are presently residents of California."

FOR MORE INFORMATION SEE: More Junior Authors, edited by Muriel Fuller, H. W. Wilson, 1963; Sam Moskowitz, *Seekers of Tomorrow,* World, 1966; *Publishers' Weekly,* July 2, 1973; *Contemporary Literary Criticism,* edited by Carolyn Riley, Gale Research, 1973; *Encyclopaedia Britannica,* 15th edition, 1974.

"The trick to jetting yourself in space lies in balancing your body on the jet—the thrust has to pass through your center of gravity. If you miss and don't correct it quickly you start to spin . . . ■ (From *Space Cadet* by Robert A. Heinlein. Illustrated by Clifford N. Geary.)

HENDERSON, LeGrand 1901-1965
(Brian Harwin, LeGrand)

PERSONAL: Born May 24, 1901, in Torrington, Conn.; son of William J. and Estelle (Toussaint) Henderson; married Kathryn Dallas, July 6, 1935. *Education:* Yale University, student, 1921-25. *Home:* R.F.D., Camden, Me.

CAREER: Free-lance writer and illustrator.

WRITINGS—Juvenile books under pseudonym LeGrand: *Why Is a Yak?*, Grosset, 1937; *Mostly About Mutt*, Garden City, 1938; *What About Willie?*, Garden City, 1939; *Saturday for Samuel*, Greystone, 1941; *Glory Horn*, McBride, 1941; *Cap'n Dow and the Hole in the Doughnut*, Abingdon, 1946; *Cats for Kansas*, Abingdon, 1948; *Here Come the Perkinses!*, Bobbs, 1949; *The Puppy Who Chased the Sun*, Wonder Books, 1950; *Why Cowboys Sing, In Texas*, Abingdon, 1950; *The Boy Who Wanted to Be a Fish*, Wonder Books, 1951; *When the Mississippi Was Wild*, Abingdon, 1952; *Are Dogs Better Than Cats?*, Wonder Books, 1953; *Tom Benn and Blackbeard, the Pirate*, Abingdon, 1954; *Matilda*, Abingdon, 1956; *The Tomb of the Mayan King*, Henry Holt, 1958; *How Baseball Began in Brooklyn*, Abingdon, 1958; *How Space Rockets Began*, Abingdon, 1960; *How Basketball Began*, Abingdon, 1962; *Samson Catches a Mystery*, Houghton, 1962.

Books in the "Augustus" Series under pseudonym LeGrand: *Augustus and the River*, Bobbs, 1939, Grosset, 1960; *Augustus Goes South*, Bobbs, 1940, Grosset, 1960; *Augustus and the Mountains*, Bobbs, 1941, Grosset, 1960; *Augustus Helps the Navy*, Bobbs, 1942; *Augustus Helps the Army*, Bobbs, 1943; *Augustus Helps the Marines*, Bobbs, 1943; *Augustus Drives a Jeep*, Bobbs, 1944; *Augustus Flies*, Bobbs, 1944; *Augustus Saves a Ship*, Bobbs,

1945, Grosset, 1960; *Augustus Hits the Road*, Bobbs, 1946, Grosset, 1960; *Augustus Rides the Border*, Bobbs, 1947, Grosset, 1960; *Augustus and the Desert*, Bobbs, 1948, Grosset, 1960; *The Amazing Adventures of Archie and the First Hot Dog*, Abingdon Press, 1964.

Under pseudonym Brian Harwin: *Home Is Upriver* (adult novel), Macmillan, 1952, republished under title, *Touch Me Not*, Monarch, 1959. Adult short stories and articles in *Saturday Evening Post, American*, other magazines.

SIDELIGHTS: Once sailed twenty-four-foot sloop, "White Wings," from Bequia, Windward Islands, to Maine. Built houseboat in Minnesota and drifted down the Mississippi River to New Orleans.

FOR MORE INFORMATION SEE: Illustrators of Children's Books: 1744-1945, Horn Book, 1947; *Junior Book of Authors*, edited by Stanley J. Kunitz & Howard Haycraft, H. W. Wilson, 2nd Edition, 1951; *Atlanta Constitution*, November 23, 1959.

(Died January 25, 1965)

HENDRICKSON, Walter Brookfield, Jr.
1936-

PERSONAL: Born August 24, 1936, in Indianapolis, Ind.; son of Walter B. and M. Dorris (Walsh) Hendrickson. *Education:* Illinois College, B.A., 1958; special courses at MacMurray College, 1958-59; University of Illinois, 1959-61. *Religion:* Episcopalian. *Home and office:* 724 West State St., Jacksonville, Ill.

CAREER: Free-lance writer, 1958—. *Member:* American Institute of Aeronautics and Astronautics, Aviation/Space Writers Association, Authors League, American Association for the Advancement of Science, Jacksonville Junior Chamber of Commerce, Gamma Nu.

WRITINGS: *Handbook for Space Travelers,* Bobbs, 1960; *Pioneering in Space,* Bobbs, 1961; *The Study of Rockets, Missiles and Space Made Simple* (junior book), Double-day, 1962; *Reach for the Moon,* Bobbs, 1962; *Satellites and What They Do,* Bobbs, 1963; *Winging Into Space,* Bobbs, 1965; *What's Going On in Space?,* Harvey House, 1968; *Wild Wings,* Harvey House, 1969; *Apollo 11, Men to the Moon,* Harvey House, 1970; *Who Really Invented the Rocket?,* Putnam, 1974; *Manned Spacecraft to Mars and Venus: How They Work,* Putnam, 1975; (co-author) *Illinois: It's People and Culture,* Denison, 1975. Weekly columnist, "Science in the News," Authenticated News International Syndicate; contributor to *Camping Horizons, Space Age, Adventure, Children's Friend, Junior Catholic Messenger, Science World, Child Life,* and other publications.

WORKS IN PROGRESS: *Any Planet in a Storm; Eagle at Cape Kennedy; Fantastic Light; Going by Plane; Homesteading in Space; How the Space Age Began; Man-Made Hummingbirds; Visit to Another Planet; Visit to Skylab; Worlds in Space; You and Space Travel.*

Finally, on one long, narrow island, the buildings reached so high that they were almost up to the flight path of the geese. (From *Wild Wings* by Walter B. Hendrickson, Jr. Illustrated by Harvey Kidder.)

HERBERT, Frank (Patrick) 1920-

PERSONAL: Born October 8, 1920, in Tacoma, Wash.; son of Frank and Eileen Marie (McCarthy) Herbert; married Flora Parkinson, March, 1941 (divorced, 1945); married Beverly Ann Stuart, June 23, 1946; children: (first marriage) Penelope (Mrs. David R. Merritt), (second marriage) Brian, Bruce. *Education:* University of Washington, Seattle, student, 1946-47. *Residence:* Port Townsend, Wash. *Agent:* Lurton Blassingame, 60 East 42nd St., New York, N.Y. 10017; and Ned Brown, P.O. Box 5020, Beverly Hills, Calif. 90210.

CAREER: Newspaperman with West Coast papers from Los Angeles to Seattle, including more than ten years on staff of *San Francisco Examiner;* novelist specializing in science fiction. Member of national council, World Without War Council, 1970-73, and member of Seattle council, 1972—. Lecturer at University of Washington, Seattle, 1970-72; consultant on social and ecological studies to Lincoln Foundation, 1971. Director-photographer of television show, "The Tillers," 1973. *Awards, honors: Dragon in the Sea* (also variously titled *Under Pressure* and *Twentieth Century Sub*) was co-winner of International Fantasy Award, 1956; *Dune* was winner of Nebula Award of Science Fiction Writers of America as best novel, 1965, and co-winner of Hugo Award of World Science Fiction Convention as best novel, 1966.

WRITINGS: *Dragon in the Sea* (originally titled *Under Pressure;* first published in *Amazing Science Fiction,* 1955), Doubleday, 1956, reissued as *Under Pressure,* Ballantine, 1973.

WALTER BROOKFIELD HENDRICKSON, JR.

FRANK HERBERT

Dune (first published in *Analog,* December 1963-February 1964 and January-May 1965), Chilton, 1965; *Great Brain* (first published in *Amazing Stories,* March 1965), Berkley Publishing, 1966; *Destination: Void* (first published in *Galaxy,* August 1965), Berkley Publishing, 1966; *Eyes of Heisenberg* (first published in *Galaxy,* June-August 1966), Berkley Publishing, 1966; *Heaven Makers* (first published in *Amazing Stories,* April-June 1967), Avon, 1968; *The Santaroga Barrier* (first published in *Amazing Stories,* February 1968), Berkley Publishing, 1968.

Dune Messiah (first published in *Galaxy,* July-September 1969), Putnam, 1970; (with others) *Five Fates,* Doubleday, 1970; *Whipping Star* (first published in *If,* January-March 1970), Putnam, 1970; (editor) *New World or No World,* Ace Books, 1970; *Worlds of Frank Herbert* (anthology), Ace Books, 1971; *The God Makers,* Berkley Publishing, 1971, hardcover edition, Putnam, 1972; *Soul Catcher* (ALA Notable Book), Putnam, 1972; *Book of Frank Herbert,* Daw Books, 1973; *Threshold: The Blue Angels Experience,* Ballantine, 1973; *Hellstrom's Hive* (first published as *Project 40* in *Galaxy,* 1972), Bantam, 1974; *The Best of Frank Herbert,* Sphere Books, 1974; *Children of Dune,* Putnam, in press.

All but one of Herbert's earlier books have been reprinted recently (in 1973 or 1974) and there have been reissues of a number of his publications of the seventies. At least five books are classified as young adult literature; that includes *Dune,* which is being made into a motion picture.

Herbert lives on the northeast corner of the northwest corner of the state of Washington, about twenty air miles from Victoria, British Columbia. One of his major projects is turning his six wooded acres into an ecological demonstration project, showing how a high quality of life can be maintained with a minimum drain on the total energy system.

HOFF, Syd(ney) 1912-

PERSONAL: Born September 4, 1912, in New York, N.Y.; son of Benjamin and Mary (Barnow) Hoff; married Dora Berman, 1937; children: Susan Hoff Gross, Bonnie Joy. *Education:* Attended New York City public schools. *Home and office:* 4335 Post Ave., Miami Beach, Fla. 33140.

CAREER: Cartoonist, 1939—. King Features Syndicate, daily cartoon panel, "Laugh It Off," 1957—. *Member:* Authors Guild.

WRITINGS—All self-illustrated, unless otherwise noted: *Muscles and Brains,* Dial, 1940; *Military Secrets,* Hillair, 1943; *Feeling No Pain* (cartoon collection), Dial, 1944; *Mom, I'm Home!,* Doubleday, 1945; *Oops! Wrong Party!* (cartoon collection), Dutton, 1951; *It's Fun Learning Cartooning,* Stravon, 1952; *Oops! Wrong Stateroom!,* Washburn, 1953; *Out of Gas!,* Washburn, 1954; *Eight Little Artists,* Abelard, 1954; *Patty's Pet,* Abelard, 1955; *Okay—You Can Look Now!,* Duell, Sloane & Pearce, 1955; *Danny and the Dinosaur,* Harper, 1958, translated as *Danielito y el*

SYD HOFF

Dinosauro, by Pura Belpre, Harper, 1969; *Sammy, the Seal,* Harper, 1959; *Julius,* Harper, 1959.

Ogluk, the Eskimo, Holt, 1960; *Where's Prancer?,* Harper, 1960; (under name Sydney Hoff) *Oliver,* Harper, 1960; *Who Will Be My Friends?,* Harper, 1960; *Little Chief,* Harper, 1961; *Albert, the Albatross,* Harper, 1961; *The*

Better Hoff (cartoon collection), Holt, 1961; *Chester,* Harper, 1961; *Upstream, Downstream and Out of My Mind,* Bobbs, 1961; *'Twixt the Cup and the Lipton,* Bobbs, 1962; *Stanley,* Harper, 1962; *So This is Matrimony,* Pocket Books, 1962; *Hunting, Anyone?,* Bobbs, 1963; *From Bed to Nurse, or What a Way to Die,* Dell, 1963; *Grizzwold,* Harper, 1963; *Lengthy,* Putnam, 1964; *Learning to Cartoon,*

(From *WHO WILL BE MY FRIENDS?* by Sid Hoff. Illustrated by the author.)

Stravon Educational Press, 1966; *Mrs. Switch*, Putnam, 1967; *Irving and Me*, Harper, 1967; *Wanda's Wand*, C. R. Gibson, 1968; *The Witch, the Cat, and the Baseball Bat*, Grosset, 1968; *Little Red Riding-Hood* (illustrated by Charles Mikolaycak), Gibson, 1968; *Jeffrey at Camp*, Putnam, 1969; *Baseball Mouse*, Putnam, 1969; *Mahatma*, Putnam, 1969; *Roberto and the Bull*, McGraw, 1969; *Herschel the Hero*, Putnam, 1969.

The Horse in Harry's Room, Harper, 1970; *Wilfred the Lion*, Putnam, 1970; *The Litter Knight*, Putnam, 1970; *Palace Bug*, Putnam, 1970; *Siegfried, Dog of the Alps*, Grosset, 1970; *When Will It Snow?*, Harper, 1971; *The Mule Who Struck it Rich*, Little, Brown, 1971; *Thunderhoof*, Harper, 1971; *My Aunt Rosie*, Harper, 1972; *Pedro and the Bananas*, Putnam, 1972; *Syd Hoff's Joke Book*, Putnam, 1972; *Giants and Other Plays for Kids*, new edition, Putnam, 1973; *A Walk Past Ellen's House*, McGraw, 1973; *Amy's Dinosaur*, Windmill Books, 1974; *Jokes to Enjoy, Draw and Tell*, new edition, Putnam, 1974; *Kip Van Winkle*, new edition, Putnam, 1974. Contributor to *New Yorker*, *Esquire* and other magazines.

Illustrator: Allan Sherman, *Hello Muddah, Hello Faddah*, Harper, 1964; Allan Sherman, *I Can't Dance*, Harper, 1964; Joan Lexau, *I Should Have Stayed in Bed*, Harper, 1965; Joan Lexau, *Homework Caper*, Harper, 1966; Joan M. Lexau, *Rooftop Mystery*, Harper, 1968; edited by Tom Mac Pherson, *Slithers*, Putnam, 1968; Jerome Coopersmith, *Chanukah Fable for Christmas*, Putnam, 1969; Mildred W. Wright, *Henri Goes to the Mardi Gras*, Putnam, 1971; Edward R. Ricciuti, *Donald and the Fish That Walked*, Harper, 1972.

SIDELIGHTS: "I was born and grew up in New York City. I attended the National Academy of Design in the hope of becoming a fine artist, but a natural comic touch in my work caused my harried instructors to advise me to try something else. I did. At eighteen I sold my first cartoon to the *New Yorker,* and have been a regular contributor to that magazine ever since.

"For twenty-five years I drew for Harold Ross [editor of the *New Yorker*] and never met him in person. Nevertheless, he was a great editor without whose criticism, relayed to me through other editors, I would never have learned how to draw—that is, *if* I have learned to draw. He taught other people to draw without meeting them, too, and he also taught a lot of other people how to write.

"In 1939, after I had been drawing for years for *Esquire, Colliers,* the *Saturday Evening Post,* etc., William Randolph Hearst selected me to do a daily comic strip for his newspapers and those of other people. For ten years I labored with the comic adventures of a little girl (Tuffy) who did not have a dog that went 'Arf! Arf!' or a stepfather with a diamond stickpin. This was a little girl who just did funny things, but I never left her hanging from a cliff or had her kidnapped by Russian agents and pretty soon (ten years) newspaper readers decided she was too tame. So we decided to kill off the strip. It's a terrible thing to kill off a comic character you've been pumping life into for ten years. The day we quit I felt like putting a notice in the obituary columns of the *New York Times.*

"The best humor has to do with events that people can identify as having happened to them, or something that has been in their subconscious. Humor, for some reason, is basically sad. There's some sort of affinity between the sad and the funny that makes it all the funnier."

Danny and the Dinosaur was made into a film strip by Weston Woods.

FOR MORE INFORMATION SEE: Young Readers' Review, April, 1967; *Best Sellers,* September 1, 1967; *New York Times Book Review,* October 8, 1967; *Horn Book,* June, 1970, December, 1971, October, 1973; *Illustrators of Children's Books: 1957-1966,* Horn Book, 1968; *Third Book of Junior Authors,* edited by Doris de Montreville and Donna Hill, H. W. Wilson, 1972.

HOFFMANN, Felix   1911-1975

PERSONAL: Born April 11, 1911, in Aarau, Switzerland; son of Emil Adolf (a music director) and Mina (Froehlich) Hoffmann; married Gretel Kienscherf, January 18, 1936; children: Sabine Hoffmann Muischneek, Christiane Hoffmann Affolter, Susanne Hoffmann Frey, Dieter. *Education:* Attended Kunstakademie Karlsruhe, Germany, 1931-33, and Kunstakademie Berlin, 1934-35. *Religion:* Protestant. *Home:* Ruetliweg 2, CH-5000-Aarau, Switzerland.

CAREER: Illustrator of books for young people and children, 1932-75; free-lance artist and painter in Aarau, Switzerland, 1935-75, executed stained glass windows for churches, school buildings, and municipal buildings, wall murals and mosaics for various structures in Switzerland;

FELIX HOFFMANN

Hans was glad at heart as he rode off happily. After a while, he decided to go faster and cried, "gee-up!" ■ (From *Hans in Luck* by Felix Hoffmann, a Margaret K. McElderry Book. Illustrated by the author.)

illustrator of bibliophile books for German and American publishers, 1951-75. *Military service:* Swiss Army. *Member:* Gesellschaft schweizer Maler, Bildhauer und Architekten, Bund deutscher Buchkunstler, Xylon, Vereinigung der Holzschneider. *Awards, honors:* Schweizer Jugendbuchpreis, 1957; Hans Christian Andersen award honor list, 1960 and 1962; Children's Spring Book Festival award, *New York Herald Tribune,* 1963; Premio Fondatione Carmine (Florence), 1969; Hans Christian Anderson Award, 1972.

WRITINGS—Illustrator: Werner Bergengruen, *Die drei Falken,* Trajanus-Presse (Frankfurt am Main), 1956; Giovanni Boccaccio, *Die Nymphe von Fiesole,* Trajanus-Presse, 1958; Hans Christian Andersen, *Der standhafte Zinnsoldat: Ein Maerchen,* Aargauer Tabblatt (Aarau), 1960; *Bilderbibel* (includes 100 lithographs by Hoffmann, text by Paul Erismann), Zwingli Verlag (Zurich), 1961; Thomas Mann, *The Magic Mountain,* Limited Editions Club, 1962; Apuleius Madaurensis, *Amor und Psyche,* Verlag Ars (Frankfurt am Main), 1963; *Das hohe Lied (The*

Song of Solomon from the Old Testament), Flamberg-Verlag (Zurich), 1964; *Die Shoepfung der Welt (Genesis,* I-II, from the Old Testament), Verlag Ars, 1965; Bram Stoker, *Dracula,* Limited Editions Club, 1965; *A Boy Went Out to Gather Pears* (old nursery rhyme; ALA Notable Book), Harcourt, 1966; Aesopus, *Drei Dutzend Fabeln von Aesop,* Angelus-Drucke (Bern), 1967; Anton Pavlovich Chekhov, *Der wartende Kutscher,* Paulus Verlag (Recklinghausen), 1968; Max Voegeli, *The Wonderful Lamp,* Houghton, 1969; *Die sieben Todsuenden* (includes seven etchings by Hoffmann, and verses from *Das Narrenschiff* by Sebastian Brant), Sauerlaender (Aarau), 1969.

Illustrator of children's picture books of fairy tales by the Grimm Brothers: *Der Wolf and die sieben Geisslein,* Sauerlaender, 1957, translation by Katya Sheppard published in Canada as *The Wolf and the Seven Kids,* Oxford University Press, 1958, Harcourt, 1959; *Dornroeschen,* Sauerlaender, 1959, translation by Peter Collier published in America as *Sleeping Beauty* (ALA Notable Book), Harcourt, 1959; *Rapunzel,* Sauerlaender, 1960, translation published in America under same title, Harcourt, 1961; *Die sieben Raben,* Sauerlaender, 1962, translation published in America as *The Seven Ravens* (ALA Notable Book), Harcourt, 1963; *Die vier kunstreichen Brueder,* Sauerlaender, 1966, translation published in America as *The Four Clever Brothers,* Harcourt, 1967; *King Thrushbeard,* Harcourt, 1970; *Tom Thumb,* Atheneum, 1973; *Hans in Luck,* Atheneum, 1975.

Also illustrated: Rene Guillot, *Elephants of Sargabal,* S. G. Phillips, 1957; Max Voegli, *Prince of Hindustan,* 1961; Adolph Haller, *He Served Two Masters,* Pantheon, 1962, included in *The Favorite Fairy Tales Told in Poland,* edited by Virginia Havilland, Little, Brown, 1963; R. Herrmann, *Christmas Crib Book,* Merry Thoughts.

WORK IN PROGRESS: Stained glass windows, mural paintings; bibliophile works.

SIDELIGHTS: Hoffmann said his Grimm fairy tale books were created for the use of his own children when they were young, between 1945 and 1951. All the picture books are composed of original chromo-lithographs, color separations which he printed himself, using either lithograph stones or acetate, both less expensive methods than photographic reproduction.

FOR MORE INFORMATION SEE: Illustrators of Children's Books: 1946-1956, Horn Book, 1958; *Philobiblon,* 1960; *Texas University Quarterly,* spring, 1962; *Illustrators of Children's Books: 1957-1966,* Horn Book, 1968; *Der Polygraph,* June, 1969; *Third Book of Junior Authors,* edited by de Montreville and Hill, H. W. Wilson, 1972; *Horn Book,* June, 1973; MacCann & Richard, *The Child's First Books,* H. W. Wilson, 1973.

(Died June, 1975)

HOPKINS, Marjorie   1911-

PERSONAL: Born May 19, 1911; daughter of Newton Fisher (a civil engineer) and Emma (Lambert) Hopkins. *Education:* Chatham College, A.B., 1933; University of Iowa, M.A., 1935. *Home:* 526 South Ardmore Ave., Los Angeles, Calif. 90005.

CAREER: Junior high school teacher of English and journalism, 1939-72, and counselor, formerly in Pittsburgh, Pa., New York State, and San Jose, Calif., now retired. Spent one year in Baghdad, Iraq, as Fulbright exchange teacher. *Military service:* U.S. Navy Women's Reserve (WAVES), 1944-46; became ensign. *Member:* National Educational Association, California Teachers' Association.

WRITINGS: The Three Visitors (picture book), Parents, 1967; *The Glass Valentine,* Parents, 1968; *And the Jackal Played the Masinko,* Parents, 1969; *A Gift for Jolum,* Parents, 1972. Contributor of short stories to juvenile magazines.

SIDELIGHTS: "Telling what happened to somebody and why and what did the somebody do *then* is forever exciting. But for *me* at least, patience is part of the game. Before *And the Jackal Played the Masinko* was published, I had studied quite a lot about Ethiopia and had written several stories about Ethiopian children. Not one did an editor

want! Then unexpectedly there came nudging up three rambunctious, headstrong animals—Ethiopian ones—and said, 'Put *us* in the story!' The animals practically took over the whole thing. I wasn't a bit surprised. With a good old uncle and an amused little girl and a hard-thinking boy working alongside, they saw to it that a story got on paper and was enjoyable enough for others to read.

"Like all authors, I am very fond of reading other peoples' stories, histories and biographies. I also love traveling to see paintings and antique pottery and modern people."

HOUGH, (Helen) Charlotte   1924-

PERSONAL: Surname is pronounced *How;* born May 24, 1924, in Brockenhurst, England; daughter of Henry Constantine (a doctor) and Helen (Littler) Woodyatt; married Richard Hough (an author), July 17, 1943; children: Sarah Garland, Alexandra, Deborah Moggach, Bryony. *Education:* Attended Frensham Heights School, 1935-40. *Religion:* Church of England. *Home:* 25 St. Ann's Ter., London N.W.8, England.

CAREER: Writer and illustrator of children's books. *Military service:* Women's Royal Naval Service, 1942-43.

WRITINGS—Juveniles; all self-illustrated: *Jim Tiger,* Faber, 1956, Bobbs, 1958; *Morton's Pony,* Faber, 1957, Transatlantic, 1958; *The Home-Makers,* Hamish Hamilton, 1957; *The Story of Mr. Pinks,* Faber, 1958; *The Hampshire*

MARJORIE HOPKINS

Now the animals all had good in them. The jackal didn't run away, the warthog didn't steal salt from the ingot, and the monkey took only his share of the roasted chick-peas. ■ (From *And the Jackal Played the Masinko* by Marjorie Hopkins. Pictures by Olivia H. H. Cole.)

Pig, Hamish Hamilton, 1958; *The Animal Game,* Faber, 1959; *The Trackers,* Hamish Hamilton, 1960; *Algernon,* Faber, 1961, A. S. Barnes, 1962; *Anna and Minnie,* Faber, 1962; *Three Little Funny Ones,* Hamish Hamilton, 1962, Penguin (Baltimore), 1966; *The Owl in the Barn,* Faber, 1964; *More Funny Ones,* Hamish Hamilton, 1965; *Red Biddy, and Other Stories,* Faber, 1966; *Educating Flora, and Other Stories,* Faber, 1968; *Sir Frog, and Other Stories,* Faber, 1968; *My Aunt's Alphabet, with Billy and Me,* Hamish Hamilton, 1969; *Abdul the Awful, and Other Stories,* McCall Publishing, 1970; *Bad Child's Book of Moral Verse,* Faber, 1970, Walck, 1971; *Queer Customer,* Heinemann, 1973; *Pink Pig, Bad Cat,* Penguin, 1974.

Illustrator: A. Stephen Tring, *Barry's Big Day,* Oxford University Press, 1954; Anita Hewett, *Elephant Big and Elephant Little, and Other Stories,* John Lane, 1955; Barbara Euphan Todd, *Boy with the Green Thumb,* Hamish Hamilton, 1956.

SIDELIGHTS: "I consider myself typically English in appearance and character, except that I lack the traditional stoicism.

"A life-long interest in medicine makes me a sympathetic listener to other people's illnesses but also, coupled with the above failing, into a fearful hypochondriac!

"From my earliest memories I loved drawing and reading and biology but had no training in anything. I was a very 'physical' child and many of my stories have something of this ancient joy still preserved (swinging in the tree-tops, jumping in sand-dunes, riding bareback, dancing alone in the moonlight, etc.).

"I live in a house in London which is full of animal momentoes, such as photographs, skulls, paintings, and also in a Lakeland farmhouse amongst marvellous wild birds, with two ponies and a collie dog, all very old.

"I believe most young children are as innocent as they used to be and should be dealt with accordingly."

FOR MORE INFORMATION SEE: Illustrators of Children's Books: 1946-1956, Horn Book, 1958; *Books and Bookmen,* November, 1968.

CHARLOTTE HOUGH

Friendship's one thing, force another.
Some folks can't tell one from t'other.
■ (From *A Bad Child's Book of Moral Verse* by Charlotte Hough. Illustrated by the author.)

HUTCHINS, Carleen Maley   1911-

PERSONAL: Born May 24, 1911, in Springfield, Mass.; daughter of Thomas William (an accountant) and Grace (Fletcher) Maley; married Morton Aldrich Hutchins (now a chemist), June 6, 1943; children: William Aldrich, Caroline. *Education:* Cornell University, B.A. (science), 1933; New York University, M.A., 1942. *Home:* 112 Essex Ave., Montclair, N.J. 07042; (summer) Box 1, Mirror Lake, N.H. 03853. *Agent:* McIntosh & Otis, Inc., 18 East 41st St., New York, N.Y. 10017.

CAREER: Woodward School, Brooklyn, N.Y., teacher of science and woodworking, 1933-37; Brearley School, New York, N.Y., teacher of science, 1937-49; All Day Neighborhood Schools, New York, N.Y., assistant director, 1943-45; self-employed in violin research, development, and construction, 1947—. Science consultant to Coward-McCann, Inc., 1956—, Girl Scouts of America, 1957—, National Recreation Association, 1962—. *Member:* Acoustical Society of America, Catgut Acoustical Society (secretary, 1963—), Viola de Gamba Society of America, International Violin Maker's Association of Arizona, Acoustical Society of America, American Association for the Advancement of Science. *Awards, honors:* Guggenheim fellowships for re-

search in violin acoustics and development of new violin family, 1959, 1961; research grant, Martha Baird Rockefeller Fund for Music, 1966; National Science Foundation travel grant, 1971 and 1974.

WRITINGS: Life's Key, DNA: A Biological Adventure into the Unknown, Coward, 1961; (science consultant) Warren Goodrich, *Science Through Recreation,* Holt, 1964; *Moon Moth,* Coward, 1965; (with Warren Goodrich) *Science through Recreation,* National Recreation Association, 1964; *Who Will Drown the Sound,* Coward, 1972; *Musical Acoustics: Part I,* 1975, *Part II,* 1976, Halsted Press. Contributor of articles and papers on violin acoustics to *Scientific American, Journal of the Acoustical Society of America, Strad* (London), and journals for musicians.

WORK IN PROGRESS: Several other life-history books on the order of *Moon Moth.*

SIDELIGHTS: "I write for young people because I believe that they deserve the best available information in any field. *Moon Moth* was taken from my own experience raising moths when I was growing up and then with my two children, and was checked very carefully with current findings in entomology.

"*Life's Key, D.N.A.* was written after I had constructed a model of the DNA molecule for the 'March of Dimes' National Foundation, and I found that nobody understood

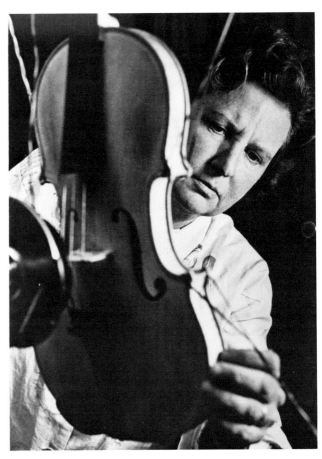

CARLEEN M. HUTCHINS

what I was talking about when I tried to explain the reason for the model configuration.

"*Science Through Recreation* came from fifteen years teaching science to grades one-through-six and making it a vital experience for them.

"*Who Will Drown the Sound* explains something of noise pollution, how sound functions and how it can be controlled, for six-to-eight-year olds. A much needed part of today's growing up."

Because friends complained that her trumpet was too loud for their chamber music sessions, Carleen Hutchins bought an inexpensive viola, "dreamed" of making a better one, spent two years (1947-49) producing the better instrument, and has since made some eighty violins, violas, and cellos—all experimental in some respect. The experimental features stem from fifteen years of work in violin acoustics with the late Frederick A. Saunders of Harvard, who pioneered violin research in America. The group that worked with Saunders forms the nucleus of the Catgut Acoustical Society, a somewhat informal organization interested in developing the "missing links" in the violin family.

FOR MORE INFORMATION SEE: Scientific American, November, 1962; *Life,* November 29, 1963; *American String Teacher,* spring, 1965; *Science News,* March, 1967; *Science Digest,* August, 1968.

HYDE, Dayton O(gden)
(Hawk Hyde)

PERSONAL: Born in Marquette, Mich.; son of Frederick Walton and Rhoda (Williams) Hyde; married Gerda Isenberg, September 23, 1950; children: Dayton, Virginia, Marsha, John, Taylor. *Education:* University of California, Berkeley, student, 1946-50. *Religion:* Episcopalian. *Home:* 1410 Pacific Ter., Klamath Falls, Ore. 97601. *Agent:* Malcolm Reiss, Paul R. Reynolds, Inc., 599 Fifth Ave., New York, N.Y. 10017. *Office:* Yamsi Ranch, Chiloquin, Ore. 97624.

CAREER: Cattle rancher at Bly, Ore., 1950-54, and Yamsi Ranch, Chiloquin, Ore., 1954—; writer and lecturer on conservation and nature subjects, 1965—. Klamath County Library, president trustee. *Military service:* U.S. Army, Signal Corps, 1944-46; served in Europe; received two battle stars. *Member:* International Wild Waterfowl Association (director), Whooping Crane Conservation Association (vice-president), Oregon Wildlife Federation (director), Defenders of Wildlife International (director). *Awards, honors:* Golden Beaver Award for conservation from Isaac Walton League of Oregon; Sears Roebuck Foundation Buffalo Award from Oregon Wildlife Federation; named Conservationist of the Year by Governor McCall of Oregon. *Awards, honors:* $10,000 Dutton Animal Book Award, 1975, for *Strange Companion.*

WRITINGS: Sandy: The Story of A Rare Sandhill Crane Who Joined Our Family (Reader's Digest condensed book), Dial, 1968; *Yamsi,* Dial, 1971; *Cranes in My Corral,* Dial, 1972; *The Last Free Man,* Dial, 1974; (editor) *Raising Wild Ducks in Captivity,* Dutton, 1974; *Strange Companion,* Dutton, 1975. Contributor of articles and editorials to nature magazines; contributor of photographs to *Life* and other magazines.

SIDELIGHTS: "I was born on Lake Superior in Northern Michigan in the days when the nightly music of timber wolves was part of our way of life. We had a camp on a little lake named Deer Lake and my summers and all possible moments were spent there in the midst of nature. The wild things were my playmates and some of my early memories are of lying on a cot on the front porch of the camp reading Thornton Burgess or Ernest Thompson Seton. I spent other hours in tree perches high atop pines and hemlocks communing with birds.

"When I was about ten, my uncle, a rancher in Oregon, wrote me that he could step out of the front door of his ranch house and scoop up enough trout for breakfast in a dishpan. On the strength of that outrageous lie I ran away from home and became a cowboy on his ranch.

"Caught up with the life, I did everything from breaking horses, riding saddle broncs, fighting brahma bulls and clowning in rodeos, and doing rodeo action photography. The photography won several awards including recognition in *Life* but what I really wanted to be was a writer. I poured out several thousand words a month on cowboy personalities and wild horses for horse magazines under the name of Hawk Hyde, illustrating the articles with my own photography. When *Life* gave me an assignment, however, I grew too big for my britches and dropped all else to work for them and help pay my way through college.

"The necessities of earning a living for my growing family took me away from writing and into ranching for a number

Walt had milked a good five inches into the bottom of the pail when one of the cranes grabbed the cow by the tail, and with one sidewinding kick the cantankerous animal drove Walt—stool, bucket, and all—out through the side of the barn. ■ (From *Cranes in My Corral* by Dayton O. Hyde. Pictures by Lorence Bjorklund.)

of years, but I continued my interest in wildlife, working on a research program of my own to try to help the greater sandhill cranes win their fight against extinction. *Audubon Magazine* published my article on my adventures with cranes, and this ended up in John Terres anthology, *The Audubon Book of True Nature Stories.*

"Thus encouraged that my prose was deathless, I wrote more and more, working by day on the ranch I had purchased from my uncle, and writing into the night. I poured out quantitites of bad stuff, never quite understanding why every story, every article came back from *Saturday Evening Post* or some such magazine rejected. I had studied writing at the University of California at Berkeley; I had nice letters from many an editor; Wessel Smitter, the prize winning novelist had even given me the chair in which he wrote *F.O.B. Detroit* in appreciation of my potential as a writer, but clearly not much was happening. But I loved to write and enjoyed the discipline of hard work. By sheer persistence I kept on, never realizing that by writing and writing I was learning a skill that came so slowly as to be almost imperceptible.

"In 1968 I wrote *Sandy,* which did well for my editor and friend, Bill Decker, at Dial Press. *Readers Digest* condensed the book and sent it flinging around the world. One classmate of mine from California, living in Norway, wrote to congratulate me on how well I wrote in Norwegian. This success was followed by television appearances, and lecture appearances and cut heavily into the time I was able to spend running the cattle operation and writing but gave me a chance to speak up of endangered species and Man's ill use of his resources, things I felt strongly about.

"*Sandy* was followed by *Yamsi, A Heartwarming Journal of a Year on a Wilderness Ranch, Cranes in My Corral,* a juvenile version of *Sandy,* and *The Last Free Man,* a historical study of an Indian family murdered in 1911 in the wilds of Northern Nevada, a book which is being filmed by Frank Capra, Jr. Next for E. P. Dutton, I edited a book, *Raising Wild Waterfowl in Captivity,* and wrote the 1975 Dutton Animal Book Award winner, *Strange Companion,* a book combining my research on cranes and a trip on which I got lost in the whooping crane nesting area of northern Canada. Already in extra printings, this book will be a Walt Disney production.

"If I could sum up my writings I would say that most are an attempt to feed some very serious ideas to the reader in as delightful and humorous a package as possible. One of the great satisfactions is hearing a reader stoutly defending my theories without the slightest idea of where he got them."

FOR MORE INFORMATION SEE: Life, November 1, 1948; *Northwest Magazine* of *Portland Oregonian,* Sunday, April 21, 1968; *New York Times Book Review,* June 9 1968.

JANSON, H(orst) W(oldemar) 1913-

PERSONAL: Born October 4, 1913, in St. Petersburg, Russia; married Dora Jane Heineberg, 1941; children: Anthony, Peter, Josephine, Charles. *Education:* University of Hamburg, student, 1932-33, 1934-35; University of Munich, student, 1933-34; Harvard University, M.A., 1938, Ph.D.,

H. W. JANSON

1942. *Home:* 29 Washington Sq. W., New York, N.Y. 10011. *Office:* Department of Fine Arts, Washington Square College, New York, N.Y. 10003.

CAREER: Worcester Art Museum, Worcester, Mass., lecturer, 1936-38; State University of Iowa, Iowa City, instructor, 1938-41; Washington University, St. Louis, Mo., assistant professor, 1941-49; New York University, Washington Square College, professor, department of fine arts, 1949—, chairman, 1949-75. *Member:* College Art Association of America (director, 1958-62; president, 1970-72), Renaissance Society of America, American Studies Association. *Awards, honors:* Guggenheim Fellow, 1948, 1955; Charles R. Morey Award, 1952, 1957.

WRITINGS: Apes and Ape Lore in the Middle Ages and the Renaissance, Warburg Institute, University of London, 1952; (with Dora Jane Janson) *The Story of Painting for Young People,* Abrams, 1952; (with Dora Jane Janson) *The Picture History of Painting,* Abrams, 1957; *The Sculpture of Donatello,* Princeton University Press, 1957; *Key Monuments of the History of Art,* Abrams, 1959; *History of Art,* Abrams and Prentice-Hall, 1962, revised edition entitled *History of Art for Young People,* Abrams and Prentice-Hall, 1969; *Sixteen Studies,* Abrams, 1974. Editor-in-chief, *The Art Bulletin,* 1962-65.

SIDELIGHTS: "I sometimes feel like a one-man United Nations when I recall that my U.S. citizenship (which I acquired more than thirty years ago) is my fourth nationality, and the only one I chose for myself. I was born a Russian subject, but my parents came from the city of Riga, which in 1919 became the capital of Latvia, so we all became Latvians automatically. Later on, we moved to Germany, and my parents became German citizens along with their children. I came to America as a student, because I did not like the Nazis, and fell in love with it, so I stayed.

"I think of myself as a teacher rather than a professional writer. I had done scholarly articles ever since I was a graduate student. In the 1940's, I devoted a good deal of research to the question of what people thought about monkeys before Darwin and the theory of evolution came along. The result was my first scholarly book. Meanwhile, however, my wife, Dora Jane, had started doing a book on the history of painting for children. We worked on it together, and the two were published the same year, 1952.

"We have found that writing for young people takes just as much thought as scholarly writing, but the kind of thinking it demands is of a different sort: how to say things simply and strikingly, how to avoid technical words that are not absolutely needed, how to draw on youngsters' everyday experience in explaining works of art, how to keep from 'talking down' to your readers.

"Friends sometimes ask us what we do for pleasure. Our answer is: everything. Looking at works of art and asking questions about them gives us such satisfaction that we do it all the time and don't feel the need for other kinds of fun. We do a good deal of traveling, though, because it enables us to see works of art in other countries and meet other people interested in art. We also both like music and good food."

JENKINS, William A(twell)   1922-

PERSONAL: Born November 18, 1922, in Scranton, Pa.; son of William A. and Thelma Marie Atwell; married Gloria Hyam, March 3, 1944 (divorced, 1974); married Alice Wyne (a secretary), November 1, 1974; children: (first marriage) William Arthur II, Darcy Ann. Education: New York University, B.S., 1948; University of Illinois, M.S., 1949, Ph.D., 1954. Politics: Independent. Religion: Protestant. Home: 8721 Southwest 137th Ave., Miami, Fla. 33183. Office: Florida International University, Tamiami Trail, Miami, Fla. 33199.

CAREER: High school teacher in Moline, Ill., 1951-53; Wisconsin State College—Milwaukee (now Wisconsin State University—Milwaukee), assistant professor of English, 1953-55, associate professor of English and elementary education, 1956; University of Wisconsin—Milwaukee, professor of education, 1958-63, chairman of department of secondary education, 1961-63, associate dean of School of Education, 1963-70; Portland State University, Portland, Ore., professor of education and dean of School of Education, 1970-74; Florida International University, Miami, vice-president for academic affairs, 1974—. Visiting summer professor at University of Hawaii, 1969, and Florida Agricultural and Mechanical University, 1951. Consultant to Educational Testing Service, Ford Foundation, and U.S. Office of Education. Chairman of Portland Development Commission (urban renewal), 1973-74. Mili-

tary service: U.S. Army, Corps of Engineers, 1943-46; became first lieutenant.

MEMBER: National Council of Teachers of English (president, 1968-69), National Conference on Research in English, Wisconsin Council of Teachers of English (president, 1967-68), Phi Delta Kappa, Kappa Delta Pi, Phi Kappa Phi, Pi Lambda Theta.

WRITINGS: (With W. Cabell Greet and Andrew Schiller) A Beginning Thesaurus: In Other Words, Lothrop, 1969; (with Greet and Schiller) A Junior Thesaurus: In Other Words, Lothrop, 1970; My Second Picture Dictionary, Scott, Foresman, 1971. Co-author or contributor to about eighty readers published by Scott, Foresman, 1963—. Contributor to professional journals. Editor, Elementary English (publication of National Council of Teachers of English), 1961-68.

WORK IN PROGRESS: A chapter on developments in the education of teachers of English in the past quarter century for National Society for the Study of Education yearbook; an evaluation of elementary school language tests.

HOBBIES AND OTHER INTERESTS: Tennis, bicycling, model railroading (HO gauge), and "puttering with a variety of tools."

FOR MORE INFORMATION SEE: Education (magazine), April-May, 1962.

JENNINGS, Gary (Gayne)   1928-

PERSONAL: Born September 20, 1928, in Buena Vista, Va.; son of Glen Edward (a printer) and Vaughnye May (Bays) Jennings; married Glenda Clarke House, August 26, 1972; children: (previous marriage) Jesse Glen. Education: New York Art Students League, student, 1949-51. Home: Apartado Postal 699, San Miguel de Allende Gto., Mexico. Agent: Curtis Brown Ltd., 60 East 56th St., New York, N.Y. 10022.

CAREER: Copywriter and account executive for advertising agencies, New York, N.Y., 1947-58; newspaper reporter in California and Virginia, 1958-61; Dude and Gent, managing editor, 1962-63. Military service: U.S. Army, 1952-54; served as correspondent in Korea; awarded Bronze Star, citation from Korean Ministry of Information. Awards, honors: Funk and Wagnalls fellowship in nonfiction, Bread Loaf Writers' Conference, 1962.

WRITINGS—Self-illustrated juvenile non-fiction: March of the Robots, Dial, 1962; The Movie Book, Dial, 1963; Black Magic, White Magic, Dial, 1965; Parades!, Lippincott, 1966; The Killer Storms, Lippincott, 1970; The Realistic Guide to Astrology, Association, 1971; The Shrinking Outdoors, Lippincott, 1972; The Earth Book, Lippincott, 1973; March of the Heroes, Association, 1975; March of the Gods, Association, 1976.

Young adult novel: The Rope in the Jungle, Lippincott, 1976.

Adult books: Personalities of Language (non-fiction),

GARY JENNINGS

Crowell, 1965; *The Treasure of the Superstition Mountain* (non-fiction), Norton, 1973; *The Terrible Teague Bunch* (novel), Norton, 1975; *Sow the Seeds of Hemp* (novel), Norton, 1976.

Contributor: *Language and Literacy Today,* edited by P. D. and M. E. Hazard, Science Research Associates, 1965; *Modern Composition,* edited by W. E. Stegner, E. H. Sauer, and C. W. Hach, Holt, 1965; *Style and Subject,* Harper, 1966; *NOW: Essays and Articles,* edited by M. L. Sutton, R. W. Puckett, and H. L. Copps, Glencoe, 1969; *People and Words,* by James B. Hogins, Science Research Associates, 1972. Stories included in *Best from Fantasy & Science Fiction: 15th Series,* and *20th Series,* Doubleday, 1966, 1973; and other anthologies. Articles and stories in *Harper's, American Heritage, Holiday, Cosmopolitan, Reader's Digest, Redbook, Ellery Queen's Mystery Magazine, Fantasy and Science Fiction, Etude, Opera News, Military Engineer,* other magazines.

WORK IN PROGRESS: Aztec, an adult novel of Mexico before the Conquest.

SIDELIGHTS: "Regarding my juvenile and young adult books—When I was a kid I had, like most kids, a great variety of interests, robots, the movies, magic, etc., but when I tried to find books dealing with those interests, I discovered that there simply weren't any, or at any rate none written for youngsters. I decided then that, when I grew up, I would write all the books I wanted to read but couldn't find when I was young. And I did. Most of the juvenile books I have written are about those precise subjects that interested and intrigued me when I was young. (Of course, I have also written a couple of others—such as *The Shrinking Outdoors*—which deal with subjects or problems that simply didn't exist when I was a youngster, but do interest the young readers of today.)

"Regarding my adult books, short stories and articles, my ideal is either to treat a subject or theme that has *never* been touched before, or a subject old, trite and threadbare that I can handle in an entirely new and unexpected way. Also, despite numerous publisher' pleas for sequels, variations, etc., 'I never write the same thing twice.'"

JONES, Diana Wynne 1934-

PERSONAL: Born August 16, 1934, in London, England; daughter of Richard Aneurin (an educator) and Marjorie (an educator; maiden name, Jackson) Jones; married John A. Burrow (a university professor), December 23, 1956; children: Richard, Michael, Colin. *Education:* St. Anne's College, Oxford, B.A., 1956. *Home:* 4 Herbert Close, Oxford, England. *Agent:* Laura Cecil, 10 Exeter Mansions, 106 Shaftesbury Ave., London, England.

CAREER: Writer.

WRITINGS—For children, except as noted: *Changeover* (adult novel), Macmillan, 1970; *Wilkins' Tooth,* Macmillan, 1973, published as *Witch's Business,* Dutton, 1974; *The Ogre Downstairs,* Macmillan, 1974, Dutton, 1975; *Eight Days of Luke,* Macmillan, 1975; *Cart and Cwidder,* Macmillan, 1975; *Dogsbody,* Macmillan, 1975.

Plays for children: "The Batterpool Business," first performed in London, England, at Arts Theatre, October, 1968; "The King's Things," first performed in London, England, at Arts Theatre, February, 1970; "The Terrible Fisk Machine," first performed in London, England, at Arts Theatre, January, 1971.

The dread black funnel of a tornado cloud churns into the city of Wichita Falls, Texas, in 1964. ■ (From *The Killer Storms* by Gary Jennings. Photograph by American Red Cross.)

DIANA WYNNE JONES

WORK IN PROGRESS: Power of Three, a novel for children; "Fred and the Bike Lamp," a play for children.

SIDELIGHTS: "I had an eccentric and unorganized childhood. When I was not balancing along rooftops hoping to learn to fly, or hatching schemes for advancement . . . I was reading avidly. There were hardly any good books . . . So nowadays, when I write for children, my first aim is to make a story—as amusing and exciting as possible—such as I wished I could have read as a child.

"My second aim is equally important. It is to give children—without presuming to instruct them—the benefit of my greater experience. I like to explore the private terrors and troubles which beset children, because they can thereby be shown they are not unique in misery. Children create about a third of their misery themselves. The other two-thirds is caused by adults—inconsiderate, mysterious, and often downright frightening adults. I put adults like this in my stories, in some firmly contemporary situation beset with very real problems, and explore the implications by means of magic and old myths. What I am after is an exciting—and exacting—wisdom, in which contemporary life and potent myth are intricately involved and superimposed. I would like children to discover that potent old truths are as much part of everyone's daily life as are—say—the days of the week."

"If you want to know what I'm like, suppose you came to visit me. You have to squeeze past the game of table tennis in the drive. The front door has a large pink notice on it: *Bell in Order.* That's right. The bell never worked for eight years, everyone just shouted. But Colin is going to be a genius when he finds out what to be a genius at, and he mended the bell. Mick put the notice up to tell people not to shout any more. Any way, come in. Yes, this is me. I look quite young. And never mind the dog. He thinks you love him. If he annoys you, just yell 'Bath!' at him, that acts as a deterrent. Will you hang up your coat? No—sorry—you can't have a light in the cloakroom. There's a blackbird nesting in the ventilator, you see, and the light activates a fan, and the fan blows the nestlings about. Just fumble about. What did you say? Noise? Yes, there is quite a noise. It's Richard and his friends having their pop-group. But this is nothing. The drummer isn't here today and they broke their amplifier over Easter.

"How did you get so wet? I don't think the roof is leaking at the moment, so someone must have shot you with a detergent bottle. There are six boys upstairs with them. Come and have coffee. Mind where you put your feet! Oh dear, that was Mick's electric trains you trod in. No, Mick isn't the one making those ten cups of coffee. That's just a visitor making it for the other visitors. We get through a lot of coffee. I drink it all the time too. This room is full of people as well. I wish they wouldn't all shout. What? My husband? No, he doesn't find it easy to work at home. He's the tallest one playing table tennis. Come outside at the back where it's quieter. The creepers are lovely. I love flowers, but I can only grow them up the walls because they get trodden on elsewhere. I think this chair will hold up if you sit in it.

"Now, how did I come to write, you say? It was a thing I decided to do at the age of eight. When we moved to the country and it was hard to get hold of books, I used to write instead of reading and then read the result to my sisters. There was an epic about a boy on rollerskates called *Rolling Rory*—which I still think is a darn good title—and another about a boy called Sandy. Always boys. I wished I was a boy. And I don't know whether my sisters or I enjoyed them most. Writing is what I enjoy most anyway.

"No, I can't write in all this noise. I like to be alone and completely comfortable, so I do it when they're out at school. They go to school next door and come home an average of ten times a day, and their friends come too. Yes, of course they provide me with no end of material, though I never use it straight. A book makes its own world. But I couldn't do it without them. Then they read what I've written and give advice, though the most valuable advice is always my husband's.

"Who do I write for? All the people who like the kind of stories I like to read. If I don't enjoy reading what I've written, I stop. Which reminds me, I have to stop and cook for everyone shortly. I don't much enjoy cooking, though I think I do it quite well. It's such a wrench to stop writing and cook. But . . .

"Here you are struck heavily by a muddy football. I *am* so sorry. I *told* them to play on the other side of the house. They never listen unless I shout. Yes, I often shout. Are you very badly hurt? Must you leave? Come again, though I'd better warn you we are moving house soon. I've no doubt the next house will be much the same. Your coat? No, that's Richard's guitarist's cousin's girlfriend's coat. We've had it six months. Here's yours. Do tell that dog 'Bath!' Mind the table tennis. Good-bye.''

JONES, Hortense P. 1918-

PERSONAL: Born January 10, 1918, in Franklin, Va.; daughter of Edgar and Cora Lee (De Loatch) Parker; married Theodore T. Jones, 1940; children: Theodora A. Jones Blackmon, Theodore T., Jr., Lawrence W. *Education:* Hampton Institute, Professional Diploma, 1936, B.S. in Ed., 1947; New York University, M.A., 1950; further graduate study at New York University, University of Chicago, and University of Puerto Rico. *Home:* 150-23 118th Ave., Jamaica, N.Y. 11434. *Office:* Board of Education, 131 Livingston St., Brooklyn, N.Y. 11201.

CAREER: City Day Care Centers, New York, N.Y., director, 1950-56; New York City Board of Education, New York, N.Y., teacher of early childhood education, 1956-63, assistant director, Bureau of Early Childhood Education, 1963-64, assistant director for more effective schools, Bureau of Early Childhood Education, 1964-69, director for more effective schools, 1969-72, assistant director, Bureau of Early Childhood Education, 1972—. Adjunct lecturer at Queens College, 1973-74, Medgar Evers College, 1974-75. Consultant on educational instruction to Peace Corps; consultant to New Jersey State Department of Education.

MEMBER: National Association for Supervision and Curriculum Development, Association for the Study of Afro-American Life and History, National Association of Elementary School Principals, Association for Childhood Education International, International Reading Association, National Association for the Education of Young Children. *Awards, honors:* Sojourner Truth Award of New York State Business & Professional Women's Association, 1968.

WRITINGS—All with Peter Buckley: *Living as Neighbors,* Holt, 1966; *William, Andy and Ramon,* Holt, 1966; *Five Friends at School,* Holt, 1966; *Our Growing City,* Holt, 1968.

KAMEN, Gloria 1923-

PERSONAL: Born April 9, 1923, in New York, N.Y.; daughter of Herman and Tillie (Kozel) Kamen; married Elliot Charney (a research scientist), June 22, 1947; children: Tina, Ruth, Juliet. *Education:* Studied at Pratt Institute, 1939-42, and Art Students' League of New York, 1942-45. *Home:* 8912 Seneca Lane, Bethesda, Md. 20034.

CAREER: Fairchild Publications, New York, N.Y., staff of promotion department, 1947-49; free-lance designer and illustrator, New York, N.Y., 1949-57, doing magazine illustration, package design, book jackets and book covers; illustrator of books for children, 1964—. Volunteer reading tutor in local schools; gives illustrated talks on books to children. *Member:* Artists Equity Association, Children's Book Guild (Washington, D.C.). *Awards, honors:* Three awards from Educational Press Association of America for magazine covers and one award for design of feature section of a National Education Association magazine; Ohio

GLORIA KAMEN

State University Award, Institute for Education by Radio, Television, 1975, for program for WETA.

ILLUSTRATOR: Hughie Call, *The Little Kingdom,* Houghton Mifflin, 1964; Elizabeth Goudge, *A Book of Comfort,* Coward, 1964; *Betty Crocker Cookbook for Boys and Girls,* Western Publishing, 1966; Ann Guy, *One Dozen Brownies,* Abingdon, 1962; Ethelyn Parkinson, *The Operation That Happened to Rupert Piper,* Abingdon, 1966; Joan Lexau, *Three Wishes for Abner,* Ginn, 1967; Phyllis Naylor, *To Shake a Shadow,* Abingdon, 1967; Barbara Klimowicz, *The Strawberry Thumb,* Abingdon, 1968; Lila Sheppard, *Wiki Wants to Read,* Whitman, 1968; Ruth Hooker, *Gertrude Kloppenberg, Private,* Abingdon, 1970; Barbara Klimowicz, *When Shoes Eat Socks,* Abingdon, 1971; Valerie Pitt, *Let's Find Out About the Family,* Watts, 1971; Ethelyn Parkinson, *Rupert Piper and Megan, the Valuable Girl,* Abingdon, 1972; Barbara Todd, *Juan Patricio,* Putnam, 1972; Ruth Hooker, *Gertrude Kloppenberg II,* Abingdon, 1974; Jean Leifheit, *Drugs Your Friends,* and *Drugs Your Enemies,* Standard Publications, 1974; Edna S. Levine, *Lisa and Her Soundless World,* Behaviorial Publications, 1974.

Has done art work for educational television programs, ''Cover-to-Cover,'' produced by WETA, Washington, D.C. Illustrations have appeared in *Woman's Day,* also in children's magazines.

by Edna S. Levine

illustrated by

Gloria Kamen

(From *Lisa and Her Soundless World* by Edna S. Levine. Illustrated by Gloria Kamen.)

they were little. When I'm not working on a book I like to draw on very large sheets of paper—out of this has come several one person shows in galleries."

KAREN, Ruth 1922-

PERSONAL: Born February 18, 1922, in Germany; daughter of David (an attorney) and Paula (Freudenthal) Karpf; married S. Alexander Hagai (now a management sciences consultant), March, 1966. *Education:* Studied at Hebrew University of Jerusalem and University of London; New School for Social Research, graduate. *Politics:* Independent. *Home:* 360 East 55th St., Apartment 5H, New York, N.Y. 10022. *Agent:* Curtis Brown Ltd., 60 East 56th St., New York, N.Y. 10022.

CAREER: War, foreign, and United Nations correspondent for *Reporter, Toronto Star,* and World Wide Press, 1947-62; full-time writer, 1962-66; Business International Corp., Latin America and Asia, senior editor, 1966-74, managing editor, New York, N.Y., 1974—. *Wartime service:* War correspondent with British Army, with assimilated rank of lieutenant colonel, 1947-48, and with U.S. Army, with assimilated rank of major, 1952-53. *Member:* Overseas Press Club of America, Authors League of America.

WRITINGS: The Land and People of Central America, Lippincott, 1965; *Neighbors in a New World: The Organization of American States,* World Publishing, 1966; *The Seven Worlds of Peru,* Funk & Wagnalls, 1969; *Hello Guatemala,* Norton, 1970; *Song of the Quail: The Wondrous World of the Maya,* Four Winds, 1972; *Brazil Today: A Case Study in Developmental Economics that Worked,* Getulio Vargas Foundation, 1974; *Kingdom of the Sun:*

RUTH KAREN

The Inca, Empire Builders of the Americas, Four Winds, 1975. Articles have appeared in *New York Times Magazine, This Week, Mademoiselle, Collier's, Business Abroad, Economic Digest,* and other periodicals.

WORK IN PROGRESS: A trilogy on the three great pre-Columbian civilizations—the Maya, the Inca and the Aztecs—and their predecessors in the American hemisphere.

SIDELIGHTS: "As I remember it, it all began one New Year's Eve in the mountains of Switzerland, when I was nine. Because it was New Year's Eve, I was allowed to take out my skis and stay up as long as I liked. Close to twelve o'clock, I was high up, looking down on the village. Snow fell in flakes so large I could see their crystal structures. The mountains glistened white, as did the gabled roofs of the village. The lights of the houses twinkled golden, returning the greetings of the stars. And the sky was ink black.

"At midnight, the bells began to peal, washing waves of sound over the roofs and mountains, up to where I stood and beyond to the sky. I remember thinking what a lovely world it was, with nature as our gift and the many fascinating things humankind itself has made. I never lost that thought.

"Later, as a journalist, a writer, an editor, I investigated some of the systems man had constructed around the gifts of nature—religion, art, science—and looked more closely at some of the structures he had wrought: politics, economics, social relations, war. I discovered in the process that looking at the here-and-now was not enough. To understand, one had to look at history, comprehend where we had started, how it all began, and grew. To peer into the future—where curiosity inevitably led—I had to search the past and know the dreams and hopes that had inspired my fellow citizens on this planet in the millenia that preceded my own.

"In this way, I came to write about people and their lives in other places, at other times. In this search for our ancestors and their ways, I came, almost by accident, across the great civilizations of the Americas: the Maya, the Inca, the Aztec and the peoples who preceded them in this hemisphere.

"Often, not much was known about them, and unearthing—sometimes literally—what could be discovered was a splendid adventure. One thing I discovered in the process was that America's great pre-Columbian civilizations shared among them the core concerns of all the great civilizations of mankind. The Mayas' civilization was focused on man's relationship to the universe; the Incas probed deeply into man's relationship to human society; the Aztecs delved into the sometimes brutal and bloody depth of man's relationship to his own will, endurance and capacity for self-sacrifice.

"This is where I am at the moment. But there are other worlds to uncover and celebrate, on other continents, in other times, perhaps even on other planets. I shall keep looking and share as best I can what I find."

FOR MORE INFORMATION SEE: Horn Book, April, 1973.

CAROLE KATCHEN

KATCHEN, Carole 1944-

PERSONAL: Born January 30, 1944, in Denver, Colo.; daughter of Samuel (owner of a tavern) and Gertrude (Levin) Katchen. *Education:* Ripon College, student, 1961-62; University of Colorado, B.A. (cum laude), 1965; further study at Hebrew University of Jerusalem, 1965, West Valley College, 1969-70, and Denver Community College, 1973-74. *Home:* 492 South Jasmine St., Denver, Colo. 80222.

CAREER: Has been welfare caseworker, shoe saleswoman, photographer's assistant, preschool teacher, and lecturer; artist whose pastels, paintings, and woodblock prints have been exhibited in one-woman shows in Bogota, Colombia (1974) and United States. *Member:* Denver Women's Press Club, *Colorado Woman Digest* (on advisory review board). *Awards, honors:* Tuttle nonfiction fellow· at University of Colorado Writer's Conference, 1966; Bread Loaf Writers' Conference, working scholarship, 1971.

WRITINGS—For young people: *I Was a Lonely Teenager,* Scholastic Book Services, 1965; *The Underground Light Bulb,* Scholastic Book Services, 1969. Contributor to Scholastic Magazines publications and *Denver Post Empire.*

SIDELIGHTS: Among Carole Katchen's more unusual travels have been hitchhiking trips across North Africa and from Texas through Mexico and Central America to Peru. She spent seven months in Israel in 1965.

"I relate best to people rather than landscapes or still lifes. So in my work I use people as subject matter, not People in the sense of Humanity, but individual human beings. I look for subjects who convey some emotion or attitude that I can relate to, usually some kind of strength, rather than physical beauty. Then when drawing the person, I work to communicate that feeling not worrying so much about physical likeness. Sometimes I've thrown away a piece that showed a great physical likeness, but lacked the spirit that I felt the person conveyed."

FOR MORE INFORMATION SEE: American Artist, September, 1975.

KEEGAN, Marcia 1943-

PERSONAL: Born May 23, 1943, in Tulsa, Okla.; daughter of Otis Claire and Mary Elizabeth (Collar) Keegan. *Education:* University of New Mexico, B.A., 1963. *Home:* Weehawken, N.J. *Office:* 140 East 46th St., New York, N.Y. 10017.

MARCIA KEEGAN

Taos Indians have always believed that the waters of Blue Lake are the source of all Taos life and the final resting place for their souls after death. ■ (From *The Taos Indians and Their Sacred Blue Lake* by Marcia Keegan. Photographs by the author.)

CAREER: Free-lance writer and photographer. *Member:* American Society of Magazine Photographers, Art Directors Club. *Awards, honors:* New Mexico Press Award, 1963.

WRITINGS—Self-illustrated with photographs: *The Taos Indians and Their Sacred Blue Lake,* Messner, 1971; *Mother Earth, Father Sky,* Grossman, 1974; *We Can Still Hear Them Clapping,* Avon, 1974.

KEEPING, Charles (William James)   1924-

PERSONAL: Born September 22, 1924, in Lambeth, South London, England; son of Charles Clark (a professional boxer) and Eliza (Trodd) Keeping; married Renate Meyer (an artist and illustrator), September 20, 1952; children: Jonathan, Vicki, Sean, Frank. *Education:* The Polytechnic, London, art studies, 1949-52, National Diploma in Design, 1952. *Politics:* "Individualist." *Religion:* None. *Home:* 16 Church Rd., Shortlands, Bromley BR2 0HP, England. *Agent:* B. L. Kearley Ltd., 59 George St., London, England.

CAREER: Began drawing as a child; apprenticed to London printer at age fourteen; later did war work (in factory and demolition corps) and was gas meter collector before joining Royal Navy at eighteen; after military service returned to meter collecting and attended night school until 1949 when he started full-time art studies; illustrator, 1952—, and author of children's books, 1966—. Teacher of lithography at The Polytechnic, London, 1956-63; visiting

lecturer in illustration at Croydon College of Art, 1963—. Lithographs have been exhibited in London, Italy, Australia, and United States, including International Exhibition of Lithography in Cincinnati, 1958; prints are in collection of Victoria and Albert Museum, London, and in other galleries; besides illustrating books has done advertising art, wall murals, posters, comic strip, and book jackets. *Military service:* Royal Navy, wireless operator.

AWARDS, HONORS: Certificate of Merit of Library Association, for British edition of *Shaun and the Cart-horse;* Certificate of Merit at Leipzig Book Fair, for *Black Dolly* (U.S. edition titled *Molly o' the Moors*); Kate Greenaway Medal of Library Association, 1968, for British edition of *Charley, Charlotte and the Golden Canary* (medal is given for most distinguished United Kingdom children's book illustration); *Joseph's Yard* was an honor book in Kate Greenaway Medal competition; *The God Beneath the Sea* was runner-up for Kate Greenaway Medal; *The Spider's Web* received honorable mention at Bratislava Biennial, 1974; Keeping was runner-up for Hans Christian Andersen International Children's Book Medal, 1974 (medal is awarded biennially for most distinguished contribution to international children's literature, based on complete works).

WRITINGS—Self-illustrated: *Shaun and the Cart-horse,* Watts, 1966; *Molly o' the Moors: The Story of a Pony,* World Publishing, 1966 (published in England as *Black Dolly,* Brockhampton Press, 1966); *Charley, Charlotte and the Golden Canary,* Oxford University Press, 1966, Watts, 1967; *Alfie Finds the Other Side of the World,* Watts, 1968 (published in England as *Alfie and the Ferryboat*, Oxford University Press, 1968); (compiler) *Tinker, Tailor: Folk Song Tales*, Brockhampton Press, 1968; (reteller) *The Christmas Story as Told on "Play School,"* BBC Publications, 1968, published in America as *The Christmas Story*, Watts, 1969; *Joseph's Yard*, Oxford University Press, 1969, Watts, 1970; *Through the Window*, Watts, 1970; *The Garden Shed*, Oxford University Press, 1971; *The Spider's Web*, Oxford University Press, 1972; *Richard*, Oxford University Press, 1973; *The Nanny Goat and the Fierce Dog*, S. G. Phillips, 1974; *Railway Passage*, Oxford University Press, 1974; (compiler of words and music) *Cockney Ding Dong*, 1975.

Illustrator: Nicholas Stuart Gray, *Over the Hills to Fabylon*, Oxford University Press, 1954, Hawthorn, 1970; Rosemary Sutcliff, *The Silver Branch*, Oxford University Press, 1957, Walck, 1958; Rosemary Sutcliff, *Warrior Scarlet*, Walck, 1958; Rosemary Sutcliff, *The Lantern-Bearers*, Walck, 1959.

John Stewart Murphy, *Roads*, Oxford University Press, 1960; Rosemary Sutcliff, *Knight's Fee*, Oxford University Press, 1960, Walck, 1961; John Stewart Murphy, *Canals*, Oxford University Press, 1961; Rosemary Sutcliff, *Beowulf*, Bodley Head, 1961, Dutton, 1962; Ruth Chandler, *Three Trumpets*, Abelard, 1962; Kenneth Grahame, *The Golden Age* [and] *Dream Days*, Bodley Head, 1962, Dufour, 1965; Barbara Leonie Picard, *Lost John*, Oxford University Press, 1962, Criterion, 1963; John Stewart Murphy, *Dams*, Oxford University Press, 1963; Hilda Hewett under pseudonym Clare Compton, *Harriet and the Cherry Pie*, Bodley Head, 1963; Martha Edith von Almedingen under

CHARLES KEEPING

E. M. Almedingen, *The Knights of the Golden Table*, Bodley Head, 1963, Lippincott, 1964; Maureen McIlwraith under pseudonym Mollie Hunter, *Patrick Kentigern Keenan*, Blackie & Son, 1963, published in America as *The Smartest Man in Ireland*, Funk, 1965; James Holding, *The King's Contest and Other North African Tales*, Abelard, 1964; John Stewart Murphy, *Railways*, Oxford University Press, 1964; Henry Treece, *The Last of the Vikings*, Brockhampton Press, 1964, published in America as *The Last Viking*, Pantheon, 1966; Maureen McIlwraith under pseudonym Mollie Hunter, *The Kelpie's Pearls*, Blackie & Son, 1964, Funk, 1966; Martha Edith von Almedingen under E. M. Almedingen, *The Treasure of Seigfried*, Bodley Head, 1964, Lippincott, 1965; John Stewart Murphy, *Wells*, Oxford University Press, 1965; Nicholas Stuart Gray, *The Apple Stone*, Dobson, 1965, Hawthorn, 1969; Alan Garner, *Elidor*, Collins, 1965; Henry Daniel-Rops, *The Life of Our Lord*, deluxe edition, Hawthorn, 1965; Rosemary Sutcliff, *Heroes and History*, Putnam, 1965; Henry Treece, *Splintered Sword*, Brockhampton Press, 1965, Duell, Sloan & Pearce, 1966; Kevin Crossley-Holland, *King Horn*, Macmillan (London), 1965, Dutton, 1966; Walter Macken, *Island of the Great Yellow Ox*, Macmillan (London), 1966; Erich Maria Remarque, *All Quiet on the Western Front*, translation by A. W. Wheen, Folio Society, 1966; James Holding, *The Sky-Eater and Other South Sea Tales*, Abelard, 1966; James Reeves, *The Cold Flame*, Hamish Hamilton, 1967, Meredith, 1969; Henry Treece, *Swords from the North*, Pantheon, 1967; Nicholas Stuart Gray, *Mainly in Moonlight: Ten Stories of Sorcery and the Supernatural*, Hawthorn, 1967; Henry Treece, *The Dream-Time*, Brockhampton Press, 1967, Hawthorn, 1968; Kenneth McLeish, *The Story of Aeneas*, Longmans, Green, 1968; Richard Potts, *The Haunted Mine*, Lutterworth, 1968; James Reeves, compiler, *An Anthology of Free Verse*, Basil Blackwell, 1968; Walter Macken, *The Flight of the Doves*, Macmillan, 1968; James Holding, *Poko and the Golden Demon*, Abelard, 1968; Margaret Jessy Miller, editor, *Knights, Beasts and Wonders: Tales and Legends from Mediaeval Britain*, David White, 1969; Roger Lancelyn Green, reteller, *The Tale of Ancient Israel*, Dent, 1969, Dutton, 1970.

Lee Cooper, *Five Fables from France*, Abelard, 1970; Leon Garfield and Edward Blishen, *The God Beneath the Sea*, Kestrel Books, 1970, Pantheon, 1971; Pamela Lyndon Travers under P. L. Travers, *Friend Monkey*, Harcourt, 1971; William Cole, compiler, *The Poet's Tales: A New Book of Story Poems*, World Publishing, 1971; Fedor Dostoevskii, *The Idiot*, Folio Society, 1971; Mary Francis Shura, *The Valley of the Frost Giants*, Lothrop, 1971; Henry Treece, *The Invaders: Three Stories*, Crowell, 1972; Robert Newman, *The Twelve Labours of Hercules*, Crowell, 1972; Roger Squire, reteller, *Wizards and Wampum: Legends of the Iroquois*, Abelard, 1972; Leon Garfield and Edward Blishen, *The Golden Shadow*, Kestrel Books, 1972, Pantheon, 1973; Ursula Synge, *Weland: Smith of the Gods*, Bodley Head, 1972, S. G. Phillips, 1973; Montague Rhodes James, *Ghost Stories of M. R. James*, Folio Society, 1973; Rosemary Sutcliff, *The Capricorn Bracelet*, Oxford University Press, 1973; Lee Cooper, *The Strange Feathery Beast, and Other French Fables*, Carousel, 1973; Helen L. Hoke, *Weirdies: A Horrifying Concatenation of the Super-sur-Real or Almost or Not-Quite Real*, Watts, 1973; Helen L. Hoke, *Monsters, Monsters, Monsters*, Watts, 1974; Lewis Jones, *The Birds, and Other Stories*, Longmans, Green, 1974; Eric Allen, *The Latchkey Chil-*

Once upon a time, a time that never was and is always, there lived in Arabia a sultan and his wife. ■ (From *About the Sleeping Beauty* by P. L. Travers. Illustrated by Charles Keeping.)

dren, Oxford University Press, 1974; Robert Swindells, *When Darkness Comes,* Morrow, 1975.

SIDELIGHTS: "In Lambeth we had a back yard, one of those tiny little ones and because my father had been brought up very poorly, his parents were costers along the street, we lived with my mother's family who were old seafaring people. There was a tremendous protectiveness for the children, and I wasn't allowed to play in the street, or associate with rough boys much. I always had to stay in this little yard you see.

"As a child I got interested in all the things that happened in that back yard. If the old cat came in I wondered if it was going to kill a bird. I watched spiders and flies and all

sorts of things. I fiddled about with the flowers and all the while I was on my own, thinking.

"To me they were all like characters in some sort of play. Next door was a stable yard. They used to have cart horses, and I knew all the horses. And at the back they used to have a great plain brick wall. Everything seemed to happen in front of it so it was like a stage, and in front of it was acted out my own little play, my own little world. *Through the Window* comes from this experience.

"You will very rarely find, unless anyone forces me, much of what I would call 'landscape' in anything I do. Figures are often isolated. I am sure this is the reason. I never saw any landscape. There was no colour, there were just horses and what are they, black, brown and white and people in those days used to dress in those dull tones too. Any colour you got was from elements like the sun, setting sun, so everything became red, but it would be all red. You'll notice in most of the things I do, I often produce a red page or a blue page, it's very rarely that I use many colours together. One review of *Alfie and the Ferryboat* said, 'This welter of colour has no meaning at all. It is completely self indulgent.' I am just influenced by the light. There are many different kinds of lighting in London streets.

"As I said to this kid the other day, 'How can you say you are wearing a red dress! It's red in this situation, it's a different red in another situation. If I take you out into the night light it'll be a different colour again. If I put you under a blue street light the dress will become mauve or purple. If we walk along a road with orange lighting your dress will become orange, and if we walk past a fish shop with neon lights outside you're going to be split up into about five different colours.'

"I think it amused, most of all, a little coloured girl who was sitting by my side. She immediately understood the idea that there is no such thing as colour. It's only relevant to the situation and therefore I tend not to use realistic colour, it's irrelevant to me. I still believe that by using discordant colours that almost jar I get something of the sounds of London.

"I was very lucky to have a family who did encourage, in their own simple way, creativity. There was my grandfather, a merchant seaman. He was a great singer of songs and teller of stories and we were never told to shut up and sit down. We were encouraged to stand up and talk. My grandfather would say, 'No *you* tell us a story, or *you* sing us a song, or *you* draw us a picture.' We lived half within the security of family and half in worlds of our own.

"My father died. I left school at fourteen. My mother thought she'd apprentice me to the newspapers and I was apprenticed in printing; but I was always drawing. I drew all the time. Soon after that of course, the war broke out and I left school. Then I left the print because the bottom fell out of it and I was supposed to be a bookbinder. I went to work in a war factory which got bombed, and I ended up on demolition, which was a very good thing because I couldn't bear working in factories. Then I was a gas meter collector in North Kensington. I joined the Navy and became a wireless operator and after four years I came out and asked for a grant to go to art college, and they said, 'No you can't have one, you left school at fourteen, you're not well educated, you are not good enough.' This absolutely infuriated me. I worked another three years as a meter collector but I studied all the time at evening school and I wrote endless stories around the people I was seeing while I was doing all this. And I was drawing, drawing, drawing. It's the only thing that ever meant anything to me.

"I eventually got to art school and was there five years. Then I left and I went into illustration. Most of us that left art schools, did. If we were decently poor, what else could we do? We had to get a living. We couldn't just sit and paint. And it was hard to get work.

"I worked in the newspapers for a while doing the cartoon. I did three years of that. It drove me mad because it couldn't develop. There's work now in illustration more than there's ever been. When I started we had to do years of line drawing before we ever got round to doing our own ideas, but now people are getting a chance to come straight in.

"There is some work that I wouldn't touch. I don't believe in doing the series kind of book like *Lassie* and then *Lassie Come Home,* and then *Lassie on Ice.* I find this kind of children's illustration, terrible. There are frustrations in drawing to someone else's words too. You might not like their story. In the past, I've had to do it for money but I don't do it much now. I don't think you can ever really understand anybody else's mind. People can stimulate ideas in me. I have done a lot of straight illustrations, really straight illustrations but unless I can extend someone else's idea, then I can't see what contribution I'm making. I don't want to do what is only 'a nice drawing.'"

Many of the illustrated books listed solely with a U.S. publisher also were published the same year in England and there have been reprints and paperback editions in both countries.

Charley, Charlotte and the Golden Canary, Alfie Finds "The Other Side of the World," and *Through the Window* were made into film strips by Weston Woods.

FOR MORE INFORMATION SEE: Illustrators of Children's Books: 1957-1966, Horn Book, 1968; *Children's Literature in Education/1,* APS Publications, Inc., March, 1970; *Children's Literature in Education/3,* APS Publications, Inc., November, 1970; *Graphis 155,* Volume 27, Graphis Press, 1971/72; *Third Book of Junior Authors,* edited by de Montreville and Hill, H. W. Wilson, 1972; *Horn Book,* October, 1974; Wintle and Fisher, *The Pied Pipers,* Paddington Press, 1975.

KELLIN, Sally Moffet 1932-

PERSONAL: Born April 21, 1932, in New York, N.Y.; daughter of Harold Leroy (an actor) and Sylvia (Field) Moffet; married Robert Dozier, January 21, 1956 (divorced, 1963); married Mike Kellin (an actor), August 3, 1966; children: (first marriage) Harold, Aaron, Brendan; (second marriage) Shauna. *Education:* Studied acting with Sanford Meisner and at Actors Studio. *Home:* 23 Clinton Ave., Nyack, N.Y. 10960. *Agent:* Maximilian Becker, 115 East 82nd St., New York, N.Y. 10028.

CAREER: Stage and television actress, 1948-58.

WRITINGS: A Book of Snails (juvenile), W. R. Scott, 1968.

WORK IN PROGRESS: Man Alive, a novel; research in paternal grandmother's family history for two projected books, a biography or novel about her paternal grandmother titled *Alberta* and a history of the family during the Civil War.

SIDELIGHTS: "I wrote the snail book because I wanted to find out about snails (they were all over our garden in California and threatened to destroy all vegetation) and had trouble finding information. I decided to fill the gap myself and wrote as I learned—or the other way round. I'm not sure which comes first, writing or learning."

FOR MORE INFORMATION SEE: New York Times Book Review, November 3, 1968.

KING, Stephen 1947-

PERSONAL: Born September 21, 1947, in Portland, Me.; son of Donald (a sailor) and Ruth (Pillsbury) King; married Tabitha Spruce (a poet), January 2, 1971; children: Naomi, Joseph Hill. *Education:* University of Maine, B.Sc., 1970. *Politics:* Populist. *Home:* RFD #2, Kansas Rd., Bridgton, Me. 04009.

CAREER: Formerly employed as janitor, in mill, and as laundry worker; also formerly high school teacher of English in Hampden, Me. *Member:* Authors Guild.

WRITINGS: Carrie (novel), Doubleday, 1974; *Jerusalem's Lot* (novel), Doubleday, 1975.

WORK IN PROGRESS: The Shine, a novel about a small boy isolated with his parents in an ominous and snowbound Colorado resort hotel.

HOBBIES AND OTHER INTERESTS: Reading (mostly fiction), jigsaw puzzles, playing the guitar ("I'm terrible and so try to bore no one but myself"), movies.

KNIGHT, Damon 1922-

PERSONAL: Born September 19, 1922, in Baker, Ore.; son of Frederick Stuart and Leola (Damon) Knight; married Gertrud Werndl; married Helen Schlaz; married Kate Wilhelm (a writer), February 23, 1963; children: Valerie, Christopher, Leslie, Jonathan. *Education:* Attended high school in Hood River, Ore. *Home address:* Box 8216, Madeira Beach, Fla. 33738. *Agent:* Robert P. Mills, 156 East 52nd St., New York, N.Y. 10022.

CAREER: Science fiction writer and editor. Milford Science Fiction Writers' Conference, co-founder, 1956, director, 1956—. *Member:* Science Fiction Writers of America (founder, 1965; president, 1965-66). *Awards, honors:* Hugo award from World Science Convention, 1965, for best science fiction criticism.

WRITINGS: Novels: *Hell's Pavement,* Lion Press, 1955; *Masters of Evolution,* Ace Books, 1959; *The People Maker,* Zenith Books, 1959, published as *A for Anything,* Berkley Publishing, 1965; *The Sun Saboteurs* (bound with Wallis G. McDonald, *The Light of Lilith*), Ace Books, 1961; *Beyond the Barrier,* Doubleday, 1964; *Mind Switch,* Berkley Publishing, 1965, published as *The Other Foot,* Whiting & Wheaton, 1965, M-B Publishing, 1971; *Three Novels: Rule Golden, Natural State, [and] The Dying Man,* Doubleday, 1967; *The Rithian Terror* (originally published as "Double Meaning," in *Startling Stories,* January, 1953), Universal Publishing & Distributing, 1972.

Collections—all stories, except as noted: *In Search of Wonder: Essays on Modern Science Fiction,* Advent, 1956, 2nd edition, 1967; *Far Out: 13 Science Fiction Stories,* Simon & Schuster, 1961; *In Deep,* Berkley Publishing, 1963; *Off Center,* Ace Books, 1965; *Turning On: Thirteen Stories,* Doubleday, 1966 (published in England as *Turning On: Fourteen Stories,* Gollancz, 1967); *World without Children [and] The Earth Quarter,* Lancer Books, 1970; *The Best of Damon Knight,* Pocket Books, 1974.

Editor of anthologies: *A Century of Science Fiction,* Simon & Schuster, 1962; *First Flight,* Lancer Books, 1963, published as *Now Begins Tomorrow,* 1969; *A Century of Great Short Science Fiction Novels,* Dial, 1964; *Tomorrow X 4,* Fawcett, 1964; *The Shape of Things,* Popular Library, 1965; (and translator) *Thirteen French Science-Fiction Stories,* Bantam, 1965; *The Dark Side,* Doubleday, 1965; *Beyond Tomorrow: Ten Science Fiction Adventures,* Harper, 1965; *Cities of Wonder,* Doubleday, 1966; *Nebula Award Stories 1965,* Doubleday, 1966; *Worlds to Come: Nine Science Fiction Adventures,* Harper, 1967; *Science Fiction Inventions,* Lancer Books, 1967; *Toward Infinity: Nine Science Fiction Tales,* Simon & Schuster, 1968; *One Hundred Years of Science Fiction,* Simon & Schuster, 1968; *The Golden Road,* Simon & Schuster, 1968; *The Metal Smile,* Belmont Books, 1968.

Dimension X: Five Science Fiction Novellas (Child Study Association book list), Simon & Schuster, 1970; *First Contact,* Pinnacle Books, 1971; (contributor) *A Pocketful of Stars,* Doubleday, 1971; *Perchance to Dream,* Doubleday, 1972; *A Science Fiction Argosy,* Simon & Schuster, 1972; *Tomorrow and Tomorrow,* Simon & Schuster, 1973; *Happy Endings,* Bobbs-Merrill, 1974; *Best Stories from Orbit, Volumes 1-10,* Berkley Publishing, in press. Also editor of "Orbit" series, Volumes 1-13, Putnam, 1966-73, Volumes 14-15, Harper, 1974, Volume 16, Harper, 1975.

Other writing: (Translator) Rene Barjavel, *Ashes, Ashes,* Doubleday, 1967; *Charles Fort: Prophet of the Unexplained* (biography), Doubleday, 1970; *A Shocking Thing,* Pocket Books, 1974. Several of Knight's novels have appeared in revised form in periodicals.

WORK IN PROGRESS: Science Fiction of the Thirties and *Westerns of the Forties,* both for Bobbs-Merrill; *The Art of Science Fiction,* for Harper; *The Futurians.*

LUCY KOMISAR

KOMISAR, Lucy 1942-

PERSONAL: Born April 8, 1942, in New York, N.Y.; daughter of David (a salesman) and Frances (Munshin) Komisar. Education: Queens College, City University of New York, B.A., 1964. Home: 100 West 12th St., New York, N.Y. 10011. Agent: Rhoda Weyr, William Morris Agency, 1350 Avenue of the Americas, New York, N.Y. 10019.

CAREER: Campaign manager for City Council candidate James McNamara, New York, N.Y., 1965; Human Resources Administration, New York, N.Y., special assistant to deputy administrator, 1967-68; press secretary, Congressional primary campaign of Allard Lowenstein, 5th District, Long Island, N.Y., 1968; WBAI Radio, New York, N.Y., writer, reporter, and producer of six one-hour documentaries on hospitals and health care in New York, 1968; Public Broadcast Laboratory, New York, N.Y., researcher reporter, 1968; National Educational Television, New York, N.Y., researcher and associate producer, 1968-69; press secretary, City Council President campaign of Elinor Guggenheimer, 1969; free-lance writer. Member: National Organization for Women (national vice president for public relations, 1970-71). Awards, honors: Center for Education in Politics grant to study political activity of International Ladies Garment Workers Union, 1963.

WRITINGS: The New Feminism (youth book), Watts, 1971; Down and Out in the U.S.A., Watts, 1973; The Machismo Factor, Macmillan, 1976. Contributor of articles on feminism and other social issues to Washington Monthly, Saturday Review, New York Magazine, Village Voice, New York Times, and Newsweek. Editor, Mississippi Free Press (weekly civil rights newspaper), 1962-63; assistant editor and contributor, Hat Worker (house organ of United Hatters, Cap and Millinery International), 1966-67.

SIDELIGHTS: "I am a product of the social conscience and political movements of the 1960's—the years of the sit-ins and freedom rides, the opposition to the House Un-American Activities Committee and the ban-the-bomb movement. In 1959, I was graduated from a suburban high school that had one black student in attendance. A year later I found myself in jail (for a few days) after trying to integrate a restaurant in Maryland. I took a year's leave after my junior year of college to go to Mississippi to work on a pro-integration newspaper called the Mississippi Free Press. That was probably the turning point in my life: it made me want to be a journalist.

"After graduation from college, I stopped being an activist and set about becoming a writer. Still, the subjects of my articles were issues I cared about—civil rights, poverty, labor unions, as well as stories about urban problems and politics. It was not until 1969 that I became a 'movement' person again, and the impetus this time was the struggle for women's rights. I realized that the job discrimination I had encountered ever since I left college was part of a historical and national pattern that had to be challenged—as I had helped challenge racism ten years before. I joined the National Organization for Women and was elected a national vice president (1970-71). Then, because it is the way I know best, I wrote a book to explain feminism to teenagers.

"Now, again, I've traded activism for journalism though the goals I have for America have not changed. All of us are private people and political people at the same time. Writing about the issues I care about, I can make those two persons into one."

HOBBIES AND OTHER INTERESTS: Films, theater, tennis, horse-back riding, skiing.

FOR MORE INFORMATION SEE: New York Times Book Review, March 28, 1971, March 17, 1974; Commonweal, May 21, 1971; Library Journal, June 15, 1971; Christian Science Monitor, May 1, 1974.

KOMODA, Kiyo 1937-

PERSONAL: Kiyoaki sometimes used as variation of his given name; born March 3, in Saijo-Shi, Ehime, Japan; son of Yasugoro (a farmer) and Hisa Komoda; married Beverly Kiku Higashida (a book illustrator), July 7, 1962; children: Paul Minoru, Danny Kiyoaki, Kurt Satoru. Education: Studied at Los Angeles City College, 1955-58, and Chouinard Art Institute (now California Institute of Art), 1958-62. Home: 14 Maple Stream Rd. E., Windsor, N.J. 08520. Office: McGraw-Hill Inc., 1221 Avenue of the Americas, New York, N.Y. 10020.

CAREER: McGraw-Hill Inc., New York, N.Y., assistant art director, 1965-67, art director, 1967—. Illustrator of books for young people. Awards, honors: Citation of Merit from Society of Illustrators for Delight in the Number and Valentina.

ILLUSTRATOR: Delight in the Number, Holt, 1965; Murray Goodwin, Alonzo and the Army of Ants, Harper, 1966; J. Caufield, The Incredible Detectives, Harper, 1966; Robert A. Rosenbaum, editor, The Best Book of True Sea Stories, Doubleday, 1966; Jay Heavilin, Fear Rides High, Doubleday, 1967; Valentina, Doubleday, 1967; Gerry Turner, Hide-Out for a Horse, Doubleday, 1967; Robert H. Redding, Aluk, an Alaskan Caribou, Doubleday, 1967; Robert A. Rosenbaum, editor, The Best Book of True Aviation Stories, Doubleday, 1967; Gail Barclay, The Little Brown Gazelle, Dial, 1968; Jean Craighead George, The Moon of the Fox Pups, Crowell, 1968; Robert H. Redding, Mara, an Alaskan Weasel, Doubleday, 1968; Lilla M. Waltch, Cave of the Incas, Parents' Magazine Press, 1968; Ruth Langland Holberg, Jill and the Applebird House, Doubleday, 1968; Beth F. Day, The World of the Grizzlies, Doubleday, 1969.

Josephine Poole, Catch as Catch Can, Harper, 1970; William B. Fink, Getting to Know the Hudson River, Coward, 1970; Alice M. Lightner, Carab, the Trap-Door Spider, Putnam, 1970; Fanny Davis, Turkey, Coward, 1971; Alice M. Lightner, Biography of a Rhino, Putnam, 1972; Edmund W. Hildick, The Doughnut Dropout, Doubleday, 1972; Barbara A. Steiner, Biography of a Wolf, Putnam, 1973.

FOR MORE INFORMATION SEE: Illustrators of Children's Books: 1957-1966, Horn Book, 1968.

"... in the department we make a point of rewarding our detectives who have performed some special task. These incredible detectives certainly are deserving." ■ (From *The Incredible Detectives* by Don and Joan Caufield. Illustrated by Kiyo Komoda.)

KORACH, Mimi 1922-

PERSONAL: Born April 25, 1922, in New York, N.Y.; daughter of Dean (an artist) and Viola (Weinberg) Korach; married Bert Lesser (a businessman), April 17, 1951; children: Steven Dean, Robin (daughter). *Education:* Yale University, student at School of Fine Arts, 1939-42. *Home:* 24 Stonewall Lane, Mamaroneck, N.Y. 10543.

CAREER: Draftsman in war plants, 1942-44; went to Europe with United Service Organizations (U.S.O.) to draw portraits of serviceman, 1944-45; started book illustration, 1945; also painter doing portraits and figure painting and exhibitor in art shows. *Member:* Silvermine Guild of Artists, Westchester Art Society (vice-president, 1972-75), Women's Museum Group, Yonkers Art Association. *Awards, honors:* Various awards for painting, inclusion in many national exhibitions.

ILLUSTRATOR: Matilda Rogers, *First Book of Cotton*, Watts, 1954; Corinne Gerson, *Like a Sister*, Funk, 1954; Alice Rogers, *The Wonderful Ice Cream Cart*, Macmillan, 1955; Emily Hahn, *Leonardo da Vinci*, Random House, 1956; Charles Dickens, *Little Dorrit*, Heritage Press, 1956; Hodding Carter, *Marquis de Lafayette: Bright Sword for Freedom*, Random House, 1958.

Donald Hall, *String too Short to be Saved*, Viking, 1960; William Dean Howells, *The Rise of Silas Lapham*, Limited Editions Club, 1961; Henry Steele Commager, *Crusaders for Freedom*, Doubleday, 1962; Nancy Faulkner, *The Secret of the Simple Code*, Doubleday, 1965; Robin Gottlieb, *The Secret of the Unicorn*, Funk, 1965; Elizabeth Black Carmer and Carl L. Carmer, *Mike Funk and the Big Turkey Shoot*, Garrard, 1965; Georgianne D. Ceder, *Reluctant Jane*, Funk, 1966; Olive Burt, *Let's Find Out About Bread*, Watts, 1966; Zena Shumsky under pseudonym Jane Collier, *A Tangled Web*, Funk, 1967; Marjory Hall, *Mystery at Lyons Gate*, Funk, 1967; Bee Lewi, *Pie for the Princess*, Garrard, 1968; Elizabeth Black Carmer and Carl L. Carmer, *Pecos Bill and the Long Lasso*, Garrard, 1968; Corinne Gerson, *The Closed Circle*, Funk, 1968; May Justus, reteller, *It Happened in No-End Hollow*, Garrard, 1969; Marjory Hall, *The Whistle Stop Mystery*, Funk, 1969; Helen Rushmore, *Look Out for Hogan's Goats*, Garrard, 1969.

William O. Steele, *Hound Dog Zip to the Rescue*, Garrard, 1970; Bee Lewi, *A Ball for the Princess*, Garrard, 1971; May Justus, *Surprise for Perky Pup*, Garrard, 1971; William O. Steele, *Triple Trouble for Hound Dog Zip*, Garrard, 1972; Donna L. Pape, *Mr. Mogg in the Log*, Garrard, 1972; Wyatt Blassingame, *How Davy Crockett Got a Bearskin Coat*, Garrard, 1972; Ida DeLage, *The Old Witch and the Wizard*, Garrard, 1974; Helen Rushmore, *Old Billy Solves a Mystery*, Garrard, 1974; Irwin Shapiro, *Dan McCann and His Fast Sooner Hound*, Garrard, 1975.

WORK IN PROGRESS: Illustrating other books for Garrard.

HOBBIES AND OTHER INTERESTS: Swimming, playing tennis, music (plays recorder in a musical group and attends many concerts).

It fitted tight and snug. Tom couldn't see a thing. He scarcely had room to holler, but holler he did for he was almighty surprised and scared. ■ (From *Hound Dog Zip to the Rescue* by William O. Steele. Illustrated by Mimi Korach.)

KORINETZ, Yuri (Iosifovich) 1923-

PERSONAL: Name also appears as Iurii Iosifovich Korinets; born January 14, 1923, in Moscow, Union of Soviet Socialist Republics; son of Josef (a diplomat) and Elly (Nagel) Korinetz; married Natalia Burlova (a translator from the English), 1964; children: Ekaterina, Yuri. *Education:* Student at Art School, Samarkand, Soviet Central Asia, 1948-51, and A. M. Gorky Institute of Literature, Moscow, 1953-57. *Home:* 125319 Krasnoarmeyskaya 21 kw. 108, Moscow, Union of Soviet Socialist Republics.

Agent: VAAP-Bolshaya Bronnaya G-A 103104, Moscow, Union of Soviet Socialist Republics.

CAREER: Full-time writer. *Member:* Union of U.S.S.R. Writers, Union of the Soviet Societies of Friendship and Cultural Relations with Foreign Countries. *Awards, honors:* First prize in U.S.S.R. children's book competition dedicated to Lenin's Centenary, 1968, for *Tam, Vdali, za Rekoi (There, Far Beyond the River); Dort weit hinter dem Fluss,* the German translation of *Tam, Vdali, za Rekoi* was runner-up tor the German prize for best youth book, 1973,

There, *Far Beyond the River* also has been published in England and translated into a total of ten languages, including Norwegian, Czech, Swedish, Italian, French, and Dutch. *Greeting from Verner* and *Volodya's Brothers* have had German editions.

FOR MORE INFORMATION SEE: Times Educational Supplement, May 10, 1973; *Horn Book,* April, 1974.

LANCASTER, Bruce   1896-1963

PERSONAL: Born August 22, 1896, in Worcester, Mass.; son of Walter Moody and Sarah Jenkins (Hill) Lancaster; married Jessie Bancroft Payne, December 12, 1931. *Education:* Harvard University, A.B., 1919. *Politics:* Republican. *Religion:* Episcopalian. *Home:* 67 Grover St., Beverly, Mass. 01915.

CAREER: Businessman in Worcester, Mass., 1919-27; U.S. Department of State, foreign service officer in Kobe and Nagoya, Japan, 1927-33; Board of Governors, Society of New York Hospital, New York, N.Y., assistant secretary, 1934-38; author, mainly of historical novels, 1938-63. Trustee, Beverly Public Library, 1958-63. *Military service:* 1st Massachusetts Field Artillery, served on Mexican border, 1916. American Expeditionary Forces, Field Artillery, 1917-19; received five battle stars. *Member:* Company of

YURI KORINETZ

and the Italian edition was named one of the best youth books of 1973 in Italy; his books were selected among the best of the year for inclusion in UNESCO International Youth Library, 1972, 1973, 1974.

WRITINGS: Cyoota Subbota v Ponedelnik (title means "Saturday in Monday"; selected verses and poems), Detskaya Literatura, 1966; *Tam, Vdali ze Rekoi* (youth novel), Detskaya Literatura, 1967, translation by Anthea Bell based on German edition published as *There, Far Beyond the River,* J. Philip O'Hara, 1973; (translator into Russian) James Krüss, *Govoriashchaia mashina* (*Die Sprechmaschine*), Detskaya Literatura, 1969; *Chetyre Sestry* (title means "Four Sisters"; selected verses and poems), Detskaya Literatura, 1970; *Privet ot Vernera* (title means "Greeting from Verner"; youth novel), Detskaya Literatura, 1972; *Volodiny Bratya* (title means "Volodya's Brothers"; youth novel), Detskaya Literatura, 1975. Writer of radio plays for children and contributor to Soviet children's magazines.

WORK IN PROGRESS: A new book for children with proposed title of *The Cleverest Horse;* a novel, *Through Fire, Water and Copper Pipes.*

SIDELIGHTS: "Being fifteen years old I wrote my first story. From that time my dream was to be a writer, or a painter (I [had] visited Moscow art school). My present interests besides writings are hi-fi stereophonic, fishing, travelling, water-colour painting."

The army left the field as darkness fell, marching in disorder toward Philadelphia. ■ (From *The American Revolution* by Bruce Lancaster. Illustrated by Lee J. Ames.)

Military Collectors and Historians (fellow), Authors League of America, P.E.N., Cambridge Historical Society, St. Botolph Club (Boston), Harvard Club (New York).

WRITINGS: The Wide Sleeve of Kwannon, Frederick A. Stokes, 1938; *Guns of Burgoyne,* Frederick A. Stokes, 1939 (published in England as *Gentleman Johnny,* Heinemann, 1939), revised and condensed edition published as *Guns in the Forest,* Atlantic-Little, Brown, 1952; (with Lowell Brentano) *Bride of a Thousand Cedars,* Frederick A. Stokes, 1939; *For Us the Living,* Frederick A. Stokes, 1940; *Bright to the Wanderer,* Little, Brown, 1942; *Trumpet to Arms,* Atlantic-Little, Brown, 1944; *The Scarlet Patch,* Atlantic-Little, Brown, 1947; *No Bugles Tonight,* Atlantic-Little, Brown, 1948.

Phantom Fortress, Atlantic-Little, Brown, 1950; *Venture in the East,* Atlantic-Little, Brown, 1951; *The Secret Road,* Atlantic-Little, Brown, 1952; *Blind Journey,* Atlantic-Little, Brown, 1953; *From Lexington to Liberty: The Story of the American Revolution,* Doubleday, 1955; *Roll, Shenandoah,* Atlantic-Little, Brown, 1956; *The American Revolution* (juvenile), Garden City Books, 1957; (author of narrative) *The American Heritage Book of the Revolution,* American Heritage Press, 1958; *Night March,* Little, Brown, 1958; *Ticonderoga: The Story of a Fort* (juvenile), Houghton, 1959; *The Big Knives,* Little, Brown, 1964. Annotated *Orderly Books and Letter Books of Col. Christian Febiger (1777-1783).* Contributor of articles and book reviews to *Atlantic* and *Saturday Review.* Editor, *Old-Time New England,* published by Society for the Preservation of New England Antiquities, 1951-56.

SIDELIGHTS: All but four of Lancaster's books deal with American history. His work pattern: "I choose my period or setting first of all, then set about learning all that I can about it and the people who figured in it. Not until all of this is as solid as I can make it, do I begin the fictional part. . . . I have been as careful as is humanly possible to bring about a blending of fact and fiction without any distortion of fact. As soon as actual writing begins, each day's work is read back to me by my wife. This began with the first book, and for me [it is] an essential part of the whole writing process."

Football was a major interest. He was a member of the Harvard team in 1916, coached there in the fall of 1919, coached the line (as an avocation) at Worcester Polytechnic Institute, 1920-26, and played with a British Rugby team in Kobe, Japan, for three seasons.

FOR MORE INFORMATION SEE: Children's Literature in the Elementary School, Charlotte S. Huck and Doris A. Young, Holt, 1961.

(Died June 20, 1963)

LASKER, Joe 1919-

PERSONAL: Born June 26, 1919, in Brooklyn, N.Y.; son of Isidore (a tailor) and Rachel (Strollowitz) Lasker; married Mildred Jaspen (a teacher), November 28, 1948; children: David, Laura, Evan. *Education:* Attended Cooper Union Art School, 1936-39. *Home and office:* 20 Dock Rd., Norwalk, Conn. 06854.

JOE LASKER

CAREER: Artist, with oil paintings in permanent collections in colleges, universities, and museums, including Whitney Museum, Philadelphia Museum, and Baltimore Museum. Art teacher at City College (now City College of the City University of New York), 1947-48, and University of Illinois, 1953-54. Illustrator of children's books. *Military service:* U.S. Army, 1941-45.

MEMBER: National Academy of Design, Authors Guild of Authors League of America, Connecticut Association for Children with Learning Disabilities (president, 1964-65). *Awards, honors:* Abbey mural painting fellowship, 1947, 1948; awards from National Academy of Design include third Hallgarten prize, 1949, first Hallgarten prize, 1955, second Altman prize, 1958, Ranger Fund purchase award, 1966, Clark prize, 1969, and Isadore medal, 1972; Prix de Rome fellowship, 1950, 1951; Guggenheim fellowship, 1954; purchase award from Springfield Art Museum, 1964; Hassam Fund purchase awards from American Academy of Arts and Letters, 1965, 1968; National Institute of Arts and Letters grant, 1968.

WRITINGS: (Self-illustrated) *Mothers Can Do Anything,* Whitman, 1972; *He's My Brother,* Whitman, 1974; *Tales of a Seadog Family,* Viking, 1974; *For Richer, for Poorer,* Viking, 1975.

Illustrator: Miriam Schlein, *The Sun, the Wind, the Sea and the Rain,* Abelard, 1960; Charlotte Zolotow, *Man with the Purple Eyes*, Abelard, 1961; Schlein, *The Way Mothers Are*, Whitman, 1963; Schlein, *Big Lion, Little Lion*, Whitman, 1964; Norman Simon, *Benjy's Bird*, Whitman, 1965; Fern Brown and Andree Grabe, *When Grandpa Wore Knickers*, Whitman, 1966; Simon, *What Do I Say?*, Whitman, 1967; Simon, *See the First Star*, Whitman, 1968; Simon, *What Do I Do?*, Whitman, 1969; Simon, *How Do I Feel?*, Whitman, 1970; Schlein, *My House*, Whitman, 1971; Joel Rothman, *Night Lights*, Whitman, 1972; Joan Fassler, *Howie Helps Himself*, Whitman, 1974; Judy Delton, *Carrot Cake*, Crown, 1975. Also illustrator of *Snow Time* by Miriam Schlein, published by Whitman.

SIDELIGHTS: "Painting is my first love. I illustrate and write to support my habit and family. As it must to (practically) all illustrators of children's books, I too have become an 'author.'"

FOR MORE INFORMATION SEE: Life, March 20, 1950; Lloyd Goodrich and John Bauer, *American Art of Our Century*, Praeger, 1961; *Parade*, September 1, 1963; *Illustrators of Children's Books: 1957-1966*, Horn Book, 1968; *New York Times Book Review*, October 20, 1974.

LAWSON, Don(ald Elmer) 1917-

PERSONAL: Born May 20, 1917, in Chicago, Ill.; son of Elmer D. and Christina (Grass) Lawson; married Beatrice M. Yates, 1945. *Education:* Cornell College, Mt. Vernon, Ia., B.A., 1939, Litt.D., 1970; attended University of Iowa Writers' Workshop, 1939-40. *Religion:* Methodist. *Home:*

DON LAWSON

1122 Lunt Ave., Chicago, Ill. 60626. *Agent:* John Schaffner, 425 East 51st St., New York, N.Y. 10022. *Office:* Tangley Oaks Education Center, Lake Bluff, Ill. 60044.

CAREER: Nora Springs Advertiser, Nora Springs, Ia., editor, 1940-41; *Compton's Pictured Encyclopedia*, F. E. Compton, Chicago, 1946-73, managing editor, 1959-65, editor-in-chief, 1965-73, vice-president, 1971-73; United Educators, Inc., Ill., executive editor, 1973-74, editor-in-chief, 1974—. *Military service:* U.S. Army Air Forces, 1941-45, served with Counterintelligence in European Theater; awarded Silver Battle Star. *Member:* Authors Guild, Cliff Dwellers, Society of Midland Authors, Chicago Press Club, Chicago Literary Club, Chicago Book Clinic. *Awards, honors:* First prize, *Story* magazine's Armed Forces contest, World War II.

WRITINGS—All for young people, except as noted: *A Brand for the Burning* (adult), Abelard, 1961; *Young People in the White House*, Abelard, 1961, revised, 1971; *The United States in World War I*, Abelard, 1963; *The United States in World War II*, Abelard, 1963; *The United States in the Korean War*, Abelard, 1964; *Famous American Political Families*, Abelard, 1965; *The War of 1812*, Abelard, 1966; *Frances Perkins: First Lady of the Cabinet*, Abelard, 1966; *The Lion and the Rock: The Story of the Rock of Gibraltar*, Abelard, 1969; *The Colonial Wars*, Abelard, 1973; *The American Revolution*, Abelard, 1974; *The United States in the Indian Wars*, Abelard, 1975.

Editor of anthologies: *Great Air Battles*, Lothrop, 1968; *Youth and War*, Lothrop, 1969; *Ten Fighters for Peace*, Lothrop, 1971. Short stories in magazines in this country and abroad.

WORK IN PROGRESS: The United States in the Spanish-American War, for Abelard.

SIDELIGHTS: "I have had a consuming interest in writing and history for as far back as I can remember. I can't recall ever wanting to be anything but an author. Fortunately, I have also been an omnivorous reader since I was a youngster. Also fortunately, I had excellent English and history teachers who encouraged me every step of the way.

"Originally I intended writing novels, but after it took me fifteen years to sell my first novel, I decided there had to be an easier way to make a living! In any event, I seem to be that horror of all publishers—the one novel novelist. Perhaps some day I'll get around to doing another.

"My interest in writing non-fiction for young people began when I started doing encyclopedia editorial work and realized what a challenge it was to write clearly, simply, dramatically on difficult subjects. My natural interest in history led me into writing books on American history. My own experience in World War II and the personal belief that to achieve peace we must first understand war, resulted in my writing mainly on military subjects. Incidentally, all of my war books for Abelard are published under the series title: *The Young People's History of America's Wars*. Unless World War III breaks out I only have a couple of books to go to complete the series. So far as I know this series will be unique.

"Aside from the above-mentioned teachers, the people who

have been the greatest help to me in my writing have been my wife, my agent, my editor, and several reference librarians—not necessarily in that order. Their totally unselfish dedication is a never-failing source of wonder to me."

LE GALLIENNE, Eva   1899-

PERSONAL: Born January 11, 1899, in London, England; daughter of Richard (an editor and poet) and Julie (a journalist; maiden name, Noerregard) Le Gallienne. *Education:* Attended College Sevigne, Paris, France, 1907-14, and Royal Academy of Dramatic Art, London, England, 1914. *Residence:* Weston, Conn.

CAREER: Actress, director. Founder and director, Civic Repertory Company, 1926-33; founder, with others, American Repertory Theatre, 1946. Has taught acting at the White Barn Theatre, Westport, Conn., 1962-63. *Member:* Actors' Equity Association, Screen Actors' Guild, Dramatists Guild, American Federation of Television and Radio Artists.

AWARDS, HONORS: Pictorial Review Award, 1926; Town Hall Club Award, 1934; Society of Arts and Sciences Gold Medal, 1934; American Academy of Arts and Letters Gold Medal for Speech, 1934; Women's National Press Club Outstanding Woman of the Year award, 1947; Norwegian Grand Cross of the Royal Order of St. Olaf, 1961; American National Theatre and Academy special award,

The little mermaid was quite frightened and dived under the water, but she soon came up again and it was as though all the stars in the sky fell in a great shower around her. ■ (From *The Little Mermaid* by Hans Christian Andersen. Translated by Eva Le Gallienne. Illustrated by Edward Frascino.)

1964; American Theatre Wing special "Tony" award, 1964; Brandeis University Award, 1966. Honorary degrees: M.A., Tufts College, 1927; Litt.D., Russell Sage College, 1930, Brown University, 1933, Mt. Holyoke College, 1937, Goucher College, 1961; D.H.L., Smith College, 1930, Ohio Wesleyan University, 1953, University of North Carolina, 1964, Barr's College, 1965, Fairfield University, 1966.

WRITINGS: (Adapter with Florida Friebus) Charles Lutwidge Dodgson, *Alice in Wonderland* (play; first produced in New York, N.Y., at the Civic Repertory Theatre, December 12, 1932), Samuel French, 1932; *At 33* (autobiography), Longmans, Green, 1934; *Flossie and Bossie* (children's book), Harper, 1949; (translator and author of preface) Henrik Ibsen, *Hedda Gabler,* Faber, 1953, New York University Press, 1955; (adapter) Fritz Hochwaelder, *The Strong Are Lonely* (play), Samuel French, 1953; *With a Quiet Heart* (autobiography), Viking, 1953; (translator and author of preface) Ibsen, *The Master Builder,* New York University Press, 1955; (translator and author of preface) *Six Plays of Henrik Ibsen,* Modern Library, 1957; (translator) *Seven Tales of Hans Christian Andersen* (ALA Notable Book), Harper, 1959; (translator and author of preface) Ibsen, *The Wild Duck and Other Plays,* Modern Library, 1961; (translator) Hans Christian Andersen, *The Nightingale,* Harper, 1965; *The Mystic in the Theatre,* Farrar, Straus, 1966; (translator) Andersen, *The Little Mermaid* (Child Study Association book list), Harper, 1971. Contributor of articles and reviews to numerous periodicals.

EVA LE GALLIENNE

SIDELIGHTS: In a career that spans more than a half a century, Eva Le Gallienne has had the opportunity of working with such theatre greats as Ethel Barrymore. Over the years, she has involved herself in virtually every phase of theatre production. When she was quite young, she once saw Sarah Bernhardt on stage, and, she writes: "From that moment on, the Theatre . . . became to me the all-important aim; all my experiences, my reading, my studies from then on were focussed toward one ultimate goal."

HOBBIES AND OTHER INTERESTS: Gardening, carpentry, reading, weaving, calligraphy, and ornithology.

LYNCH, Patricia (Nora) 1898-1972

PERSONAL: Born June 7, 1898, in Cork City, Ireland; daughter of Timothy Patrick (a businessman) and Nora (Lynch) Lynch; married Richard Michael Fox (an author), October 31, 1922. *Education:* Educated at convent school, and at secular schools in Ireland, Scotland, England, and Belgium. *Home:* Dublin, Ireland. *Address:* c/o J. M. Dent & Sons Ltd., Aldine House, 10-13 Bedford St., London W.C.2, England.

CAREER: Author of children's books, 1925-72. *Christian Commonwealth,* London, England, staff member, writing feature stories, other articles, 1918-20. *Member:* P.E.N. (Dublin; delegate to P.E.N. Congress in Vienna), Irish Women Writers' Club. *Awards, honors:* Silver Medal of Aonac Tailtean for *The Cobbler's Apprentice;* London Junior Book Club annual award for *The Turf-Cutter's Donkey;* Irish Women Writers' Club annual award for *Fiddler's Quest.*

WRITINGS: The Green Dragon, Harrap, 1925; *The Cobbler's Apprentice,* Talbot Press, 1931; *The Turf-Cutter's Donkey,* Dent, 1934, Dutton, 1935; *The Turf-Cutter's Donkey Goes Visiting,* Dent, 1935, Dutton, 1936; *King of the Tinkers,* Dent, 1938; *The Turf-Cutter's Donkey Kicks Up His Heels,* Dutton, 1939; *The Grey Goose of Kilnevin,* Dent, 1939, Dutton, 1940.

Fiddler's Quest, Dent, 1941, Dutton, 1943; *Long Ears,* Dent, 1943; *Knights of God,* Hollis & Carter, 1945, Regnery (Children's Book Club selection), 1955; *Strangers at the Fair,* Browne & Nolan, 1945; *A Story-Teller's Childhood* (autobiographical), Dent, 1947, Norton, 1962; *The*

Its eyes were red jewels and its slender tongue flicked in and out. ∎ (From *Brogeen and the Bronze Lizard* by Patricia Lynch. Illustrated by H. B. Vestal)

Mad O'Haras, Dent, 1948 (published in United States under title *Grania of Castle O'Hara,* L. C. Page & Co., 1952); *Lisbeen at the Valley Farm, and Other Stories,* Gayfield Press, 1949.

The Seventh Pig, and Other Irish Fairy Tales, Dent, 1950, new edition published as *The Black Goat of Slievemore, and Other Irish Fairy Tales,* 1959; *The Dark Sailor of Youghal,* Dent, 1951; *The Boy at the Swinging Lantern,* Dent, 1952, Bentley, 1953; *Tales of Irish Enchantment,* Clonmore & Reynolds, 1952; *Delia Daly of Galloping Green,* Dent, 1953; *Orla of Burren,* Dent, 1954; *Tinker Boy,* Dent, 1955; *The Bookshop of the Quay,* Dent, 1956; *Fiona Leaps the Bonfire,* Dent, 1957; *Shane Comes to Dublin,* Criterion, 1958; *The Old Black Sea Chest: A Story of Bantry Bay,* Dent, 1958; *Jinny the Changeling,* Dent, 1959; *The Runaways,* Basil Blackwell, 1959.

Sally from Cork, Dent, 1960; *Ryan's Fort,* Dent, 1961; *The Golden Caddy,* Dent, 1962; *The House by Lough Neagh,* Dent, 1963; *Holiday at Rosquin,* Dent, 1964; *The Twisted Key, and Other Stories,* Harrap, 1964; *Mona of the Isle,* Dent, 1965; *The Kerry Caravan,* Dent, 1967; *Back of Beyond,* Dent, 1967.

"Brogeen" series; all published by Burke Publishing, except as indicated: *Brogeen of the Stepping Stones,* Kerr-Cros, 1947, *Brogeen Follows the Magic Tune,* 1952, Macmillan (New York), 1968, *Brogeen and the Green Shoes,* 1953, *Brogeen and the Bronze Lizard,* 1954, Macmillan (New York), 1970, *Brogeen and the Princess of Sheen,* 1955, *Brogeen and the Lost Castle,* 1956, *Cobbler's Luck* (short stories), 1957, *Brogeen and the Black Enchanter,* 1958, *The Stone House at Kilgobbin,* 1959, *The Lost Fisherman of Carrigmort,* 1960, *The Longest Way Round,* 1961, *Brogeen and the Little Wind,* 1962, Roy, 1963, *Brogeen and the Red Fez,* 1963, *Guests at the Beech Tree,* 1964.

WORK IN PROGRESS: A book with Isle of Man background, for Dent; another "Brogeen" book for Burke Publishing Co.

SIDELIGHTS: Patricia Lynch's fantasies, most of them based in Ireland, have reached children of many lands. In French editions, Brogeen (a leprechaun) has been renamed Korik, a creature of Bregon folklore. Eight books have been translated into French, four into Gaelic, five into Dutch, others into German, Swedish, and Malay. *Brogeen and the Little Wind* was dramatized in six installments for the British Broadcasting Corporation "Children's Hour," and *The Mad O'Haras* was dramatized for a television series; other stories have been adapted for radio and issued in Braille.

FOR MORE INFORMATION SEE: Junior Bookshelf, March, 1943, and March, 1949; Patricia Lynch, *A Story-Teller's Childhood,* Dent, 1947; Brian Doyle, *The Who's Who of Children's Literature,* Schocken, 1968; *Horn Book,* June, 1970.

(Died September, 1972)

MacPHERSON, Margaret 1908-

PERSONAL: Born June 29, 1908, in Colinton, Midlothian, Scotland; daughter of Norman (a minister) and Shina (Macaulay) Maclean; married Duncan MacPherson, June 28,

MARGARET MacPHERSON

1929 (died, 1971); children: Lachlan, Alasdair, Neil, William, Allan, Andrew, Kenneth. *Education:* University of Edinburgh, M.A., 1929. *Politics:* Labour Party. *Home:* Torvaig, Portree, Isle of Skye.

CAREER: Free-lance writer. Member of Commission of Inquiry into Crofting, 1951-54, and Consultative Council of Highlands and Island Development Board, 1970—. *Member:* P.E.N. *Awards, honors: The Rough Road* was chosen among the "fifty best children's books published in the United States" in 1965.

WRITINGS—Juveniles: *The Shinty Boys,* Harcourt, 1963; *The Rough Road* (Horn Book honor list), Harcourt, 1965; *Ponies for Hire,* Harcourt, 1967; *The New Tenants,* Harcourt, 1969; *The Battle of the Braes,* Collins, 1971; *The Boy on the Roof,* Collins, 1974.

SIDELIGHTS: "I write for children between the ages of ten to fourteen. I write from my own experience. We went through hard times in the 30's bringing up a family on the land. I only started writing when my family was almost all grown-up. My grandchildren take a great interest, wanting to know the names of the characters in the new one. They report when the book is being read aloud in school and tell me what their friends say—useful criticism."

"Good life! Falling off doesn't matter one bit. Jockeys are always falling off . . ."
"Oh grand, just my idea of fun." (From *Ponies for Hire* by Margaret MacPherson. Illustrated by Robert Parker.)

Charlie wasn't sure he understood why someone would work for so long just to build something beautiful. But he was sure that he liked what the old man built. ■ (From *Beautiful Junk* by Jon Madian. Photographs by Barbara and Lou Jacobs, Jr.)

MADIAN, Jon 1941-

PERSONAL: First syllable of surname rhymes with "played"; born April 10, 1941, in New York, N.Y.; son of Sydney (an administrator) and Anna (a teacher; maiden name, Leiber) Madian; married Gisele Marosi, July 14, 1960 (divorced, 1974); children: Lorraine, Andrea. *Education:* University of California, Riverside; Dartmouth College; University of California, Los Angeles, further study, 1962-67. *Politics:* Democratic free socialist. *Home and office:* 27 Voyage St., Venice, Calif. 90291.

CAREER: Southern California Counseling Center, Los Angeles, supervisor, 1974—. Private practice as marriage, family, and child counselor.

WRITINGS—Juvenile: Beautiful Junk: The Story of the Watts Towers, Little, Brown, 1968; *Two Is a Line,* Platt, 1971; *Lines Make Me Lonely,* Ginn, 1972.

WORK IN PROGRESS: A children's science-fiction adventure.

SIDELIGHTS: "I was always a poor student in school. I had great difficulty learning to write my name and read. I always wanted to be a psychoanalyst. I find that literature and psychotherapy are like two sides of a coin, i.e. personal images and history on one side, cultural images on the other. The writer creates images. The therapist, like the critic or historian, analyzes and catalyzes them."

FOR MORE INFORMATION SEE: Commonweal, November 22, 1968; *National Review,* December 17, 1968.

MALMBERG, Carl 1904-
(Timothy Trent)

PERSONAL: First syllable of surname rhymes with "calm"; born June 26, 1904, in Oshkosh, Wis.; son of Anton Martin (superintendent of a mining plant) and Kirsten Marie (Jensen) Malmberg; married Elizabeth Newhall, January 10, 1940. *Education:* Studied at Lawrence College, Appleton, Wis., 1921-23, and Columbia University, 1924-27. *Address:* Route 1, Warner, N.H. 03278. *Agent:* Barthold Fles Literary Agency, 507 Fifth Ave., New York, N.Y. 10017.

CAREER: American Telephone & Telegraph Co., New York, N.Y., writer, 1928-29; New York Telephone Co., New York, N.Y., clerk in accounting department, 1930-32; free-lance work, 1933-36; H. & H. Publishing Co., New York, N.Y., editor of *Health & Hygiene* (monthly magazine), 1936-38; Works Progress Administration Writers' Project, New York, N.Y., supervisor, later managing supervisor, 1938-39; American Optometric Association, New York, N.Y., writer in public health bureau, 1940-41; U.S. Public Health Service, Washington, D.C., writer, 1941-45, assigned as chief investigator to Subcommittee on Wartime Health and Education of U.S. Senate Committee on Education and Labor, 1944-45; Democratic National Committee, Washington, D.C., writer (of speeches and other campaign materials), 1945-46; free-lance writer, 1947-48; Will, Folsom & Smith, Inc. (public relations and fund-raising firm serving nonprofit hospitals), New York, N.Y., writer, 1948-69; retired, 1969. Free-lance writer, translator from the Danish, Norwegian, and Swedish, and reader for pub-

Scandinavians in America observe October 9 as Leif Eriksson Day, equally firm in the conviction that their hero, an adventuresome Viking chieftain, got here almost 500 years ahead of Columbus. ■ (From *America is Also Scandinavian* by Carl Malmberg. Illustrated by Tran Mawicke.)

lishers. *Member:* American Translators Association, New Hampshire Historical Society, Warner (N.H.) Historical Society.

WRITINGS—Nonfiction: *Diet and Die,* Hillman-Curl, 1935; *140 Million Patients,* Reynal & Hitchcock, 1947; *America Is Also Scandinavian* (Child Study Association of America book list; ALA book list), Putnam, 1970; (editor) *Warner, New Hampshire: 1880-1974,* Warner Historical Society, 1974.

Fiction under pseudonym Timothy Trent: *Night Boat,* Godwin, 1934; *All Dames are Dynamite,* Godwin, 1935; *Fall Guy,* Godwin, 1936.

Translations from the Danish: Leif Panduro, *Kick Me in the Traditions (Rend mig i traditionerne),* Eriksson, 1961;

Carl Erik Soya, *Seventeen (Sytten),* Eriksson, 1961, reprinted as *The Rites of Spring,* Pyramid Publications, 1962, and as *17,* Pyramid Publications, 1967; Jacob Paludan, *Joergen Stein,* University of Wisconsin Press, 1966; Leif Panduro, *One of Our Millionaires Is Missing (Vejen til Jylland),* Grove, 1967; Tom Kristensen, *Havoc (Haervaerk),* University of Wisconsin Press, 1968; Jens Kruuse, *War for an Afternoon (Som vanvid),* Pantheon, 1968; Jens August Schade, *People Meet (Mennesker moedes),* Dell, 1969. Also translator of short stories and articles for *American-Scandinavian Review.*

Writer of radio scripts. Contributor of more than one hundred articles to magazines, including *Woman, New Republic, Reader's Digest, Cunarder, Parents' Magazine, Equality, Health and Hygiene, Consumer Union Reports,* and *Popular Psychology Guide.*

WORK IN PROGRESS: Research in American and Scandinavian history and in Scandinavian literature.

HOBBIES AND OTHER INTERESTS: Maintaining and improving about sixty acres of woodland and field that once were a New Hampshire farm.

MARCUS, Rebecca B(rian) 1907-

PERSONAL: Born November 26, 1907, in New York, N.Y.; daughter of William and Mary (Steinberg) Brian; married Abraham Marcus (a writer); children: Daniel, Judith. *Education:* Hunter College, A.B., 1928; City College of New York, student; Columbia University, student, 1929-31. *Home:* 73-08 184th St., Flushing, N.Y.

CAREER: Junior high schools, New York, N.Y., teacher of science, 1934-54; now professional writer. *Member:* Authors Guild.

WRITINGS: First Biography of Galileo, 1960, *First Biography of Joseph Priestly,* 1961, *Science in the Bathtub,* 1961, *Science in the Garden,* 1961, *First Book of Glaciers,* 1962, *Immortals of Science: William Harvey,* 1962, *First Book of Volcanoes and Earthquakes,* 1963, *Antoine Lavoisier and the Revolution in Chemistry,* 1964, *Prehistoric Cave Paintings,* 1965, *The Cliff Dwellers,* 1968, *Biography of Moses Maimonades,* 1969, (with Judith Marcus) *Fiesta Time in Mexico,* Garrard, 1974, *Survivors of the Stone*

REBECCA MARCUS

As the charros, sitting straight and proud in their saddles, tug ever so slightly at the reins, their horses respond with dancing rhythms and fancy steps that draw an admiring "oh" and "ah" from the crowd. ■ (From *Fiesta Time in Mexico* by Rebecca B. and Judith Marcus. Illustrated by Bert Dodson.)

Age: Nine Primitive Tribes, Hastings House, 1975 (all published by Watts, unless otherwise noted). Associate science editor, *Book of Knowledge,* Grolier.

SIDELIGHTS: "Although my greatest interest for years was in the fields of chemistry, physics, and geology, I have become increasingly interested in the way people, past and present, live. Thus, my last four books have been about people—Cro-Magnon man and his cave paintings, the Cliff Dwellers of the Southwestern part of the United States, the people of Mexico, and the Stone Age people living today. Where I could do so, I spent some time among these people. Thus, I have been to Mexico eight times, and have seen most of the observances of their holiday times at first hand. For my latest book, *Survivors of the Stone Age,* I spent some time in Papua–New Guinea, seeing how the people are slowly emerging from the Stone Age to a system of self-government.

"The reading I do to write these books about people gives me many hours of enjoyment: poring over both old and new books, deciding what should go into the book and what might be left out. I have taken photographs of some of the places I have visited, and some of the photographs are used to illustrate my books."

HOBBIES AND OTHER INTERESTS: Traveling, camping, hiking, cooking, baking, reading.

Mama learned so many things about San Francisco. The cable cars were an endless delight, and Mama's idea of a perfect Sunday afternoon was for Papa to take us riding on them from one transfer point to another. Papa would tell of the time Mama took out her citizenship papers and astounded the solemn court by suddenly reciting the names of the streets. "Turk, Eddy, Ellis, O'Farrell," Mama said proudly, "Geary, Post, Sutter, Bush, and Pine." ■ (From the movie "I Remember Mama," © 1948, RKO Radio.)

McLEAN, Kathryn (Anderson)   1909-1966
   (Kathryn Forbes)

PERSONAL: Born March 10, 1909, in San Francisco, Calif.; daughter of Leon Ellis and Della (Jesser) Anderson; married Robert McLean (a contractor), 1926 (divorced, May, 1946); children: Robert, Jr., Richard. *Education:* Graduated from Mount View High School, San Francisco, 1925. *Residence:* Burlingame, Calif.

CAREER: Full-time professional writer.

WRITINGS—Under pseudonym Kathryn Forbes: *Mama's Bank Account* (short stories), Harcourt, 1943; *Transfer Point,* Harcourt, 1947. Also wrote articles for magazines and scripts for radio.

SIDELIGHTS: Kathryn Forbes' semi-autobiographical *Mama's Bank Account* concerns a Norwegian-American family in the early years of the 20th century and a mother's financial strategem for giving her children a sense of security when times were hard and it seemed almost impossible to stretch the father's earnings to cover expenses. A *Book Week* reviewer noted that although the book was frankly sentimental it was not offensively so. "It's amusing, gently ironic and well written, making real people of Mama, Papa, the girls and Nels, and all the aunts. If there are any who may excusably be called 100 per cent American, they are people like this Norwegian family, who brought with them from the old country traits of courage, honesty and straight thinking which we like to think make up the American character."

Mama's Bank Account was dramatized by John Van Druten, produced by Richard Rodgers and Oscar Hammerstein II, and reached the Music Box Theater on Broadway as "I Remember Mama" in 1944. It was filmed by RKO as "I Remember Mama" in 1948 and became a popular television show for the Columbia Broadcasting Company which ran from July 1, 1949 to June 1, 1957.

FOR MORE INFORMATION SEE: Book Week, March 21, 1943; *New York Times,* May 17, 1966.

(Died May 15, 1966)

KATHRYN McLEAN

MEYER, Carolyn   1935-

PERSONAL: Born June 8, 1935, in Lewistown, Pa.; daughter of H. Victor (a businessman) and Sara (Knepp) Meyer; married Joseph Smrcka, June 4, 1960 (divorced, 1973); children: Alan, John, Christopher. *Education:* Bucknell University, B.A., 1957. *Politics:* Liberal. *Religion:* "Questioning." *Home:* 16 Murray St., Norwalk, Conn. 06851. *Agent:* Joan Daves, 515 Madison Ave., New York, N.Y. 10022.

CAREER: Free lance writer. Institute of Children's Literature, instructor, 1973—.

WRITINGS: Miss Patch's Learn-to-Sew Book, Harcourt, 1969; *Stitch by Stitch,* Harcourt, 1971; *Bread Book* (ALA Notable Book), Harcourt, 1972; *Yarn,* Harcourt, 1973; *Saw, Hammer, and Paint,* Morrow, 1973; *Milk, Butter, and Cheese,* Morrow, 1974; *Christmas Crafts,* Harper, 1974; *People Who Make Things,* Atheneum, 1975; *Rock Tumbling,* Morrow, 1975; *Amish People,* Atheneum, in press: *The Needlework Book of Bible Stories,* Harcourt, in press; *Lots and Lots of Candy,* Harcourt, in press. Author of monthly book review column, "Chiefly for Children," *McCall's,* 1968-72. Contributor to magazines.

SIDELIGHTS: "I was born in Lewistown, Pennsylvania. An only child, I spent most of my childhood reading, writing stories about caterpillars, sewing doll clothes, and concocting things in the kitchen. I wore glasses and hated sports but sometimes agreed to play softball if my teammates would allow me six strikes. If they needed me badly enough, they did. By high school the glasses were thicker and I had braces on my teeth. There was small comfort in

Something about the Author

In the early part of the nineteenth century, English school children were often required to produce "Christmas pieces" for their parents. ■ (From *Christmas Crafts* by Carolyn Meyer. Illustrated by Anita Lobel.)

being class valedictorian without a Saturday night date in those pre-lib days.

"I worked summers in the local radio station in high school and then went on to Bucknell University, graduating in 1957 with a B.A. in English, a few secretarial courses taken at my father's insistence, lest I starve, and a continuing desire to write that had cropped up when I first learned to read and to print my own name. I went to New York, told the employment agency that I was there to be a writer, and got a job as a secretary. After marriage and two children, I quit working and stayed at home to be a good housewife. That lasted a few months. While the children took naps, I began to write. When they stopped taking naps, I kept on writing. My first story was sold to a secretarial magazine and published in shorthand. But I was the only one in the family who could read it. My secretarial training came in handy for something.

"Later I wrote a book about sewing for little girls, mostly because my children were, boys. Then I went on to the next book and the next, always getting more involved with crafts.

"We moved to Connecticut from New York ten years ago, and not long after that a third son was born. Still no daughters but more craft books—for both sexes. I now have nine books in print, three in production, one in the typewriter, and several more cooking in my head.

"I like to read, listen to music, cook, eat, travel, sew, swim, dance, watch movies, see plays. I don't like to play softball, even with six strikes."

FOR MORE INFORMATION SEE: Horn Book, August, 1971, June, 1973.

MEYER, F(ranklyn) E(dward)   1932-

PERSONAL: Born February 9, 1932, in St. Louis, Mo.; son of Franklyn Edward, Sr. and Gladys (Dishman) Meyer; married Janice Monola Kindorf, January 31, 1953; children: James August, John Andrew, Lyn Ashley. Education: Student at Dartmouth College, 1949-50, Missouri Valley College, 1950-51, Washington University, St. Louis, Mo., 1951-52; University of Missouri, A.B., 1954. Religion: Protestant. Home: 264 Gardenia Rd., Venice, Fla. Office address: P.O. Box 1719, Sarasota, Fla.

CAREER: Out of Door School, Sarasota, Fla., athletic director, social studies teacher, 1957-64, English teacher, 1964—. Out of Door School summer camp, Sarasota, Fla., director, 1958-60; Eagle's Nest Camp, Pisgah Forest, N.C., director of boys' unit, 1961. Military service: U.S. Marine Corps, 1954-56; became first lieutenant. Awards, honors: Juvenile story award from Follett Publishing Co., 1962.

WRITINGS: Me and Caleb (juvenile), Follett, 1962; Me and Caleb Again, Follett, 1969. Sarasota Herald Tribune, outdoor editor, 1972-75.

WORK IN PROGRESS: Contemporary adult novels, humorous and serious; short stories; articles.

SIDELIGHTS: "As a kid and an adult I have always been hung-up on nature—especially animals. I've always had dogs and it seems natural to write about them. Right now I am being chewed on by a nine-week-old German Shepherd pup whose name is Nikolai. He is all white. I raised his mother and grandmother from pups too. His grandmother died when Nik's mother was ten days old and we had to feed the ten pups goat milk from doll bottles.

"I presently write an outdoor column for a local newspaper and get to go fishing a lot. Recently we anchored offshore about thirty-five miles and fished in one-hundred feet of water. We caught thirty-one barracudas, ten sharks and five amberjacks that weighed thirty-five pounds.

"My fiction ideas usually start with something real. Then I make up the rest of the story to fit around it. I think day dreaming helps develop imagination. I like telling stories as well as writing them, and most of the time I don't know where they are going to end when I start. I do a lot of re-writing and revising. Sometimes after going over material many times I find the original idea has gone but a new and better one has taken its place."

HOBBIES AND OTHER INTERESTS: "Off-beat type" travels with family, fishing, skin diving, camping, science fiction, drama, working with children.

MIKOLAYCAK, Charles 1937-

PERSONAL: Surname is pronounced *Mike*-o-lay-chak; born January 26, 1937, in Scranton, Pa.; son of John Anthony and Helen (Gruscelak) Mikolaycak; married Carole Kismaric (a picture editor and author), October 1, 1970. *Education:* Pratt Institute, B.F.A., 1958; New York University, further study, 1958-59. *Home:* 115 East 90th St., Apt. 1-E, New York, N.Y. 10028.

CAREER: Du Crot Studios, Hamburg, Germany, illustrator and designer, 1959; free-lance illustrator and designer, 1962—; Time-Life Books, New York, N.Y., designer, 1963—. Illustrations for three children's books are in Kerlan Collection at University of Minnesota; other illustrations are in permanent collection of International Youth Library, Munich, Germany. Group show, Contemporary Arts Museum, Houston, Tex., 1975. *Military service:* U.S. Army, 1960-62; became sergeant.

MEMBER: American Institute of Graphic Arts. *Awards, honors:* Books he designed or illustrated were included among the Fifty Best Books of the Year in American Institute of Graphic Arts Shows, 1967, 1968, 1970, 1973, 1974, and in Chicago Book Clinic Best of the Year Show, 1967, 1971, 1972; Printing Industries of America Graphic Design Awards for *Great Wolf and the Good Woodsman,* 1967, *Mourka, the Mighty Cat,* 1970, *Fabulous Century 1960-1970,* 1971, *Grand Canyon,* 1972, and *Great Divide,* 1973; Society of Illustrators Gold Medal for book art direction, 1970; *How the Hare Told the Truth About His Horse* was among the twenty-one books from which American Institute of Graphic Arts selected illustrations to enter in Biennial of Illustrations Bratislava, 1973, and also was nominated for Caldecott Medal of American Library Association, 1973; *Shipwreck* and *The Feast Day* were included in American Institute of Graphic Arts Children's Book Show for 1973-74; *Shipwreck* was among twenty-seven books selected for Children's Book Showcase of Children's Book Council, 1975.

WRITINGS: (Adapter with wife, Carole Kismaric, from Norwegian folktale, and illustrator) *The Boy Who Tried to Cheat Death,* Doubleday, 1971.

Illustrator—Adult books: Fedor Dostoevski, *Crime and Punishment,* Kawade Shobo (Tokyo), 1966; Fedor Dostoevski, *The Brothers Karamazov,* Kawade Shobo, 1967.

Illustrator and designer—Children's books: Helen Hoover, *Great Wolf and the Good Woodsman,* Parents' Magazine Press, 1967; Brothers Grimm, *Little Red Riding Hood,* C. R. Gibson, 1968; Brothers Grimm, *Grimm's Golden*

Goose, Randon House, 1969; Jane Lee Hyndman under pseudonym Lee Wyndham, *Mourka, the Mighty Cat,* Parents' Magazine Press, 1969; Jane Lee Hyndman under pseudonym Lee Wyndham, *Russian Tales of Fabulous Beasts and Marvels,* Parents' Magazine Press, 1969.

Cynthia King, *In the Morning of Time,* Four Winds, 1970; Barbara Rinkoff, *The Pretzel Hero,* Parents' Magazine Press, 1970; Eric Sundell, *The Feral Child,* Abelard-Schuman, 1971; Margaret Hodges, reteller, *The Gorgon's Head,* Little, Brown, 1972; Barbara K. Walker, *How the Hare Told the Truth About His Horse,* Parents' Magazine Press, 1972; Edwin Fadiman, Jr., *The Feast Day,* Little, Brown, 1973; Vera Cumberlege, *Shipwreck,* Follett, 1974; Mirra Ginsburg, translator, *How Wilka Went to Sea and Other Tales from West of the Urals,* Crown, 1975; Marion L. Starkey, *The Tall Man From Boston,* Crown, 1975.

Editor and designer: Ken Dallison, *When Zeppelins Flew,* Time-Life, 1969; Fred Freeman, *Duel of the Ironclads,* Time-Life, 1969; Paul Williams, *The Warrior Knights,* Time-Life, 1969.

CHARLES MIKOLAYCAK

The old women sat huddled together, their thin, gray hair blown by the North Wind, while one of them, with the wonderful eye in her forehead, told the others everything she was seeing in countries far away. ▪ (From *The Gorgon's Head* by Margaret Hodges. Illustrated by Charles Mikolaycak.)

WORK IN PROGRESS: Writing and illustrating two books, *The Rumor of Pavel and Paali* and *And So He Kissed Her*.

SIDELIGHTS: "I am an illustrator because I must illustrate, and I am a book designer because I love books. Obviously the field in which the two meet is the one which makes me most happy—children's books. I can usually find something in most stories which makes me excited; be it a locale or period of time requiring great research, or a sense of fantasy which permits me to exercise my own fantasies pictorially, or great writing which forces me to try to match it in visual images.

"I am particularly fond of epics and folk tales. I don't care how many times they have been illustrated before; the challenge is to find the truth for myself and depict it. When I illustrate I am aware of many things; storytelling, graphic design, sequence of images and my own interests in which I can indulge. I never 'draw-down' to a projected audience. I feel children are most surprisingly capable of meeting a challenge and instinctively understand a drawing. Perhaps it will lead them to ask a question or wonder in silence—either will help them to learn or to extend themselves. I have experienced that if I am satisfied with one of my books, both children and adults will often get from it more than I ever realized I was putting into it.

"My interests include reading, theatre, films and travel. I find each in its own way provides inspiration when I begin to illustrate a book. A sight, sound, idea or anything-you-want is very often the key to a drawing. If it is experienced and remembered, all that is necessary is to put it to work for you. That is why I enjoy all of the above."

FOR MORE INFORMATION SEE: Publisher's Weekly, May 14, 1973, August 19, 1974; *Horn Book,* October, 1973; Sebesta and Iverson, *Literature for Thursday's Child,* Science Research Associates, 1975; *Children's Book Showcase Catalogue 1975,* Children's Book Council.

MILLER, Mary Beth 1942-
(Mary Beth)

PERSONAL: Born December 18, 1942, in Louisville, Ky.; daughter of Chester F. (a printer) and Nellie (Logston) Miller. *Education:* Kentucky School for the Deaf, Diploma, 1961; Gallaudet College, B.A., 1967; Connecticut College, M.A., 1974. *Residence:* New York, N.Y. *Office:* Deafness Research and Training Center, New York University, 80 Washington Sq. E., New York, N.Y. 10003.

CAREER: Actress with National Theatre of the Deaf and Little Theatre of the Deaf, Waterford, Ct., 1967-74; New York University, New York, N.Y., associate research scientist at Deafness Research and Training Center, 1974—. *Awards, honors:* Member of National Theatre of the Deaf troupe which received *Mademoiselle* Special Recognition Award.

WRITINGS: (Under name Mary Beth; with Remy Charlip) *Handtalk: An ABC of Finger Spelling and Sign Language* (juvenile), Parents' Magazine Press, 1974.

WORK IN PROGRESS: More books on sign language for young people.

SIDELIGHTS: "My life was never dull or lonely. Coming from deaf parents, our lives were filled with memories of

MARY BETH MILLER

storytelling in Sign Language, Christmas carols and the togetherness of a family. My world may be silenced by sickness but there's music inside me playing all day and I enjoy life tremendously."

MORTON, Miriam 1918-

PERSONAL: Born June 14, 1918, in Kishinev, Rumania (now Russian territory); brought to United States, 1921; became citizen through father's naturalization, 1926; married Lewis Morton (an editor and writer), April 24, 1937; children: two daughters. *Education:* New York University, B.S., 1942. *Home:* 61 Stockton Rd., Kendall Park, N.J. 08824.

CAREER: Worked full time while attending evening school for seven years, mostly at Modern Library, Inc. and Random House, Inc., both New York, N.Y.; after receiving degree continued working in New York, N.Y., as investigator for Department of Public Welfare, as social worker for the Board of Child Welfare, and visiting teacher for Bureau of Attendance, Department of Education; later nursery school teacher, script reader for 20th Century-Fox Films, and manuscript editor for University of California Press and University of Chicago Press: translator and author, 1963—.

AWARDS, HONORS: Program for Cultural Communication grant, 1962; *From Two to Five* was included on Child Study Association of America's Best Books of the Year List, 1964; *A Harvest of Russian Children's Literature* was an American Library Association Notable Book, 1967, and a *School Library Journal* Distinguished Book, also 1967; *Fierce and Gentle Warriors* was an Honor Book in *Book Week's* Children's Spring Festival, 1967; Child Study Association of America's Best Books of the Year List included *Twenty-Two Tales for Young Children by Leo Tolstoy,* 1969, *Voices from France,* 1969, and *The Moon Is Like a Silver Sickle,* 1972; Special Recognition Citation from American Children's Theatre Association, 1973, for *The Arts and the Soviet Child.*

WRITINGS: (Editor and translator from the Russian) Kornei Chukovsky, *From Two to Five* (foreword by Frances Clarke Sayers), University of California Press, 1963; (editor, principal translator, and author of introduction and commentary) *A Harvest of Russian Children's Literature,* University of California Press, 1967; (editor, translator from the Russian, and author of introduction) Mikhail Sholokhov, *Fierce and Gentle Warriors* (juvenile), Doubleday, 1967; (translator from the Russian and author of introduction) Semyon E. Rosenfield, *The First Song* (juvenile), Doubleday, 1968; (editor, translator from the Russian, and author of introduction) *Shadows and Light: Nine Stories by Anton Chekhov* (juvenile), Doubleday, 1969; (editor, translator from the Russian, and author of afterword) *Twenty-Two Tales for Young Children by Leo Tolstoy,* Simon & Schuster, 1969.

The Arts and the Soviet Child: The Esthetic Education of Children in the USSR, Free Press, 1972; *Pleasures and Palaces: The After-School Activities of Soviet Children* (juvenile), Atheneum, 1972; (editor and translator) *The Moon Is Like a Silver Sickle: A Celebration of Poetry by Soviet Children,* Simon & Schuster, 1972; (translator from the Russian) Samuel Marshak, *Zoo Babies* (poems for children), Ginn, 1973; *Said the Racoon to the Moon* (juvenile),

Ginn, 1974; *The Making of Champions: Soviet Sports for Children and Teenagers,* Atheneum, 1974; *Our World Series: The Soviet Union* (juvenile), Messner, in press.

Translator from the French: Colette Vivier, *The House of the Four Winds* (documentary novel for children), Doubleday, 1969; (editor, and author of introduction and separate commentaries) *Voices from France: Ten Stories by Eight French Nobel Laureates in Literature* (juvenile), Doubleday, 1969; (editor and author of introduction) *Fifteen by Maupassant* (juvenile), Doubleday, 1972.

Contributor to *Horn Book, Detskaia Literatura , P.T.A. Magazine, Reading Perspectives,* and other periodicals and newspapers.

SIDELIGHTS: "Consistent with earlier interest and work concerning the welfare of children (Board of Child Welfare, nursery school teaching, editing of books on child psychology and sociology), the themes and purpose of the books translated and published have been child culture and child guidance, exclusively. Knowledge of the French and Russian languages enabled me to translate from both languages into English works *for* and *about* children and youth. Children's literature is my primary specialty.

"The credo inspiring and guiding my publishing work is that cultural exchange of proved knowledge about, and of

MIRIAM MORTON

There are forty-two children's railroads in the Soviet Union. They are widely scattered over the length and breadth of the country, and are run by as well as for children. ■ (From *Pleasures and Palaces* by Miriam Morton.)

creative work for and with children, result in great benefits to the growth and development of the world's citizens to be."

Miriam Morton made her first trip to France in 1933, visited France, England, and Italy in 1963, France and the Soviet Union in 1965, 1969, France and England in 1971, and France in 1974. She attended the International Conference of Translators in the Soviet Union in 1972 and the International Children's Film Festival, also in the Soviet Union, 1973. Since 1965 her travels abroad have been made for the purpose of research and the acquisition of materials for her publications.

MYERS, Bernice

PERSONAL: Born in Bronx, N.Y.; daughter of Leonard (a jewelry designer) and Anna (a dressmaker; maiden name, Marer) Kaufman; married Lou Myers (cartoonist and writer), June 5, 1947; children: Marc Lee, Danny Alan. *Education:* Brooklyn College (now part of City University of New York), student in degree program sponsored by Ford Foundation for adults, 1966. *Home:* 58 Lakeview Ave. W., Peekskill, N.Y. 10566.

CAREER: After high school worked at various jobs in garment industry, including model, designer assistant, and sketcher, 1943-45; Columbia Pictures, New York, N.Y., employee in photostat department and illustrator of spots for movie ads, 1945-47; author and illustrator of children's books. Occasional advertising illustrator. *Member:* Authors Guild.

WRITINGS—Self-illustrated juveniles: *Olivier, l'ours savant,* Hachette, 1956; *Voilá Le Facteur,* Hachette, 1957; *Les Quatre Musiciens,* Hachette, 1957; *Not This Bear!,* Four Winds, 1968; *My Mother Is Lost,* Scholastic Book Services, 1971; *Come Out Shadow, Wherever You Are,* Scholastic Book Services, 1971; *The Apple War,* Parents' Magazine Press, 1973; *Shhhh! It's a Secret,* Holt, 1973; *Chicken Feathers,* Holt, 1973; *The Safest Place,* Holt, 1973; *Nobody Knows Me,* Macmillan, 1974; *Where's a*

That kind of person would understand right away—I'm almost positive—and help! ■ (From *A Lost Horse* by Bernice Myers. Illustrated by the author.)

Dog?, Holt, 1974; *A Lost Horse*, Doubleday, 1975; *Herman and the Bears Again*, Scholastic Book Services, 1976. Writer of stories for readers published by Holt, 1972, Macmillan, 1973.

Illustrator: Mary Elting under pseudonym Benjamin Brewster, *It's a Secret*, Grosset, 1950; Inez McClintock, *Billy and His Steam Roller*, Grosset, 1951; *Sailing on a Very Fine Day*, Rand, 1954; (with husband, Lou Myers) adapted from Charles Perrault, *Puss-in-Boots*, Rand McNally, 1955; Samuel Epstein and Beryl Williams, *First Book of Mexico*, Watts, 1955; Caroline Horowitz under pseudonym Jane K. Lansing, *Being Nice Is Lots of Fun*, Hart, 1955; Rose Wyler, *First Book of Weather*, Watts, 1956; Rose Wyler and Gerald Ames, *What Makes It Go?*, McGraw, 1958; Margaret O. Hyde, *Off into Space! Science for Young Space Travelers*, McGraw, 1959, 3rd edition, 1969; Irving A. Leitner, *Pear Shaped Hill*, Golden Press, 1960; Beulah Tannenbaum and Myra Stillman, *Understanding Food: The Chemistry of Nutrition*, McGraw, 1962; Benjamin Elkin, *Six Foolish Fisherman*, Scholastic Book Services, 1970; John Lawrence Peterson, *How to Write Codes and Send Secret Messages*, Four Winds, 1970; Mel Cebulash, *The See-Saw*, Scholastic Book Services, 1972.

Also illustrator of science series by Tillie S. Pine and Joseph Levine, published by McGraw: *Sounds All Around*, 1959; *Water All Around*, 1959; *Air All Around*, 1960; *Friction All Around*, 1960; *Light All Around*, 1961; *Electricity All Around*, 1962; *Gravity All Around*, 1963; *Heat All Around*, 1963; *Simple Machines and How We Use Them*, 1965; *Weather All Around*, 1966; *Rocks and How We Use Them*, 1967; *Trees and How We Use Them*, 1969.

SIDELIGHTS: "My early childhood was brief because that's the way I like to think of it. I stuttered through junior high and high school and had impossible hang-ups about my

BERNICE MYERS

BERNICE MYERS, by Lou Meyers

long thin arms and big feet, as well as my straight hair which refused to grow longer than my ear lobes. Adulthood couldn't arrive soon enough for me.

"My early years were spent in Washington Heights. After high school I attended some fashion institutes followed by subsequent jobs of various sorts in the garment industry as model, designer assistant, sketcher, etc. after which I worked five years in the photostat department of Columbia Pictures, at the same time doing occasional 'spots' for the press books. It was here I met my husband.

"At a meeting I attended, attempting to organize the commercial artists, Jan Balet gave a talk on how he had started doing children's books. The lecture gave me a direction. I sat down and wrote a children's book, illustrated it and went off to try and sell it. The publishers never bought it but within one day two publishers commissioned me to illustrate a book for them—*Artist and Writers Press*. And so it all began.

"It was when my husband and I lived in Paris for four years that I became a writer as well as an illustrator.

"I rarely write with a theme in mind. I begin with a sentence, any sentence which should lead to a second and then a third and so forth finally culminating in a children's story. There are times I can only come up with five or ten sentences, unable to carry the story further. I have drawers full of sentences. All kinds of sentences. Sentences that can stand alone in their perfection. Some of these I am able to incorporate finally into other structures and be able to come up with a complete story. Then it begins . . . the process of

honing and grooming these sentences, rearranging them within the context of the story, adding words and eliminating others. . .all this with the pictures in mind. In this way I eliminate much description that I know will appear in the drawings and so keeps the story moving at a good pace.

"I began playing tennis a few years ago to relieve a bad back condition and it has continued to keep me fully exercised and physically fit. Even more, I play for the town in inter-county tournaments in North Westchester, and have a great deal of fun participating. On to Wimbledon!

"I've done some speaking to large groups of school administrators divulging inner-most secrets of the artist-author, her hates, her loves, her angers, and her frustrations. It was an interesting experience and both sides had a lot of laughs."

OLDS, Helen Diehl   1895-

PERSONAL: Born April 29, 1895, in Springfield, Ohio; daughter of William Wallace and Henrietta (Zammert) Diehl; married Phelps Olds (deceased); children: Bob, Jerry. *Education:* University of Texas, student, two years; Wittenberg University, B.A., 1921. *Politics:* Democrat. *Religion:* Unity School of Christianity. *Home:* 251-32 43rd Ave., Little Neck, N.Y. 11363.

CAREER: Former editor, *The Ledger*, Little Neck, N.Y.;

HELEN DIEHL OLDS

Back and forth she went across the cement driveway, from one house to the other. She fell a couple of times but that did not bother her. ■ (From *Kate Can Skate* by Helen D. Olds. Illustrated by Carol Beech.)

Queens College, Flushing, N.Y., teacher of juvenile writing, 1954-69. Teacher, Huckleberry Workshop, Hendersonville, N.C., 1950-61, Cherryfield Camp, Brevard, N.C., 1962, Dixie Council of Writers, Young Harris, Ga., 1962, McKendree College writers' workshop, McKendree, Ill., 1959, 1961. *Member:* Women's National Book Association, Kappa Kappa Gamma.

WRITINGS: Joan of the Journal, D. Appleton, 1930; *Barbara Benton, Editor,* D. Appleton, 1932; *Victoria Clicks,* Messner, 1942; *Jill, Movie Maker,* Messner, 1944; *Lark, Radio Singer,* Messner, 1946; *Come In, Winifred,* Messner, 1947.

You Can't Tell about Love, Messner, 1950; *Fisherman Jody,* Messner, 1951; *Christmas-tree Sam,* Messner, 1952; *Krista and the Frosty Packages,* Messner, 1952; *Sharing is Fun,* Koinonia Foundation, 1953; *Sara's Lucky Harvest,* Messner, 1953; *Peanut Butter Mascot,* Messner, 1953; *Don and the Book Bus,* Knopf, 1956; *The Silver Button,* Knopf, 1958; *Miss Hattie and the Monkey,* Follett, 1958; *Detour for Meg,* Messner, 1958.

Kate Can Skate, Knopf, 1960; *What Will I Wear?,* Knopf,

1961; *The Little Ship that Went to Sea,* Reilly & Lee, 1962; *What's a Cousin?,* Knopf, 1962; *Jim Can Swim,* Knopf, 1963; *Christopher Columbus,* Putnam, 1964; *Lyndon Baines Johnson,* Putnam 1965; *Richard Nixon,* Putnam, 1970.

SIDELIGHTS: "One of five children, I was born and brought up in a middle-sized town in Ohio. My oldest brother was a great help to me when I was small. He believed I would do all the fascinating things I planned when I was grown—such as living in New York City and writing books.

"But it was my twin brother who helped me unknowingly to become a writer. He did not read a word I'd written but he always felt competent to write his criticism across the first page. It was always the same word. 'Rotten.' His comments only made me more determined.

"I can't remember when I didn't write. I remember my mother pulling me away from a book and shooing me outdoors. I was small for my age and skinny as well. My grandmother wailed that they'd never raise me. I have outlived all my brothers and sisters.

"I remember our tenth birthday. My twin wrapped up his library card and gave it to me as a birthday gift. At that time, you had to be ten years old to have a library card. And you could take out only one book on a card! Now, with my twin's card (he was definitely a nonreader) I could and I did take out two books each day and read them too. I remember trying to return them the same day, but the librarian said No. My book, *Don and the Book Bus* is dedicated to my twin brother.

"I began writing and mailing out manuscripts as soon as I was old enough. I wrote romances, and none of them sold. Then one day, I was coming out of our church and someone handed me a copy of the Sunday School paper, 'The Classmate.'

"I had never seen a copy of 'The Classmate,' and I read it from cover to cover. One story intrigued me. It was about a group of college students. 'I can write a story as good as that!' I told myself, and I wrote it that very afternoon. "Classmate' accepted it, and paid me the sum of fifteen dollars. I was launched into the juvenile writing field. After a good many magazine sales to teen-age magazines, I tried a book, *Joan of the Journal*. After that I wrote over a dozen books for the teenage girl, each one around a career.

"One day my good friend Margaret Sutton, author of the Judy Bolton series, said, 'Why don't you try a picture book?' So I wrote *Miss Hattie and the Monkey*. It sold for over sixteen years! I guess that's why it's my favorite book!"

FOR MORE INFORMATION SEE: The Ledger, Little Neck, N.Y., August 20, 1959.

PANTER, Carol 1936-

PERSONAL: Born January 19, 1936, in New York, N.Y.; daughter of Irving J. (an investment analyst) and Rosalie (Kluge) Yeckes; married Gideon G. Panter (a physician), February 2, 1956; children: Danielle, Ethan, Abigail. *Education:* Attended Juilliard School of Music, 1947-53, and Bennington College, 1953-54; New York University, A.B., 1957; City College of the City University of New York, M.S., 1961. *Home:* Ludlow Lane, Palisades, N.Y. 10964. *Agent:* Russell & Volkening, 551 Fifth Ave., New York, N.Y. 10017.

CAREER: Harpsichordist. Palisades Free Library, Palisades, N.Y., member of board of trustees, 1968-75, president of board, 1969-70; member of board of directors, Montessori Associates School, Englewood, N.J., 1972-77, and Juvenile Diabetes Association, 1973-75.

WRITINGS: (With Kathleen Lukens) *Thursday's Child Has Far to Go,* Prentice-Hall, 1969; *Beany and His New Recorder,* Four Winds, 1972; (with Ellen Liman) *Decorating Your Room,* Watts, 1974. Short stories and articles have appeared in *Good Housekeeping, Ladies' Home Journal,* and *Redbook.*

WORK IN PROGRESS: A book with Samuel Basch, *Life Island* (tentative title), publication by Harper expected in 1976.

He picked one of his favorite places to sit, a smooth, flat rock that jutted out of the trees—a fine forest seat for a boy and a cat. ■ (From *Beany and His New Recorder* by Carol Panter. Pictures by Imero Gobbato.)

PAYSON, Dale 1943-

PERSONAL: Born June 3, 1943, in White Plains, N.Y.; daughter of Henry and Frances T. Payson. *Education:* Endicott Junior College, graduate, 1963; attended School of Visual Arts, summers, 1961 and 1962, and 1963-64. *Home and office:* 800 West End Ave., New York, N.Y. 10025.

CAREER: Sylvor Display Co., New York, N.Y., window display designer, 1965; Famous Artists, Westport, Conn., teacher of correspondence course, 1967; Encore Fashions, New York, N.Y., fabric designer, 1969-70; Fairfield Co., New York, N.Y., colorist, 1970-71.

WRITINGS: Almost Twins (for children), Prentice-Hall, 1974; (compiler with Karen M. Wyant) *The Sleepy Time Treasury* (children's book), Prentice-Hall, 1975.

Illustrator: *Ann Aurelia and Dorothy,* Harper, 1967; *The Silver Crown,* Atheneum, 1968; *Next Door to Xanadu,* Harper, 1969; *Amish Boy,* Putnam, 1969; *Amish Wedding,* Putnam, 1970; *If You Listen,* Atheneum, 1971; *Tatu and the Honey Bird,* Putnam, 1972; *The Seven Stone,* Holiday House, 1972; *The Friendship Hedge,* Dutton, 1973; *The Mystery of the Spider Doll,* Watts, 1973; *On Reading*

150

Something about the Author

ALMOST TWINS

In the same village, on the same road, in the same house lived two sisters, Nellie and Annabelle . . . Everyone thought they were almost twins. ■ (From *Almost Twins* by Dale Payson. Illustrated by the author.)

story and pictures by Dale Payson

Palms, Prentice-Hall, 1973; *The Magic of the Little People,* Messner, 1973.

WORK IN PROGRESS: Poems compiled with Karen Maxwell Wyant.

PEARE, Catherine Owens   1911-

PERSONAL: Born February 4, 1911, in Perth Amboy, N.J.; daughter of Eugene J. and Georgie (Owens) Peare. *Education:* New Jersey State Teachers College, B.A., 1933; New York University, graduate student, 1946-47. *Address:* C/o Thomas Y. Crowell Co., 201 Park Ave. South, New York, N.Y.

CAREER: Duke Endowment, New York, N.Y., investment department, 1942-51; National Urban League, New York, N.Y., public relations department, 1951-52; became free-lance writer, 1952. *Member:* Authors League, Society of Women Geographers, P.E.N., Women's International League for Peace and Freedom. *Awards, honors:* Boys' Club of America Award, 1951; Sequoyah Award, 1962, for *The Helen Keller Story.*

WRITINGS—All youth books except where noted: *Albert Einstein,* Holt, 1949; *Mahatma Gandhi,* Holt, 1950; *Mary McLeod Bethune,* Vanguard, 1951; *Stephen Foster,* Holt, 1952; *The Lost Lakes* (fiction), Holt, 1953; *John James Audubon,* Holt, 1953; *Henry Longfellow,* Holt, 1953; *John Woolman,* Vanguard, 1954; *Louisa May Alcott,* Holt, 1954; *Mark Twain* (Junior Literary Guild selection), Holt, 1954; *Robert Louis Stevenson,* Holt, 1955; *Rosa Bonheur,* Holt,

1956; *Jules Verne,* Holt, 1956; *William Penn* (adult), Lippincott, 1957; *Washington Irving,* Holt, 1957; *Louis Agassiz,* Lippincott, 1958; *William Penn,* Holt, 1958; *The Helen Keller Story,* Crowell, 1959; *Charles Dickens,* Holt, 1959.

John Keats: A Portrait in Words (young adult), Dodd, 1960; *The FDR Story,* Crowell, 1962; *The Woodrow Wilson Story,* Crowell, 1963; *Melor: King Arthur's Page* (fiction), Putnam, 1963; *Painter of Patriots: Charles Wilson Peale,* Holt, 1964; *The Herbert Hoover Story,* Crowell, 1965; *Aaron Copland: His Life,* Holt, 1969; *Mahatma Gandhi: Father of Non-Violence,* Hawthorne, 1969; *The Louis Brandeis Story,* Crowell, 1970.

SIDELIGHTS: "I can't remember when I did not want to be a writer. In high school at Tenafly, New Jersey, I produced a profusion of themes and stories and was editor of the school paper in my senior year. At New Jersey State Teachers College, I was a frequent contributor of poetry and plays to the campus quarterly. In later years, I wrote in my spare time until I was at last able to free-lance.

"Eventually my background drew me into the newly developing juvenile book field, and my first series was for young adults.

"I invented William Penn. What I mean is that my full-scale adult biography is the most definitive life of the colonizer ever written. The book, based on hundreds of rare manuscripts never before investigated, was the result of

Gandhi prayed for light, divine light. He sat cross-legged in meditation in the daytime and sometimes prayed the entire night through. ■ (From *Mahatma Gandhi* by Catherine Owens Peare. Illustrated by Paul Frame.)

three and a half years of writing and research in the United States, England, Ireland and the Continent. Travel is vital to my work, and so far my writing has led me to thirteen foreign countries.

"Any story, fiction or non-fiction, has a truer ring if the author was *there*. A classroom of children finds Longfellow much realer when I can assure them that Spain is just as the poet described it. And it gives them a real thrill to hear that I explored the caves that Sam Clemens loved near Hannibal, Missouri."

FOR MORE INFORMATION SEE: Wilson Library Bulletin, October, 1959; *More Junior Authors*, edited by Muriel Fuller, H. W. Wilson, 1963.

POTTER, Marian 1915-

PERSONAL: Born January 9, 1915, in Blackwell, Mo.; daughter of Samuel and Flora (Bookstaver) McKinstry; married David Potter, October 18, 1943; children: Andrew, Pamela, Rebecca. *Education:* University of Missouri, B.J., 1939. *Politics:* Democrat. *Religion:* Presbyterian. *Home:* 124 Beaty St., Warren, Pa. 16365.

CAREER: Jefferson County, Mo., teacher, elementary schools, 1932-35; *Monroe City News,* Monroe City, Mo., reporter, 1939; University of Missouri, Columbia, editor, extension division, 1940-41; *St. Louis Globe-Democrat,* St. Louis, Mo., copyreader, 1942-43; United Nations Information Office, New York, N.Y., assistant press officer, 1944; WNAE and WRRN (radio stations), Warren, Pa., editorial writer, 1962-74. Member of board of directors of Northern Allegheny Broadcasting Co., 1965-74. *Member:* Kappa Tau Alpha. *Awards, honors:* Outstanding contribution to children's literature, 1971, from Central Missouri State College.

WRITINGS: The Little Red Caboose, Golden Press, 1953; *Milepost 67,* Follett, 1965; *Copperfield Summer,* Follett, 1967. Stories and articles published in children's and adult magazines.

SIDELIGHTS: "My father was an agent for the Missouri Pacific Railroad Company and was assigned to small shipping stations in rural Missouri. The railroad was an exciting part of my childhood as I grew up in the country.

"I worked as a journalist and did not consider writing for children until I had children of my own. We read and looked at bushels of picture books from Warren, Pa., public library. When I wrote a book for little children, it was about a freight train. A second generation of children now reads *The Little Red Caboose.* I wrote *Milepost 67* because I wanted to share with children events of a childhood lived close to a railroad depot. *Copperfield Summer* is a story of

MARIAN POTTER

ALICE and MARTIN PROVENSEN

family emergency and farm life: but again, the children travel by train. Vivid memories of childhood and a wish to make a response to those experiences have been my reasons for writing for children.''

HOBBIES AND OTHER INTERESTS: Horticulture and travel.

PROVENSEN, Alice 1918-

PERSONAL: First syllable of surname rhymes with "grow"; born August 14, 1918, in Chicago, Ill.; daughter of Jay H. (a broker) and Kathryn (an interior decorator; maiden name, Zelanis) Twitchell; married Martin Provensen (a writer and illustrator of children's books), April 17, 1944; children: Karen Anna. *Education:* Studied at Art Institute of Chicago, University of California at Los Angeles, and Art Students League, New York. *Home address:* Rural Delivery, Staatsburg, N.Y. 12580.

CAREER: Walter Lantz Studios, Hollywood, Calif., employed in animation, 1942-43; Office of Strategic Services, Washington, D.C., graphics, 1943-45; writer and illustrator of children's books, 1946—.

WRITINGS—All self-illustrated children's books, with husband, Martin Provensen: *The Animal Fair,* Simon & Schuster, 1952, revised edition, 1974; *Karen's Curiosity,* Golden Press, 1963; *Karen's Opposites,* Golden Press, 1963; *What Is a Color?,* Golden Press, 1967; *Who's in the Egg?,* Golden Press, 1968; (editors) *Provenson Book of Fairy Tales,* Random House, 1971; *Play on Words,* Random House, 1972; *My Little Hen,* Random House, 1973; *Roses Are Red,* Random House, 1973; *Our Animal Friends,* Random House, 1974.

Illustrator, with Martin Provensen: Margaret Bradford Boni, editor, *Fireside Book of Folksongs,* Simon & Schuster, 1947; Boni, editor, *Fireside Book of Lovesongs,* Simon & Schuster, 1954; James A. Beard, *Fireside Cook Book,* Simon & Schuster, 1949.

All published by Golden Press: Dorothy Bennett, editor, *The Golden Mother Goose,* 1948; R. L. Stevenson, *A*

Child's Garden of Verses, 1951; Elsa Jane Werner, adapter, *The New Testament,* 1953; Jane Werner Watson, adapter, *Iliad and Odyssey,* 1956; Anne Terry White, adapter, *Treasury of Myths and Legends,* 1959; *The First Noel,* 1959; George Wolfson, editor, *Shakespeare: Ten Great Plays,* 1962; Alfred Lord Tennyson, *The Charge of the Light Brigade,* 1964; Louis Untermeyer, adapter, *Aesop's Fables,* 1965; Untermeyer, editor, *Fun and Nonsense,* 1967; Untermeyer, adapter, *Tales from the Ballet,* 1968.

SIDELIGHTS: "Our lives almost touched at many points before we finally met. Both of us were born in Chicago and grew up loving books and book illustration. We decided at an early age to make beautiful books; both won scholarships to the Art Institute of Chicago; both transferred to the University of California and spent a year there, I in Los Angeles and Martin in Berkeley. I went to New York and studied for a while at the Art Students League. Returning to California, I began to work for Walter Lantz Studios. Martin worked for five years for Walt Disney on such films as *Fantasia* and *Dumbo.* During his three and a half years in the Navy he worked on training movies. While working on a film for the Navy on the Universal lot with Lantz he and I discovered each other. We were married in Washington, D.C. in 1944."

"In 1945 we moved to New York and began to illustrate children's books together. Our first book was *The Fireside Book of Folksongs* with five hundred illustrations."

"After traveling throughout Europe in 1950 collecting material for illustrations, we returned to the United States, bought a farm near Staatsburg, New York, and converted the barn into a studio. In 1952 we illustrated *The Golden Bible: The New Testament,* taking their models from color photographs of the Holy Land and from illuminated manuscripts. Many books followed, including our own favorite, *The Illiad and the Odyssey.* For this we traveled to Greece for three months in 1954, filling sketchbook after sketchbook with what the eye could see and the camera could not.

"*Karen's Opposites,* was both written and illustrated by us and our own daughter Karen, then four years old, is the Karen of the story about two little girls, one dark and one light, one shouting and one whispering, doing exactly opposite things.

"We work together on all our illustrations, much as the medieval scribes and scriveners did, passing the drawings back and forth between us, adding this and taking out that, until each is satisfied. We discard sketch after sketch, until finally we obtain the effect we feel will most delight the young eye. We completed a set of illustrations for *The Charge of the Light Brigade* and then, unhappy with its complexity, redid the whole book. This stern self-criticism results in a deceptively easy, spontaneous-looking style.

"The farm supplies many models for our work: cows, cats, horses, lambs. Our daughter, who shares our art enthusiasm, contributes her criticism to our work and her drawings hang in our studio among those of ours.

"Our profession is drawing and painting, our hobbies are drawing and painting. Our enthusiasms are drawing and painting. Outside of that, our interests are doing it better."

FOR MORE INFORMATION SEE: Illustrators of Children's Books: 1946-1956, Horn Book, 1958; *Illustrators of Children's Books: 1957-1966,* Horn Book, 1968; *The Who's Who of Children's Literature,* Brian Doyle, Schocken Books, 1968; *Third Book of Junior Authors,* edited by de Montreville and Hill, H. W. Wilson, 1972; *McCall's,* November, 1974.

PROVENSEN, Martin   1916-

PERSONAL: Surname is pronounced *Proh*-ven-sen; born July 10, 1916, in Chicago, Ill.; son of Marthin (a musician) and Berendina (a teacher; maiden name, Kruger) Provensen; married Alice Twitchell (a writer and illustrator of children's books), April 17, 1944; children: Karen Anna. *Education:* Studied at Art Institute of Chicago and University of California at Berkeley. *Home address:* Rural Delivery, Staatsburg, N.Y. 12580.

CAREER: Walt Disney Studios, Hollywood, Calif., member of story board, 1938-42; writer and illustrator of children's books, 1946—. *Military service:* U.S. Navy, 1942-45.

WRITINGS—All self-illustrated children's books, with wife, Alice Provensen: *The Animal Fair,* Simon & Schuster, 1952, revised edition, 1974; *Karen's Curiosity,* Golden Press, 1963; *Karen's Opposites,* Golden Press, 1963; *What Is a Color?,* Golden Press, 1967; *Who's in the Egg?,* Golden Press, 1968; *Play on Words,* Random House, 1972; *My Little Hen,* Random House, 1973; *Roses Are Red,* Random House, 1973; *Our Animal Friends,* Random House, 1974.

Illustrator, with Alice Provensen: Margaret Bradford Boni, editor, *Fireside Book of Folksongs,* Simon & Schuster, 1947; Boni, editor, *Fireside Book of Lovesongs,* Simon & Schuster, 1954; James A. Beard, *Fireside Cook Book,* Simon & Schuster, 1949.

All published by Golden Press: Dorothy Bennett, editor, *The Golden Mother Goose,* 1948; R. L. Stevenson, *A Child's Garden of Verses,* 1951; Elsa Jane Werner, adapter, *The New Testament,* 1953; Jane Werner Watson, adapter, *Iliad and Odyssey,* 1956; Anne Terry White, adapter, *Treasury of Myths and Legends,* 1959; *The First Noel,* 1959; George Wolfson, editor, *Shakespeare: Ten Great Plays,* 1962; Alfred Lord Tennyson, *The Charge of the Light Brigade,* 1964; Louis Untermeyer, adapter, *Aesop's Fables,* 1965; Untermeyer, editor, *Fun and Nonsense,* 1967; Untermeyer, adapter, *Tales from the Ballet,* 1968.

FOR MORE INFORMATION SEE: Illustrators of Children's Books: 1946-1956, Horn Book, 1958; *Illustrators of Children's Books: 1957-1966,* Horn Book, 1968; *The Who's Who of Children's Literature,* Brian Doyle, Schocken Books, 1968; *Third Book of Junior Authors,* edited by de Montreville and Hill, H. W. Wilson, 1972; *McCall's,* November, 1974.

PYNE, Mable Mandeville   1903-1969

PERSONAL: Born January 15, 1903, in Mount Vernon, N.Y.; daughter of Arthur William and Emma (Walter) Mandeville; married John Pyne, March 2, 1924 (deceased);

children: Jennifer (Mrs. Robert C. Oliver). *Education:* Pratt Institute Art School, student, 1922; Columbia University, student, 1946. *Home and Office:* 51 Sunset Rd., Darien, Conn.

CAREER: Fashion artist, various companies and agencies, 1921-29; illustrator of children's books, New York, N.Y., 1929-30; free-lance author and illustrator, 1940-69. Civil Defense, Darien, Conn., executive secretary, 1950-51; Save the Children Federation, Norwalk, Conn., correspondent, 1957-58; Norwalk Community Hospital, volunteer worker, 1959-69. *Member:* Daughters of the American Revolution.

WRITINGS: From Morning to Night, Stokes, 1929; *The Little History of the United States,* Houghton, 1940; *The Little Geography of the United States,* Houghton, 1941; *The Little History of the World,* Houghton, 1947; *The Story of Religion,* Houghton, 1954; (with Emma Mandeville and Jennifer Pyne Oliver) *When We Were Little,* Hastings, 1957; *The Hospital,* Houghton, 1962.

SIDELIGHTS: Her books about the United States were translated into Turkish, Korean, and Malay for distribution by the U.S. Information Agency. Interests included children, birds, swimming.

(Died September 19, 1969)

EDITH RASKIN

RASKIN, Edith Lefkowitz 1908-

PERSONAL: Born October 17, 1908, in New York, N.Y.; daughter of Maximillian (in real estate) and Sara (Brown) Lefkowitz; married Joseph Raskin (an artist), October 30, 1936. *Education:* Hunter College, B.A., 1930; Cornell University, graduate study, 1939-40; New York University, M.A., 1941; American Museum of Natural History, postgraduate courses. *Home:* 59 West 71st St., New York, N.Y. 10023.

CAREER: New York City (N.Y.) Board of Education, teacher of science, 1930-37, biology laboratory teacher, 1937-67. *Member:* United Federation of Teachers, Authors Guild.

WRITINGS: (Co-author) *Home-Made Zoo,* McKay, 1952; *Many Worlds, Seen and Unseen,* McKay, 1954; *Watchers, Pursuers and Masqueraders* (about animals), McGraw, 1964; *The Pyramid of Living Things,* McGraw, 1967; *The Fantastic Cactus, Indoors and in Nature,* Lothrop, 1969; (with Joseph Raskin) *Indian Tales,* Random House, 1969; *World Food,* McGraw, 1971; (with Joseph Raskin) *Tales Our Settlers Told,* Lothrop, 1972; (with Joseph Raskin) *Ghosts and Witches Aplenty: More Tales Our Settlers Told,* Lothrop, 1973; (with Joseph Raskin) *The Newcomers, Ten Tales of American Immigrants,* Lothrop, 1974; (with Joseph Raskin) *Guilty or Not Guilty: Tales of Justice in Early America,* Lothrop, 1975; (with Joseph Raskin) *Spies and Traitors: Tales of the Revolutionary and Civil Wars,* Lothrop, 1976. Contributor to anthologies: *Literature, Mythology and Folklore: Two Stories From Tales Our Settlers Told,* Science Research Associates, 1973, 1974; *Rhetoric and Literature,* McGraw, 1974.

SIDELIGHTS: "Although I was born in midtown New York, I somehow developed a love of nature ever since early childhood. At first I explored the city parks, then as a girl, scouted the nearby woodlands and later the flora and fauna of the ocean and countryside of New England.

"I was always fascinated by words and when I was ten years old I used my mother's library card and took out books from the adult library starting with Tolstoi and working my way through to Jane Austin.

"However, I never thought of writing myself until I married an artist, Joseph Raskin, and we went off to spend our first summer on Monhegan Island, Maine. Mingling with the artists and writers on the island, I was tempted to try to create something of my own. My first try was a dismal failure, but later when I combined my feeling for words and nature, I succeeded in writing my first published book and several science books thereafter.

"A chance present of a nineteenth-century book from our charming ninety-odd-year-old landlady in Pigeon Cove, Massachusetts, inspired my husband and myself to dig into the life of early America. From this came our joint venture of writing a series of books on tales of early America for young readers.

"At present, my husband and I are engaged in writing another book dealing with the same epoch."

Many Worlds was translated into Arabic and Persian.

MARGARET RAU

HOBBIES AND OTHER INTERESTS: Plastic arts, the theatre, opera, hiking, swimming, and watching baseball.

RAU, Margaret 1913-

PERSONAL: Surname rhymes with "now"; born December 23, 1913, in Swatow, China; daughter of George Wright (a missionary) and Mary Victoria (Wolfe; also a missionary) Lewis; married Neil Rau (a writer), 1935 (died, 1971); children: Robert, Peter, Peggy, Frank, Thomas. *Education:* Studied under private tutor in China; attended University of Chicago, 1931, Columbia University, 1932, and University of Redlands, 1933-34; Riverside Library College, degree, 1934. *Home:* 823 South Plymouth Blvd., Apt. 12, Los Angeles, Calif. 90005.

CAREER: Writer. *Member:* Photographic Society of America, United States-China People's Friendship Association, National Writers Guild.

WRITINGS—Juvenile books: *Band of the Red Hand,* Knopf, 1938; *Dawn from the West,* Hawthorn, 1964; *The Penguin Book,* Hawthorn, 1968; *The Yellow River,* Messner, 1969; *The Yangtze River,* Messner, 1970; (self-illustrated with photographs) *Jimmy of Cherry Valley,* Messner, 1973; *Our World: The People's Republic of China,* Messner, 1974.

Adult books with husband, Neil Rau: *My Father, Charlie*

Toward the end of the summer, Mr. Haydt showed Jimmy a special way of getting his trees to bear fruit. All he had to do was rip off the tips of some of the branches. This would hold the sap back, and fruit buds would develop instead of leaf buds. ■ (From *Jimmy of Cherry Valley* by Margaret Rau. Photographs by the author.)

Chaplin, Random House, 1960; *Act Your Way to Successful Living,* Prentice-Hall, 1966; *My Dear Ones,* Prentice-Hall, 1971. Collaborator with husband on material used by Norman Lear for film, "Cold Turkey", United Artists, 1972.

Writer of pamphlets on China. Contributor to *Parents' Magazine* and *Cricket.*

WORK IN PROGRESS: A book on the musk ox, for Crowell; a picture-text book about modern China based on her own observations and illustrated with her own photographs; a book about the panda in the wild, for Knopf.

SIDELIGHTS: "I grew up in China where I spoke Chinese for four years before learning English. I have always felt a deep and abiding love for the countryside in which I grew up and for the people among whom I found myself. Now with China taking a new and ever-growing role in the modern world I feel it imperative that our young people know something about this great country and the Chinese—their aims, dreams and hopes.

"In 1974 I paid a visit to the People's Republic of China and hope it will be the first of many which will enable me to bring an even deeper and more vital understanding of China to American children. As I feel that photography as well as the written word carries a tremendous impact I hope to illustrate my books with copious pictures.

"I am also working on a book in the adult field which will help to explain current activities and outlooks in the People's Republic of China in the light of the country's long past. Only by having an understanding of that past, I believe, will Americans be able to grasp what is going on in China today.

"Have traveled widely in Europe and Soviet Union."

RAY, JoAnne 1935-

PERSONAL: Born June 19, 1935, in Duluth, Minn.;

JO ANNE RAY

daughter of Robert Earl (a railroad inspector) and Trudie (Burford) Green; married Glenn H. Ray (administrator in a state agency), May 25, 1957; children: Christian, Anne, Andrew. *Education:* University of Minnesota, B.A., 1957, M.A., 1966. *Home:* 14624 Woodhill Ter., Minnetonka, Minn. 55343.

CAREER: University of Minnesota, Minneapolis, an editor, 1958-62; Minnesota Association for Retarded Children, Minneapolis, public information director, 1962-64; National University Extension Association, Minneapolis, Minn., editor, 1964-71; Minnesota State Horticultural Society, St. Paul, editor, 1974—.

WRITINGS—Juvenile books: *American Assassins,* Lerner, 1974; *Careers With a Television Station,* Lerner, 1974; *Careers in Football,* Lerner, 1974; *Careers in Hockey,* Lerner, 1974; *Careers in Computers,* Lerner, 1974; *Careers With a Police Department,* Lerner, 1974.

WORK IN PROGRESS: Biography of Maud Hart Lovelace, author of children's books, for a volume on women in Minnesota history.

RIKHOFF, Jean 1928-

PERSONAL: Born May 28, 1928, in Chicago, Ill.; daughter of Harold Franklin (a businessman) and Blanche (a teacher; maiden name, Bowlus) Rikhoff; divorced; chil-

dren: Allison, Jeffrey. *Education:* Mount Holyoke College, B.A., 1948; Wesleyan University, M.A., 1949. *Politics:* Democrat. *Home:* R.D.2, Salem, N.Y. 12865. *Agent:* Barthold Fles Literary Agency, 507 Fifth Ave., New York, N.Y. 10017. *Office:* Adirondack Community College, Glens Falls, N.Y. 12801.

CAREER: Gourmet magazine, editorial assistant; Adirondack Community College, Glens Falls, N.Y., assistant professor of English, 1969—. Chairman of university awards committee, State University of New York. *Awards, honors:* Eugene Saxton Fellowship for Creative Writing, 1958; National Endowment for the Humanities fellowship, 1972; State University of New York Creative Writing Award, 1973.

WRITINGS—Juvenile: *Writing About the Frontier: Mark Twain,* Encyclopedia Britannica, 1963; *Robert E. Lee: Soldier of the South,* Putnam, 1968.

Adult: *Dear Ones All,* Viking, 1961; (editor) *Quixote Anthology,* Grosset, 1962; *Voyage In, Voyage Out,* Viking, 1963; *Rites of Passage,* Viking, 1966; *Buttes Landing,* Dial, 1973; *One of the Raymonds,* Dial, 1974.

WORK IN PROGRESS: The Sweetwater, publication expected in 1976.

FOR MORE INFORMATION SEE: Library Journal, September, 1968.

ROACH, Marilynne K(athleen) 1946-

PERSONAL: Born July 15, 1946, in Cambridge, Mass.; daughter of William Lawrence (a house painter) and Priscilla (Dunbar) Roach. *Education:* Massachusetts College of Art, B.F.A., 1968. *Religion:* Christian. *Residence:* Watertown, Mass.

Come with me to Rome and enjoy the glories of city life.
■ (From *Two Roman Mice* by Horace. Retold and illustrated by Marilynne K. Roach.)

CAREER: Mosaic Tile Co., Boston, Mass., designer of bathrooms and tile wall murals, 1968-70; free-lance writer and illustrator, Watertown, Mass., 1970—. *Awards, honors: The Mouse and the Song* was selected as Children's Book Showcase Title, 1975.

WRITINGS: The Mouse and the Song (juvenile), Parents' Magazine Press, 1974; *Two Roman Mice*, Crowell, 1975. Contributor of illustrations to *Boston Globe.*

WORK IN PROGRESS: New England ghost stories.

SIDELIGHTS: "I was introduced to libraries almost at the beginning of my life, and came to love books even before I could read them. I enjoyed remembering stories and drawing pictures—now I can begin to do this in earnest. Favorite subjects are: Nature, history (ancient and local), mythology and folklore."

FOR MORE INFORMATION SEE: New York Times Book Review, November 3, 1974.

RODMAN, Selden   1909-

PERSONAL: Born February 19, 1909, in New York, N.Y.; son of Cary Selden and Nannie Van Nostrand (Marvin) Rodman; married Eunice Clark, 1933 (divorced); married Hilda Clausen, 1938 (divorced); married Maja Wojciechowska, 1950 (divorced); married Carole Cleaver, 1962; children: (third marriage) Oriana, (fourth marriage) Carla Pamela, Van Nostrand. *Education:* Yale University, B.A., 1931. *Home:* 659 Valley Rd., Oakland, N.J.; also, Jaemel, Haiti.

CAREER: Common Sense (monthly political magazine), co-founder and co-editor, 1932-43; Centre d'Art, Port-au-Prince, Haiti, co-director, 1949-51; Haitian Art Center, New York, N.Y., former president and organizer of traveling exhibits; poet, free-lance writer, art critic, art collector. Lecturer at colleges and universities. New Jersey Tercentenary Commission, member of fine arts committee, 1962-63. New Jersey State Art Commission, chairman, 1963. *Military service:* U.S. Army, 1943-45; became master sergeant in foreign nationalities section of Office of Strategic Services. *Awards, honors:* Commander, Haitian Legion of Honor.

WRITINGS: Mortal Triumph and Other Poems, Farrar & Rinehart, 1932; *Lawrence, the Last Crusade* (narrative poem), Viking, 1937; *The Airmen* (narrative poem), Random, 1941; *The Revolutionists* (play, produced in Port-au-Prince, by the government of Haiti, 1941), Duell, Sloan & Pearce, 1942; *Horace Pippin: A Negro Painter in America,* Quadrangle, 1947; *The Amazing Year, May 1, 1945-April 30, 1946* (diary in verse), Scribner, 1947; *Renaissance in Haiti: Popular Painters in the Black Republic,* Pellegrini and Cudahy, 1948.

Portrait of the Artist as an American: Ben Shahn, Harper, 1951; *Haiti: The Black Republic,* Devin, 1954, revised edition, 1973; *The Eye of Man: Form and Content in Western Painting,* Devin, 1955; *Conversations with Artists,* Devin, 1957; *Mexican Journal: The Conquerors Conquered* (travel), Devin, 1958; *The Insiders: Rejection and Rediscovery of Man in the Arts of Our Time,* Louisiana State

University Press, 1960; *The Heart of Beethoven,* Shorewood, 1962; *Death of the Hero* (poem), Shorewood, 1963; *Quisqueya, 1492-1962: A History of the Dominican Republic,* University of Washington Press, 1964; *The Road to Panama* (travel), Hawthorn, 1966; *The Peru Traveler,* Meredith, 1967; *The Caribbean,* Hawthorn, 1968; *The Mexico Traveler,* Meredith, 1969; *The Guatemala Traveler,* Meredith, 1967.

South America of the Poets, Hawthorn, 1970; *The Colombia Traveler,* Hawthorn, 1971; (with Carole Cleaver) *Horace Pippin: The Artist as a Black American,* Doubleday, 1972; *Tongues of Fallen Angels,* New Directions, 1974; *The Miracle of Haitian Art (School Library Journal* book list), Doubleday, 1974; *100 British Poets,* New American Library, 1974.

Editor: (With Alfred Mitchell Bingham) *Challenge to the New Deal,* McGraw, 1935; *A New Anthology of Modern Poetry,* Random, 1938, 2nd revised edition, Modern Library, 1946; *The Poetry of Flight* (anthology), Duell, Sloan & Pearce, 1941; (with Richard Eberhart) *War and the Poet,* Devin, 1945; *One Hundred American Poems,* New American Library, 1948; *One Hundred Modern Poems,* Pelligrini & Cudahy, 1949.

Contributor of travel articles on Latin America to magazines, including *Harper's Bazaar.*

SIDELIGHTS: During his postwar residence in Haiti, Rodman fostered a mural painting movement, and directed the painting of the Episcopal cathedral in Port-au-Prince by

SELDEN RODMAN

nine primitive artists. His private collection of non-abstract contemporary paintings and sculpture is housed in a gallery in his contemporary New Jersey home. The gallery's exterior murals were painted by Seymour Leichman, 1961-64.

FOR MORE INFORMATION SEE: New York Times Book Review, May 7, 1972; *Horn Book,* August, 1974, October, 1974.

ROGERS, Pamela   1927-

PERSONAL: Born October 8, 1927, in Horsham, Sussex, England; daughter of Rex Owen (a banker) and Doris (Haygarth) Folkard; married Clifford Rogers (a teacher), August 15, 1951; children: Gabrielle, Andrew, Matthew, Imogen. *Education:* Bedford College, London, B.A. (with honors), 1949; Institute of Education, London, diploma in teaching, 1950. *Home:* 32 Yew Tree Rd., Turnbridge Wells, Kent, England.

CAREER: Teacher; writer of children's books.

WRITINGS—All juveniles; all published by Lutterworth: *The Runaway Pony,* 1961; *The Rag and Bone Pony,* 1962; *Dan and His Donkey,* 1964; *Secret in the Forest,* 1964; *Thomasina,* 1966; *The Lucky Bag,* 1969; *The Magic Egg,* 1971; *The Weekend,* Nelson, 1972; *The Rare One,* Hamish Hamilton, 1973, Nelson (Junior Literary Guild Selection), 1974.

SIDELIGHTS: "I think that a writer for children must hook them on to reading at an early age; therefore, I believe that more emphasis should be placed on writing and the importance of it for the earlier age group, six to twelve. After that it is too late. More awards, financial and otherwise, are given to books for older children, to my mind not so essential."

"I believe in the absolute importance of writing for children, and like to write mainly for the younger sections—six-to-fourteen. I do not believe in the writer salting himself away and being a WRITER in capitals. Writers must live first and write afterwards.

"I write my books in the bath, through television westerns, amid the litter of dolls' tea parties and football boots. I let the ideas simmer for a long time in my mind before pen meets paper. My happiest days are when a new idea has begun to grow. My worst are when I actually *have* to put it down.

"*The Rare One,* like all my other books, was the coming together of several unrelated incidents. First, the characters of Toby and his sister, Olly. Then an episode, based on fact, when an old man was discovered living rough in some deep local woods four years ago. The episode lay dormant at the time, until suddenly incident and character joined. Then, the book *The Rare One* emerged."

HOBBIES AND OTHER INTERESTS: "Children, all sorts and sizes, gardening, reading, training and showing horses and ponies, and, oh, yes, talking!"

RUTH, Rod   1912-

PERSONAL: Born September 21, 1912, in Benton Harbor,

ROD RUTH

Mich.; son of Dwight M. (a banker) and Grace (McCord) Ruth; married Mary Spencer, June 25, 1938; children: Eric Spencer, Bradford Eastman, Peter McCord. *Education:* Chicago Academy of Fine Arts, graduate; further study at Frederick Mizen School of Art and Institute of Design, both Chicago. *Politics:* Independent liberal. *Religion:* Liberal Protestant. *Home and studio:* 620 Vine Ave., Park Ridge, Ill. 60068.

CAREER: Graphic artist in Chicago art studios and as free lance; designer and illustrator of trade and textbooks; other art work includes comic strip, series of Greyhound Bus travel posters, charts of species of fish for National Marine Fisheries, and national advertising. Watercolors have been exhibited in Artists Guild of Chicago shows. *Member:* Artists Guild of Chicago, National Audubon Society, Wilderness Society, Chicago Ornithological Society, Art Institute of Chicago (life member), Field Museum of Natural History (life member), Chicago Council on Foreign Relations, Chicago Zoological Society. *Awards, honors:* Awards from Society of Illustrators, Printing Industry of America, and Artists Guild of Chicago.

ILLUSTRATOR: Julian May, *Alligator Hole,* Follett, 1969; Julian May, *Cactus Fox,* Creative Educational Society, 1971; Julian May, *Cascade Couger,* Creative Educational Society, 1972; Tom McGowen, *Album of Dinosaurs,* Rand McNally, 1972; Julian May, *Eagles of the Valley,* Creative Education Society, 1972; Julian May, *Glacier*

Other dinosaur eggs have since been found. But little Protoceratops will always be famous as the dinosaur that first showed us how dinosaur babies were born. ∎ (From *Album of Dinosaurs* by Tom McGowen. Illustrated by Rod Ruth.)

Grizzly, Creative Educational Society, 1972; Julian May, *Islands of the Tiny Deer,* W. R. Scott, 1972; Tom McGowen, *Album of Prehistoric Animals,* Rand McNally, 1974. Illustrations have appeared in readers, science fiction magazines, and popular magazines.

WORK IN PROGRESS: Illustrating Tom McGowen's *Album of Prehistoric Man,* for Rand McNally.

SIDELIGHTS: "Boyhood shaped by ready access to nearby Lake Michigan, two rivers, many inland lakes and streams, dunes, ravines, woods, marshes, one grandfather's farm and another grandfather's carpenter shop and garden.

"At present almost entirely devoted to first love: drawing and painting animals, birds, all wildlife, and outdoor subjects chiefly for book illustrations.

"In 1936-37 spent several months in a fur trading post above the Arctic Circle in Yukon Territory as caribou hunter and dog-team driver. Favorite recreation has included camping, hunting, fishing and canoing in Alaska, Canada, Mexico, the North Woods, western deserts and Rocky Mountains; and sailing, cycling and birdwatching closer to home. One current obsession: preserving what is left of wilderness."

SCHICK, Eleanor 1942-

PERSONAL: Born April 15, 1942, in New York, N.Y.; daughter of William (a psychiatrist) and Bessie (a social worker; maiden name, Grossman) Schick; children: Laura, David. *Education:* Attended high school in New York, N.Y. Studied modern dance with Martha Graham, Alvin Ailey, and others. *Religion:* Jewish. *Home:* 41 West 96th St., New York, N.Y. 10025. *Office:* Behrman House Publishers, 1261 Broadway, New York, N.Y. 10001.

CAREER: Author and illustrator of children's books; professional dancer, giving solo performance with Tamaris-Nagrin Dance Company and the American Dance Festival, and member of Juilliard Dance Theatre; lectured and taught dance at Hofstra University, Bryn Mawr College, and Connecticut College. Parent chairman of St. Matthew and St. Timothy Day Care Center, 1972-73.

WRITINGS—All self-illustrated children's books; all published by Macmillan, except as indicated: *Surprise in the Forest,* Harper, 1964; *The Little School in Cottonwood Corners,* Harper, 1965; *The Dancing School.* Harper, 1966; *I'm Going to the Ocean,* 1966; *5A and 7B,* 1967; *Katie Goes to Camp,* 1968; *Jeanie Goes Riding,* 1968; *City in the*

Summer, 1969; *Making Friends,* 1969; *Peggy's New Brother,* 1970, *City in the Winter,* 1970; *Andy,* 1971; *Peter and Mr. Brandon,* illustrated by Donald Carrick, 1973; *Student's Encounter Book for When a Jew Celebrates,* Behrman House, 1973; *City Green,* 1974; *City Sun,* 1974.

Illustrator: Jan Wahl, *Christmas in the Forest,* Macmillan, 1967.

SIDELIGHTS: City in the Winter and *City in the Summer* have been made into filmstrips.

SANDRA SCOPPETONE

SCOPPETTONE, Sandra 1936—

PERSONAL: Born June 1, 1936, in Morristown, N.J.; daughter of Casimiro R. and Helen (Greis) Scoppettone. *Home:* 149 6th St., Greenport, N.Y. 11944. *Agent:* Gloria Safier, 667 Madison Ave., New York, N.Y. 10021.

CAREER: Full time professional writer. *Member:* Actors' Studio Playwrights Unit (1968-1973). *Awards, honors:* Eugene O'Neill Memorial Theatre Award, 1972, Ludwig Vogelstein Foundation grant, 1974.

WRITINGS: Suzuki Beane, Doubleday, 1961; *Bang Bang*

You're Dead, Harper, 1968; (with Louise Fitzhugh) *Trying Hard to Hear You* (ALA Best Young Adult book list) Harper, 1974; *The Late Great Me,* Putnam, 1976.

Plays: "Three One-Act Plays," first produced at Sheridan Square Playhouse, 1964; "One-Act Play," first produced at Sheridan Square Playhouse, 1965; "Two One-Act Plays," first produced at Cubiculo Theater, 1968; "Home Again, Home Again Jiggity Jig" (full length play), first produced at Cubiculo Theater, 1969, Tosos Theater, 1975; "Two One-Act Plays," first produced at Assembly Theater, 1970; "Something for Kitty Genovese" (one-act play), first performed by Valerie Bettis Repertory Company, 1971; "Stuck," first produced at Eugene O'Neill Memorial Theater, Waterford, Connecticut, 1972, Open Space, New York, N.Y., 1976.

Films: "Scarecrow in a Garden of Cucumbers," Independent, 1972; "The Inspector of Stairs," Independent (short subject), 1975.

Television: "CBS Playhouse," 1968; "Where the Heart Is," 1970; "CBS Playhouse," 1972; "Love of Life," 1972; "A Little Bit Like Murder," ABC Wide World of Entertainment, 1973.

WORK IN PROGRESS: Novel set in 1931 based on a true crime, *Some Unknown Person.*

SIDELIGHTS: "I have no idea what to say about myself as a writer except that I started out at the age of twenty as a novelist then switched to writing for the theater—had some success writing for film and television—none for theater. I believe that at this time there is no room for women as playwrights. Therefore, I have given up writing plays. I have returned to the novel where I get satisfaction plus publication plus money. I enjoy writing and don't find it painful. I work four hours a day, five days a week. I write in the morning. Well, I did find something to say after all!

"As a person? I live in the country in a house that I bought with money earned writing books and that is a very good feeling. My house is third from the Bay. I live with Linda Crawford who is also a writer. We don't compete. Tansy and Max (two Yorkies), and Gilda, Putnam and Vivian (three cats) also live with us.

I wrote *Trying Hard To Hear You* because during the summer of 1973 I directed a production of 'Anything Goes' with about sixty teenagers. The kids and an incident and the fact that I am a lesbian led me to write this book that deals with homosexuality.

"My new book, *The Late Great Me,* is about a sixteen-year-old alcoholic. Alcoholism among teenagers is a very serious problem. I am a recovered alcoholic and that is what led me to write this book.

"I am interested in antiques, love going to auctions and yard sales. I'm crazy about old movies and suspense novels. And I constantly have to watch my weight."

FOR MORE INFORMATION SEE: Cosmopolitan, April, 1961; *Newark Sunday News,* April 23, 1961; *Newsday,* May 11, 1961; *Village Voice,* December 16, 1974; *New York Times Book Review,* January 12, 1975; *Psychology Today,* March, 1975.

... and celebrated the end of the war. ■ (From *Bang Bang You're Dead* by Sandra Scoppetone and Louise Fitzhugh. Illustrated by Louise Fitzhugh.)

SEAMANDS, Ruth (Childers) 1916-

PERSONAL: Born December 15, 1916, in Herrin, Ill.; daughter of Henry (a civil servant) and Pearl (Gibbs) Childers; married John Thompson Seamands (professor of missions at Asbury Theological Seminary), June 5, 1938; children: Sylvia Ruth (Mrs. Rae Phillips), Sheila Ellen (Mrs. James W. Lovell), Sandra Joan (Mrs. Richard Sheppard), Linda Helen (Mrs. Pedro De Los Santos). *Education:* Asbury College, B.A., 1941; further study at Asbury Theological Seminary. *Politics:* Republican. *Home:* 407 Talbott Dr., Wilmore, Ky. 40390.

CAREER: Methodist missionary in Belgaum, Bombay, India, 1941-60; Asbury College, Wilmore, Ky., typesetter, 1967-75; now self-employed typesetter.

WRITINGS: Missionary Mama, Greenwich, 1957; *House by the Bo Tree* (Word Book Club selection), Word Books, 1969; *Land of the Snake Charmer* (juvenile), Moody, 1970; *The Pearl of Warrior Island,* Beacon Hill, 1972. Former writer for children's page of *Herald* (of Asbury Theological Seminary).

WORK IN PROGRESS: Pilgrim with a Blueprint (tentative title), a biography of the author's father-in-law, a missionary to India; a novel, *Isa Lei.*

RUTH SEAMANDS

SIDELIGHTS: "I grew up in the small town of Herrin, Illinois, which during my childhood was notorious as 'Bloody Herrin,' in 'Bloody Williamson County.' That was because of the coal-mine riots and also because of the war between the bootleggers and the law. For a time my father was a deputy sheriff (I still have his badge) and one of the 'good guys' so the 'bad guys' were out to get him. There were bombings, stabbings, and killing in the streets in those days, and one of my earliest memories is not being allowed to walk alone anywhere. I also grew up during the depression—which hit when I was about thirteen. My parents were religious and saw to it that our family was in church every time the doors opened. So my life was shaped by learning to stand and fight for what one believed, and by a deep faith in God. I'm still that way.

"My husband and I went to India as missionaries just before World War II, and then I came home with my first baby during the war while my husband stayed in India. That meant a hard separation of three years. After the war we all went back to India where our missionary career lasted until 1960. It was cut short because of the illness of one of our children, so my husband took a position as Professor of Christian Missions in Asbury Theological Seminary. We have been here ever since.

"While in India I learned to speak the Kanarese language of Mysore State, in South India, to know and love the Kanarese village people, as well as getting acquainted with many of the ruling class of Rajahs and British Government officials in India before Independence there. We have many good friends in India in all classes and castes, and have visited India several times since our missionary career was over. I have written many stories based on Indian situations and culture. The only children's book I wrote, *Land of the Snake Charmer,* was a collection of some of these short stories.

"I wrote my first book, *Missionary Mama,* because I was

alone so much in the huge mission bungalow in Belgaum, India. My husband used to travel and preach in the villages a great deal and I was alone with the current baby. That was because from the age of seven, we had to send our children 800 miles away from home to the nearest American boarding school. Not much happens after dark on a mission compound so after dark was the lonely time. I'd read every book in the house a dozen times, I didn't like the radio music, so there was nothing else to do but write. Our unusual experiences were meant to be written about anyhow. *House By the Bo Tree,* my second book, is also about our life in India. From then on, writing has become a big part of my life. It is only a part, however, because I also do a good deal of speaking in churches. Therefore my writing output is not as great as it ought to be. Whenever I travel, I always gather material and facts about the places we visit, and usually a plot begins to form even before I leave the country. This was true of my novel, *The Pearl of Warrior Island,* and my latest novel, *Isa Lei,* which is set in the Fiji Islands.

"My husband also writes—he wrote two books in the Kanarese Language in India, and has had six books published here in the States. His books are all Christian oriented. I could not write as he writes, and neither could he write as I do, but we encourage each other."

SHAFER, Robert E(ugene) 1925-

PERSONAL: Born March 30, 1925, in Beloit, Wis.; son of James Vaughn (a contractor) and Harriet Ethel (Sewards) Shafer; married Susanne Mueller (a professor of educa-

ROBERT E. SHAFER

Something about the Author

tion), June 19, 1953. *Education:* University of Wisconsin, B.S., 1950, M.S., 1953; Columbia University, Ed.D., 1958. *Home:* 3021 Fairway Dr., Tempe, Ariz. 85282. *Office:* Department of English, Arizona State University, Tempe, Ariz. 85281.

CAREER: Teacher in public schools of Arlington, Va., 1950-53; San Francisco State College (now San Francisco State University), San Francisco, Calif., instructor, 1955-56, assistant professor of English, 1956-58; Wayne State University, Detroit, Mich., associate professor of English, 1958-62; Columbia University, Teachers College, New York, N.Y., associate professor of English, 1962-66; Arizona State University, Tempe, professor of English, 1966—. Consultant in reading and English to school systems in nine states. *Military service:* U.S. Marine Corps, 1942-46; became staff sergeant; served in China and elsewhere in Pacific theater; received Presidential Unit Citation.

MEMBER: National Council of Teachers of English (vice-president, 1968), International Reading Association (co-chairman of committee on linguistics and reading, 1974-75), Linguistic Society of America, Modern Language Association of America, English-Speaking Union, Arizona Civil Liberties Union, Arizona Four Keys Democratic Club. *Awards, honors:* Grants for research at Max-Planck Institute of Education, West Berlin, 1972, and Oxford University, 1973.

WRITINGS: (With others) *Success in Reading,* Silver Burdett, Books 1-2, 1966, Books 3-4, 1967, Books 5-6, 1968; *Personal Values,* Scholastic Book Service, 1975; (with Karen M. Hess and Lanny Morreau) *Developing Reading Efficiency,* Wiley, 1975.

SHEEHAN, Ethna 1908-

PERSONAL: Born November 22, 1908, in Castletown Berehaven, County Cork, Ireland; daughter of John Vincent (a businessman) and Christina (O'Dwyer) Sheehan. *Education:* Hunter College (now part of City University of New York), student, 1928-29, evening courses, 1929-38, A.B., 1938; Columbia University, part-time courses, 1938-45, M.S. in L.S., 1945. *Politics:* "In general, Republican." *Religion:* Roman Catholic. *Home:* 179 Linden St., Rockville Centre, N.Y. 11570.

CAREER: Queens Borough Public Library, Jamaica, N.Y., staff member, 1930-63, advancing from children's librarian to head of central children's room, coordinator of Children's Services, 1952-63; St. John's University, School of Education, Jamaica, N.Y., assistant professor of children's literature and secondary school literature, 1966-75; retired as full-time teacher, June, 1975, currently adjunct professor as well as self employed. Part-time instructor at various times between 1950-63 at Queens College, City University of New York, at Library School of Pratt Institute, at School of Library Services, Columbia University, and at St. John's University. Consultant to publishers and distributors of literary materials for young people.

MEMBER: American Library Association, Catholic Library Association (honorary life member), American Association of University Professors, National Council of Teachers of English, North Shore Literary Guild (Long Island), Books for Brotherhood Committee, National Con-

ETHNA SHEEHAN

ference of Christians and Jews. *Awards, honors:* Named librarian of the year by Catholic Library Association, 1975.

WRITINGS: (Compiler) *A Treasury of Catholic Children's Stories,* M. Evans, 1963; (reviser and author of introduction) Kate Douglas Wiggin and N. A. Smith, original editors, *The Fairy Ring,* new edition, Doubleday, 1967; (compiler) *Folk and Fairy Tales from Around the World,* Dodd, 1970. Contributor to *Grolier's Encyclopedia, New Catholic Encyclopedia,* and professional and literary periodicals; book reviewer for *New York Times Book Review, America,* and other publications.

WORK IN PROGRESS: A selection of folktales and modern tales for storytelling; research into sources for a collection of Irish folktakes.

SIDELIGHTS: "I was born in a little seaside town in the south of Ireland. My father and his father before him were businessmen, but they handed down their love for books and history to all the family. My mother's people (though in business and professions), had a tradition of adventure and romance. War-like O'Dwyers had been outlawed from the Irish midlands by Queen Elizabeth I. Three of their equally rebellious descendants made a dramatic escape from the exile to which the young Queen Victoria had had them sentenced. A late-19th century O'Dwyer sent his own trading vessel to Argentina and contacts were maintained with friends in that country for a long time afterward.

"As a child I loved not only to read all the books I could find but also to produce family newspapers and magazines. My friends and I loved to put on plays—many of which we made up ourselves. We explored the lovely Bantry Bay region with its historical associations and prehistoric remains. I longed to see over the surrounding mountains, and I had my wish when I went away to boarding school and ultimately crossed the ocean to live on Long Island. Since then I have traveled extensively through the U.S. and Canada. I have been to Iceland and North Africa as well as to the Continent of Europe and—many times—to England and Ireland. I now spend my summers on the shores of Bantry Bay, about a mile from the town in which I was

Who should come to meet her on the bridge but her twelve sons; and before the mother could cry out to them the wicked witch threw her spell upon them, and turned them into twelve ducks.
■ (From *Folk and Fairy Tales from Around the World* compiled by Ethna Sheehan. Illustrated by Mircea Vasiliu.)

born. From my house—called Harbour Lights—I can see a ruined castle which was the centre of a great battle in Elizabethan times, several lighthouses, and a mountainous island; and I can watch ships from far-away places coming and going.

"My interest in people and books led me into the library profession. Here I could introduce good books to young people, and could tell stories to children. Some of my happiest memories are of storytelling times at various libraries and schools. I find that the children of today enjoy stories as much as their parents did. It is a great thrill to have modern-day boys or girls tell me that they recognize a story from Grimm or Perrault as a variant of one they have heard at home as a tale from Lithuania or Puerto Rico. I have put many of the stories into collections for reading and storytelling. To do this I had to undertake considerable research in reference libraries to be sure I had the correct sources. I often have to re-work some of the material to make it enjoyable in style for modern readers and listeners.

"Writing is always hard work, whether one is composing a book review, or writing a literary or technical article, or inventing an original story. It takes discipline and perseverance to work and re-work one's prose and to smooth out awkward or confusing passages. The preliminary research can be fun if one enjoys seeking out half-forgotten materials

and comparing early versions of traditional tales. But it can be tiring and at times discouraging. And yet, isn't there a satisfaction in overcoming obstacles? And isn't there some drudgery in every worthwhile and enjoyable undertaking?"

SILVERMAN, Mel(vin Frank) 1931-1966

PERSONAL: Born January 26, 1931, in Denver, Colo.; son of Harry and Goldie (Hellerstein) Silverman; married Sydel Finfer (an anthropologist), December 27, 1953; children: Eve Rachel, Julie Beth. *Education:* Chicago Art Institute, B.F.A., 1953, B.A.E., 1954. *Religion:* Jewish. *Home:* 276 Riverside Dr., New York, N.Y.

CAREER: Artist, New York, N.Y., 1956-63; painter-member, Salpeter Gallery, New York, N.Y.; one-man shows, 1956, 1958, 1962; graphic artist, one-man shows at Associated American Artists Gallery, Butler Art Institute, Zanesville Art Institute (Zanesville, Ohio), Ein Hod Gallery (Israel), University of Maine; exhibited at Chicago Art Institute, Denver Art Museum, Minnesota University, Southern Methodist University, University of Kentucky, University of Oklahoma, and Philadelphia Print Club; work represented in numerous public and private collections. *Member:* Society of American Graphic Artists, Creative Graphic Workshop. *Awards, honors:* Bryan Lathrop traveling fellowship; fellowship from American Israeli Cultural Foundation.

WRITINGS: (Author, illustrator) *Ciri Biri Bin*, World, 1957; *Good-for-nothing Burro*, World, 1958; *Hymie's Fiddle*, World, 1960.

Illustrator: *The Two Uncles of Pablo*, Harcourt, 1959; *Roderick*, Harcourt; *My First Geography of the Panama Canal*, Little; *Jade Jaguar Mystery*, Abingdon; *Songs Along the Way*, Abingdon, 1960; *Apprentice to Liberty*, Abingdon; *Women Who Made America Great*, Lippincott; *The Still Small Voice*, Behrman; *Portals to the Past*, Viking, 1963; *Tuchin's Treasure*, Morrow, 1963; *Flight to the Promised Land*, Harcourt; *Awani*, Morrow, 1964; *Fire in the Sky: Story of a Boy of Pompeii*, Abingdon, 1965.

WORK IN PROGRESS: Many projects; also painting and printmaking for shows.

HOBBIES AND OTHER INTERESTS: Travel, theater and movies, all sports, conversation, and reading.

FOR MORE INFORMATION SEE: Illustrators of Children's Books: 1957-1966, Horn Book, 1968.

(Died September 16, 1966)

SIMONT, Marc   1915-

PERSONAL: Born November 23, 1915, in Paris, France; first came to United States, 1927, but later went back to Europe with parents, returning to America, 1935; naturalized citizen, 1936; son of Jose (a draftsman on staff of *L'Illustration*) and Dolores (Baste) Simont; married Sara Dalton (a teacher of handicapped children), April 7, 1945; children: Marc Dalton. *Education:* Studied art in Paris at Academie Ranson, Academie Julien, and with Andre Lhote, 1932-35, and in New York at National Academy of Design, 1935-37. *Home:* Town St., West Cornwall, Conn. 06706. *Office:* 31 West 11th St., New York, N.Y. 10011.

CAREER: Did portrait painting and advertising art in late 1930's; illustrator of children's books, 1939—. Also author and translator of books for children. *Military service:* U.S. Army, 1943-46; became sergeant. *Awards, honors:* Tiffany fellow, 1937; Caldecott Medal of American Library Association for best illustrated book for children, 1957, for *A Tree Is Nice.*

*WRITINGS—*Self-illustrated: *Opera Souffle: 60 Pictures in Bravura*, Schuman, 1950; *Polly's Oats*, Harper, 1951; (with Red Smith) *How to Get to First Base: A Picture Book of Baseball*, Schuman, 1952; *The Lovely Summer*, Harper, 1952; *Mimi*, Harper, 1954; *The Plumber Out of the Sea*, Harper, 1955; *The Contest at Paca*, Harper, 1959; *How Come Elephants?*, Harper, 1965; *Afternoon in Spain*, Morrow, 1965; (translator) Federico Garcia Lorca, *The Lieutenant Colonel and the Gypsy*, Doubleday, 1971; (with members of staff of Boston Children's Medical Center) *A Child's Eye View of the World*, Delacorte, 1972.

Illustrator: Emma G. Sterne, *The Pirate of Chatham Square: A Story of Old New York*, Dodd, 1939; Ruth Bryan Owens, *The Castle in the Silver Woods*, Dodd, 1939.

MARC SIMONT

Albert Carr, *Men Of Power*, Viking, 1940; Mildred Cross, *Isabella, Young Queen of Spain*, Dodd, 1941; Charlotte Jackson, *Sarah Deborah's Day*, Dodd, 1941; Richard Hatch, *All Aboard the Whale*, Dodd, 1942; *Dougal's Wish*, Harper, 1942; Meindert DeJong, *Billy and the Unhappy Bull*, Harper, 1946; Margaret Wise Brown, *The First Story*, Harper, 1947; Iris Vinton, *Flying Ebony*, Dodd, 1947; Robbie Trent, *The First Christmas*, Harper, 1948; Andrew Lang, editor, *The Red Fairy Book*, new edition, Longmans, Green, 1948; Ruth Krauss, *The Happy Day*, Harper, 1949; Ruth Krauss, *The Big World and the Little House*, Schuman, 1949.

Meindert DeJong, *Good Luck Duck*, Harper, 1950; Ruth Krauss, *The Backward Day*, Harper, 1950; James Thurber, *The Thirteen Clocks*, Simon & Schuster, 1951; Marjorie B. Paradis, *Timmy and the Tiger*, Harper, 1952; Miriam Powell, *Jareb*, Crowell, 1952; *The American Riddle Book*, Schuman, 1954; Elizabeth H. Lansing, *Deer Mountain Hideaway*, Crowell, 1954; Jean Fritz, *Fish Head*, Coward, 1954; Elizabeth H. Lansing, *Deer River Raft*, Crowell, 1955; Fred Gipson, *The Trail-Driving Rooster*, Harper, 1955; Julius Schwartz, *Now I Know*, Whittlesey House, 1955; Janice May Udry, *A Tree Is Nice*, Harper, 1955; Julius Schwartz, *I Know a Magic House*, Whittlesey House, 1956; Thomas Liggett, *Pigeon Fly Home*, Holiday House, 1956; Chad Walsh, *Nellie and Her Flying Crocodile*, Harper, 1956; James Thurber, *The Wonderful "O"*, Simon & Schuster, 1957; Maria Leach, *The Rainbow Book of American Folk Tales and Legends*, World Publishing, 1958; Alexis Ladas, *The Seal That Couldn't Swim*, Little, Brown, 1959.

and the squirrels sleep in the trees,
the ground hogs sleep in the ground.
(From *The Happy Day* by Ruth Krauss. Illustrated by Marc Simont.)

James A. Kjelgaard, *The Duckfooted Hound*, Crowell, 1960; Ruth Krauss, *A Good Man and His Wife*, Harper, 1962; Julius Schwartz, *The Earth Is Your Spaceship*, Whittlesey House, 1963; David McCord, *Every Time I Climb a Tree*, Little, Brown, 1967; Janet Chenery, *Wolfie*, Harper, 1969; Janice May Udry, *Glenda*, Harper, 1969.

Marjorie Sharmat, *Nate the Great*, Coward, 1972; Marjorie Sharmat, *Nate Goes Undercover*, Coward, 1974.

SIDELIGHTS: Marc Simont was born in Paris and spent his childhood in France, Spain, and the United States, drawing pictures wherever he was. He feels that those early years of traveling sharpened his faculties of observation. His most important teacher was his artist father. Mr. Simont and his wife, a teacher of remedial reading, divide their time between New York City and West Cornwall, Connecticut, where he is the "chief instigator" of community soccer.

HOBBIES AND OTHER INTERESTS: Skiing and other sports.

FOR MORE INFORMATION SEE: Caldecott Medal Books: 1938-1957, edited by Miller and Field, Horn Book, 1957; *More Junior Authors*, edited by Muriel Fuller, H. W. Wilson, 1963; *Newbery and Caldecott Medal Books: 1956-1965*, edited by Lee Kingman, Horn Book, 1965; Diana Klemin, *The Art of Art for Children's Books*, Clarkson Potter, 1966; Lee Bennett Hopkins, *Books Are by People*, Citation Press, 1969; *Christian Science Monitor*, November 11, 1971; *Junior Literary Guild Catalog*, September, 1974.

SINCLAIR, Upton (Beall)   1878-1968 (Clarke Fitch, Frederick Garrison, Arthur Stirling)

PERSONAL: Born September 20, 1878, in Baltimore, Md.; son of Upton Beall (a traveling salesman) and Priscilla S. (Harden) Sinclair; married Meta H. Fuller, 1900 (divorced, 1911); married Mary Craig Kimbrough, (a poet), April 21, 1913 (died, 1961); married Mary Elizabeth Willis, October 14, 1961 (died, 1967); children: (first marriage) David. *Education:* City College of New York, A.B., 1897; graduate studies at Columbia University, 1897-1901. *Politics:* Formerly Socialist; then left-wing Democrat. *Residence:* Monrovia, Calif. *Agent:* Bertha Klausner, 130 East 40th St., New York, N.Y. 10016.

CAREER: Supported himself while an undergraduate by writing jokes and doing other hack writing; wrote nearly 100 "nickel novels" while studying at Columbia; established a theater company for the performance of Socialist plays; assisted government in Chicago stock yard investigation, 1906; founded Helicon Home Colony, Englewood, N.J., 1906; founded Intercollegiate Socialist Society, now League for Industrial Democracy; Socialist congressional candidate, 1906 and 1920; Socialist candidate for U.S. Senate, California, 1922, for governor of California, 1926 and 1930; Democratic candidate for governor of California, 1934; united segments of progressives to form EPIC (End Poverty in California) League. Full-time writer. Lectured occasionally.

MEMBER: Authors League of America (a founder),

American Institute of Arts and Letters, American Civil Liberties Union (founder of Southern California branch, 1923). *Awards, honors:* Pulitzer Prize for *Dragon's Teeth,* 1943; award of American Newspaper Guild and of United Automobile Workers, 1962.

WRITINGS: Saved by the Enemy, Street & Smith, 1898; *Wolves of the Navy; or, Clif Faraday's Search for a Traitor,* Street & Smith, 1899; (as Clarke Fitch) *A Soldier Monk,* Street & Smith, 1899; *A Soldier's Pledge,* Street & Smith, 1899.

Springtime and Harvest, Sinclair Press, 1901, later published as *King Midas,* Funk, 1901; (as Clark Fitch) *Clif, the Naval Cadet; or, Exciting Days at Annapolis,* Street & Smith, 1902; *The Journal of Arthur Stirling* ("The Valley of the Shadow"), revised and condensed, Appleton, 1903, Doubleday, Page & Co., 1906; (as Clarke Fitch) *From Port to Port; or, Clif Faraday in Many Waters,* Street & Smith, 1903; (as Clarke Fitch) *The Cruise of the Training Ship; or, Clif Faraday's Pluck,* Street & Smith, 1903; (as Frederick Garrison) *Off for West Point; or, Mark Mallory's Struggle,* Street & Smith, 1903; (as Frederick Garrison) *On Guard; or, Mark Mallory's Celebration,* Street & Smith, 1903; (as Clarke Fitch) *A Strange Cruise; or, Clif Faraday's Yacht Chase,* Street & Smith, 1903; *Prince Hagens: A Phantasy,* L. C. Page & Co., 1903; *Manassas: A Novel of the War,* Macmillan, 1904, Scholarly Press, 1968, revised edition published as *Theirs be the Guilt: A Novel of the War Between the States,* Twayne, 1959; *A Captain of Industry,*

The Appeal to Reason, 1906; *The Jungle,* privately printed, 1906, Doubleday, 1906; *The Moneychangers,* B. W. Dodge & Co., 1908, Gregg Press, 1968; *The Metropolis,* Moffat, Yard & Co., 1908.

American Outpost: A Book of Reminiscenses, Farrar & Rinehart, 1932 (published in England as *Candid Reminiscences: My First Thirty Years,* Laurie, 1932); *The Way Out: What Lies Ahead for America,* Farrar & Rinehart, 1933; *An Upton Sinclair Anthology,* compiled by I. O. Evans, Farrar & Rinehart, 1934, revised Murray & Gee, 1947; *The Gnomobile: A Gnice Gnew Gnarrative with Gnonsense, but Gnothing Gnaughty,* Farrar & Rinehart, 1936; *Little Steel,* Farrar & Rinehart, 1938.

Another Pamela; or, Virtue Still Rewarded, Viking, 1950; *My Lifetime in Letters,* University of Missouri Press, 1960; *Affectionately, Eve,* Twayne, 1961; *Autobiography of Upton Sinclair,* Harcourt, 1962.

"Lanny Budd series: *World's End,* 1940, *Between Two Worlds,* 1941, *Dragon's Teeth,* 1942, *Wide Is the Gate,* 1943, *Presidential Agent,* 1944, *Dragon Harvest,* 1945, *A World to Win,* 1946, *Presidential Mission,* 1947, *One Clear Call,* 1948, *O Shepherd Speak!,* 1949, *The Return of Lanny Budd,* 1953 (all published by Viking; for complete list of works see *Contemporary Authors-5/8*).

SIDELIGHTS: Sinclair, who began as a hack, had been a pamphleteer, a muckraker, a best-selling novelist, and always a reformer. Some of his novels have succeeded both as propaganda and as literature. His first important novel, *The Jungle,* created a sensation which led directly to the passage of the Pure Food and Drug Act. The causes he has promoted include socialism, world peace, teetotalism, women's rights, special diets, justice for Sacco and Vanzetti, endowments for poets, and spelling reform.

He began, he said, as a "perfect little snob and tory," who had received a capitalist education. Yet even this "could not keep me from realizing that the rule of society by organized greed was an evil thing; but it managed to keep me from knowing that there was anybody else in the world who thought as I did; it managed to make me regard the current movements, Bryanism and Populism, which sought to remedy this evil, as vulgar, noisy, and beneath my cultured contempt." He was not to be duped again. When many American liberals became Communist sympathizers, Sinclair remained a vigorous opponent of Communism.

All of the books published by Street & Smith are reissues of stories written prior to 1901 and first published in *Starry Flag Weekly* and *True Blue Library.* Sinclair considered these stories his "juvenile" work, not to be confused with his serious writing.

The Lilly Library at Indiana University is the depository of Sinclair's personal papers, books, manuscripts, and other materials, an accumulation which weighs eight tons. On October 18, 1963, on his eighty-fifth birthday, the library honored him with a convocation. Reflecting at that gathering on his life-long concern with social justice, Sinclair said: "When I was very young, I remember asking my mother: 'Why should some people be rich and others poor?'" And after eighty-five years, he said, he still had not found out.

UPTON SINCLAIR

"We call it an automobile. That means something which moves itself. When it moves gnomes,
I suppose it should be called a gnomobile."
I am the gnifty gnomobile,
Before my gname all gnations gneel;
And when I have a gnut that loosens
Then I can be a gnawful gnuisance. ■ (From the movie *"The Gnome-Mobile,"* © MCMLXVI Walt Disney Productions.)

The following films have been based on his works: "The Adventurer," U.S. Amusement Corp., 1917; "The Money Changers," Pathe Exchange, 1920; "Marriage Forbidden," Criterion, 1938; "The Gnome-Mobile," Buena Vista, 1967.

FOR MORE INFORMATION SEE: Georges Schreiber, editor, *Portraits and Self-Portraits,* Houghton, 1936; James Lambert Harte, *This Is Upton Sinclair,* Rodale Press, 1938; *New Republic,* September 29, 1958; *New York Herald Tribune,* February 11, 1960; *Harper's,* March, 1961; *New York Times Book Review,* May 13, 1962; *Time,* December 14, 1962, December 6, 1968; *Christian Century,* September 25, 1968; *New York Times,* November 26, 1968, November 27, 1968; *London Times,* November 27, 1968; *National Observer,* December 2, 1968; *Publishers' Weekly,* December 9, 1968; *Nation,* December 9, 1968; *Current Biography,* January, 1969; *Books Abroad,* spring, 1969; *Current Biography Yearbook,* 1969.

(Died November 25, 1968)

SINGER, Susan (Mahler) 1941-

PERSONAL: Born July 30, 1941, in Brooklyn, N.Y.; daughter of Ernest (a lawyer) and Pearl (Smith) Mahler; married Marshall R. Singer (a professor), January 1, 1960; children: Shepherd, Paul. *Education:* Studied at Brooklyn College, 1958-60, Hunter College, 1961-62, New School for Social Research, 1962-64, and University of Pittsburgh, at intervals, 1964—. *Religion:* Jewish. *Home:* 1520 Shady Ave., Pittsburgh, Pa. 15217. *Agent:* McIntosh & Otis, Inc., 18 East 41st St., New York, N.Y. 10021.

CAREER: Worked in former years as secretary and editorial assistant for professional journals and a publishing firm; free-lance writer and editor. *Awards, honors:* Bread Loaf Writers' Conference fellowship, 1972.

WRITINGS: Kenny's Monkey (juvenile), Scholastic Book Services, 1963.

WORK IN PROGRESS: The Magic Radio, a book about the adventures of children who find an old radio in a trash pile.

SIDELIGHTS: "I have always liked to read and loved to write. In addition to my children's stories, I have written many stories for adults, as well as half a novel. I do believe

SUSAN SINGER

Go through the grass. ■ (From *I'm Going on a Bear Hunt* by Sandra S. Sivulich. Illustrated by Glen Rounds.)

that art imitates life, and my writing tends to follow closely behind my life expereince—not too closely, of course. It takes several years for the full meaning of events to filter into my imagination. . . .

"I've had the benefits of the academic life without being in it myself, and thus have had much opportunity for travel in Europe, Central America, and a two-year stay in Southeast Asia. Travel provides a new world view, new tastes, vivid memories. But the writer's work is done anywhere, anywhere his energies are taxed, anywhere his mind is stimulated.

"I write because it is my way of interpreting life."

SIVULICH, Sandra (Jeanne) Stroner   1941-

PERSONAL: Surname is pronounced Siv-*o*-lich; born April 8, 1941, in Berwyn, Ill.; daughter of Frank Joseph (a policeman) and Helen (Rench) Stroner; married Kenneth G. Sivulich (director of Erie Metropolitan Library), May 22, 1971. *Education:* Marygrove College, B.A., 1962; Rosary College, M.A.L.S., 1963. *Politics:* Democratic. *Religion:* Roman Catholic. *Home:* 1238 West Ninth, Erie, Pa. 16502.

CAREER: Chicago Public Library, Chicago, Ill., branch children's librarian, 1963-66; Skokie Public Library, Skokie, Ill., children's librarian, 1966-68; Evanston Public Library, Evanston, Ill., director of children's services, 1968-71; Mercyhurst College, Erie, Pa., lecturer in children's literature, 1971—. Lecturer and conductor of workshops on children's books; consultant to Encyclopaedia Britannica

Educational Corp. *Member:* American Library Association, Catholic Library Association, Pennsylvania Library Association, League of Women Voters.

WRITINGS: I'm Going on a Bear Hunt (Junion Literary Guild selection), Dutton, 1973. Contributor to library journals.

WORK IN PROGRESS: A chapter for National Council of Teachers of English book about literary experience for preschool children.

SLADE, Richard   1910-1971

PERSONAL: Born July 19, 1910, in England; son of Richard Simon (a chef) and Ellen (Reardon) Slade. *Education:* Weymouth Teacher Training College, Ministry of Education Certificate, 1947. *Residence:* Barking, Essex, England.

CAREER: Waiter in Belgium and Austria, 1928-31; Gascoigne Junior School, Barking, Essex, England, teacher, 1948-69. Elementary exchange teacher in Los Angeles, Calif., 1965-66. *Military service:* British Army, Royal Signals, 1941-46; took part in Normandy invasion.

WRITINGS: You Can Make a String Puppet, 1957, *Clever Hands,* 1959, *Your Book of Heraldry,* 1960, *Masks and How to Make Them,* 1964, *Take an Egg Box,* 1965, *Your Book of Modelling,* 1967, published in America as *Modeling in Clay, Plaster, and Papier-mache,* Lothrop, 1968, *Toys from Balsa,* 1968, *Tissue Paper Craft,* 1968, *Patterns in Space,* 1969, *Geometrical Patterns,* 1969, *Paper Aero-*

RICHARD SLADE

planes, 1970, *Carton Craft,* 1972, *Take a Tin Can,* 1973 (all published in England by Faber). Contributor to *Art Craft and Education;* also contributor of travel articles to *Lady,* and articles on photography and motorcycling to British national magazines.

WORK IN PROGRESS: Other books on handicraft.

SIDELIGHTS: Constance Nankivell, Slade's sister wrote: "After Richard's visit to Los Angeles in 1965/66 he used the return journey as a means to complete his first circumnavigation. In 1970, he once more embarked on a round-the-world trip, having retired from Gascoigne primary school, an early retirement due to ill-health. During this trip he revisited Los Angeles, to renew his friendships formed in 1965/66 and continued his journeying to New Zealand and Australia.

"Richard Slade spent his final school years in the picturesque fishing village of St. Ives, Cornwall, where his parents and I lived. Among the articles written by him was one published in the *Lady Magazine,* entitled 'White Gold' illustrating the rugged beauty of the St. Austell china clay area. It was to this area of Cornwall that he retired in 1969, taking up residence with my husband and I.

"I would like to end this letter by saying that my brother had a very great feeling for children, the royalties of his books have been donated to the 'Pestalozzi Childrens Trust'. Richard held a very strong view that children with low academic qualifications could make a more than meagre contribution to the 'WORLD' if they expressed themselves, as the title of his second book suggests, *With Clever Hands.''*

Competent in French and German. Covered most of Europe by motorcycle during school holidays, and traveled in Russia, Palestine, Egypt, Japan, India, Hawaii, Central America, and most of North America.

(Died October, 1971)

SNOW, Dorothea J(ohnston)   1909-

PERSONAL: Born April 17, 1909, in McMinnville, Tenn.; daughter of Fred Russell and Theresa Ella (Mosher) Johnston; married Clarence A. Snow, 1929; children: Donald M. *Education:* Attended art school in Fort Wayne, Ind., for two years. *Religion:* Methodist. *Home:* 1519 Locust Circle, Huntsville, Ala. 35801.

CAREER: Taught art in public schools in Tampa, Fla., 1927-28, Des Moines, Iowa, 1928-29; Art Publishing Co., Chicago, Ill., art director, 1933-36; writer of children's books and illustrator for children's magazines. *Member:* Society of Midland Authors (Children's Reading Round Table, Chicago). *Awards, honors:* Top juvenile award, Friends of American Writers, 1961, for *Sequoyah, Young Cherokee Guide;* Indiana University Hoosier Author Award, 1968, for *Tomahawk Claim.*

DOROTHEA J. SNOW

This could not be happening, he reasoned. Not here. Not now. Would they torture him, scalp him, burn him at the stake?
■ (From *The Mystery of Ghost Burro Canyon* by Dorothea J. Snow. Illustrated by David Stone.)

WRITINGS: *No-Good, the Dancing Donkey*, Rand, 1942; *Puddlejumper*, Rand, 1944; *Eli Whitney, Boy Mechanic*, Bobbs, 1947; *Peter the Lonesome Hermit*, Whitman, 1948; *Goofy*, John Martin, 1948; *Samuel Morse, Inquisitive Boy*, Bobbs, 1950; *John Paul Jones, Salt-Water Boy*, Bobbs, 1950; *Ralph Semmes, Tidewater Boy*, Bobbs, 1952; *Come, Chucky, Come*, Houghton, 1952; *The Whistling Mountain Mystery*, Bobbs, 1954; *Jeb and the Flying Jenny*, Houghton, 1956; *Roy Rogers' Favorite Western Stories*, Whitman, 1956; *Lassie and the Mystery at Blackberry Bog*, Whitman, 1956; *Circus Boy Under the Big Top*, Whitman, 1957; *Circus Boy and Captain Jack*, Whitman, 1957; *Circus Boy and War on Wheels*, Whitman, 1958; *Lassie and the Secret of the Summer*, Whitman, 1958; *Indian Chiefs*, Whitman, 1959; *Secret of the Stone Frog*, Bobbs, 1959.

Sequoyah, Young Cherokee Guide, Bobbs, 1960; *A Doll for Lily Belle*, Houghton, 1960; *Donald Duck on Tom Sawyer's Island*, Whitman, 1960; *Henry Hudson, Explorer of the North*, Houghton, 1962; *The Charmed Circle*, Whitman, 1962; *The Mystery of Ghost Burro Canyon*, Bobbs, 1962; *A Sight of Everything*, Houghton, 1963; *That Certain*

Girl, Whitman, 1964; *Tomahawk Claim*, Bobbs, 1968; *Billy's Secret*, Rand, 1972. Contributor to *Children's Activities, Child Life, Wee Wisdom*, other youth magazines.

WORK IN PROGRESS: An adult gothic suspense novel, *Run, Danghter, Run*.

SIDELIGHTS: "I had a wonderful childhood spent in a small cotton town, Huntsville, in northern Alabama, which has since become an important center of the space effort.

"My father owned a small sawmill and we lived on top of Monte Sano, a mountain just outside Huntsville, where he cut and hauled timber to his mill and, being versatile, planed and finished it and built houses of it. Being a long-suffering and patient man, he often let his small daughter run the carriage which sent the log into the big, round, whirling blade, though for my safety, he always stood at my elbow when he did so. How I loved sliding down the huge mounds of clean-smelling sawdust that was always piled around the mill!

"The nearest, and only, school was in Huntsville and, while it is hard to believe now, there were no school buses to pick me up at my door in the morning and deposit me there in the afternoon. So I did the next best thing, went by way of 'shank's horses,' as dad called them, meaning my own legs. Yes, I walked up and down the mountain to school, a distance of four miles each way, often leaving before daybreak and arriving home after dark.

"Strangely, though, I never considered myself an underpriviledged child, nor do I think that today. I really enjoyed those walks to and fro, and rarely missed a day in school, nor was I often tardy. It is to that childhood experience that I credit my love of walking today and the superb health I have enjoyed all my life.

"Living on that mountain was a wonderful childhood experience and I can remember gathering nuts in the fall, berries in the spring and summer, and all sorts of exciting activities that kept me and my brother and small nephew busy without benefit of TV or radio, swimming pool or even a bicycle. We thought we were the luckiest kids in the world. I still think so and now like nothing better than to hike again the woodland areas I knew as a child.

"Now, I have a son in the administration branch of the University of Alabama at Tuscaloosa and sometimes he brings his own little son and wife and we hike them together.

"I still paint and write within view of Monte Sano (Spanish for Health Mountain) where I grew up."

SPEARING, Judith (Mary Harlow) 1922-

PERSONAL: Born November 29, 1922, in Boston, Mass.; daughter of Ralph Volney (a historian and writer) and Judith (Moss) Harlow; married Edward A. Spearing (a chemical engineer), September 21, 1942; children: Peter, Sara, Diana, Janet. *Education:* Attended Syracuse University, 1940-42. *Politics:* Independent. *Religion:* Episcopalian. *Home:* 18310 Shaw Road, Hiram, Ohio 44234. *Agent:* Carolyn Willyoung Stagg, Lester Lewis Associates, 156 East 52nd St., New York, N.Y. 10022.

JUDITH SPEARING

CAREER: Free Public Library, Elizabeth, N.J., reference assistant, 1946-51; Chagrin Falls Branch, Cuyahoga County Library, Chagrin Falls, Ohio, adult and children's services assistant, 1961—.

WRITINGS—Children's books: *Ghosts Who Went to School,* Atheneum, 1966; *Museum House Ghosts,* Atheneum, 1969. Contributor of short stories to *Episcopalian, New Ingenue,* and *American Girl.*

WORK IN PROGRESS: A mystery for children.

SIDELIGHTS: "I have been making up stories ever since I can remember. My mother was a superb story teller, who could hold an audience with an account of what happened when my father invited the dean to dinner, or any other household event. My father was a professor who wrote books of history and biography. They both enjoyed reading aloud, not only to us children but to their friends. I can remember dinner parties where the after-dinner entertainment was hearing my father read a story he had discovered in a second-hand shop. Growing up in this atmosphere, it was as natural to learn to tell stories as to tie your own shoes, and not only tell them, but make them up. My sister and I improved the fifteen-minute walk to school with a long story, beginning in September and ending in June, about a beautiful, rich girl who lived in a house full of secret passages, priests' holes, caskets of jewels, and anything else we thought would improve our own quite ordi-

nary house. When I married and had children of my own, I made up stories for them for quite a long time before I thought of turning the stories into a book.

"When I am writing, I usually begin by asking, 'What if—?' What if a teacher looked across the room and saw a pencil writing by itself? What if a boy wanted to learn Morse code and decided to try flashing messages out his bedroom window? What if a dog ran across the ice and it broke? Then I work backwards and forwards. Why was the boy trying to learn Morse? What kind of boy is he; studious, impulsive, cautious, lonesome, gregarious? Does his mother lose her temper easily? What will his father think when the police arrive? For that matter, why are the police going to arrive? I mull these questions over while I iron or clean. Having a story in mind is the only incentive for ironing I know of, unless you count needing something to wear at once.

"Then I write, and read the story over, and cross out (or tear up in serious cases), and write again. And again. Sometimes I write a story six times before the story on paper is as good as the tone in my mind.

"When I am really thinking hard about a story, my patient family sometimes suffers. Once, when my second daughter was learning to drive and had reached the stage of driving me everywhere we went, I got a marvelous idea on the way home from the dentist. This was a trip we had made dozens of times and it never took more than twenty minutes, even in winter. She said, 'We turn here, don't we?' and I, thinking of my plot, said no. We found ourselves in a place we had never seen before and it took us forty-five minutes to get home. Even when the story sold, she still felt rather resentful. I had caused her to miss gym, which she loved, and we got back in time for physics, which she detested.

"Writing takes me a long time, because I never get anything right the first time, but I don't know of anything more fascinating than getting to know the characters and their world. There is surely nothing more satisfying than reading the completed story when everything is as right as I can

"I wanted to pet the kittens," Louise sobbed. ■ (From *Ghosts Who Went to School* by Judith Spearing. Illustrated by Marvin Glass.)

174   **Something about the Author**

make it, except actually seeing it in print. That doesn't always happen. Sometimes I think a story is perfect but no editor needs it or wants it. That can be discouraging, but I have a folder full of ideas I haven't even written yet, just waiting for me to get moving and have some free time again.

"I couldn't write anything worth publishing if my husband didn't overlook deficiencies in the housekeeping when a story is going well and take the time to listen while I read a completed story aloud. Reading aloud, even to oneself, always brings out unsuspected flaws; a sympathetic listener will always notice and tell me if I have accidentally left out something crucial to the story, which can easily happen because I know the characters and their environment so well. My husband is a very sympathetic listener."

HOBBIES AND OTHER INTERESTS: Gardening and sewing.

SPENCER, William   1922-

PERSONAL: Born June 1, 1922, in Erie, Pa.; son of Herbert Reynolds (a manufacturer) and Rachel (Davis) Spencer; married Martha Jane Brown, February 6, 1948 (divorced); married Helen Elizabeth Bouvier (artist, teacher), May 18, 1969; children (first marriage): Christopher, Meredith, Anne. *Education:* Phillips Exeter Academy, student, 1937-41; Princeton University, A.B., 1948; Duke University, A.M., 1950; American University,

WILLIAM SPENCER

Ph.D., 1965. *Politics:* Democrat. *Religion:* Presbyterian. *Home:* 1037 Betton Rd., Tallahasee, Fla. *Office:* 478 Bellamy, Florida State University, Tallahasee, Fla. 32306.

CAREER: Middle East Journal, Washington, D.C., assistant editor, 1956-57; George Washington University, Washington, D.C., associate professor of political science, 1957-60; U.S. Office of Education, Washington, D.C., international programs specialist, 1960-62; UNESCO, Paris, France, chief of publications, 1962-64; American University, Washington, D.C., director of Institute of Non-Western Studies, 1965-68; Florida State University, Tallahasee, professor of Middle East history, 1968—. Consultant to Historical Evaluation and Research Organization and Special Operations Research Office; adviser to Government of Morocco (for UNESCO). *Military service:* U.S. Army, 1943-46; cryptanalyst in India; received Presidential Citation. *Member:* Middle East Studies Association (fellow), Florida Heritage Foundation (director), Phi Alpha Theta, Phi Kappa Phi, Pi Sigma Alpha. *Awards, honors:* Distinguished Service Award, U.S. Junior Chamber of Commerce, 1958; Title V award, U.S. Office of Education; Fulbright-Hays grant; Carnegie fellowship.

WRITINGS: The Land and People of Turkey, Lippincott, 1958, revised, 1963, 2nd edition 1972; *Political Evolution in the Middle East*, Lippincott, 1962; *The Land and People of Morocco*, Lippincott, 1965; *The Land and People of Tunisia*, Lippincott, 1967; *The Land and People of Algeria*, Lippincott, 1969; *The Story of North Africa*, McCormick-Mathers, 1975; *Algiers in the Age of the Corsairs*, University of Oklahoma Press, in press. Annual articles for *World Book Encyclopedia, World Book Year Book, Grolier Encyclopedia Year Book;* articles and reviews in leading newspapers and magazines; studies for U.S. Department of Defense, "Cuba" and "The Congo," both in *Strategic Concepts and the Changing Nature of Modern War*, and *Trends in North Africa: Politics, Society, The Economy 1970-1980*.

WORK IN PROGRESS: Mediterranean Africa.

SIDELIGHTS: "My first book was written after returning from a year's residence in Turkey, and developed out of personal recollection plus a genuine interest in providing for young people a true picture of a land relatively unknown to them. Since then I have written three other books in the same series, all based on personal visits followed by reflection and careful research, and much labor in the writing. I am particularly excited about *The Story of North Africa* because it will tie together the stories of four nations for very young readers, not merely introducing them to an unfamiliar region, but hopefully making them feel they are a part of North African life.

"Writing is an avocation rather than a career for me, but it is an absorbing one that has taken up a large part of my time for more than twenty years. As to how it began there is no easy explanation. However, an interest in geography, history, and languages developed in school and at home probably was a determining factor. Chance led me to various parts of the world and I became aware of the cultural values that conditioned other societies and made them different from our own. The combination of teaching and writing has been invaluable—teaching forces one to focus writing ideas into coherent form, and writing develops analysis toward the achievement of better teaching."

STEINBECK, John (Ernst)   1902-1968

PERSONAL: Born February 27, 1902, in Salinas, Calif.; the son of John Ernst (a county treasurer) and Olive (a schoolteacher; maiden name, Hamilton) Steinbeck; married Carol Henning, 1930 (divorced 1943); married Gwyn Conger, 1943 (divorced 1949); married Elaine Scott, 1950; children (by second marriage) Tom, John. *Education:* Stanford University, special student, 1919-25. *Agent:* McIntosh and Otis, 18 East 41st St., New York, N.Y. 10017.

CAREER: Worked at several jobs before becoming writer, including hod-carrier, apprentice painter, laboratory assistant, ranch hand, fruitpicker, construction worker at Madison Square Garden, New York, N.Y., and reporter for the *New York American.* Special writing for U.S. Army Air Forces during World War II; correspondent in Europe for New York *Herald Tribune*, 1943. *Awards, honors:* Three-time winner of Commonwealth Club of California general literature gold medal for work by a California author, for *Tortilla Flat*, 1936, *In Dubious Battle*, 1937, *The Grapes of Wrath*, 1940; New York Drama Critics Circle silver plaque for play, "Of Mice and Men," 1938; Pulitzer Prize for novel, *The Grapes of Wrath*, 1940; Nobel Prize for Literature, 1962.

WRITINGS: Cup of Gold: A Life of Henry Morgan, Buccaneer, R.M. McBride, 1929; *Pastures of Heaven*, Brewer, Warren & Putnam, 1932; *To a God Unknown*, Covici-Friede, 1933; *Tortilla Flat*, Covici-Friede, 1935; *In Dubious Battle*, Covici-Friede, 1936; *St. Katy the Virgin* (short story), Covici-Friede, 1936; *Nothing So Monstrous* (short story), Pynson Printers, 1936; *Of Mice and Men*, Covici-Friede, 1937; *The Red Pony*, Covici-Friede, 1937; *The Long Valley*, Viking, 1938; *The Grapes of Wrath*, Viking, 1939.

A Letter to the Friends of Democracy, Overbrook Press [Stamford], 1940; *The Forgotten Village*, Viking, 1941; (with Edward F. Ricketts) *Sea of Cortez*, Viking, 1941, reissued as *The Log From the Sea of Cortez*, Viking, 1951; *Bombs Away: The Story of a Bomber Team*, Viking, 1942; *The Moon Is Down*, Viking, 1942; *How Edith McGillcuddy Met R.L.S.* (short story), Rowfant Club (Cleveland), 1943; *Steinbeck*, edited by Pascal Covici, Viking, 1943, enlarged edition published as *The Portable Steinbeck*, Viking, 1946 (published in Melbourne, Australia, as *Steinbeck Omnibus*, Oxford University Press, 1946); *Cannery Row*, Viking, 1945; *The Wayward Bus*, Viking, 1947; *The Pearl*, Viking, 1947; *A Russian Journal* (with pictures by Robert Capa), Viking, 1948.

Burning Bright (a play in story form), Viking, 1950; *East of Eden*, Viking, 1952; *Sweet Thursday*, Viking, 1954; *The Short Reign of Pippin IV: A Fabrication*, Viking, 1957; *Once There Was a War*, Viking, 1958; *The Winter of Our Discontent*, Viking, 1961; *Travels With Charley in Search of America*, Viking, 1962, large type edition, Watts, 1965;

His mother looked after him for a moment . . . Her eyes were brooding and quiet. Now and then her mouth smiled a little but without changing her eyes at all. ■ (From the movie, "The Red Pony," © Republic, 1949.)

The Short Novels of John Steinbeck, Viking, 1963; *America and Americans*, Viking, 1966; *Journal of a Novel: East of Eden Letters*, Viking, 1969; *Steinbeck: A Life in Letters*, Viking, 1975. Author of syndicated column, written during stay in Viet Nam, 1966-67.

Scripts: *Of Mice and Men: A Play in Three Acts*, Covici-Friede, 1937; *The Forgotten Village* (film), Viking, 1943; "*Lifeboat*" (original author), 20th Century-Fox, 1944; *The Moon is Down: A Play in Two Parts*, Viking, 1943; "A Medal for Benny", in *Best Film Plays-1945*, edited by John Gassner and Dudley Nichols, Crown, 1946; *Burning Bright* (acting edition), Dramatists Play Service, 1951; "Viva Zapata" (film), abridged in *Argosy*, February, 1952.

Screenplays: *The Pearl*, RKO Radio, 1948; *The Red Pony*, Republic, 1949.

SIDELIGHTS: "The writers of today, even I, have a tendency to celebrate the destruction of the spirit, and God knows it is destroyed often enough. But the beacon thing is that sometimes it is not.... It is the duty of the writer to lift up, to extend, to encourage. If the written word has contributed anything at all to our developing species and our half developed culture, it is this.

"The mountain labors and groans and strains and the tiniest of rodents comes out. And the greatest foolishness of all lies in the fact that to do it all, the writer must believe that

JOHN STEINBECK

He hooked his foot in the loop on his rock and his hands worked quickly, tearing the oysters loose, some singly, others in clusters. ■ (From *The Pearl* by John Steinbeck. Illustrated by José Clemente Orozco.)

what he is doing is the most important thing in the world. And he must hold to this illusion even when he knows it is not true."

When asked to name his favorite writer, Steinbeck said: "Oh, it's very broad, Mark Twain, Dostoevsky, Tolstoi. The King James Version of the New Testament. And Cervantes. Certainly Cervantes; he's the best." The play "Molly Morgan", by Reginald Lawrence, 1961, was based on The Pastures of Heaven; the Rodgers and Hammerstein musical "Pipe Dream", 1956, was based on Sweet Thursday; the musical "Here's Where I Belong" based on East of Eden, opened at the Billy Rose Theater, March 3, 1968 (one performance); Of Mice and Men was first produced as an opera by the Seattle Opera Association, January 21, 1970. A TV movie, "The Harness," was based on a short story.

FOR MORE INFORMATION SEE—Books: Harry Thornton Moore, The Novels of John Steinbeck: A First Critical Study, Normandie House, 1939; Edmund Wilson, The Boys in the Back Room, Colt Press, 1941; Maxwell Geismar, Writers in Crisis, Houghton, 1942; Alfred Kazin, On Native Grounds, Harcourt, 1942; George Snell, The Shapers of American Fiction: 1798-1947, Dutton, 1947; W. M. Frohock, The Novel of Violence in America, University Press in Dallas, 1950; E. W. Tedlock, Jr., and C. V. Wicker, editors, Steinbeck and His Critics, University of New Mexico Press, 1957; Peter Lisca, The Wide World of John Steinbeck, Rutgers University Press, 1958; Joseph Warren Beach, American Fiction: 1920-1940, Russell & Russell, 1960; Warren French, John Steinbeck, Twayne, 1961; F. W. Watt, John Steinbeck, Grove, 1962; Joseph Fontenrose, John Steinbeck, Barnes & Noble, 1963; Walter Allen, The Modern Novel, Dutton, 1965; Twentieth Century Literature, October, 1967.

Recent articles: Saturday Review, November 1, 1958; New York Times Book Review, November 16, 1958, June 25, 1961; New Statesman, June 30, 1961; Times Literary Supplement, July 7, 1961, New Republic, August 21, 1961; Yale Review, December,. 1961; Life, November 2, 1962; Newsweek, November 5, 1962, January 30, 1967, December 30, 1968; American Literature, January, 1965; Detroit Free Press, January 9, 1967; Ramparts, July, 1967; Antioch Review, spring, 1967; The New Yorker, March 9, 1968; Washington Post, December 21, 1968, December 22, 1968, February 23, 1969; The Observer, December 22, 1968, January 19, 1970; London Times, December 21, 1968; New York Times, March 13, 1967, December 3-4, 1967, December 21, 1968, June 2, 1969; National Observer, December 23, 1968; Time, December 27, 1968; Variety, January 1, 1969; Publishers' Weekly, December 30, 1968; Antiquarian Bookman, January 6-8, 1969; Washington Post, February 23, 1969; Books Abroad, spring, 1969; Commonweal, May 9, 1969; New York Times, June 2, 1969; National Observer, January 19, 1970; Christian Science Monitor, January 30, 1970; Writer, May, 1970.

(Died December 20, 1968)

STEINBERG, Alfred 1917-

PERSONAL: Born December 8, 1917, in St. Paul, Minn.; son of Harry (a salesman) and Libby (Baron) Steinberg; married Florence Louise Schoenberg, September 16, 1940; children: Arne, Lise, Polly. Education: University of Minnesota, B.A., 1938, M.A., 1940. Home and office: 904 Highland Dr., Silver Spring, Md.

CAREER: U.S. Government Agencies, Washington, D.C., economist, 1941-46; Food and Agricultural Organization of United Nations, Washington, economist, 1947; Economic and Political Weekly News-Letter on Far East, Washington, editor and publisher, 1946-47; Committee for Equality in Naturalization, public relations, 1948; free-lance writer, 1948—.

WRITINGS: (With Senator Tom Connally) My Name is Tom Connally, Crowell, 1954; Mrs. R.: The Life of Eleanor Roosevelt, Putnam, 1958; (with Paul Siple) Ninety Degrees South, Putnam, 1958; Man From Missouri: Life and Times of Harry S Truman, Putnam, 1962; The First Ten: The Founding Presidents and Their Administrations, Doubleday, 1967; Sam Johnson's Boy, Macmillan, 1968; The Bosses, Macmillan, 1972; Sam Rayburn, Hawthorn, 1975.

Teen-age biographies: Eleanor Roosevelt, 1959, Daniel Webster, 1959, Richard E. Byrd, 1960, Douglas MacArthur, 1961, Woodrow Wilson, 1962, John Marshall, 1962, Harry Truman, 1963, James Madison, 1965, Herbert Hoover, 1966; Dwight D. Eisenhower, 1967, John Adams, 1967, The Kennedy Brothers (Junior Literary Guild selection), 1969 (all published by Putnam).

Over 200 magazine articles on politics, history, and economics. Contributor to encyclopedias.

SIDELIGHTS: "My continuing interest in history began when I was a small boy in Minneapolis and dug up some Indian arrowheads in my back yard. A patient librarian helped me choose books on Indian lore and life, and from there I expanded my readings in history. Similarly, my interest in politics began when I stumbled onto a political rally on a corner not far from home while returning from an evening of monthly collections on my paper route. The speakers and the cheering and jeering crowd of partisan listeners fascinated me. So from early youth I had these interests, when I was not playing football, baseball and hockey.

"There was never any doubt in my mind that one day I would write about past and present events and about 'important' people. I had hardly begun to write when I was fortunate enough to have the editors of the Saturday Evening Post ask me to go to the White House and write a series of articles on President Harry Truman. Later I got to know him even better when I went to Independence, Missouri for further talks with him for a biography I was writing. One morning in a discussion with him on Character, I asked how his mother and father had influenced him. 'I don't buy that,' he said. 'That's a lot of nonsense. The only thing that matters is what's in you.'

"When I wrote books for 'Putnam's Lives to Remember' series for young people, I intended them for my three children. I am still writing for their younger images frozen in time and memories, for son Arne has his Ph.D., my daughter Lise is a practicing attorney, and Polly is in medical school."

STONE, D(avid) K(arl) 1922-

PERSONAL: Born March 24, 1922, in Reedsport, Ore.; son of Karl R. (a dairy county supervisor) and Genevive (Rogers) Stone; married Peggy Lee Barker (a model), February 14, 1952; children: Kelly, Jamie. *Education:* University of Oregon, B.A., 1947; also studied at Art Center College of Design, Los Angeles, and in Mexico at University Michoacana de San Nicolas de Hidalgo. *Home:* 6 Farm View Rd., Port Washington, N.Y. 11050. *Agent:* (Illustration) Bette Mandel, Estelle Mandel Co., Inc., 65 East 80th St., New York, N.Y. 10021.

CAREER: Hay baler, sign painter, and farm hand, 1930-40; Springfield Creamery, Springfield, Ore., truck driver, 1938-40; Westfir Lumber Co., Westfir, Ore., lumber stacker, 1940-41; illustrator and painter, 1950—; professional artist (civilian) for U.S. Air Force, Washington, D.C., 1960—. Vice-president of Craven Evans Stone Creative Graphics, New York, N.Y., 1970-72. Member of village board of governors, Flower Hill, Port Washington; member of board of directors, Port Washington Community Relations Council and Port Washington Coalition for Racial Concern. *Military service:* U.S. Army, Infantry, 1941-46; became first lieutenant. *Member:* Society of Illustrators (president, 1968-69), Graphic Artists Guild (board of directors), Art Advisory Council. *Awards, honors:* Society of Illustrators Certificate of Merit, 1964, 1966, 1969, 1971, 1974; First Award at Artist and Book Show, 1965; St. Louis Art Directors' Club Medal, 1969; U.S. Air Force Plaque, 1970; Graphic Artists Guild Commendation, 1975.

WRITINGS—Author and illustrator: *Art in Advertising*, Pitman, 1961; *Thanksgiving*, Holt, 1968.

Illustrator: Louisa May Alcott, *Little Women*, Whitman, 1965; Louisa May Alcott, *Little Men*, Whitman, 1965; Gladys Baker Bond, *Patrick Will Grow*, Whitman Publishing, 1966; Katherine J. Hardie and Pauline P. Meek, *The Birth of God's People*, CLC Press, 1968; Kenneth Grahame, *The Wind in the Willows*, Golden Press, 1968; Glenn P. Crone, *There Really is a Santa Claus*, John Knox Press, 1968; Veronica Nash, *Carlito's World: A Block in Spanish Harlem*, co-published by McGraw and Rutledge Books, 1969; *Three Little Pigs*, Platt, 1969; Robert F. Burgess, *Where Condors Fly*, World Publishing, 1969; Walt Whitman, *Miracles: The Wonder of Life*, Rand, 1969.

Tom McGowen, *Hammett and the Highlanders*, Follett, 1970; Eleanor L. Clymer, *We Lived in the Almont*, Dutton, 1970; Lois Elizabeth Johnson, editor, *Christmas Stories Round the World*, Rand, 1970; Eleanor Harder, *Darius and the Dozer Bull*, Abingdon, 1971; Eleanor L. Clymer, *Me and the Eggman*, Dutton, 1972; Ewan Clarkson, *The Running of the Deer*, Dutton, 1972; Ernest Hemingway, *For Whom the Bell Tolls*, Sho Ku Kan (Tokyo), 1972; Dion Henderson, *Algonquin*, Whitman, 1972; Ewan Clarkson, *In the Shadow of the Falcon*, Dutton, 1973; Frank Martin, *How Do You Say It? In English, Spanish and French*, Platt, 1973; Bernice W. Carlson and Ristina Wigg, retellers, *We Want Sunshine in Our Houses*, Abingdon, 1973; Norman Mailer, *The Naked and the Dead*, Shogo Ku Kan, 1973; Morton Grosser, *The Snake Horn*, Atheneum, 1973; June L. Shore, *What's the Matter with Wakefield*, Abingdon, 1974; Glen A. Hodges, *The Lost Bear*, Dutton, 1975; Ewan Clarkson, *Wolf Country*, Dutton, in press; Elizabeth Rider Montgomery, *Duke Ellington: King of Jazz*, Dell, in press.

He was hungry, scared, wet, and lost. But he was alive. And like all creatures he wanted to stay alive. ■ (From *Lost Bear* by Glen A. Hodges. Illustrated by David K. Stone.)

WORK IN PROGRESS: Wagon train painting for the Commonwealth of Pennsylvania Bicentennial; illustrating *The Cat that Never Died,* by William MacKellar, for Dodd.

SIDELIGHTS: "I am, by nature, a narrative painter and hence enjoy nothing more than visualizing an author's characterizations."

FOR MORE INFORMATION SEE: Saturday Review, January 23, 1971.

STOREY, (Elizabeth) Margaret (Carlton) 1926-

PERSONAL: Born June 27, 1926, in London, England; daughter of Harold (an editor) and Lyn (a chemist; maiden name, Bramwell) Storey. *Education:* Girton College, Cambridge, B.A., 1948, M.A., 1953.

CAREER: Teacher of English language and literature in London, England, 1957—. Has also done secretarial and publicity work. *Member:* Institute for Comparative Study of History, Philosophy, and the Sciences.

WRITINGS—All for children; all published by Faber, except as indicated: *Kate and the Family Tree*, Bodley Head, 1965, published as *The Family Tree*, Nelson, 1973; *Pauline*, 1965, Doubleday, 1967; *Timothy and Two Witches*, 1966, Dell, 1974; *The Smallest Doll*, 1966; *The Smallest Bridesmaid*, 1966; *The Stone Sorcerer*, 1967; *The Dragon's Sister, and, Timothy Travels*, 1967, Dell, 1974; *A Quarrel of Witches*, 1970; *The Sleeping Witch*, 1971; *The Mollyday Holiday*, 1971; *Wrong Gear*, 1973; *Keep Running*, 1974, published in America as *Ask Me No Questions*, Dutton, 1975.

WORK IN PROGRESS: More books for children.

SIDELIGHTS: "It is intensely difficult to write about me-as-a-person; mostly I think that gets into my books, and that indirect way of expressing myself is far easier than trying to say what I'm like. As to how and why I write, there are two main kinds of authors, and great writers have belonged to either, so one need not feel either is superior; naturally I do feel that my way is superior all the same.

"I have a dazed admiration for those who can sit down and write their so many hundred words a day, and I think probably that is the way to earn a living by writing. My method is the one where you don't write a thing unless you have something to say, which leads to rather slow production except at those times when there really is something to say; at those times I wouldn't eat or sleep if I was left to it, and

Being kidnapped was such an entirely unlikely thing that she had no idea how to behave, but obviously, and although the idea frightened her, she ought to consider how to get away.
■ (From *Ask Me No Questions* by Margaret Storey. Illustrated by Robert Clayton.)

getting to school to teach is like stepping out of a space ship or another dimension.

"Teaching is something I like doing. It's a communication too, and that's what I'm most interested in. One of the best writers for children, E. Nesbit, used to pray when she was a child that she never would forget what childhood was like. So many adults do—you can hear it when they talk to and of children. I, too, don't want to forget."

STORR, Catherine (Cole) 1913-
(Irene Adler, Helen Lourie)

PERSONAL: Born July 21, 1913, in London, England; daughter of Arthur Frederick (a lawyer) and Margaret (Gasealee) Cole; married Anthony Storr (a psychiatrist and writer), February 6, 1942; children: Sophia, Cecilia, Emma. *Education:* Studied at St. Paul's Girls' School, London, England, 1925-31, Newnham College, Cambridge, 1932-36 and 1939-41, and West London Hospital, 1941-44. *Religion:* Agnostic. *Home:* 14 High St., Hampstead, London N.W.3, England. *Agent:* A. D. Peters, 10 Buckingham St., London W.C.2, England.

CAREER: West London Hospital, London, England, assistant psychiatrist, 1948-50; Middlesex Hospital, London, England, assistant psychiatrist, 1950-62; now full-time writer. *Member:* Society of Authors.

WRITINGS: Ingeborg and Ruthy, Harrap, 1940; *Clever Polly*, Faber, 1951; *Stories for Jane*, Faber, 1952; *Clever Polly and the Stupid Wolf*, Faber, 1955; *Polly, the Giant's Bride*, Faber, 1956; *The Adventures of Polly and the Wolf*, Faber, 1957; *Marianne Dreams*, Faber, 1958; *Marianne and Mark*, Faber, 1960; *Magic Drawing Pencil*, A. S. Barnes, 1960; *Lucy*, Bodley Head, 1961; *Lucy Runs Away*, Bodley Head, 1962; (under pseudonym Helen Lourie) *A Question of Abortion*, Bodley Head, 1962; *Robin*, Faber, 1962; (under pseudonym Irene Adler) *Freud for the Jung*, Cresset, 1963; *Catchpole Story*, Faber, 1965; *The Merciful Jew* (adult), Barrie and Rockcliff, 1968; *Rufus*, Faber, 1969, Gambit, 1971; *Puss and Cat*, Faber, 1969; *Thursday*, Faber, 1971, Harper, 1973; *Black God, White God* (adult), Barrie and Rockcliff, 1972; *Kate and the Island*, Faber, 1972; *The Chinese Egg*, Faber, 1975, McGraw-Hill, 1975; *Growing Up*, Hutchinson, 1975; *Unnatural Fathers* (adult), Quartet, 1976. Contributor of reviews to *Times Literary Supplement*.

SIDELIGHTS: "I started writing when I was ten years old and it has become an addiction. I write very fast and almost always too much, then have to cut. I can write anywhere and against a lot of background noise, apart from music that I want to listen to and being talked at. I'm basically a story teller, I think in story form and my dreams often take the form of stories, though hardly ever useful as plots. I enjoy writing dialogue and find it comes very easily. I don't write with a child readership in mind, I write for the childish side of myself, and find it often acts as psycho-therapy. I can't think of any greater piece of good fortune than to find myself paid for what I so much enjoy doing."

FOR MORE INFORMATION SEE: Children's Literature in Education/1, APS Publications, Inc., March, 1970; *New York Times Book Review*, October 1, 1972; *Horn Book*, April, 1973.

STOVER, Marjorie Filley   1914-

PERSONAL: Born June 23, 1914, in Lincoln, Neb.; daughter of H. Clyde (a college professor) and Creta (Warner) Filley; married John F. Stover (a professor at Purdue University), August 21, 1937; children: John C., Robert V., Charry E. *Education:* University of Nebraska, A.B., 1935. *Religion:* Methodist. *Home:* 615 Carrolton Blvd., West Lafayette, Ind. 47906.

CAREER: Nebraska School of Agriculture, Curtis, instructor in English and speech, 1935-37; Bergen Junior College, Teaneck, N.J., instructor in speech and drama, 1937-41. *Member:* Chicago Round Table, Creative Writers. *Awards, honors:* Dorothy Canfield Fisher master award list, 1973-74.

WRITINGS: Trail Boss in Pigtails, Atheneum, 1972; *Chad and the Elephant Engine,* Atheneum, 1975.

WORK IN PROGRESS: A story about a girl who was a telegrapher in the late 1870's.

SIDELIGHTS: "Both of my parents came from Nebraska pioneer families. The stories of those early days were a part of my growing years. Perhaps this is why I am fascinated by historical stories. When I was in school, however, I did not find my history classes particularly interesting. Now I have discovered that when I start to research the background for a story, I am interested in all kinds of details. I must know how people dressed in that time and place, what kinds of food they ate, how they talked, what kind of trans-

portation was used, and what the problems were in their every-day living. All of these affect what the characters do and say.

"Since I did not grow up in a horse and buggy age, I had to learn a great deal about horses before I could write *Trail Boss In Pigtails*. Information about oxen, covered wagons, longhorns, and trail driving suddenly became very important to me.

"*Trail Boss* is based on one of the stories from my own family history. The bones of the story are true, but it is fleshed out with imagination guided by research.

"*Chad and the Elephant Engine* was sparked by a circus train legend that my husband, who teaches American History and writes books about railroads, found in his research. Learning about circuses was a great deal of fun.

"Even more important than writing is my role as housewife. The words, 'She's just a housewife,' irritate me no end. A good homemaker is the key to a comfortable and happy home for husband and children. The family is the basic unit of our civilization, and if the family disintegrates, so does our civilization.

The band played on, and the music had been timed to fit—so many flip-flaps, handstands, somersaults, and balancing acts. ■ (From *Chad and the Elephant Engine* by Marjorie Filley Stover. Illustrated by Judith Gwyn Brown.)

"Modern household equipment has freed us from much of the old household drudgery. With self-discipline and planning even the woman with small children can and should find time to develop special interests. Many are ideal for the housewife.

"It is the delicate balance between family life and personal interests that make the happy and harmonious life we all seek."

SWINBURNE, Laurence   1924-

PERSONAL: Born July 2, 1924, in New York, N.Y.; son of Laurence T. (an artist) and Marie-Louise (a teacher; maiden name, Floris) Swinburne; married Irene Kallini (collaborator on her husband's books), June 14, 1947; children: Virginia Louise (Mrs. Thomas Bowman), Susan Elizabeth. *Education:* Princeton University, A.B., 1949; Rutgers University, M.Ed., 1958. *Politics:* Independent. *Religion:* Roman Catholic. *Home:* 49 Cord Pl., East Norwich, N.Y. 11732. *Office:* de Merlier Swinburne Associates, 49 Cord Pl., East Norwich, N.Y. 11732.

CAREER: Textbook salesman after finishing Princeton; American Educational Publications, Middletown, Conn., educational sales promotion manager, 1959-61; Doubleday & Co., Inc., Garden City, N.Y., educational sales promotion manager, 1961-64; Great Society Press (educational materials), East Norwich, N.Y., vice-president, 1964-65; McGraw-Hill Book Co., New York, N.Y., an editor, 1965-68; Educreative Systems, Inc., New York, N.Y., vice-president, 1968-72; de Merlier Swinburne Associates (educational materials), East Norwich, N.Y., vice-president, 1974—. Writer of juvenile books and textbooks, 1964—. Library trustee, Oyster Bay, N.Y., 1965-68. *Military service:* U.S. Marines, infantryman, 1943-45; served in Pacific theater.

MEMBER: Authors Guild. *Awards, honors: Detli* was among the thirty best books for children in grades four through eight on list for Dorothy Canfield Fisher Memorial Children's Book Award, 1970; Nice Book Fair Award for "Crossroads" series, 1970.

WRITINGS: Joe, the Salesman, McGraw, 1966; (editor and contributor) *Ramblers, Gamblers and Lovers* (poems), McGraw, 1968; (adapter), *Dark Sea Running,* McGraw, 1968; (adapter), *Art Arfons: Fastest Man on Wheels,* McGraw, 1968; (adapter) *Stories by Jesse Stuart,* McGraw, 1968; *Angelita Nobody* (junior high novel for slow readers), McGraw, 1968; (adapter), *Follow the Free Wind,* Ballantine, 1969; (co-author with Eric Broudy and Warren Halliburton) *They Had a Dream,* Pyramid Publications, 1969; *RFK: The Last Knight* (biography), Pyramid Publications, 1969; *Detli,* Bobbs, 1970; *Robby on Ice,* Creative Educational Society, 1972; *Cows and Cowboys,* Parents' Magazine Press, in press.

(Editor with James Olsen) "Crossroad" program (for inner city junior high students), published by Noble & Noble, 1969, and co-editor of following books in program: *Love's Blues; Me, Myself and I; Dreamer of Dreams; He Who Does; Tomorrow Won't Wait; Breaking Loose; In Other's Eyes: Playing It Cool.*

In N.O.W. program (filmstrips and books), published by

LAURENCE SWINBURNE

Simon & Schuster, 1970: *Timmy Timms, a Perfect Man; Timmy Timms and His Floating Bed; Timmy Timms and the Suction Shoes; Timmy Timms and the Forest Fire; Timmy Timms Builds a Kite; Johnny Hope and the Deserted Apartment House; Johnny Hope and Old Man Corrigan; Johnny Hope, the Campaign Manager; Johnny Hope and the Great Snowball Fight; Johnny Hope's Thanksgiving; Bernardo the Detective; Bernardo the Baseball Player; Bernardo's Halloween; Bernardo at the Amusement Park; Bernardo at the Beach; Saltine Keeps Cool; Saltine Goes Fishing; Saltine the Cowboy; Saltine's New House; Saltine and the Skiis.*

(With Sister Agnes A. Pastva) "Composing with Words," published by Cambridge Book Co., 1974: Unit I: *Slippery Words;* Unit 2: *Making a Difference;* Unit 3: *The Writer Sees.*

"Audobook" series (cassette and print for slow or unmotivated students), published by Swinburne Press, 1974: *Ragnar and the Winged Horses; The Ice Dragon; The Jungle of Evil; The High Poet of Ireland; Tin Lion on a Roof; The Tin Lion and His Friends; The Boy Who Had No Name and Other Stories; The Girl Who Took Care of Her Parents and Other Stories; 1-2-3! And Other Stories.*

In "Series R" (basal readers), published by Macmillan, 1975: *Pastimes; Birds and Beasts; Journeys.*

Filmstrips: "Career Education Planning," six filmstrips, Appalachia Research Laboratory, 1967; "American Folktales," five filmstrips, Audio-Visual, Inc., 1968; "Middle American Folktales," five filmstrips, Audio-Visual, Inc., 1968; "Black Leaders," six filmstrips, Audio-Visual, Inc., 1968; "City Streets," twelve filmstrips, McGraw, 1972; and others.

SIDELIGHTS: "As long as I can remember, I wanted to write—even *before* I could write. I recall that before I went to school, my mother would write the poems and stories that I made up. The other day, I ran across one of these poems (it concerned looking at the moon as I lay in bed). It was fairly good and left me with the odd feeling that it might have been the best piece I have done in my life.

"All through elementary and high school, I wrote almost anything that came into my head. I also did an enormous amount of reading, a necessary task for a would-be writer. Following World War II, I went to college and there I was on the staff of the campus literary magazine. For the first time, I saw my stories in print.

"When I graduated from Princeton, I became a textbook salesman, but continued to write and was published several times in literary magazines. However, to this point, I had never written any stories for children.

"Finding myself at loose ends in late 1964, I decided to write for two markets: 1) the so-called juvenile market (the books found in libraries and bookstores), and; 2) the textbook market, especially for reading and language arts classes. It has been a long and sometimes rough road, but as of this date, I have had published fifty-two books, over 300 short stories, articles, and poems, and sixty-three filmstrips. Two more books will be published soon.

"I love writing for kids and believe with Isaac Singer that they are the most receptive reading audience in the country. How do I get my ideas? Why, usually by asking the kids themselves. Over the past four years, I have given talks to about 40,000 children here on Long Island. They ask a lot of good questions about the writing craft, and they also tell me what they would like to read.

"I think that there ought to be more professional writers in the reading and language arts fields. It is all very well to teach children the rudiments of reading, but they are liable to become 'turned-off' if their textbooks do not include interesting and entertaining stories, articles, poems, and plays. If their educational materials were more 'fun,' perhaps more than a small minority would use the library as a steady habit—because they have been taught to like reading.

"I collaborate with my wife in writing nowadays. She does a great deal of research and gives me invaluable criticism. I also ask kids for their reactions; their comments are most helpful. I believe that a great deal of problems in the school and library publishing field would be eliminated if publishers took the time to ask the children what they think.

"I don't exactly know where I got the yen for writing. My father and brother became artists. The poet Algernon Charles Swinburne is a very, very distant cousin, but I discount him as an influence. Perhaps it is primarily due to an aunt, who was a professional lecturer and gave fascinating talks on historical subjects."

SYNGE, (Phyllis) Ursula 1930-

PERSONAL: Surname rhymes with "thing"; born April 8, 1930, in Minehead, Somersetshire, England; daughter of Walter John Reginald (a chartered accountant) and Kath-

URSULA SYNGE

leen Phyllis (Vowles) Synge; married Bernard Alfred Gordon Perrin (an artist), 1950; children: Jonathan, Abigail. *Education:* Studied at convent school, 1935-41, country grammar school, 1941-44, and West of England College of Art, Bristol, 1944-46. *Politics:* None. *Religion:* "A sort of paganism." *Home:* 10 Highbury Villas, St. Michael's Hill, Bristol BS2 8BX, England.

CAREER: After leaving school worked at various short-duration jobs, such as photographer's assistant, accounts clerk, and bookseller's assistant; bookseller specializing in art books and books for children, The Pied Piper Bookshop, Bristol, England, 1957—; author of books for young people, 1972—.

WRITINGS: Weland, Smith of the Gods, Bodley Head, 1972, S. G. Phillips, 1973; *The People and the Promise,* S. G. Phillips, 1974; *Audun and the Bear,* Bodley Head, 1975. Editor, quarterly publication of Bristol branch of Society for Mentally Handicapped Children, 1958-61.

WORK IN PROGRESS: A book about a prince with a swan's wing for an arm and how variously people react to him; research in folktale, legends, and mythology.

SIDELIGHTS: "Reading has always been my ruling passion and as a child I read widely and omnivorously but, in those days, I never thought of writing as a possible career. I wanted to be an artist—there was no question of any other life. So, when I left school I went to art college and it was there I started writing. Very seriously. But I could never finish anything. Circumstances changed—I married, had children and read—but put my writing away. Reading aloud those stories that I had most enjoyed, I began to think again of writing, and this time, after so long an interval, it went well. I was no longer trying to write the definitive twentieth-century novel, but had returned to my earliest influences—mythology, legend, the folk-tale. These stories are re-created for each generation and contain, I believe, important truths that we would be foolish to ignore.

"My earliest memory (from a book) is of the three grey sisters with one eye and one tooth between them in Charles Kingsley's telling of the Perseus story. When I read that

But his own voice was snatched away by the wind and carried out to sea, while the voice in his head grew louder and yet louder. ■ (From *Weland: Smith of the Gods* by Ursula Synge. Illustrated by Charles Keeping.)

passage now, as an adult, my mind contains the same picture it held when I was a child—a picture that was perhaps purely my own for our copy of the book was not illustrated. It was a tiny limp-covered schoolbook that my father had had when he was a child (and I have it still). And I shall never be able to re-tell that story.

"I was brought up in a small sea-side town in Somerset, England—a clean bright little town with a harbour and surrounded by hills, the edge of Exmoor which is, I am quite sure, one of the most beautiful places in England. But, even apart from the hills, Minehead had something very special of its own—the Hobby-horse, a folk-survival so ancient that not even the families who held the tradition and brought out the Hobby-horse each May, could say certainly how it originated. The Hobby-horse itself is a vaguely boat-shaped frame worn on the shoulders, with a covering of sacking painted in circles and decorated with rags and ribbons, having a long rope tail. The mask was terrifying. For three days at the beginning of May (each year) the Hobby-horse dances through the town, accompanied by a man with a drum and a man with an accordian. On the third day (in the evening) is the Booty. The whole town turns out to follow the horse to its traditional sites. . . . In the old days it was an occasion of great drunkenness but has long since dropped that aspect though there is still tension in the air, and an excitement I have never encountered at any other time.

"Surely the Hobby-horse (which is, in fact, the remnant of a fertility rite), its music and the Booty have been great influences on my later reading, my own writing, and my beliefs.

"I describe myself as 'a sort of pagan' because most of my beliefs date from a pre-Christian era—but truly I am fascinated by religious belief in all its forms, and I revere it in all its forms. I write of heroes (in the literal sense of the word) because these are, to me, inspired men—men who, in seeking, become a little larger than life.

"In writing about heroes for children I am, perhaps, trying to share with them the excitements and glories of my own childhood reading, in the way that one always wishes to share a treasured book with a friend."

TANNER, Louise S(tickney) 1922-

PERSONAL: Born February 16, 1922, in New York, N.Y.; daughter of Henry Austin (a lawyer) and Helen (a poet; maiden name, Frith) Stickney; married Edward E. Tanner (an author best known as Patrick Dennis), December 17, 1948 (separated, 1962); children: Michael, Elizabeth. *Education:* Vassar College, B.A., 1944. *Politics:* Democrat. *Religion:* Roman Catholic. *Agent:* McIntosh & Otis, Inc., 18 East 41st St., New York, N.Y. 10021.

CAREER: Conde Nast Publications, New York, N.Y., editorial copywriter, 1944-46; *Good Housekeeping,* New York, N.Y., editorial copywriter, 1946-47; Franklin Spier, Inc., New York, N.Y., advertising copywriter, 1947-57; author. *Member:* Authors League, P.E.N., New York Civil Liberties Union. *Awards, honors: Reggie and Nilma* received first prize for a juvenile (older reader division) in *Chicago Tribune Children's Spring Book Festival* awards, 1972.

LOUISE S. TANNER

WRITINGS—Adult books: *Here Today*, Crowell, 1959; *Miss Bannister's Girls*, Farrar, Straus, 1963; *All the Things We Were*, Doubleday, 1968.

Juvenile books: *Reggie and Nilma*, Farrar, Straus, 1971.

WORK IN PROGRESS: Dr. IRT a juvenile based on the New York subway system, for Coward; and *Put Me in the Picture*, a collection of plays, classroom activities, and slide shows which have successfully encouraged participation in an East Harlem classroom.

SIDELIGHTS: "Each generation is influenced by the pop art idols of its adolescence. I was lucky to have some good ones: Garbo, Carole Lombard, Benny Goodman, Cole Porter, Duke Ellington and 'Our Gal Sunday.' I still thrill to the memory of the train whistles of Thomas Wolfe. They all ended up in my book on the Thirties, *All the Things We Were*. The left-wing movements of the decade gave me a kinship with the revolutionaries of the sixties. I had less respect for the archetypal figures of the forties and fifties. I can never understand why anyone would want to revive the Cold War with Richard Nixon and Joe McCarthy riding high. I have no nostalgia for Checkers or Johnnie Ray. Patti Page inspires me with no yen to buy a record of 'How Much Is That Doggie in the Window?' The same goes for revivals featuring the movie stars of the late fifties, who posed for fan magazines amid wet-bottomed babies and Early American furniture. No swinger I, in those days I thought it was a scandal what Elvis did with his pelvis.

"Youth and its changing fashions, however, always fascinated me. It took an editor to talk me into writing a juvenile, though he promptly turned down the resulting opus. By 1960 I had children of my own, who played baseball in the street, attended rock concerts, rode the Staten Island ferry, and learned to play seven-card stud from the wonderful lady who was the Nilma of *Reggie and Nilma*. *Reggie and Nilma* and *Dr. I.R.T.* show New York kids in an urban setting, increasingly polarized between the very rich and the very poor. For *Dr. I.R.T.* I took a step, which for many Manhattanites is as novel as a trip to the moon. I boarded a subway bound for Brooklyn.

"Music as a theme runs through both juveniles. My son was part of the Woodstock generation. He introduced me to Bob Dylan, the Rolling Stones and Beatles. Like Helen Morgan, they hit a chord. Their dissatisfaction with the machine age took me back to *The Wasteland*. Their debt to the South took me back to jam sessions on Fifty-Second Street. Today Woodstock is as remote as the Stone Age. I for one am sorry. If the young don't sing songs of rebellion, who else will? All too soon comes the struggle to get into Med School.

"The struggle to get into Med School has taken over the campus. Like bygone campus fixtures such as the hip flask, the Oxford Oath, the G.I. Quonset hut and the bullhorn, it tells a lot about the times. I long for the days when it was still possible to believe that youth could change the System. I also remember when every kid in the United States dreamed of making it on Broadway. I'll believe again in the possibility of change when 'Fun City' is no longer a pejorative term, or when they write another New York musical like *Wonderful Town*.

"I studied French for twelve years in school, Russian for one at the Berlitz School. My reading knowledge of Spanish was acquired during ten trips to Mexico and from peering over peoples' shoulders at *El Diario* in the New York subway. (See *Dr. I.R.T.*) Spoken performance in any of the above languages inspires guffaws in Mexico City, Moscow and Montmartre.

"I'm a confirmed Manhattan cliff dweller, though Mexico City and Los Angeles strike me as safer places to retire, as well as a good deal warmer. When I say this, my children retort, 'You know you'll be carried out of this apartment in a pine box.' In the interim I take heart and literary inspiration from the fact that Huckleberry Finn is alive and well in New York City."

FOR MORE INFORMATION SEE: Best Sellers, March 1, 1968; *New York Times Book Review*, May 12, 1968; *Commonweal*, May 21, 1971; *Horn Book*, August, 1971.

TARSHIS, Jerome 1936-

PERSONAL: Born June 27, 1936, in New York, N.Y.; son of Benjamin (a postal worker) and Freda (Wiener) Tarshis. *Education:* Columbia University, A.B., 1957. *Home:* 1315 Polk St., San Francisco, Calif. 94109.

CAREER: Dancer-Fitzgerald-Sample, Inc. (advertising agency), New York, N.Y., research analyst, 1957-59; Pageant Press, New York, N.Y., editorial assistant, 1959-60; *Television* (magazine), New York, N.Y., assistant editor,

1960; Physicians Publications, Inc., New York, N.Y., writer and editor, 1962-67; free-lance writer, 1967—; art critic, 1970—.

WRITINGS: Claude Bernard: Father of Experimental Medicine (youth book), Dial, 1968; *Andreas Vesalius: Father of Modern Anatomy* (youth book), Dial, 1970. Contributor of reviews and articles to *Boys' Life, Evergreen Review, Village Voice, Art Forum, Art News, Studio International,* and other publications.

WORK IN PROGRESS: A book on art and literature of the 1960's.

SIDELIGHTS: "I came to write my biographies of Claude Bernard and Andreas Vesalius by what might be called a series of accidents. Taking them in no particular order, I can begin by saying that I spent the middle sixties working on a magazine published for doctors. This magazine tried to present the latest news of medicine—if possible, so late that it had not yet been published elsewhere—and often not even a recent event, but only a proposal for the future.

"Before long I despised the worship of the new. To do my job I had to suppress my understanding that many of the promising new lines of research I was writing about would come to nothing; I wished I could write about research that would still stand us 25 years later.

"By 1964 I had decided to move from New York to San Francisco, and I thought I should sell a high-priced magazine article to ease the transition period in which I would be looking for a new job. Bearing in mind my interest in medical research, I wrote an article for *Reader's Digest* about the 19th-century physiologist Claude Bernard. My article was rejected, whereupon I decided that someone had better pay me for my time. That article turned into my first book, and when the editor who bought it asked me what else I'd like to write for him, I suggested Andreas Vesalius, and he said yes.

"As for how I decided to write juveniles, that is another story. I had read a life of Louis Pasteur, by John Mann, and hadn't realized at the time that it was a book for young people. . . . I thought that if Mann could write a juvenile biography I had read with pleasure, then I myself could write a juvenile biography without compromising my standards as a writer. I spoke about this idea with Robert Silverberg, a college classmate of mine who has written many juveniles, and he encouraged me to go ahead. . . .

"For a variety of reasons, I stopped writing books in 1969, and have only recently started again. I've been an art critic since 1970, and I'm pleased to be able to turn my interests into books. As I write this, I don't have any clear vision of the future of book publishing, or of my own future, and I can't say whether I will someday write more books for young people."

FOR MORE INFORMATION SEE: New York Times Book Review, May 19, 1968; *Best Sellers,* July 15, 1968, April 1, 1970.

TASKER, James

PERSONAL: Born December 5, in Kimberley, South Af-

JAMES TASKER

rica; son of James (a company director) and Edith Elizabeth (Lark) Tasker; married Elaine English (a novelist), October 3, 1946. *Education:* Attended high school in Port Elizabeth, South Africa. *Home:* Peartree Cottage, Park St., Greyton, Cape 7233, South Africa. *Agent:* Evelyn Singer Agency, P.O. Box 163, Briarcliff Manor, N.Y. 10510.

CAREER: J. Walter Thompson Co. (advertising agency), New York, N.Y., manager of branches in Port Elizabeth, South Africa, 1946-50, and Frankfurt-am-Main, Germany, 1951, account executive in New York, N.Y., 1951-52, associate director of branch in London, England, 1952-62; artist and writer, 1962—. Has lectured at Principia College, Elsah, Ill., and University of California, Riverside. *Military service:* South African Army, intelligence officer, 1940-46, served in Abyssinia, Egypt, Libya, and Italy. *Member:* Botanic Society of South Africa, Royal Horticulture Society (Great Britain; fellow).

WRITINGS: African Treehouse (for children), Harvey House, 1974. Contributor to local newspapers.

WORK IN PROGRESS: A children's book in verse on Australian animals.

SIDELIGHTS: "Africa is no longer Darkest Africa, but it still provides ample opportunity for one to study the wild life of animals and birds. Antelope still roam freely in the open spaces and occasionally marauding leopards raid ranches for sheep near where I live.

This fox is a fennec,
a silver-grey fellow.
(From *African Torchouse* by James Tasker. Illustrated by Kathleen Elgin.)

Other: Ninety short stories, articles, and poems for Educational Development Laboratories "Learning 100" (adult reading program), 1964-65; more than forty stories and articles for "Springboards" program, Great Society Press and Portal Press, 1965-67; sixty stories for "Mission Read," Random House, 1970; twenty-five stories for "Listen and Read" program, Heath, 1970-71; ten stories for "Urban Reading" program, Heath, 1970-71; twenty-five stories and articles for Reader's Digest Services, 1973-74; and other stories and articles in texts. Also contributor of stories and articles to popular magazines in 1940's and 1950's.

WORK IN PROGRESS: The Horse Children, about the first people to ride horses, circa 3000 B.C., for Parents' Magazine Press; short stories and articles.

"South Africa set the example to the rest of Africa in providing vast areas of wilderness as reserves for wild game where no hunting is allowed and highly-trained game wardens supervise the protection of the wild life.

"As a young boy, therefore, I had every chance in this great country of familiarizing myself with African animals and their habits. It was natural, too, for me to hunt in season but somehow I could not now get any pleasure out of shooting these magnificent animals or beautiful game birds. Of course, during the war in East Africa, I was often called upon to provide meat for my Scottish battalion when other fresh meat was unobtainable, so I had to go hunting then. But thas was a long time ago.

"An incident during World War II in the Libyan Desert had quite a bearing on my incentive to write. With one or two other officers, after a tank battle at Sidi Rezegh, I had managed to escape from my German captors. We were almost taken again as we lay under a full moon on a completely flat and shelterless plain with a number of the enemy in an armoured vehicle immediately behind us—about twenty yards away! So still did we lie, in various grotesque positions, that it must have appeared to them that we had been shot. This must have convinced the man behind us for they left a few minutes later. I think this experience made me realize how a hunted animal must feel, how it feigns death in its stillness. I believe then I became attuned to the wild in a greater degree than ever before and I know, too, that I couldn't hunt any more. Now I prefer to write about such things.

"I had the good fortune to visit Australia a few years back and saw many of that continent's extraordinary animals and birds. My latest manuscript deals with them so let's hope it will one day be in book form.

"My other vocation is painting—not animals this time, but mostly landscape or portraits in oils, acrylics or watercolors. By the time this is printed, I shall have had a one-man exhibition of watercolors of 'Cape Cottages and Chimneys'—structures which are peculiarly South African."

TATE, Joan 1922-

PERSONAL: Born in 1922; married; three children. *Home:* 32 Kennedy Rd., Shrewsbury SY3 7AB, England.

CAREER: Writer. *Member:* Society of Authors, PEN International, Translators Association, Amnesty International.

WRITINGS—All teenage or children's fiction, except as noted; all published by Heinenmann except as noted: *Jenny,* 1964; *The Crane,* 1964; *The Rabbit Boy,* 1964; *Coal Hoppy,* 1964; *The Silver Grill,* 1965; *The Next Doors,* 1965; *Picture Charlie,* 1965; *Lucy,* 1965.

The Tree, 1966, published as *Tina and David,* Nelson, 1973, Scholastic, 1974; *The Holiday,* 1966; *Tad,* 1966; *Bill,* 1966; *Mrs. Jenny,* 1966; *The Lollipop Man,* Almqvist & Wiksell, (Stockholm), 1967, Macmillan, 1969; *The Wild Boy,* Almqvist & Wiksell, 1967, Harper, 1973, published as *Wild Martin,* Heinemann, 1968; *The Train,* Almqvist & Wiksell, 1967.

Bits and Pieces, 1968; *The Circus and Other Stories,* 1968; *Letters to Chris,* 1968; *The Crow,* 1968; *Luke's Garden,* 1968; *The New House,* Almqvist & Wiksell, 1968; *The Soap Box Car,* Almqvist & Wiksell, 1968; *Jenny and Mrs. Jenny,* 1968 (published as *Out of the Sun,* 1968); Sam and Me, *Macmillan, 1968, Coward, McCann, 1969;* Polly, *Almqvist & Wiksell, 1969;* The Great Birds, *Almqvist & Wiksell, 1969;* Whizz Kid, *Macmillan, 1969, published as* An Unusual Kind of Girl, *Scholastic Book Services;* Clipper, *1969, published as* Ring on My Finger, *1971;* The Old Car, *Almqvist & Wiksell, 1969;* The Nest, *Macmillan, 1969;* The Cheapjack Man, *Macmillan, 1969;* The Gobbleydock, *Macmillan, 1969;* The Tree House, *Macmillan, 1969;* The Ball, *Macmillan, 1969; (with Sven Johansson and Bengt Astrom)* Going Up One *(nonfiction; language text) with* Workbook and Key, *Almqvist & Wiksell, 1969;* The Letter and Other Stories, *Almqvist & Wiksell, 1969;* Puddle's Tiger, *Almqvist & Wiksell, 1969;* The Caravan, *Almqvist & Wiksell, 1969;* Edward and the Uncles, *Almqvist & Wiksell, 1969;* The Secret, *Almqvist & Wiksell, 1969;* The Runners, *Almqvist & Wiksell, 1969.*

(With Johansson and Astrom) *Going Up Two* (nonfiction) with *Workbook and Key,* Almqvist & Wiksell, 1970; *Night Out and Other Stories,* Almqvist & Wiksell, 1970; *The Match and Other Stories,* Almqvist & Wiksell, 1970; *Dinah,* Almqvist & Wiksell, 1970; *The Man Who Rang the Bell,* Almqvist & Wiksell, 1970; *Ginger Mick,* Almqvist & Wiksell, 1970; *Luke's Garden,* Almqvist & Wiksell, 1970; *Journal for One,* Almqvist & Wiksell, 1970; *Gramp,* Chatto & Windus, 1971; *The Long Road Home,* 1971.

Your Town (nonfiction), David & Charles, 1972; *Wump Day,* 1972; *Dad's Camel,* 1972; *Ben and Annie,* Doubleday, 1972; *Jock and the Rock Cakes,* Brockhampton, 1972; *Grandpa and My Little Sister,* Brockhampton, 1972; *Taxi!,* Schoeningh, 1973; *How Do You Do* (nonfiction), Schoeningh, 1974; *The Living River* (nonfiction), Dent, 1974; (with Johansson and Astrom) *Going Up III* with *Workbook and Key,* Almqvist & Wiksell, 1974; *The Runners,* David & Charles, 1974; *Dirty Dan,* Almqvist & Wiksell, 1974; *Sandy's Trumpet,* Almqvist & Wiksell, 1974.

Zena, Almqvist & Wiksell, 1975; *The Think Box,* Almqvist & Wiksell, 1975; *Disco Books* (for adult nonreaders), Cassell/Collier/Macmillan, 1975; *Club Books,* Cassell/Collier/Macmillan, 1975; *Your Dog* (nonfiction), Pelham, 1975; *Apple Books* (for adult nonreaders), Cassell/Collier/Macmillan, in press; *The House That Jack Built,* Pelham, in press.

Translator: John Einar Aberg, *Do You Believe in Angels,* Hutchinson, 1963; Dagmar Edqvist, *Black Sister,* Doubleday, 1963; Maertha Buren, *A Need to Love,* Dodd, 1964; Berndt Olsson, *Noah,* Hutchinson, 1964; Buren, *Camilla,* Dodd, 1965; Per Wahloo, *The Assignment,* Knopf, 1965; Ralph Herrmanns, *River Boy: Adventures on the Amazon,* Harcourt, 1965; Mika Waltari, *The Roman,* Putnam, 1966; Folke Henschen, *History of Diseases,* Longmans, 1966, published as *The History and Geography of Diseases,* Dial, 1967; Nan Inger, *Katrin,* Hamish Hamilton, 1966; Maria Lang, *Wreath for the Bride,* Hodder & Stoughton 1966; Lang, *No More Murders,* Hodder & Stoughton, 1976; Lang, *Death Awaits Thee,* Hodder & Stoughton, 1967; Sven Gillsaeter, *From Island to Island,* Allen & Unwin, 1968; Per Wahloo, *A Necessary Action,* Pantheon, 1968 (published in England as *The Lorry,* M. Joseph); Margit Fjellman, *Queen Louis of Sweden,* Allen & Unwin, 1968; Wahloo and Maj Sjoewall, *The Man Who Went Up in Smoke,* Pantheon, 1969; Carl Nylander, *The Deep Well,* Allen & Unwin, 1969; Hans Heiberg, *Ibsen,* Allen & Unwin, 1969.

Wahloo, *The Steel Spring,* Knopf, 1970; Goeran Bergman, *Why Does Your Dog Do That?,* Hutchinson, 1970; Anders Bodelsen, *Freezing Point,* Knopf, 1970; Wahloo and Sjoewall, *The Fire-Engine That Vanished,* Pantheon, 1970; Gunnel Beckman, *Admission to the Feast,* Macmillan, 1971; Doris Dahlin, *The Sit-In Game,* Viking, 1972; Beckman, *A Room of His Own,* Viking, 1972; Wahloo, *The Generals,* Pantheon, 1973; Beckman, *Mia,* Bodley Head, 1974, Viking, 1975; Astrid Lindgren, *That Emil,* Brock-

JOAN TATE (with family)

hampton, 1974; Barbro Lindgren, *Alban,* A. & C. Black, 1974; Olle Hoegstrand, *The Debt,* Pantheon, 1974; Astrid Lindgren, *The Lionheart Brothers,* Brockhampton, 1974, Viking, 1975; Lennart Frick, *The Threat,* Brockhampton, 1975; Merete Kranse, *Scatty Ricky,* Pelham, 1975; *The Bjorn Borg Story,* Pelham, 1975; Kare Holt, *The Race,* Michael Joseph, in press; Anders Bodelson, *Operation Cobra,* Pelham, in press.

SIDELIGHTS: "There is nothing about me that is of interest or use to anyone in the world of books. Most of the books listed here are not for children, but for those people who have grown away from childhood but cannot yet tackle adult books. I write on the principle (always, though not always with the same success, alas) that if a story does not interest an intelligent fast-reading adult, however briefly, it is useless to any young reader too. I feel there are few concepts that a reading child cannot understand. It depends on how a book is written.

"I do not plan stories systematically. I have an idea, brood on it, sometimes for years, then one day sit down and write it. I sometimes shorten stories, or lengthen them, but I never change the central core of a story to suit anyone. A story is a story is a story, or should be.

"Naturally one's life experience comes into what one writes, but no person in any of my stories is based on a real person. They are imaginary characters, experiencing life in some way or other, against backgrounds which are so varied, in so many combinations of human experience, that it is impossible to generalize. But through them all, perhaps, runs a strain that people are much the same all over the world, underneath their different languages and customs, and what we have in common are the same delights, pleasures, sorrows, miseries and terrors.

"I write all the time and read when I am not writing. We have a large shambly house, the door is always open. I

When they get to Woolworth's, Ben pushes the chair up to one of the glass doors and shouts, "Make way for the Queen." ■ (From *Ben and Annie* by Joan Tate. Illustrated by Judith Gwyn Brown.)

listen to everyone (a writer is always *there,* so people are apt to come and talk). I make no judgments, but feel that talking something out alone helps people sort out their rights and wrongs for themselves. Books can sometimes act in the same way. I personally think there is no such thing as ultimate right or wrong.

"Translation is like writing, except that million dollar nerve-wracking process of inventing a series of characters who live and interact on each other has been done for you. So translation is easier. It is more important to be able to write than it is to have a perfect knowledge of the language. Many people can help you with unknown words. No one can help you to write so that the reader enjoys it. That you have to do yourself.

"I have written a book on the habits and behavior of dogs. It is based on what the animal behaviorists have found out about dogs by studying wolves. It is a kind of translation of adult scientific knowledge for young readers. Our own dogs (we have always had one or two) sit on the chairs when they shouldn't, chew things they oughtn't to, behave in a way which shows that we have not studied the behavior of dogs well enough. Perhaps all my stories are translations of what life is about, what people are about, to readers who are younger than me?

"I have been reading since I was four, often indiscriminately, but gradually discovering that there is always some-

thing new to be learnt about human kind. Thus, I feel that tolerance is the greatest of all virtues, the most difficult to achieve, and the one worth striving for. But we have to get rid of our fears before we can be tolerant.

"I talk too much, dress to please myself, share everything with my other half with whom I have lived for over thirty years, as he does with me, have been a person in my own right since I was very young, which you have to be if you are to be a writer, or indeed if you are to survive in life.

"I started writing when I was forty, and have always worked since our youngest went to school and would probably simply wither away if I didn't have a lot to do."

FOR MORE INFORMATION SEE: Horn Book, December, 1974.

TAYLOR, Florance Walton

PERSONAL: Born in Danville, Ill.; daughter of Thomas E. (a physician) and Elizabeth (Burke) Walton; married Mack Taylor (a dental surgeon); children: Thomas E., Betsy, Alan. *Education:* Northwestern University, B.A., 1920; University of Illinois, M.A., 1933. *Politics:* Republican. *Religion:* Presbyterian. *Home:* 2 North Shore Ter., Danville, Ill. 61832.

CAREER: Once a high school teacher; writer, mainly of

historical fiction for young people. Member of board, Vermilion County Children's Home, 1954-60. *Member:* Children's Reading Round Table, Kappa Kappa Gamma, Delta Kappa Gamma, P.E.O. Sisterhood. *Awards, honors:* Merit Award, Northwestern University, 1940.

WRITINGS: With Fife and Drum, Albert Whitman, 1938; *Vermilion Clay,* Albert Whitman, 1939; *Salt Streak,* Revell, 1939; *Towpath Andy,* Albert Whitman, 1940; *Owen of the Bluebird,* Albert Whitman, 1942; *Navy Wings of Gold,* Albert Whitman, 1955; *Carrier Boy,* Abelard, 1956; *Jim Longknife,* Albert Whitman, 1959; *Gold Dust and Bullets,* Albert Whitman, 1962; "Felipe Adventure" series, Lerner, 1971, seven books, titled *Ball Two, Corn Festival, From Texas to Illinois, Plane Ride, School Picnic, What Is a Migrant?,* and *Where's Luis?*

WORK IN PROGRESS: A juvenile book based on William Henry Harrison's victory at the Battle of Tippecanoe.

HOBBIES AND OTHER INTERESTS: Gardening.

TAYLOR, Florence M(arian Tompkins) 1892-

PERSONAL: Born March 4, 1892, in Brooklyn, N.Y.; daughter of Edward Osborn and Ruth (Flandreau) Tompkins; married George Russell Taylor, December 18, 1916; children: Edward Osborn, Elizabeth Anne (Mrs. Willard B. Fernald), Margaret Flandreau (Mrs. Robert C. West, Jr). *Education:* Graduated from Montclair State Normal School (now Montclair State College). *Religion:* Protestant. *Home:* 261 North Drexel Ave., Columbus, Ohio 43209.

CAREER: Kindergarten teacher at school for retarded children and in New Jersey public schools, 1909-17; Protestant Council of the City of New York, New York, N.Y., associate in Christian education for fifteen years; writer of textbooks for church schools, 1938—.

WRITINGS: Neighbors at Peace, Abingdon, 1938; *Child*

FLORENCE M. TAYLOR

Life in Bible Times, Bethany, 1939; *Their Rightful Heritage,* Pilgrim Press, 1942; *Thine is the Glory,* Westminster, 1948; *Growing Pains,* Westminster, 1948; *Good News to Tell,* Westminster, 1949; *Your Children's Faith: A Guide for Parents,* Doubleday, 1964; *The Autumn Years,* Seabury, 1968; *A Boy Once Lived in Nazareth* (child study Association book list), Walck, 1969; *From Everlasting to Everlasting,* Seabury, 1972; *Hid in My Heart,* Seabury, 1974; *The Bridled Tongue,* Keats, 1975. Author with Imogene M. McPherson of series of interdenominational church school textbooks; six teacher's books and twelve pupil's books, for use in released-time classes in New York, N.Y., Abingdon-Cokesbury, 1947-49.

He liked the peaceful hours when work was done

(From *A Boy Once Lived in Nazareth* by Florence M. Taylor. Illustrated by Len Ebert.)

WORK IN PROGRESS: All the Days of My Life: Spiritual Supplies for Daily Needs, for Keats; *As for Me and My House: The Christian Family—A Redemptive Fellowship,* for Word, Inc.

THACHER, Mary McGrath 1933-

PERSONAL: Born December 20, 1933, in New York, N.Y.; daughter of Raymond D. (an investment banker) and Anne (Serre) McGrath; married Peter Shaw Thacher (an official of United Nations), March 2, 1957; children: Anne, Linda, Shaw. *Education:* Bryn Mawr College, B.A. (cum laude), 1954; Ecole des Beaux Arts, Geneva, Switzerland, further study, 1973—. *Religion:* Roman Catholic. *Home:* 29e Chemin de Grange Canal, 1208 Geneva, Switzerland. *Agent:* Curtis Brown Ltd., 60 East 56th St., New York, N.Y. 10022.

CAREER: Graphic artist and photographer; also designer of decorative needlework.

ILLUSTRATOR: Phyllis Busch, *A Walk in the Snow,* Lippincott, 1971; Phyllis Busch, *Exploring as You Walk in the Meadow,* Lippincott, 1972; Phyllis Busch, *Exploring as You Walk in the City,* Lippincott, 1972.

WORK IN PROGRESS: A series of wood engravings illustrating the year 1066.

HOBBIES AND OTHER INTERESTS: Botany and bird watching.

UNRAU, Ruth 1922-

PERSONAL: Second syllable of surname rhymes with "now"; born February 28, 1922, in Kouts, Ind.; daughter

RUTH UNRAU

of A. E. (a farmer) and Martha (Zook) Baughman; married Walter D. Unrau (an accountant), August 1, 1953; children: Susan (Mrs. Greg Stucky), Paula. *Education:* Ball State University, B.S., 1943; Indiana University, M.C.S., 1945. *Religion:* General Conference Mennonite. *Home address:* Box 214, North Newton, Kan. 67117. *Office:* Bethel College, North Newton, Kan. 67117.

CAREER: Bethel College, North Newton, Kan., associate professor of business, 1947—. *Member:* American Association of University Women (local chapter treasurer, 1974-75).

WRITINGS: Buckwheat Summer, Herald Press, 1962; *Who Needs an Oil Well?,* Abingdon, 1968.

WORK IN PROGRESS: A book about her experiences in India.

SIDELIGHTS: "Writing is my avocation, since teaching takes almost full time. I started with children's stories, thinking after having read one hundred books to my older daughter that surely I could write stories like those, and I found I could. Then I told the story of my own growing up in *Buckwheat Summer,* and then my husband's story in *Who Needs an Oil Well?* Our family spent four years working in Woodstock School in northern India, and when I have stopped making speeches about the experience, I will start writing."

VECSEY, George 1939-

PERSONAL: Surname is pronounced Vessy; born July 4, 1939, in Jamaica, N.Y.; son of George (a copy editor with Associated Press) and May (a society editor; maiden name, Spencer) Vecsey; married Marianne Graham (an artist and teacher), October 1, 1960; children: Laura, Corinna, David. *Education:* Hofstra College (now Hofstra University), B.A., 1960. *Religion:* Christian. *Home:* 9 Chelsea Dr., Port Washington, Long Island, N.Y. 11050. *Agent:* Philip Spitzer, 111-25 76th Ave., Forest Hills, N.Y. 11375.

CAREER: Newsday, Garden City, Long Island, N.Y., sportswriter, 1956-68; *New York Times,* New York, N.Y., sportswriter, 1968-70, Appalachian correspondent, based in Louisville, Ky., 1970-72, Long Island correspondent, based in Port Washington, 1972—.

WRITINGS: Baseball's Most Valuable Players, Random House, 1966; (with John Biever) *Young Sports Photographer With the Green Bay Packers,* Norton, 1969; *The Baseball Life of Sandy Koufax,* Scholastic Book Services, 1969; *Joy in Mudville: Being a Complete Account of the Unparalled History of the New York Mets from Their Most Perturbed Beginnings to Their Amazing Rise to Glory and Renown,* McCall Publishing, 1970; *Pro Basketball Champions,* Scholastic Book Services, 1970; *The Harlem Globetrotters,* Scholastic Book Services, 1971; *Frazier/Ali,* Scholastic Book Services, 1972; *One Sunset a Week: The Story of a Coal Miner,* Saturday Review Press, 1974; (editor) *The Way It Was,* McGraw, 1974; (with wife, Marianne Vecsey) *The Bermuda Triangle: Fact or Fiction?,* Macmillan, 1975; (with Loretta Lynn) *Coal Miner's Daughter,* Geis, in press.

SIDELIGHTS: "I have always been interested in people. My first sports hero was Jackie Robinson, who made such

GEORGE VECSEY

an impact on major-league baseball. I loved reading the travel adventures of Richard Halliburton, who was always swimming some forbidden canal, or climbing a mountain. Perhaps the first biography I ever read was about Franklin Delano Roosevelt. I loved to read how men and women behaved in difficult times—what made one person great.

"As a writer, I have tried to get close to people, to really understand them. I started out as a sportswriter, and found I was more interested in the players than in the facts of the game. How did big stars handle their sudden fame? Why did some players last a dozen years, and others burn out in a year or two?

From age 21 to 31, I travelled around the country, covering the New York Mets and Yankees, meeting interesting people like Casey Stengel and Bill Russell, seeing all the great cities I had dreamed about. In 1970, I decided I had seen enough games for a while—it was time to learn about other people. So I became a correspondent for *New York Times,* based in Louisville, Kentucky. I was privileged to meet coal miners, farmers, small-town people in Appalachia and the South. They were two of the best years in this city boy's life. . . .

"We live in Port Washington, an old town on Long Island Sound. We love the hills and fog and sunny days by the water. It has small-town atmosphere but we are only forty-five minutes from the Museums and restaurants of New York City. My wife paints pictures and decorates our home in bright colors. We ride bicycles and swim and fish, and we enjoy travelling almost anywhere.

"Some of our best adventures have come while travelling—chatting in an old country store in Tennessee, talking politics with an old soldier in Italy, poking around villages in New England. I hope to write about different parts of the world in my future books.

"I was raised in a newspaper family. My father was the sports editor and my mother was the society editor at the same paper when they met. My first job was delivering newspapers. Later I was an errand boy at several newspapers before I got my chance to write for *Newsday* on Long Island. I admire some of my colleagues who can dig out important news 'scoops.' I prefer doing interviews with people to determine *why* they did what they did, and how they *feel* about themselves and their role in the news.

"My favorite writers are Thomas Wolfe, Charles Dickens and Joyce Carol Oates. My children *adore* the work of Louise Fitzhugh and Laura Ingalls Wilder."

FOR MORE INFORMATION SEE: Christian Science Monitor, June 25, 1970.

WALKER, Diana   1925-

PERSONAL: Born April 24, 1925, in Stoke Poges, Buckinghamshire, England; daughter of George Frederick (a civil servant) and Lillian (Loring) Taylor; married Barrie Neil Walker (a technical engineer), June 4, 1960. *Education:* Attended Blackpool Art College, Blackpool, England, 1944-46. *Address:* R.R. 1, Bolton LOP IAO, Ontario, Canada. *Agent:* Paul R. Reynolds, Inc., 599 Fifth Ave., New York, N.Y. 10017.

CAREER: Secretary, at various times, 1945-65.

WRITINGS—Juvenile: *Caterpillar Capers,* Thomas Nelson, 1947; *Singing Schooners,* Abelard, 1965; *An Eagle for Courage,* Abelard, 1967; *Mystery of Black Gut,* Abelard, 1968; *Skiers of Ste. Celeste* (Junior Literary Guild selection), Abelard, 1970; *Never Step on an Indian's Shadow,* Abelard, 1973.

WORK IN PROGRESS: The Year of the Horse, for Abelard, a story set on Prince Edward Island.

SIDELIGHTS: "My love of the countryside and the excitement of discovering small miracles of nature, such as the first daffodils blooming in the woods after a long winter, has stayed with me all of my life. I have never enjoyed living in cities and deplore progress which is swallowing up and mutilating our countryside. My husband and I both share the same ambition: to live in Nova Scotia, an area still comparatively unspoiled and isolated. In all my books I try to convey some of the delight of simple things, which in a commercially-minded world is sadly lacking today.

"As far back as I can remember I have possessed a very fertile imagination which sometimes got me into trouble as a child. When I was about eleven, my sister and I discovered writing as an outlet for our imaginations. We wrote avidly, mostly school stories, in a fierce state of competition. It was a wonderfully absorbing pastime, but then my sister, reaching her teens, discovered boys and the fact that real life could be as interesting as fiction. That was the end of her literary aspirations."

LELA WALTRIP

WALTRIP, Lela (Kingston) 1904-

PERSONAL: Born February 2, 1904, in Coleman, Tex., daughter of Ollie Bennet and Elon (Johnson) Kingston; married Rufus Charles Waltrip (a writer and teacher); children: Rufus Charles, Jr. *Education:* Highlands University, B.A., 1935; Eastern New Mexico University, M.A., 1955; additional study at Southern Methodist University, McMurry College, University of New Mexico. *Politics:* Democrat. *Religion:* Methodist. *Home:* 811 South Fourth St., Artesia, N.M. 88210.

CAREER: Public school teacher of English and music, secondary grades, twelve years; now teacher of bi-lingual children in elementary grades. *Member:* Business and Professional Women's Club, Writers League of America, American Association of University Women, National Education Association, Delta Kappa Gamma. *Awards, honors:* First-prize for juvenile novel manuscript, awarded by Southwestern Writers' Conference for "Navajo Pony," 1959.

WRITINGS—All with husband, Rufus Waltrip: *White Harvest,* Longmans, Green, 1960; *Quiet Boy,* Longmans, Green, 1961; *Purple Hills,* Longmans, Green, 1961; *Indian Women,* McKay, 1964; *Cowboys and Cattleman,* McKay, 1967; *Contemporary Indian Women,* Shield, 1975; *Mexican American Story,* Shield, 1975.

Has contributed educational articles, short stories, and poetry to magazines and newspapers.

WORK IN PROGRESS: Dear Teacher and *Waterways of the Southwest.*

SIDELIGHTS: "My husband, Rufus, and I have lived in the West and Southwest all of our lives and love it. We know the country and the people, and are especially interested in the young people of this area as well as all others. There are many cultures in the Southwest—Indian, Spanish, Anglo and others, who are all basically the same, with the same interests and needs. In our stories we try to point up this fact in an interesting and unique way, so that the readers may identify with the characters in the stories. (Black, brown, red, yellow or white) they are there and can participate in the action and life of the story, and can say, 'That is just the way I think and do.

"We write about the Indian, Mexican, Spanish American, Black and Anglo, sometimes all in the same book, and when we get letters from young readers who say, 'Are you an Indian? You write like one.' or 'Are you Spanish? You write and speak Spanish fluently!' this gives us a good feeling and inspires us to write more and better stories about them all. We read and answer all the letters we receive. We love it! And we love the boys and girls we write about, they are real to us."

HOBBIES AND OTHER INTERESTS: Music, travel.

RUFUS WALTRIP

Something about the Author

Down on one knee, Quiet Boy aimed steadily. Just as his thumb flipped out the agate, a loud snort burst in his ear. It was Tall Boy blowing his nose again. Quiet Boy winced 'and the agate missed its mark. ■ (From *Quiet Boy* by Lela and Rufus Waltrip.)

WALTRIP, Rufus (Charles)   1898-

PERSONAL: Born September 26, 1898, in Rosenburg, Tex.; son of John William (a farmer and rancher) and Cynthia (Nicholson) Waltrip; married Lela Kingston (a public school teacher); children: Rufus Charles, Jr. *Education:* Highlands University, B.A., 1936; University of New Mexico, M.A., 1947; additional study, Southern Methodist University, McMurry College, Eastern New Mexico University. *Politics:* Democrat. *Religion:* Methodist. *Home:* 811 South Fourth St., Artesia, N.M.

CAREER: New Mexico public schools, English teacher, principal, director of guidance and testing. Co-sponsor of local writer's workshop; extensive local and state Boy Scout work. *Member:* National Education Association (life member), New Mexico Education Association (organizer; former chairman of creative writing section), Rotary Club. *Awards, honors:* First prize for juvenile novel manuscript, awarded by Southwestern Writers' Conference for "Navajo Pony," 1959.

WRITINGS—All with wife, Lela Waltrip: *White Harvest,* Longmans, Green, 1960; *Quiet Boy,* Longmans, Green, 1961; *Purple Hills,* Longmans, Green, 1961; *Indian Women,* McKay, 1964; *Cowboys and Cattleman.* McKay, 1967; *Contemporary Indian Women,* Shields, 1975; *Mexican American Story,* Shields, 1975. Has contributed articles and stories to magazines and to education publications.

HOBBIES AND OTHER INTERESTS: Photography, fishing, travel.

WARNER, Gertrude Chandler   1890-

PERSONAL: Born April 16, 1890, in Putnam, Conn.; daughter of Edgar Morris and Jane Elizabeth (Carpenter) Warner. *Education:* Attended Yale University summer school for many years. *Politics:* Republican. *Religion:* Congregationalist. *Home:* 22 Ring St., Putnam, Conn. 06260.

CAREER: Grade school teacher, Putnam, Conn., 1918-50; free-lance writer, 1919—. Publicity work, American Red Cross, 1917—; service chairman, Connecticut Cancer Society, 1950—. *Awards, honors:* Emblem Club, woman of the year, 1965; American National Red Cross, 50-year pin, and citation.

WRITINGS—Juvenile: *The House of Delight,* Pilgrim Press, 1916; *Star Stories,* Pilgrim Press, 1918; *The Boxcar Children,* Rand McNally, 1924, revised, Scott, 1942; *The World in a Barn,* Friendship, 1927; *Windows into Alaska,* Friendship, 1928; *The World on a Farm,* Friendship, 1931; *Children of the Harvest,* Friendship, 1940; *Surprise Island,* Scott, 1949.

The Yellow House Mystery, Whitman, 1953; *1001 Nights (Arabian Nights* revised), Scott, 1954; *Mystery Ranch,* Whitman, 1958; *Mike's Mystery,* Whitman, 1960; *Blue Bay Mystery,* Whitman, 1961; *Woodshed Mystery,* Whitman, 1962; *The Lighthouse Mystery,* Whitman, 1963; *The Mountain Top Mystery,* Whitman, 1964; *The Schoolhouse Mystery,* Whitman, 1965; *The Caboose Mystery,* Scott, 1966; *Peter Piper,* Zondervan, 1967; *Mystery Behind the Wall,* A. Whitman, 1973.

Adult: (With Frances Warner) *Life's Minor Collisions,* Houghton, 1921; (with Frances Warner) *Pleasures and Palaces,* Houghton, 1933; *Henry Barnard—An Introduction,* Connecticut State Teachers Association, 1937; *History of Connecticut,* Connecticut State Teachers Association, 1948. Contributes essays and articles to magazines.

GERTRUDE CHANDLER WARNER

On and on went the thing in the trees. On and on went Benny.
■ (From *Blue Bay Mystery* by Gertrude Chandler Warner. Illustrated by Dirk Gringhuis.)

WORK IN PROGRESS: Traveling Parakeet, for Zondervan; *Department Store Mystery.*

SIDELIGHTS: "I am telling the exact truth when I say that my sister and I began to write when we were just able to hold a pencil. (She later was known as an essay writer, author of *Endicott and I,* and more than once was compared favorably with a renowned essayist.) As children, we received from our mother a ten-cent blank book to prevent the house from being littered with scraps of paper containing a 'good word' or a full sentence, or even a whole article.

"My first book was an imitation of the 'Uptons Gollwag' book, consisting of verses illustrated with watercolors of the two Dutch docks and the Gollwag, a bestseller of that day. I always said I could write better if I had a decent pencil, and this was true. It seemed that our household never had a new pencil, but the worst old stubs, sharpened with a kitchen knife. I gave the Gollwag book to my grandfather, a born child lover, and every Christmas thereafter gave him a handmade book. The second one being an imitation of Gelett Burgess 'Goops'.

"When we girls were eighteen and twenty, my mother had a serious talk with us saying it was a nice idea to write but not to anticipate earning any money from it. She would be surprised if she knew how wrong she was.

"My writing seems to coincide with an illness. Finally, I discovered that writing coincided with enforced leisure. The *Boxcar Children* was the most important of these efforts. I had to stay at home from school because of an attack of bronchitis. Having written a series of eight books to order for a religious organization, I decided to write a book just to suit myself. What would I like to do? Well, I would like to live in a freight car, or a caboose. I would hang my wash out on the little back piazza and cook my stew on the little rusty stove found in the caboose. I do not know how many editions this book has come to. I rewrote the *Boxcar Children* from ordinary childish language in a prescribed vocabulary of six-hundred words and 15,000 running words. This is used as a school book for non-readers up to age eighteen.

"Most of this writing has been done in spite of frequent ill health. At one time or another, I have broken my back in an auto accident and have broken first one hip and then the other. I am still home from the last hip and walk with a cane.

"I have had spells of making a butterfly and moth collection, a la *The Girl of the Limberlost,* collecting pressed wild flowers, and I learned all the birds by sight and sound which are indigenous to this region at age eight.

"I played the piano for the Pages of Arthur and learned the planets and constellations in order to teach them to the boys. The result of this sortie was a book called *My Star Book.*

"At times I had beautiful gardens, spaded and planted by me. Sweet williams, sweet alyssum, zinneas, phlex, forget-me-nots, holly hocks and petunias interspersed with carrots, radishes, parsnips and all varieties of tomatoes, staked and tied up. My best parsnips were dug out of the frozen ground of February with an axe.

"With every occupation, I wrote about it and am still doing so. Yes, I have a procedure. When setting about a new book, I have a dozen black 'Sharpie' pens and a one-hundred-page notebook. I have a special workroom furnished, typewriter, paper cutter, easy chair etc., with violets on the wallpaper and in artificial bouquets.

"Almost all my writing started in copying someone elses style without plagarism. I live with a congenial housemate who is a retired nurse and own a shingled house with garage in the basement, surrounded by woods and good neighbors.

"I find Talking Book records of infinite importance, as I cannot see to read. I can listen to Adam Bede again, or the latest modern novel which I find unnecessarily vulgar. I have faith that this is a trend which will soon swing back into a well-written good story."

HOBBIES AND OTHER INTERESTS: Engrossing, crewel embroidery.

WARREN, William Stephen 1882-1968 (Billy Warren)

PERSONAL: Born September 6, 1882, in Carrollton, Ark.; son of James Henry (a cattleman) and Mary Lou (Eddelman) Warren; married Agnes Kirkland, May 14, 1913 (deceased); married Anne Kirkland, March 5, 1952. *Education:* Academy of Fine Arts, Chicago, Ill., student, 1918-20. *Politics:* Democrat. *Religion:* Episcopalian. *Home:* 483 University Circle, Claremont, Calif. 91711.

CAREER: Cowboy on Colorado range, 1895-1910; Colorado State Penitentiary, Canon City, superintendent of road construction by convict labor, 1910-18; political cartoonist for *Chicago Tribune*, part-time, 1920-22, *Cleveland News*, 1922-28, *Philadelphia Morning Public Ledger*, 1928-32, and *Buffalo Evening News*, 1932-40; owner of a peach orchard at Palisade, Colo., and a cattle ranch at Collbran, Colo., 1941-48; writer and illustrator of books for young people, 1942-68. *Member:* Authors Guild, University Club (Claremont). *Awards, honors:* Boys' Clubs of America Junior Book Award, 1950, for *Tony Gay on the Longhorn Trail*.

WRITINGS—All under name Billy Warren and all self-illustrated, except as indicated: *Ride, Cowboy, Ride!*, Reynal, 1946; *Saddles Up! Ride 'em High*, McKay, 1948; *Tony Gay on the Longhorn Trail*, McKay, 1949; *Silver Spurs*, McKay, 1950; *The Golden Palomino*, McKay, 1951; *Ride West into Danger* (Junior Literary Guild selection), McKay, 1953; *Headquarters Ranch*, McKay, 1954; *Black Lobo* (illustrated by Bernard Garbutt), Golden Gate, 1967.

Contributor: *All Around Me*, Macmillan, 1951; *Time to Read: Finding Favorites*, edited by Bernice E. Leary, Edwin C. Reichert, and Mary K. Reely, Lippincott, 1953; *Aboard the Story Rocket*, L. W. Singer, 1960; *Stories of Fun and Adventure*, Copp Clark, 1964; "Around the World Readers," Book I, A. H. and A. W. Reed, 1967.

WORK IN PROGRESS: *Rosita*, a sequel to *Black Lobo*, the life story of an old Indian woman with a sixth sense.

SIDELIGHTS: *Ride, Cowboy, Ride!* was made into a movie and was published in Braille. Warren is competent in Spanish.

HOBBIES AND OTHER INTERESTS: Golf and bridge.

(Died October 18, 1968)

WEIL, Ann Yezner   1908-1969

PERSONAL: Born August 31, 1908, in Harrisburg, Ill.; daughter of David (a merchant) and Rose (Shedorshy) Yezner; married Sam Weil, August 17, 1930 (deceased); children: Jon, Robert. *Education:* Attended University of Illinois, Southern Illinois University, and Evansville College. *Home:* 100 Fielding Rd., Evansville, Ind.

CAREER: Elementary school teacher in Eldorado, Ill., and Evansville, Ind., 1926-30; writer of books for children, 1939-69. University of Indiana, member, children's literature staff for writer's workshop, 1947; Evansville College, lecturer in English, 1950-51. *Member:* Planned Parenthood (board, 1933-1943), Children's Theatre Association (board, 1940-45), League of Women Voters (board, 1940-47), Musicians Club of Evansville (vice-president, 1960-62). *Awards, honors:* Runnerup for John Newbery Medal, for *Red Sails to Capri*, 1953.

WRITINGS: *The Silver Fawn*, Bobbs, 1939; *My Dear Patsy*, Bobbs, 1941; *Pussycat's Breakfast*, Greenberg, 1944; *John Quincy Adams: Boy Patriot*, Bobbs, 1945; *The Very First Day*, Appleton, 1946; *Animal Families*, Greenberg, 1946; *Franklin Roosevelt: Boy of the Four Freedoms*, Bobbs, 1947; *Red Sails to Capri*, Viking, 1952; *Betsy Ross:*

"Marching! You're always marching! But even you, John Philip Sousa, can't march with a lighted candle." ■ (From *John Philip Sousa: Marching Boy* by Ann Weil. Illustrated by Katherine Sampson.)

Girl of Old Philadelphia, Bobbs, 1954; *John Philip Sousa: Marching Boy*, Bobbs, 1959; *Eleanor Roosevelt: Courageous Girl*, Bobbs, 1965. Parts of *The Silver Fawn* anthologized in six other books.

WORK IN PROGRESS: A book on architecture.

SIDELIGHTS: Various books have been translated into French, Swedish, and Chinese.

HOBBIES AND OTHER INTERESTS: Architecture, travel, including southeast Asia, the Soviet Union, and some of its European satellite nations, and a recent three-month tour in France, Italy, Greece, and Turkey.

(Died, 1969)

WELS, Byron G(erald)   1924-

PERSONAL: Born April 20, 1924, in New York, N.Y.; son of Joseph and Henrietta (Schreiber) Wels; divorced; children: Joshua, Deborah, Heather. *Education:* Brooklyn College (now Brooklyn College of City University of New York), student; also studied at Cleveland Institute of Electronics and various military radio and radar schools. *Home:* 32-L Riverview Gardens, North Arlington, N.J. 07032. *Office: Magic* Magazine, 381 Park Ave. S., New York, N.Y. 10016.

BYRON G. WELS

CAREER: Prior to 1963 worked as advanced research and developmental electronics technician for such firms as Potter Instruments, Amperex, and Fairchild Engine Division, and in publications departments of other firms, including Radio Engineering Laboratories, Westbury Electronics, and Eldico Electronics; *Popular Mechanics,* electronics editor based in New York, N.Y., and Chicago, Ill., 1963-66; Davis Publications, Inc., New York, N.Y., editor-in-chief of *Radio-TV Experimenter* and *Elementary Electronics* and also electronics editor of sister magazine, *Science and Mechanics,* 1964-66; *Popular Electronics,* New York, N.Y., feature editor, 1966-67; Conover-Mast, Inc., New York, N.Y., 1967-69, started as engineering editor for *Mill & Factory,* became managing editor of *Construction Equipment; Data Products News,* New York, N.Y., editor-in-chief, 1969-70; writer or executive for public relations firms in New York, N.Y., and Princeton, N.J., 1970-72; Singer Communications Corp., Little Falls, N.J., public relations and advertising and writer of correspondence courses, 1972—; *Magic,* New York, N.Y., editor-in-chief. Holds Federal Communications Commission second class radiotelephone license, amateur radio operator's license, and pilot certificate. *Military service:* U.S. Army Air Forces; received Air Medal. *Member:* Flying Engineers, New York Advertising Sportsmen's Club, Masons.

WRITINGS: Getting the Most from Your Hi-Fi and Stereo System, Foulsham, 1967; *Here Is Your Hobby:* *Magic* (juvenile), Putnam, 1967; *Here Is Your Hobby: Amateur Radio* (juvenile), Putnam, 1968; *Transistor Circuit Guidebook,* TAB Books, 1968; *Electronics in Photography,* Sams, 1968; *Fell's Guide to Guns and How to Use Them Safely—Legally—Responsibly,* Fell, 1969; *Computer Circuits and How They Work,* TAB Books, 1970; *Fire and Theft Security Systems,* TAB Books, 1971; *How to Build Clocks and Watches,* Auerbach, 1971; *Science Fair Experiments* (juvenile), Auerbach, 1971; *Simple Wall Paneling,* Doubleday, 1971; *How to Repair Musical Instrument Amplifiers,* TAB Books, 1973.

Contributor to about eighty popular, technical, and trade magazines, including *Argosy, Popular Photography, Reader's Digest, Bachelor, Guns and Hunting, True, Holiday, National Wildlife, Skiing, Boys' Life, American Sportsman,* and *Civil Engineering.*

WORK IN PROGRESS: Revising *Fire and Theft Security Systems,* for TAB Books; a book on how to upholster furniture, also for TAB Books; a book on candle making, for Putnam; a book on hot air balloons, for Drake.

SIDELIGHTS: "Mort Persky, of *Family Weekly* calls me his 'man of perilous adventure,' and continually gives me assignments that his staffers won't touch. It was Mort that got me to solo in a balloon for the first time, and has had me in race cars at Daytona, and Lord knows what he'll have for me in the future. I'm a licensed pilot, and love to use my writing skills to explore new and different areas that I might never have been able to expose myself to had I to depend on my own finances.

"Writing is not a suitable career for anybody, as there are so few who are howlingly successful. I've received royalty checks for as little as 68¢, and would actively discourage any who would pursue this as a full-time career. Once, I tried freelancing on a full-time basis, was writing a book, and my daughter was approached by a nosy neighbor who asked, 'Honey, what does your daddy do?' Debbie knew I was writing a book, so she said, 'He's a book-maker!' Try to live THAT down!

"But the *cacothes scrivendi* is a strong urge, and once you start, you can't stop. I simply stumble along, doing my best, and wishing I could do better. The *Magic Magazine* certainly looks promising, and I'm working diligently at making it a success. If all it took was hard work, we'd be over the top now. Still, it IS my best shot, and I'm giving it my all."

WELTY, Susan F. 1905-
(S. F. Welty)

PERSONAL: Born January 20, 1905, in Fairfield, Iowa; daughter of Charles Jacobs and Hermine (Stichter) Fulton; married Joel Carl Welty (professor emeritus, Beloit College), September 2, 1930. *Education:* Parsons College, B.S., 1926; University of Utah, M.A., 1927; summer graduate study at University of Southern California, 1929, and University of Iowa, 1930. *Politics:* Independent. *Religion:* Congregational (United Church of Christ). *Home:* Rural Route 1, Beloit, Wis. 53511. *Agent:* McIntosh & Otis, Inc., 18 East 41st St., New York, N.Y. 10017.

CAREER: High school speech teacher and drama coach in

SUSAN FULTON WELTY

Oklahoma City, Okla., 1928; Parsons College, Fairfield, Iowa, speech instructor and drama coach, 1928-34; Washington State College, Pullman, instructor in English, 1946-47; instructor in parliamentary procedure at Community College, Beloit, Wis., 1955-56, and Beloit Vocational School, 1961; free-lance writer. *Member:* Wisconsin Academy of Sciences, Arts, and Letters, Beloit College Faculty Women's Club, Ned Hollister Bird Club, Spring Brook Watershed Association.

WRITINGS: (Under name S. F. Welty) *Knight's Ransom,* Wilcox & Follett, 1951; *Look Up and Hope: The Life of Maud Ballington Booth,* Thomas Nelson, 1961; *Birds with Bracelets: The Story of Bird-Banding,* Prentice-Hall, 1965; *A Fair Field, in Jefferson County, State of Iowa,* Harlo Press, 1968, Bicentennial edition, 1975.

Plays: *The Light Shines,* David C. Cook, 1938; *St. Francis Spreads Christmas Joy,* Row, Peterson & Co., 1944; *A Candle for the Christmas Guest,* Row, Peterson & Co., 1945.

Contributor of short stories, plays, and articles to various magazines.

WORK IN PROGRESS: Boy With Wise Hands, a story of prehistoric inventions.

SIDELIGHTS: "In the delightful town of Fairfield, Iowa,

where I grew up, my parents and their closest friends were all book-lovers, sponsors and patrons of the popular Carnegie Library. Several of the group, my parents among them, wrote occasionally. My mother had published a few poems and essays; my father wrote in connection with his political career, and spent years on spare-time scholarly local history. This culminated in a *History of Jefferson County, Iowa,* still in demand, though out of print. I was so enchanted by additional stories of Fairfield as I grew up that I meant to write a novel about it, but when I reached the now-or-never stage, my book turned into *A Fair Field,* a shorter and more anecdotal version of my father's work, updated fifty years. The real stories were too good to resist.

"Quite naturally, my parents' three children were voracious readers; my sister eventually became a university librarian; and my brother, professionally a chemist in government service specializing in alcohol and drugs, has written widely in his field. I started writing verses when I was in the third grade, filling a little tablet. Some of the older kids got hold of it, and teased me by quoting it with such glee that I hid my scribbles from then on, except from my mother, who encouraged me to try to write better. A summer playmate who visited regularly from Chicago liked to make verses, too; we competed, and by the time we were thirteen we were quite proficient at rhymes and meters, and could compose on short order sonnets that were technically respectable.

"But my chief interest was in putting on plays: I corralled neighborhood children in vacation time to help me, from the time I was eight until I was through high school and studied dramatics in college. This led to my writing and producing short sketches for special occasions in church school and public school, later to studying speech in college. That involved debate, oratory, interpretive reading and extemporaneous speaking, all helpful in developing the use of words and communicating ideas. I studied journalism, wrote for the college paper and later edited it; for a short time read proof on the town newspaper.

"After graduate work in speech, I became a teacher of speech and dramatics. I loved teaching, and I could earn my living that way. I still wanted to write, but had only the vaguest notions of how to get anything published. When I stumbled on the *Writer's Digest,* that helped. But even when I had a few stories and plays in print, the payment was chiefly in knowing that they were used. Even when I stopped teaching, a few years after my marriage, and had more time for writing, my published work would not have paid for my bread and butter. But my husband, Joel Carl Welty, encouraged me to go ahead with my hobby, and he provided the bread and butter, plus some jam, by his biology teaching. Both the books *Knights' Ransom* and *Birds With Bracelets* stemmed from his interest in ornithology and from watching him band birds for over thirty years, and they were preceded by two serials called 'The Bird Banders' and 'Apprentice Game Manager' based on adventures of some of his college students.

"Incidentally, I don't like to write anything that does not contain some worthwhile information, or some suggestion of constructive action or admirable feeling. *Birds With Bracelets* and the serials, for instance, all, I hope, make conservation and ecology more interesting. My biography of Maud Ballington Booth grew out of an intense admiration for her, sparked by her visits to my mother, during which I sat enthralled by her conversation, about her early social work and prison reform. This work was basic in the romantic story of her life, and is pertinent to problems today.

"When my husband retired, he became immersed in bringing up to date his own book, *The Life of Birds*. It demanded increasingly long hours of concentrated research with masses of references. He does not love writing as I do—he would rather work on our country place—but he is much more successful than I am. So I left our shared study to him, concentrated on a highway fight to save land in our area, and on gardening and handcraft, until I could help with his mechanical chores of proof reading, bibliography, and indexing. With his revised *Life of Birds* issued in May, 1975, he rejoiced in being out of 'literary jail' and I began thinking of serving a new sentence in the study."

WILBUR, Richard (Purdy)   1921-

PERSONAL: Born March 1, 1921, in New York, N.Y.; son of Lawrence Lazear (a portrait artist) and Helen Ruth (Purdy) Wilbur; married Mary Charlotte Hayes Ward, June 20, 1942; children: Ellen, Christopher, Nathan, Aaron. *Education:* Amherst College, A.B., 1942; Harvard University, A.M., 1947. *Politics:* Independent. *Religion:* Episcopal. *Residence:* Portland, Conn. *Agent:* Gilbert Parker, Curtis Brown, Ltd., New York, N.Y. (for theatre only). *Office:* Department of English, Wesleyan University, Middletown, Conn.

CAREER: Harvard University, Cambridge, Mass., Society of Fellows, junior fellow in Society of Fellows, 1947-50, assistant professor of English, 1950-54; Wellesley College, associate professor of English, 1955-57; Wesleyan University, Middletown, Conn., professor, 1957—. Lecturer at colleges, universities, and Library of Congress. Traveled to Russia, September, 1961, as an American specialist for the Department of State. *Military service:* U.S. Army, 1943-45, technician, third class. *Member:* National Institute of Arts and Letters, American Academy of Arts and Sciences, Dramatists' Guild, American Academy of Arts and Letters (president), Academy of American Poets (chancellor), Chi Psi. *Awards, honors:* Harriet Monroe Prize of *Poetry* Magazine, 1948; Oscar Blumenthal Prize, 1950; Guggenheim grant, 1952, 1963; Prix de Rome, 1954; Edna St. Vincent Millay Memorial Award, 1957; Pulitzer Prize for poetry, 1957, for *Things of This World;* National Book Award, 1957, for *Things of This World;* Boston Festival Award, 1959; Ford Fellow, 1960; Cane Award, 1962; Bollingen Prize for translation, co-recipient, 1963, for *Tartuffe;* honorary L.H.D., Lawrence College, 1960, Washington University, 1964; M.A., Amherst College; D.Litt., Amherst, 1967, Williams, 1975.

WRITINGS: Beautiful Changes and Other Poems, Reynal, 1947; *Ceremony and Other Poems,* Harcourt, 1950; (editor and contributor) *A Bestiary* (anthology), Pantheon, 1955; (translator) Moliere, *The Misanthrope,* Harcourt, 1955; *Things of This World* (poems), Harcourt, 1956; (contributor) *The New Landscape in Art and Science,* edited by Gygory Kepes, Theobald, 1956; *Poems, 1943-1956,* Faber, 1957; (author of lyrics with John Latouche and Dorothy Parker) *Candide* (comic opera based on the satire by Voltaire), Random, 1957; (editor) Edgar Allan Poe, *Com-*

plete Poems of Poe, Dell, 1959; (with Robert Hillyer and Cleanth Brooks) *Anniversary Lectures,* U.S. Government Printing Office, 1959.

(With Louise Bogan and Archibald MacLeish) *Emily Dickinson: Three Views* (criticism), Amherst College Press, 1960; *Advice to a Prophet, and Other Poems,* Harcourt, 1961; (editor of section on Poe) *Major Writers of America,* Harcourt, 1962; (contributor) *The Moment of Poetry,* edited by Don C. Allen, Johns Hopkins Press, 1962; *Loudmouse* (juvenile), Collier, 1963; (translator) Moliere, *Tartuffe* (play), Harcourt, 1963; *The Poems of Richard Wilbur,* Harcourt, 1963; (introduction) *Poems of William Shakespeare,* Pelican, 1966; *Walking to Sleep: New Poems and Translations,* 1969; *Digging for China* (Child Study Association book list), Doubleday, 1970; (translator) Moliere's *School for Wives,* 1971; *Opposites* (poems and drawings for children and others; *Book World's* Children's Spring Book Festival Award), Harcourt, 1973; (introduction) Poe's *The Narrative of Arthur Gordon Pym,* Godine, 1973. General editor, "Laurel Poet" series published in original paperback editions by Dell. Contributor to anthologies.

WORK IN PROGRESS: Collection of occasional prose pieces, and a new book of poems.

SIDELIGHTS: Wilbur has recorded for the Library of Congress and for Spoken Arts.

FOR MORE INFORMATION SEE: Northwest Review, spring, 1957; *Voices,* May-August, 1957; *New York Times Book Review,* October 29, 1961; *New York Herald Tribune Books,* December 3, 1961; *Commonweal,* December 22, 1961; *Yale Review,* March, 1962; *Times Literary Supplement,* April 23, 1964; *Virginia Quarterly Review,* winter, 1964; M. L. Rosenthal, *The Modern Poets,* Oxford University Press, 1965; Donald L. Hill, *Richard Wilbur,* Twayne, 1967; John Field, *Richard Wilbur: A Biographical Checklist,* Kent State University Press, 1971; *Horn Book,* June 6, 1973; *New York Times Book Review,* July 1, 1973.

WILSON, Ellen (Janet Cameron)

PERSONAL: Born in Pittsburgh, Pa.; daughter of Henry Nesmith (a clergyman) and Belle (Morgan) Cameron; married William E. Wilson (a writer), June 29, 1929; children: William E. III, Cameron and Douglas (twins). *Education:* Ohio Wesleyan University, A.B., 1924; Radcliffe College, A.M., 1927; Universite Aix-Marseille, School for Foreign Students, graduate study, 1956-57. *Politics:* Democrat. *Religion:* Protestant. *Home:* 1326 Pickwick Pl., Bloomington, Ind. 47401.

CAREER: Rhode Island School of Design, Providence, teacher of English, 1931-33; Katherine Gibbs School, Providence, R.I., teacher of English, 1933-37; Indiana University, Bloomington, teacher of independent study courses in history of children's literature, 1953—. Leader of children's literature workshop, University of Colorado Writers Conference, 1967. *Member:* National Society of Arts and Letters, Kappa Alpha Theta, Theta Sigma Phi. *Awards, honors:* Indiana Author's Day Award for best biography for young people, 1972, for *American Painter in Paris: A Life of Mary Cassatt.*

WRITINGS—Juvenile fiction; with Nan Agle, "Three

ELLEN WILSON

Boys'' series, published by Scribner: *Three Boys and a Lighthouse*, 1951; *... and the Remarkable Cow*, 1952; *... and a Tugboat*, 1953; *... and a Mine*, 1954; *... and a Train*, 1956; *... and a Helicopter*, 1958; *... and Space*, 1962; *... and H2O*, 1968.

Biographies for children, except where otherwise noted: *Ernie Pyle: Boy from Back Home*, Bobbs, 1955; *Annie Oakley: Little Sure Shot*, Bobbs, 1958; *Robert Frost: Boy with Promises to Keep*, Bobbs, 1967; *American Painter in Paris: A Life of Mary Cassatt* (for young adults), Farrar, Straus, 1971; *They Named Me Gertrude Stein* (for young adults), Farrar, Straus, 1973.

Contributor of stories and articles to *Cricket*, *American Heritage*, and *Horn Book*. Book reviewer, *Providence Journal*, 1951—, Louisville *Courier Journal*, 1963—.

WORK IN PROGRESS: A biography of Margaret Fuller, focusing on her part in literature and in women's liberation, for Farrar, Straus.

SIDELIGHTS: Ellen Wilson began writing fiction books for children some time after her own three boys were in school. "It was an artist friend and neighbor in Baltimore who gave me the initial push. Nan Agle and I wrote our first book together—*Three Boys and a Lighthouse*. By the time that Scribner's told us that we should make our manuscript longer, we Wilsons had moved to Boulder, Colorado. Nan and I finished the *Lighthouse* book by correspondence, and have since written seven more 'Three Boys' books by mail between Bloomington and Baltimore.

"For all of those children's books we developed a workable theory and procedure: give children both facts and adventure. Whether we wrote of the three boys and a train, a tugboat, or a helicopter, we separately not only did thorough library research, but rode in diesel engines, tugboats, and in helicopters so that we would know what it felt like to have the adventures our three boys had."

Now concentrating on biographies for young adult readers, Wilson continues to do extensive research for each book. "When people say 'You put all that work and research in writing just for children?,' I resent it. I resent the implication that young people deserve less than adults. I feel strongly that they deserve an author's best work both in research and in writing." In the process of writing her biography of Mary Cassatt, for example, she not only read books about her life and work, but interviewed relatives, borrowed letters she had written home from France, studied her paintings, and visited her chateau in France. She followed the same procedure in writing her biography of Gertrude Stein, using libraries in America and Europe, as well as visiting Stein's various homes in France.

FOR MORE INFORMATION SEE: Horn Book, October, 1971.

WILWERDING, Walter Joseph   1891-1966

PERSONAL: Surname is pronounced *Will*-wording; born February 13, 1891, in Winona, Minn.; son of John (a mill owner) and Albertine (Muller) Wilwerding; married Nan Barrett, November 30, 1916 (died, February, 1932); married Sylvia Grace Novotny, May 23, 1933. *Education:* Studied at Minneapolis Art School, 1910-15. *Politics:* Republican. *Home:* 5644 Chowen Ave. South, Edina, Minn. 55410.

CAREER: Art Instruction Schools, Minneapolis, Minn., vice-president and director of education, 1948-61; painter of animal life; writer and illustrator. Made expeditions to Africa to study and paint animals, 1929, 1933, 1953; also sketched in Europe, Alaska, and the American West; paintings exhibited at one-man shows in New York, Chicago, Los Angeles, Minneapolis, and other cities. *Member:* Society of Animal Artists (vice-president, 1956-58), American Geographical Society (fellow), Association of Professional Artists (Minneapolis).

WRITINGS: Jangwa, the Story of Jungle Prince, Macmillan, 1935; *Keema of the Monkey People*, Macmillan, 1936; *Punda the Tiger Horse*, Macmillan, 1937; *Tembo the Forest Giant*, Macmillan, 1939; *Animal Drawing and Painting*, Watson, 1946; *Book of Wild Beasts*, Putnam, 1963; *The Cats in Action*, Foster Art Service, 1963; *How to Draw and Paint Hoofed Animals*, Foster Art Service, 1964; *How to Draw and Paint Animal Textures*, Foster Art Service, 1965; *The Big One: A Second Book of Wild Beasts*, Putnam, 1966.

Regular contributor of articles and illustrations to *Sports Afield*, 1930–66. Also writer of articles and short stories for *Field and Stream*, *Boy's Life*, *This Week*, *Blue Book*, *Nature*, *Jack and Jill*, *Story Parade*, and *Audubon Magazine*.

SIDELIGHTS: Spoke German and KiSwahili.

(Died September 19, 1966)

Lowering his large head, the giraffe touched noses with Tommy. ▪ (From *The Big One and Other Beasts* by Walter J. Wilwerding. Illustrated by the author.)

Something about the Author

SOMETHING ABOUT THE AUTHOR

CUMULATIVE INDEXES, VOLUMES 1-9
Illustrations and Authors

ILLUSTRATIONS INDEX

(In the following index, the number of the volume in which an illustrator's work appears is given *before* the colon, and the page on which it appears is given *after* the colon. For example, a drawing by Adams, Adrienne appears in Volume 2 on page 6, another drawing by her appears in Volume 3 on page 80, and another drawing in Volume 8 on page 1.)

AUTHORS INDEX

(In the following index, the number of the volume in which an author's sketch appears is given *before* the colon, and the page on which it appears is given *after* the colon. For example, the sketch of Aardema, Verna, appears in Volume 4 on page 1).